Walls Without Cinema

Walls Without Cinema

State Security and Subjective Embodiment in Twenty-First-Century US Filmmaking

Larrie Dudenhoeffer

BLOOMSBURY ACADEMIC
NEW YORK · LONDON · OXFORD · NEW DELHI · SYDNEY

BLOOMSBURY ACADEMIC
Bloomsbury Publishing Inc
1385 Broadway, New York, NY 10018, USA
29 Earlsfort Terrace, Dublin 2, Ireland

BLOOMSBURY, BLOOMSBURY ACADEMIC and the Diana logo are trademarks of
Bloomsbury Publishing Plc

First published in the United States of America 2021
This paperback edition published in 2022

Copyright © Larrie Dudenhoeffer, 2021

For legal purposes the Acknowledgments on p. xi constitute an extension
of this copyright page.

Cover design: Eleanor Rose
Cover image © Vince Cavataio/Getty Images

All rights reserved. No part of this publication may be reproduced or transmitted
in any form or by any means, electronic or mechanical, including photocopying,
recording, or any information storage or retrieval system, without prior
permission in writing from the publishers.

Bloomsbury Publishing Inc does not have any control over, or responsibility
for, any third-party websites referred to or in this book. All internet addresses given in
this book were correct at the time of going to press. The author and publisher regret any
inconvenience caused if addresses have changed or sites have ceased to exist, but can
accept no responsibility for any such changes.

A catalog record for this book is available from the Library of Congress.

ISBN: HB: 978-1-5013-6419-8
PB: 978-1-5013-7097-7
ePub: 978-1-5013-6418-1
ePDF: 978-1-5013-6417-4

Typeset by Newgen KnowledgeWorks Pvt. Ltd., Chennai, India

To find out more about our authors and books visit www.bloomsbury.com
and sign up for our newsletters.

*To my grandparents,
all of them immigrants, all of them dreamers*

CONTENTS

List of Figures ix
Acknowledgments xi

1 Conceptual Borders: An Introduction to *Walls Without Cinema* 1

2 Green Zones: Beside the Walls on the Cinema Screen 35

3 Safe Spaces: Inside the Walls on the Cinema Screen 77

4 Gated Communities: Outside the Walls on the Cinema Screen 119

5 Interface Areas: Beyond the Walls on the Cinema Screen 161

Conclusion: The Walls Came Tumbling Down 203

Bibliography 209
Index 231

FIGURES

1.1 The Berlin Wall in *The Spy Who Came in from the Cold* 9
1.2 The Berlin Wall in *Atomic Blonde* 12
1.3 The Security Fencing Near the Wastelands in *Code 46* 16
1.4 Raven's Gate Bridge in *Resident Evil: Apocalypse* 17
1.5 The City Walls in *Troy* 19
2.1 Greater Los Angeles Sentries in *Southland Tales* 40
2.2 The Karkh District in *Green Zone* 45
2.3 The Fortress City of Erebor in *The Hobbit: The Battle of the Five Armies* 52
2.4 The Magic Bubble in *Fantastic Beasts and Where to Find Them* 56
2.5 The Makeshift Security Embankment in *The Wall* 61
3.1 The Transparent Dome over Springfield in *The Simpsons Movie* 84
3.2 Zombies Climbing the Israeli Separation Wall in *World War Z* 87
3.3 The Dark Portal in *Warcraft* 93
3.4 The Engines of Nation-State Security in *The Great Wall* 98
3.5 The Office Tower in *The Belko Experiment* 102
4.1 The US–Mexico Separation Wall in *Monsters* 125
4.2 The Gates of Heaven in *This Is the End* 131
4.3 The Wall of Outer Space in *Elysium* 133
4.4 The Force Dome Surrounding and Concealing Wakanda in *Black Panther* 137
4.5 The Orb of Osuvox in *Ready Player One* 145
5.1 The City Walls in *Warm Bodies* 166
5.2 The Walls Surrounding the Glade in *The Maze Runner* 171
5.3 The Antenna Arrays Atop the City Walls in *The Divergent Series: Allegiant* 177
5.4 The Village Walls in *Kong: Skull Island* 183
5.5 The California Border Quarantine Facility in *War for the Planet of the Apes* 186

ACKNOWLEDGMENTS

For the sake of *building bridges, not walls*, I wish to reach out and thank the friends, colleagues, and students who were instrumental in the conceptualization, writing, and revision of this manuscript. First, many thanks to my editor, Katie Gallof, as well as Erin Duffy, Haaris Naqvi, Steven Shaviro and my anonymous readers, and the rest of the team at Bloomsbury, for their encouragement, support, and useful suggestions in seeing my work to completion. I am also thankful to Cal Thomas for recommending me to Bloomsbury and for being an inspiration and a mentor to me.

David Marsh, Marvin Severson, Mitch Olson, Sueyoung Park-Primiano, Jeff Greene, Daniel Singleton, Jordan Carroll, Thomas Johnson, Jeremy Simpson, and Jerome Dent deserve credit for taking the time to share their thoughts with me about twenty-first-century Hollywood filmmaking. My thanks also to Keith Botelho and Darren Crovitz for their advice and for still remaining friends with me throughout my incessant ramblings about the forty-fifth president.

The coolest video store in Atlanta, Georgia, made it easy for me to capture and compile the screenshots for each chapter. My thanks to John Robinson, Matt Booth, Matt Owensby, and the rest of the staff at Videodrome for their assistance, conversation, and understanding.

Early drafts of sections of *Walls Without Cinema* made their first appearance at the 2018 Society for Cinema and Media Studies Conference in Toronto, Ontario, and the 2019 International Conference on the Fantastic in the Arts in Orlando, Florida. I am grateful to the conference organizers and the scholars in attendance for engaging with my ideas, asking thoughtful questions, and making valuable suggestions toward the improvement of my manuscript.

Finally, none of this work is imaginable without my family, Camille, Larrie, Juanita, Claudio, Grant, Anna, Becky, and my many aunts, uncles, cousins, and relatives. Love all of you so much always. Special thanks to Joe for reminding me of the security walls in *Pacific Rim* and for being the best brother anyone could have. And I might have been crawling up the walls, so to speak, at certain times during the writing of the chapters to follow if it were not for my wife Terri—my dearest love and deepest admiration for all that she is and does.

1

Conceptual Borders: An Introduction to *Walls Without Cinema*

> *We, in this country, in this generation, are—by destiny rather than by choice—the watchmen on the walls of world freedom.*
> PRESIDENT JOHN F. KENNEDY, UNDELIVERED SPEECH, DALLAS, TX, NOVEMBER 23, 1963

> *We go into wars to defend [other countries'] borders. We don't defend our own borders. And we're going to start defending our country; we're going to start defending our borders.*
> PRESIDENT DONALD J. TRUMP, NRA CONVENTION SPEECH, DALLAS, TX, MARCH 4, 2018

"*Build the wall!*" At several rallies for Donald J. Trump throughout 2016–18, in such far-flung areas as East Otay Mesa in San Diego, California; the State Fairgrounds Expo Hall in Tampa, Florida; Olantengy Orange High School in Lewis Center, Ohio; and the Federal Building in Greenville, South Carolina, several supporters were to chant that slogan over and over in an effort to convince the forty-fifth president to fulfill a campaign oath to construct a security wall along wide stretches of the almost 2,000-mile region of deserts, uplands, river valleys, and municipalities that separate the United States from Mexico.[1] At the outset of the campaign season, Trump spoke openly about exploiting the Secure Fence Act of 2006—which, according to then-president George W. Bush, was meant to curb terrorist attacks and stimulate "immigration reform"[2]—in order to install a wall made of concrete, steel, and rebar that will rise anywhere from 30 to 55 feet in the air. "I would build a great wall," the famous real estate developer was to declare in a 2015 presidential announcement speech,[3] "and nobody builds them better than me, believe me, and I'll build them very inexpensively." Despite serious objections that the effort to construct such a wall is xenophobic and only appealing to white supremacists, that it might cause flooding and other environmental damage, and that it might embolden agents to question, detain, and accost Hispanics, Muslims, and noncitizens without moral constraint, Trump set forth shortly after taking office Executive Order 13767, which calls for funding for five thousand additional border patrol officers and a "secure, contiguous, and impassable physical barrier" to discourage illegal immigration, stem the trade of drug cartels, and facilitate the repatriation of aliens to their countries of origin.[4] On October 12, 2018, Senator Kevin McCarthy, echoing the favorite slogan of Trump's supporters, spoke in favor of the "Build the Wall, Enforce the Law Act," a measure that asks the Department of Homeland Security for $23,400,000,000 to oversee construction of the wall, outfit it with the newest surveillance technologies, cover its infrastructure and daily operations costs, and finally squelch sanctuary city resistance to it.[5]

The inflaming of fears over "unfair" trade agreements causing factory outsourcing and massive unemployment, "illegals" taking the work that remains away from citizens, terrorists entering the country, and traffickers impudently funneling opioids and sex slaves into it speaks to Naomi Klein's analysis of the workings of "disaster capitalism." She argues that the invention or exploitation of a crisis, such as those surrounding issues of nation-state security, creates certain market opportunities so that, for example, state officials, in concert with their corporate cronies and sponsors, strip us of civil rights at the same time as they finance watchlist informatics; video surveillance systems; iris, retina, voice, DNA, face, fingerprint, and other "biometric" scanners; web tracking devices; data mining software; spy drones; and security walls, fences, checkpoints, roundups, and detention centers.[6] However, in concentrating on the economics of these sorts of measures, Klein, along with more mainline media scholars, neglects an important component in moving citizen-voters to support their construction, staffing, and maintenance, or at least to register them on their cultural radar: *the near ubiquity of these border walls* in much twenty-first-century US cinema.

Timothy Corrigan, writing about the similar cultural, economic, and technological shake-ups wrought in the aftermath of the Vietnam War, argues that our contemporary viewing experiences involve a crisis of "legibility and interpretation."[7] The "movie rituals and formulas" in the classical era tendentially serve to "supplement, reflect, and support relatively stable social identities and ideologies," according to Corrigan.[8] However, after Hollywood's experimentation with the techniques of the "new waves and counter-cinemas" of the 1960s and 1970s, its conglomeratization in the

1980s and the resulting fragmentation of its audiences, and its acquiescence to the time-shifting, "zapping" (channel-changing), and cross-promotional regimes of VCRs, cable television, and music videos, the cinema underwent a series of sweeping changes in terms of its formal qualities, experiential meanings, and narrative codes.⁹ The cinema, after Vietnam and the countercultural revolution, times that saw the steady destabilization of our collective "identities and ideologies," was to suffer the decay of its structural coherence, unambiguous spectator alignments, and archiving of sociohistorical memories, offering its audience only "a minimal amount of textual engagement" in favor of slick, surface-level visual designs and manic action set pieces.¹⁰ Corrigan, though, also argues that the market ambitions and international reach of Hollywood companies, as well as other national cinemas, make their output inevitably cosmopolitan in flavor so that "a cinema without walls" appears (contextually speaking, after the collapse of the Berlin Wall) that might undo cultural chauvinism, collapse older forms of textual and interpretive sensemaking, and make space for new ones to emerge.¹¹

The attacks on the World Trade Center on September 11, 2001, in which al-Qaeda terrorists flew airliners into the sides of the Twin Towers, demolishing them, set in motion a series of changes in cross-border relations, US state security measures, and their recoding and representation in the media, chiefly cinema. George W. Bush spoke in 2006 to the nation about expanding the National Guard from twelve thousand to eighteen thousand agents, arguing that the "border should be open to trade and lawful immigration, and shut to illegal immigrants, as well as criminals, drug dealers, and terrorists."¹² President Barack Obama, after requesting $500 million to reinforce the nation's defenses and revamp its immigration system, in 2010 similarly sent south 1,200 more forces to secure it.¹³ Donald Trump, though, in a series of tweets on October 18, 2018, went against Bush's vow never to "militarize the southern border,"¹⁴ threatening to immediately cut financial assistance to Honduras, El Salvador, and Guatemala and to deploy US troops to Mexico to aggressively thwart any attempts at illegal immigration:

> In addition to stopping all payments to these countries, which seem to have almost no control over their population, I must, in the strongest of terms, ask Mexico to stop this onslaught—and if unable to do so I will call up the U.S. Military and CLOSE OUR SOUTHERN BORDER!¹⁵

The catastrophic effects of the 9/11 attacks on the ethicopolitical decision-making of the United States, as well as its treatment of those from different races, creeds, classes, and cultures, show up on cinema screens, sometimes explicitly, sometimes metaphorically, in several different twenty-first-century (sub)genres, including war films, zombie films, monster films, fantasy films, superhero films, romance films, science fiction films, action thrillers, and dark comedies.

However, unlike the mainstream films that came out after the Vietnam War that Corrigan discusses, these more recent films call attention to a different sort of crisis that afflicts the post-9/11 era: that of *an excess of the legible*, or what we might rather term the *spatio-legible*, taking the form of an all-too-clear demarcation, articulation, surveilling, and management of certain diegetic spaces at once meant to fence some characters inside of their confines and exclude others. However, these films do more than dehumanize their antagonists; use fear tactics to tacitly argue for the construction of security walls or surveillance nets; or uncritically repeat the ideologemes that serve the racist, fascist, and xenophobic agendas of recent US administrations (and their international counterparts). Many of these films, through their complex narrative, representational, and compositional rhetorics, frustrate the development of any sort of *sensus communis* that might universally and imprudently support, owing to their fear of terrorism, crime, or economic disadvantage, Bush's, Obama's, or Trump's solutions to the issues facing immigrants, refugees, and members of certain outgroups. These films, in other words, move us to rethink and counter the implementation of these apartheidist measures, most explicitly the construction of those aesthetic and architectural monstrosities, the real-life security walls outside of the cinema—the "walls without it." As Michael J. Shapiro might argue, the films under discussion in the following chapters, rather than simplistically capitalizing on racist or reactionary attitudes to national, cultural, racial, ethnic, or religious "others," actually serve to introduce their viewers to the operations of "dissonance and disjuncture that break down walls."[16]

Something There Is That Doesn't Love a Wall

To appreciate the extent to which twenty-first-century Hollywood films depart from the diegetic constructions, ideological commitments, and compositional strategies of the cinema of the Cold War era, all we must do is compare a few of them to their mid-century counterparts. Many of the films from the 1950s and 1960s—the time of rising counterinsurgent US intervention in Southeast Asia, the announcement of President John F. Kennedy's New Frontier myth, and the completion of the Berlin Wall—mostly take to task separation fences; security auxiliaries, such as roadblocks, checkpoints, and sentry nests; and the isolationist mentalities that result from them. Richard Slotkin describes the US foreign affairs doctrine at the time as calling for military action against communist nations on the "frontiers" of the Third World, "a stage for the expansion of American influence" and a testing site for the advancement of democratic values and neoliberal economic development.[17] He further describes John Wayne, arguably the most recognizable star of the era, as a "folk hero" to scores of Americans, who saw the actor as a spokesman for these distinct American virtues; a supporter of initial US counterguerrilla efforts; and, although a staunch Republican, a fellow traveler of Kennedy's anti-communist New Frontier thesis.[18] Thus, such films as John Huston's *The Barbarian and the Geisha* (1958) advocate nonobservance of strict state demarcations and *even breaching international barriers* in favor of robust intercontinental trade, cultural exchange, and sociopolitical cooperation.[19]

The film, set in 1856 in a Japan suffering from the ravages of earthquakes, typhoons, and cholera outbreaks, opens with the approach of US consul general Townsend Harris's (John Wayne) ships to the coastlines of the nation. The representatives of the Shimoda Prefecture run down to the shore, forbidding the ships from docking, even as Harris ignores their warnings, saluting them and reminding them of their earlier trade agreement with the United States. The Japanese at first refuse to recognize Harris's diplomatic status, although they offer the consul general's cohort quarters in a shack, apologizing for its shabbiness while explaining the troubles they face with natural disasters. Harris, in a formulation that speaks to US anti-barrier attitudes at a time when Soviet authorities were restricting east-west European travel and emigration, tells the Japanese, "No one stays as he was, nor any country. This will do. Home, sweet home." However, over the course of the film, Harris must fight for official recognition, and even decent treatment in the marketplace, in order to win their trust and negotiate with the Shogunate for the opening of Japan. He does so with the assistance of Okichi (Eiko Ando), who, as romantic interest and cultural attaché, announces in voice-over, "This is my story too."

The film therefore enacts the violation and dissolution of state identity- and territory-markers in three significant and overlapping ways. Of course, in terms of *diegetic construction*, despite censure, social shunning, and the continual threat of arrest, Harris defies isolationist thinking and crosses over into Japanese waters, a movement that we might characterize as sadly one-way and thus imperialist, if it were not for the other two ways through which the film counters the impulse to create or refortify nation-state "walls." The film, in its *narrative content*, also depicts the crossing of certain cultural divides: apart from the interracial romance that informs its overarching storyline, one scene features a Japanese man embarrassing macho icon John Wayne in a martial arts demonstration, a turn of events unthinkable in the work of Howard Hawks or Henry Hathaway, some of the star's other famous directors. Finally, the film's *textual form* resembles the spirit of international cooperation that its main characters advocate. Although its image track in the main focuses us on Harris's diplomatic mission, the film reserves the voice-over narration for Okichi, who mediates and controls the telling of these events, so distant in time—in doing so, she figures the "now" of US–Japanese comity. *The Barbarian and the Geisha*, then, in tune with its release context and anticipating the crisis in Berlin in the following months, ultimately valorizes *exploring frontiers over shoring up borders*.[20]

Contrast the ideological tenor and diegetic construction of Huston's film to Martin Scorsese's *Silence* (2016), a film also set in Japan, in this case close to the time of the Catholic resistance to the Tokogawa Shogunate in the 1630s. The film depicts the efforts of two Jesuits, Sebastião Rodrigues (Andrew Garfield) and Francisco Garupe (Adam Driver), as they attempt to minister in secret to the converts of the villages of Tomogi and Gotō, whom the samurai of the magistrates, suspicious of the foreign missionaries and set on restoring the traditional cultural identity of Japan, routinely torture, terrorize, and repress. The Jesuits throughout the film struggle with their consciences, as they realize that satisfying the Shogunate's demands that they openly renounce their faith might abate some of the suffering they witness and endure themselves. Ultimately, Garupe dies and Rodrigues apostatizes, stepping on a *fumi-e* (an effigy of Jesus), inspecting trade ships for religious artifacts, and meeting with the inquisitor a final time to discuss the fate of Christianity in Japan. *Silence* thus surprisingly follows much of the same narrative arc as *The Barbarian and the Geisha*, each film culminating with an audience in front of a Japanese official concerning the opening of the nation to international and intercultural commerce. However, Scorsese's film, reflecting the emphasis on security walling in the world-systems of the twenty-first century, shifts its focus to the closing of Japan off from other territories and regimes, as well as the effects of such a decision on the social unicity, cultural normativity, and internal dynamics of the nation-state.

Silence opens in a very different manner than *The Barbarian and the Geisha*, with Japanese ministers and their samurai standing in the mists and carrying their standards up a mountainside near a series of volcanic springs. There the Japanese torture five Catholic missionaries with scalding water; one of them, the Jesuit Cristóvão Ferreira (Liam Neeson), informs us in voice-over that they constantly "live in fear," since "all [their] progress has ended in new persecution, new repression, new suffering." As the missionaries scream and Ferreira despairs, the camera captures the mountaintops in the distance that form a stratigraphic carapace—a natural set of walls—surrounding the coastlines of the nation. Once Rodrigues and Garupe arrive in Japan, they come ashore at night, disappearing into a cave under the mountains, in clear contradistinction to Townsend Harris's much cheerier disembarkation in Huston's film. These opening scenes in *Silence* offer clear parallels to the situation facing immigrants and refugees as they attempt to enter other countries in the new millennium, fully understanding that there they must maintain a furtive existence, counting on the assistance of sympathizers or fellow members of the same ethnicity, religion, or sociolinguistic cast to elude those authorities that wish to entrap, ostracize, or inflict some form of sanction on them. Philip Horne, in fact, aptly describes the film as a movement from the "epic sweep" of its "seething volcanoes" and "threatening waves" to a much tighter, almost claustrophobic focus on the confinement of its main characters to a series of "huts, bamboo cages, compounds, prison cells, [and] palanquins."[21] True to this description, *Silence* ends with Rodrigues's funeral, a train of Buddhists setting fire to the casket with torches reminiscent of the ones the villagers of Tomogi use to dispel the darkness of the cave for the Jesuits earlier in the film. The camera then digitally zooms in on the inside of the casket, revealing a crude wooden crucifix in the folds of the corpse's palms.

The implosive qualities of the film mark the radical departure of twenty-first-century US cinema from the internationalism and cultural rapprochement of *The Barbarian and the Geisha*, again in three ways. *Silence*, in terms of its *diegetic construction*, dramatizes the closing of the "walls" surrounding the nation in on the main characters, specifically Rodrigues, so much so that the final shot of the film consists of the snug interior of the man's casket as the torchbearers cremate it. As for its *narrative content*, the film, unlike its counterparts from the Cold War era, suggests the reversion of US cinema in the new millennium to isolationist feeling and ethno-national chauvinism, as the most of the Japanese remain Buddhists and the missionaries, although tacitly, in silence, remain Christian, the only open cross-cultural exchange occurring through the shipping trade. Finally, regarding its *textual form*, the film insists that its narrative and its image-flow do not move in the direction of a mutual "story," with Ferreira in voice-over calling the oppression of the converts and the confinement of the Jesuits to the island's natural and carceral borders a series of "hells." The Shogunate speaks to these men in Japanese, the film conventionally subtitling their words so as to suggest the inexorable nonidentity of the one to the other, each of their cultural rituals unable to truly touch the other's "inner being." *Silence*, coming out at a moment that saw the engineering of security walls to separate Hungary from Serbia, China from North Korea, Egypt from Gaza, and the United States from Mexico, contemplates *the shoring up of borders and their isolating influence on the individual along with the nation-state*.

Other films from the mid-twentieth century advocate for more than the opening of nation-states; some take to task the concrete walls, anti-vehicle trenches, anti-tank obstacles, observation towers, and meshwork fences that separate them, restricting civilian movement, international travel, and ideological commerce. The most conspicuous of these structures, the Berlin Wall, the climax of a decade's worth of Soviet demarcation efforts meant to stem emigration and defection from East Germany and other satellite states, made appearances in some of the spy films of the "New Frontier" era. J. Hoberman, comparing President John Kennedy to secret agent James Bond, describes the August 13, 1961, construction scene as an effort of the

Soviets and East Germans to seal "the border between East and West Berlin" with a "double-tiered wall," turning the area into an exclave, with alien and unfriendly territory surrounding it on either side.[22] Although certain films of the era in the James Bond vein, such as *Funeral in Berlin* (Guy Hamilton, 1966) and *Casino Royale* (Ken Hughes, John Huston, Joseph McGrath, Robert Parrish, and Val Guest, 1967), feature the Wall, the most thoughtful cinematic representation of it comes from an adaptation of a John le Carré novel, the quite unglamorous *The Spy Who Came in from the Cold* (Martin Ritt, 1965).

The film opens with a shot overlooking the Wall, with the camera scanning the ashen, mortar-and-steel Checkpoint Charlie site and focusing on a sign that reads, "You Are Leaving the American Sector." The first sequence of the film depicts its main character, Secret Intelligence Service (MI6) member Alec Leamas (Richard Burton), watching the death of another operative attempting to move through the checkpoint on a bicycle. Midway through the death strip, the Germans activate the sirens and floodlights, shooting down the agent, who unsuccessfully tries to weave from side to side in order to dodge the fire of their machine guns. More than a stark treatment of the ugliness of East-West relations, this sequence depicts one of the worst consequences of state security walling and other similar devices: their delimitation of our freedom of movement, of the easy flow of our arms, torsos, and feet as they force us to curtail our motions or cramp them in such a way as to make them seem unwieldy, irregular, spasmodic, or, in this case, serpentine. Of course, the movement of these characters onscreen, the charm and stylishness of their actions, distinguishes the cinema from the older visual arts.[23] However, in this sequence, the movements of the spy that the Germans assassinate appear clumsy, erratic, and unheroic; if anything, the alarms, signals, and machinegun nests off-screen function much more smoothly, meaning that these instruments of war, oppression, and mutual suspicion seem to function more "naturally" than the men and women in the film do. The Berlin Wall, in other words, represents *an affront to the moving image*, or rather to *the fundamentally human movement* that makes it of interest to us.[24]

The rest of the film focuses on Leamas's attempts to enter East Berlin so as to frame Hans-Dieter Mundt (Peter van Eyck), the officer responsible for the cyclist's death, for counterespionage and treason. The film emphasizes the circuitous routes that Leamas must negotiate in order to do so, impersonating an alcoholic ex-convict; developing romantic ties with an idealistic communist sympathizer, Nan Perry (Claire Bloom); meeting the recruiters of the Link, a chain of spies seeking out informants and defectors; and finally traveling to the GDR to convince the interrogator Fiedler (Oskar Werner) that Mundt serves the UK as a secret intelligence asset. En route to Germany, Leamas drives through a series of checkpoints, iron gates, and troop stations that make the entire countryside seem an expansion of the death strip, with miniature Wall-like ramparts and soldiers with combat rifles cropping up throughout it. At one of the East German compounds, Mundt manages to escape character assassination and conviction, convincing a tribunal to arrest Fiedler as the real traitor, Leamas as a confusion agent, and Nan Perry as their accomplice and dupe. However, in another twist—narratively matching the circuitous movements it took to reach the German manor—Mundt, who serves as a mole for the UK, frees the couple from their cells during the night, furnishes them with a car, and instructs them to race to Berlin to flee the country. The couple complies, reaching the city and moving again in roundabout ways through its dark alleys, warehouse interiors, and desolate sidewalks near the outer strip of the Wall, which they must scale while avoiding the searchlight that scans its surface, much in the way the camera slides over it in the opening scenes of the film (Figure 1.1).

The two scramble toward the Wall, clamber over it, and freeze as the searchlight spots them. Then a sniper in an over-the-shoulder composition shoots down Nan, and Leamas, after a moment of indecision, descends to the East German side to implicitly assist the woman or even retrieve the corpse. The sniper shoots once more and Leamas crumples over and dies. The circular ray that draws attention to the couple in this final sequence resembles nothing so much as the cone of xenon arc light that commonly came from the movie projectors of the era. This final touch underlines the ways that nation-state walling infringes on our capacities to move about unselfconsciously, to interact with those whom we wish, and to catch sight of distant objects or scenes of interest to us without something obstructing our view of them. By extension, then, these sorts of security walls also infringe

FIGURE 1.1 *The Berlin Wall in* The Spy Who Came in from the Cold.

on cinematic expression, in that it relies on near-constant movement, the dynamic interrelation of the characters on-screen, and the illusion of depth in its wide or establishing shots. The searchlight, though, stops shining as the main characters die and the film ends. *The Spy Who Came in from the Cold* thus aligns the cinema with them, its opto-mechanical functions clearly in the service of free movement and very much able to critique the tools of alienation, fear, murder, and repression—whether sirens, sniper rifles, or searchlights—as inimical to the moving image's operational values. As Leamas's decision to assist Nan rather than reenter West Berlin shows us, such structures as the Wall reduce each nonconformist individual who rejects the thinking that occasions Cold War containment to the status of *an exclave of one*.

David Leitch's spy action film *Atomic Blonde* (2017) serves as a new millennial counterpart to *The Spy Who Came in from the Cold* in several ways. Set in 1989, right on the cusp of the fall of the Berlin Wall, *Atomic Blonde* follows secret agent Lorraine Broughton (Charlize Theron), who, much as with Leamas in the earlier film, seeks revenge for the murder of another MI6 operative, James Gascoinge (Sam Hargrave), who was attempting to smuggle out of East Berlin "the List," a microfilm document that contains the names, identities, and affiliations of everyone working for an intelligence service throughout the Cold War arena. The List thus functions as an informational analogue to the Link, the order of communist agents that Leamus must infiltrate in Martin Ritt's 1965 film, in which the villain Mundt turns out to serve as double agent for the British. *Atomic Blonde* offers an additional twist on this scenario: the MI6 undercover agent David Percival (James McAvoy), Lorraine Broughton's contact in Berlin, at first appears the traitor whom the British codename "Satchel," as we see this man make self-serving deals with the KGB and then assassinate a Stasi defector thought to memorize the contents of the entire List. However, the antihero Broughton actually serves as the double agent in this film, as she murders Percival, retrieves the List, impersonates a Russian, and massacres the KGB agents, the epilogue revealing that, as Satchel, she was working for the CIA, spreading misinformation to manipulate Soviet opinion. She even frames Percival as the rouge Satchel, using audiovisual evidence taken from Delphine Lasalle (Sofia Boutella), a French agent and Broughton's romantic interest who thus functions as a counterpart to Nan Perry—not only do the two of them fill similar forensic roles, they also die in the course of their respective story arcs. Leamus, in a fit of despair, chooses to die alone with Nan Perry on "neither" side of the Cold War dispute, whereas Broughton eventually retires the Satchel deception[25] after Percival strangles Lasalle to death, flying off with a senior official from the CIA after at once repudiating MI6 and the KGB in the film's epilogue sequence. However, *Atomic Blonde* also differs in significant ways from *The Spy Who Came in from the Cold*, as it speaks to twenty-first-century feelings of ambivalence toward nation-state walling.

The film opens with footage of President Ronald Reagan's 1987 "Tear Down this Wall" speech, and from there it segues into an action sequence involving Gascoigne attempting to escape East Berlin in foot. A KGB agent drives into Gascoigne and then shoots the man down in the streets in an act reminiscent of the death of the cyclist that opens *The Spy Who Came in from the Cold*. The agent steals Gascoigne's wristwatch, which contains a copy of the List on microfilm. This opening sequence, more than slyly alluding to an older spy film, establishes the aesthetic of *acceleration* central to understanding the diegetic construction of a film set during the collapse of the Berlin Wall and the restructuring of US international relations.[26] The film contains a number of similarly dizzying set pieces; for instance, after immediately arriving in West Berlin, Broughton fights off two assassins in a speeding car. Then she fights off Stasi and KGB agents in Gascoigne's apartment, in a movie theater, on a stairwell in East Berlin, and in an opulent suite in Paris, all after receiving a final "message" from a vision of the former MI6 operative in a dream: "You need to run." The disorienting composition of these sequences, along with the extreme fast-motion insert shots of Berlin's streets, autobahn, nightlife, and freedom marches, speaks to accelerating changes in the film's diegetic-ideological coordinates with the immanent tearing down of the Berlin Wall and the decommunization of the East, changes that we can intuit, if not directly sense, from these sorts of images.

Lisa Purse argues that viewers of action cinema "can be imaginatively oriented towards particular diegetic trajectories without having to continuously *see* them," since these velocities express cultural concerns over the "negation of space" that accompanies moments of intense social, economic, and technological change.[27] This accent on fastness finds its complement in the film's directional axes of movement: unlike with the circuitous crossings in *The Spy Who Came in from the Cold*, the agents in *Atomic Blonde* enter East and West Berlin in a mostly *straightforward* manner. Broughton, wearing a crimson wig, merely consults a checkpoint officer and walks right into the Alexanderplatz; moreover, while teenagers from the GDR drink, dance to rap music, and trade for illegal merchandise, Percival evades the Stasi forces raiding the scene and crawls into a duct under the Berlin Wall to easily cross into West Berlin. These twin forces, accelerating motion and forward momentum, explode in the film's climax in the dismantlement of the Berlin Wall, during which Germans chip away at its ramparts, scale them without retaliation from soldiers, and set off fireworks while chanting "Down with the Wall" in unison. Broughton, in these moments, shoots Percival in the streets near the Wall (much as Leamas dies near it) and afterward takes advantage of the opening of the East to entrap and murder the KGB agents seeking the List (Figure 1.2).

FIGURE 1.2 *The Berlin Wall in* Atomic Blonde.

These two forces, as they mutually inform these final sequences, also nicely characterize the film's twenty-first-century release context, in that the acceleration of socioeconomic change in it dovetails with further escalations of violence. It is no accident that the straightforwardness of the movement of the characters in *Atomic Blonde* seems to contradict its narrative structure; unlike its 1965 forerunner, it "retells" its main narrative threads over the course of a series of debriefings with MI6 and CIA chiefs. This film, even as it reenacts the transgression and collapse of the twentieth century's most notorious security structure, at the same time *fantasizes its recursion*. The fall of the Berlin Wall in *Atomic Blonde* might then represent another instance of the "false intel" that its main character, the real Satchel, appears so expert at—in other words, while on the surface dramatizing and acknowledging the internal pressures that make state security apparatuses so unstable and unpopular, the film also unmistakably couches them *in an air of nostalgia*.[28] Thus, if anything, the film expresses the conflicting temptations to erect walls, as well as demolish them, and in any case to contemplate their return and their effects at times of swift cultural, ideological, and socioeconomic transformation. Without these walls, the world-system devolves into a set of shifting allegiances and *conclaves*, such as the conspiratorial CIA and the now-capitalist remnants of the KGB.

These sets of films, as symptomatic of the cultural attitudes toward nation-state security in two different centuries, clearly differ from each other in significant respects. The films from the Cold War era, for example, disparage natural barriers and separation walls as anathema to free movement, trade, cultural dialogue, and romantic attachment, as an invention only dear to militarists, isolationists, and apparatchiks.[29] Typically these films treat these sorts of security measures as a challenge for their main characters to defy or outmaneuver, as with *The Barbarian and the Geisha* or Alfred Hitchcock's spy thriller *Torn Curtain* (1966).³⁰ Some of these films rue the construction of security walls as a cause for ideological despondency and an affront to freedom of association, self-determination, and open and transparent communication, as in the case of *The Spy Who Came in from the Cold*. However, the films from the 2010s coming out after the 9/11 attacks and the Secure Fencing Act, and at about the same time as President Donald Trump's January 2017 Border Security and Immigration Enforcement Improvements Order, reflect changes in US attitudes toward the issue of nation-state walling.³¹ These films do not accede to the US development of separation walls so much as they express a certain cultural ambivalence about them, criticizing their violent effects while also representing them as *established facts*, as concretizations of twenty-first-century realpolitik over contentious issues of immigration reform, national security, and cultural identity. These films often suggest the crushing, coarsening, or deindividualizing effects of natural or man-made barriers on those inside of them, or the ways that these security measures create an atmosphere of social mistrust that tends to other characters *who do not appear to belong* to the nation-state.³² Although these films depict security walls and other such mechanisms as failures of the sociopolitical imagination, they nonetheless inure viewers to the act of seeing them and therefore to conceivably seeing them outside the movie theater or television room—to seeing walls without cinema. It is indisputable that much twenty-first-century mainstream Hollywood cinema works to normalize the very sight of these walls in US artistic, cultural, and critical discourse, their frequent reappearance from film to film making their real-life construction seem inevitable, almost a foregone conclusion. However, the ambivalence of these films to their subject matter, diegetic construction, and sociohistorical context also makes them extremely valuable tools for us to use in thinking through the dangers these walls represent to refugees, immigrants, citizens, military servicepersons, US government officials, and other nation-state actors, as well as to the environment, farmlands, wildlife, and the world's commercial traffics, shipping routes, capital flows, and overall economic well-being. These walls do not wait to show up on cinema screens until after the 2006 approval of the Secure Fence Act, though. Right after 9/11, a number of Hollywood releases and coproductions from 2003 to 2005 set about introducing their audiences to state security techniques, including the use of separation walling to *exclude certain bodies from certain spaces*. These films anticipate those that came to theaters after the installation of over 600 miles of wire and steel fencing on US–Mexican territories, during the course of its extension under President Barack Obama, and throughout Trump's efforts to finish the wall that the Bush administration, a GOP majority Congress, and the US Department of Homeland Security set about constructing.

For Yonder Walls, That Pertly Front Your Town

The impulse to security walling, according to Wendy Brown, invariably responds to a crisis in nation-state sovereignty. She argues that walls first and foremost serve a theatrical function, constituting a "screen for fantasies of restored sovereign potency and national purity" and offsetting fears of terrorism, mass immigration, demographic change, and the vagaries of transnational corporate finance.[33] Thus, these walls react not to the threat of invading armies or rival nation-state interests so much as represent an effort to stem the flow of certain social, economic, ethnoracial, and religious forces that the neoliberal order displaces from certain countries into others.[34] These walls resemble "shoals," as they attempt to divert, channel, reroute, or quiet the flow into a sovereign territory of the immigrants seeking work, the refugees seeking sanctuary, and the criminal elements (coyotes, drug runners, terrorists) concealing themselves among them.[35] These security measures—separation walls, surveillance webs, rapid-response networks—combine in their material effects and their theatrical qualities the functional with the chauvinistic, and in doing so they operate as "potent organizers" of cultural-political identities.[36]

Brown returns to the "shoal" metaphor to describe the sphere of activity of state security apparatuses, as they attempt to root out insurgent cells and at the same time control mass minorities: "Security requires not only the ability to survey, inspect, process, count, and record, but the ability to channel, transfer, relocate, or simply drive out certain populations."[37] However, as she further argues, these setups, in classing desperate workers and asylum seekers with "cultural-religious" aggressors, conduce to certain negative consequences.[38] These walls increase the cunning of those attempting to circumvent them and therefore the expense of tracking their movements through mountains, deserts, and tunnels. Also, these walls inadvertently finance terrorist organizations that turn to migrant smuggling to cover their own costs of operation.[39] Finally, Brown observes that, in the service of a ruthless neoliberalism, security walling tends to create a cheap, disposable workforce without any civil rights, citizenship entitlements, or union representation, thereby subjecting vulnerable families, communities, and alliances to violence and exploitation.[40] The theatrical surfaces of these walls more than offer the illusion of a once-again triumphant nation-state at times of crisis. They also cover over the cruelty that occurs on their other sides.

Concurring with this analysis, Inderpal Grewal argues that such cultures of security, surveillance, militarization, and ultra-nationalism set in motion further "insecurities, threats, and fears"; cast a shadow over the affects, desires, and social feelings of citizens; and at the same time empower certain agencies, all in the name of "safety," to continue to "work through violence" against outsiders.[41] However, she also argues that these insecurities make visible the material, economic, and sexual violence that state security mechanisms implement, as well as the ways they discipline the actions, movements, and sense-experiences of those they enclose and call on for support.[42] She then makes a case for the value of "corporate media" and implicitly US mainstream cinema, claiming that its "transnational reach and rapid circulation of images" makes it an ideal vehicle for exposing the contradictions inherent in neoliberal, imperialist, and colonizing ventures that necessitate separation walling for national defense and securitization.[43]

The films of the early 2000s, unlike much twentieth-century Hollywood cinema, spectacularize the construction, maintenance, and institutionalization of separation walls in their diegeses, as they at once anticipate the Secure Fence Act and root the use value of the measures it recommends in the theatrical. However, what distinguishes these films from those that appear after 2006 and into Trump's tenure in office is the fact that the walls in them represent more a reaction to the trauma of 9/11 than to crises of immigration, national identity, and cultural-demographic changeover. These films still trace the facticity of these walls to sovereign inaction or inadequacy—specifically, to the failure of the US government to thwart or intercept the al-Qaeda terrorists—and therefore these defense measures often come under attack, appearing throughout these narratives as at risk of infiltration, collapse, or some form of siege. Although these films do not focus on the same concerns as those coming out after 2006, they nevertheless depict the security walls in them serving a "shoal" or valve function, marking outsiders clearly as such and checking their flow into the sovereign territories of a city, village, or safe zone. These walls, as targets for destruction, more than function as metaphors of "Fortress America"; more importantly, they suggest that citizens' dependence on them only sets the stage for further war, terror, violence, unease, and moral depravation.

One of the first films to make state security one of its central conceits, Michael Winterbottom's *Code 46* (2003) focuses on insurance crime investigator William Geld (Tim Robbins), who travels to Shanghai for work and falls for Maria Gonzalez (Samantha Morton), a forger of "covers," travel documents that regulate the movement of citizens from city to city. The film, set in the near-future, divides its diegesis in two. The "inside" refers to its cityscapes, multicultural, multilingual, and neoliberal in character, and under the control of such sovereign corporate entities as the Sphinx that work in concert to enforce Code 46, an expansive set of sexual restrictions for citizens who share identical DNA due to wide-scale experimentation with cloning and other medical therapies. The "outside" refers to the desert wastelands surrounding these cities, accessible only through traffic and post-9/11-style airport security checkpoints, and the

FIGURE 1.3 *The Security Fencing Near the Wastelands in* Code 46.

settlement site for indigent nomads, street merchants, and those caught in violation of Code 46 (Figure 1.3). Maria, after spending a decade in the "outside" as an exile, drudges away assembling covers for the Sphinx. Thus, the film suggests that nation-state fencing and surveillance enables the further exploitation of workers, who constantly face more than the threat of unemployment or impoverishment—they face the threat of total expulsion from the wealth, comfort, technological affordances, and aesthetic charms of the cities and, along with this fate, the total revocation of their rights under the nation-state.

Moreover, the security infrastructure in the film only exacerbates the radical insecurity of its characters, as state forces make the couple feel ill at ease and ultimately discipline them for their "incestuous" tryst, erasing William's memories and sentencing Maria to exile in the desert. The film's security technosphere seems to cause serious environmental damage, namely the intense ultraviolent radiation that the couple describes as toxic and unbearable. Accordingly, those "inside" the cities only walk the streets at night and otherwise take shelter in workplaces, nightclubs, and apartment complexes, while those "outside" of them reside in shacks and suffer from fuller exposure to the sun. Finally, the security state offers its stooges access to viral treatments that can increase their empathetic skills or even turn them into mindless informants, suggesting that the sovereign corporations in the film aspire to shape and control citizens' affects, desires, and unconscious conduct. However, narrative circumstances function as a form of counterprogramming: William, whose travel clearance expires, must ask Maria to fabricate a cover, a turn of events, rather than a medical enhancement, that enables these characters to *truly empathize* with each other. The film solicits from its viewers, then, a similar affective reorientation toward those on the outside: it asks that they empathize with those who subsist right *beside* the safe, affluent cities near the Middle East,[44] a region so desolate that it does not even require a cover to visit. Hence, William declares in one scene that, under this system, citizens remain "prisoners of [their] genes," a warning that those subject to the security state must face the unpleasant fact that its carceral structures and regulatory overreach might come to seem as determinative and inescapable as their DNA codes, as it strives to control what even they can express.

Code 46 offhandedly makes reference to Baghdad as an uninhabitable site. The zombie science fiction film *Resident Evil: Apocalypse* (Alexander Witt, 2004), the first sequel in a series of them to a successful videogame adaptation, seems much more direct in its 9/11 overtones. The film, for example, features a woman making the Catch-22 decision to either turn into a zombie or dive off an office tower in the manner of the World Trade Center victims; an explosion that devastates the downtown area of a city, causing its skyscrapers to shatter and crumple; and a snippet of dialogue in its opening scenes consonant with the nation's sense of unease since the terror attacks: "We thought we had survived the horror, but we were wrong." *Apocalypse* follows Alice (Milla Jovovich), a superhuman test subject and former security director of the Umbrella Corporation, as she tries to escape Raccoon City, the site of The Hive, a secret research facility responsible for a zombie outbreak. Government forces order the evacuation of the city, since it is overrun with zombies, monsters, and other super-spreaders as a result of Umbrella's unethical testing of the mutagenic T-virus on its employees. The soldiers immediately seal off Raven's Gate Bridge, the main access point into the city, fortifying it with steel entry doors, cyclone fencing, and floodlights and stationing their snipers atop it to watch over the zombies. This security wall functions to screen the virus's survivors out from the zombies, with *Apocalypse*, unlike *Code 46*, othering them visually, as well as stylistically— slow motion effects distinguish the zombies from Alice's cohort, and the film additionally ramps its antiheroes' movements so that they appear quicker, effortless, and more impactful (Figure 1.4).

FIGURE 1.4 *Raven's Gate Bridge in* Resident Evil: Apocalypse.

The soldiers, though, cannot eliminate the zombies or rescue the survivors, so the Umbrella Corporation and the US government order a nuclear strike in order to contain the virus, a sign of nation-state inefficacy and misadministration that compels Alice and the other main characters to seek an airlift to the city's outskirts on their own. Even after their escape, Umbrella scientists recapture and implant satellite uplinks into Alice's flesh, so as to track their most valuable test subject throughout future installments of the series. Unlike in *Code 46*, then, most of *Apocalypse*'s narrative transpires *inside* the walled-in Raccoon City, with no clear means of escape from its state corporate regulation and control: no matter the quickness of their movements, Alice's cohort cannot elude the satellites orbiting the Earth and monitoring their activities. The "outside" of Umbrella's domain, in other words, remains its "inside." Although the film thus makes the security state seem almost ineluctable, it also suggests that walling, surveillance, and other forms of civil defense might also set in motion the conditions of its internal decay. After all, what are the zombies in the film, if not citizens unwilling to further acquiesce[45] to the whims of a technocratic order, to allow state forces and their corporate ancillaries to seize them with so much terror that they submit to imprisonment in the suburbs and shopping districts of their own city?

The inverse in some significant ways of *Resident Evil: Apocalypse*, Wolfgang Petersen's *Troy* (2004) also features an "inside" and an "outside," namely the city of the Trojans and the coastal wilderness surrounding its walls. This retelling of *The Iliad* follows King Agamemnon's (Brian Cox) efforts to recruit a cohort of Greek armies, including those of Odysseus (Sean Bean) and the redoubtable Achilles (Brad Pitt), in order to topple the city of Troy in spite of its unbreachable walls, ostensibly out of revenge for the abduction of Queen Helen (Diane Kruger). However, true to the film's release context in the aftermath of 9/11, the motives of the Greeks do not really center on Helen. A stand-in for George W. Bush, Agamemnon actually wages war on Troy for imperialist reasons, assembling a "coalition of the willing," so to speak, and only feigning to seek revenge on the Trojans for their slight to King Menelaus (Brendan Gleeson), the unfaithful Helen's consort. Over the course of the siege, Agamemnon accuses the ruler of the Trojans, the religiously observant Priam (Peter O'Toole), of "hiding behind [his] high walls," even though at times the Greek soldiers reconfigure themselves into a "wall" of shields to deflect the arrows and spears of their enemies. Ultimately, through the subterfuge of the Trojan Horse, the Greeks enter the city, rape and murder its residents, and, taking their direction from Agamemnon, sack its interiors, desecrate its temples, and attempt to "smash its walls to the ground." Their victories, though, cost the deaths of Agamemnon, Menelaus, and Achilles, along with Priam and the Trojan champion Hector (Eric Bana).

The walls of Troy, as well as the formations of the Greeks, increase the insecurity of those they mean to enclose and protect. The Trojans,

FIGURE 1.5 *The City Walls in* Troy.

for example, as they mass outside the city, *come to defend the walls more than the walls defend them* in the film's epic fighting sequences. Moreover, the walls make it impossible for the two opposing sides to see what the other is up to, compelling the Greeks to steal into the city in inglorious fashion and the surviving Trojans to sneak out of it at night—ultimately in order to establish the capital of Rome, more of an imperial threat to Agamemnon than Troy ever was. Over the course of its runtime, then, *Troy* suggests that security walls only tempt further dislocation, resettlement, and attritional warfare, and with them continual fear of infiltration and internal collapse (Figure 1.5). Much of the action in the film takes place *outside* these walls, and in a sense the Greeks over the course of the narrative seek to transform the city too into an "outside," destroying its sanctuaries and compelling its inhabitants to flee to the uplands. Unlike in *Resident Evil: Apocalypse*, then, the "inside" of the city retains the traces of its "outside," for its Greek occupiers and its native inhabitants. *Troy* thus underlines for viewers the untenable situation of those nation-states that must resort to constant terror alerts and tighter access checks to maintain their sovereign status and stop Trojan Horses (an apt metaphor for the 9/11 attackers) from foiling their security designs.

Troy and *Resident Evil: Apocalypse*, each in their own way, offer no discernible means of escape from the security state and its support industries, which, as Naomi Klein reports, after 9/11 "exploded to a size that is now significantly larger than" Hollywood.[46] M. Night Shyamalan's *The Village* (2004), though, dares to motion toward an alternative to the engineering and construction of detention centers, surveillance networks, facial recognition software, and separation walls in the aftermath of 9/11. The film introduces its viewers to the small mid-nineteenth-century village of Covington, a series of chicken wire fences, watchtowers, oil flares, and alarm clappers mysteriously surrounding this otherwise idyllic farm community. Soon an animal-like shriek emanates from Covington Woods, and in another scene one of the village elders, Edward Walker (William Hurt), explains the situation to a room full of children: "Those We Don't Speak Of have not breached our borders in many years. We do not go into their woods. They do not come into our valley. It is a truce. We do not threaten them." However, these "creatures" start to menace the community, slaughtering farm animals and marking the doors with a reddish streak, the color that attracts them and moreover signifies the most severe terror alert in the US Department of Homeland Security's advisory scale. The villagers take refuge in their cellars, and the elders warn their children against crossing "the forbidden line into Covington Woods." Nonetheless, after Noah Percy (Adrian Brody), a man suffering from mental and emotional disabilities, almost murders Lucius Hunt (Joachim Phoenix), the suitor of Ivy Walker (Bryce Dallas Howard), she finds that she must venture into the woods to ask the neighboring towns for medicine. The elders acquiesce, only since she cannot see; and over the course of the excursion we come to discover their ruse, as they wear monster suits to scare the villagers into reclusion and use chimes to simulate the moans and shrieks that came from the woods during the film's opening sequence.

This "farce," as the Walkers call it, anticipates the film's most controversial narrative twist: after crossing over to the other side of the woods, Ivy stumbles across a forest ranger driving in an automobile. She asks for medicine, and we come to realize that the village is actually set in a twenty-first-century wildlife sanctuary that the elders underwrote so as to assuage their traumas and shelter their children from the insecurities that the rest of the nation faces. The ranger chief repeats the message of Edward Walker, advising the others to "maintain and protect the border" and to "not get into conversations." *The Village*, then, unlike *Resident Evil: Apocalypse*, does not visually or stylistically mark those on the other side of its security fence as monstrous in appearance or inhuman in their movements. The film distinguishes the village from the ranger station only in terms of atmospherics, its two worlds—a quaint techno-primitive one within walking distance to a more modern counterpart—distinct in terms of tone and feel. Ivy then returns to Covington with the medicine for Lucius, as the film exposes the deception, self-delusion, and sociocultural retardation that security walling entails for those communities that decide to cut themselves off from their neighbors. *The Village*, in showing that the men and women of these two worlds do not differ that much in terms of their appearances or common needs, aspires to a *beyond* to the security state, to an intercultural conversation opening the way to new freedoms while at the same time exorcising older fears and intolerances. The film, it seems, enjoins us to create the conditions that might enable us to envision a sequel to it, one that we might christen *The Global Village*.

Slavoj Žižek asks, "What if the true evil of our societies" consists in "our attempts to extricate ourselves" from its "capitalist dynamics," through "carving out self-enclosed communal spaces," such as the one in *The Village*?[47] The films conspicuously featuring separation walls in their *mise-en-scène* that came out after the early 2000s retain their antecedents' critique of the insecurity and dishonesty that accompanies the neoliberal security state. However, in them we can detect a subtle shift away from some of the other concerns of those earlier films, as the walls in them, addressing the 9/11 attacks, the wars in the Middle East, and the US fretfulness toward Muslims, function in one of two ways: to constrain the movement of security threats or to establish the theater of operations for colonialist enterprises, analogous to the ones in Iraq and Afghanistan at the time. The films that came out after the authorization of the Secure Fence Act of 2006, though, start to focus more on other issues, such as immigration, sex slavery, and the risk of terrorists, drug traffickers, or other criminals entering the United States from the south. These films move away from colonial attitudes toward other sovereign nation-states and more toward a sense of nationalism, as the sovereign entities in them decide to wall their territories off from the world's other spheres of influence. Moreover, the security walls in these films do not simply regulate the movements of those inside them; they mainly function to exclude some characters from these areas in the first place, designating them as unacceptable due to their racial differences, inhuman traits, or monstrous appearances. The year 2006–7 appears to mark the moment of this shift. Thus the films that feature security walls in them that came out closer to the time of the questionable responses of the Bush administration to the 9/11 attacks, we might argue, represent at the most Trump-style solutions to fears over the weakening national defense, sociopolitical cachet, and cultural mythologies of the US *avant la lettre*.

Pictures Deface Walls Oftener Than They Decorate Them

Challenging the cultural and economic dominance of the Global North's neoliberal consensus, Julie Reid argues that the effort to reverse its imperialist tendencies "demands a far-reaching exercise of countermythologization" to expose "the fallacies" in those narratives, traditions, and modes of thinking that sustain it.[48] While it is doubtlessly crucial for decolonial efforts[49] to critique texts supportive of military adventurism, uneven development, and resource exploitation, it is also important that we do not forget or ignore those mainstream cultural discourses and media representations that might contain their own anti-imperialist messages. More to the point, we must ensure that these efforts do not dovetail with calls for a return to nationalism, "America First" exceptionalism, or commitments to deglobalization—in other words, with calls to militarily secure the state, wall it off from noncitizens, "purify" its ethnoracial identity, and force its retreat from the rest of the world's cultures. Nonetheless, Reid is correct to ask that we "counter-mythologize" the images in commercially dominant forms of cinematic expression, those with the most studio investment in spectacular special effects and marketing, access to theatrical distribution circuits worldwide, and value for downstream media venues (optical discs, streaming services, and television showings) and ancillary markets (toys, clothing, videogames, etc.).

Therefore, rather than simply root out elements of racism, apartheidism, or xenophobia in films that depict security fences, walls, and digital surveillance nets—rather than relegate these films to the "must-see" queues of the alt-right—this survey will focus on the deceptive surfaces of their diegeses, which seem to make it simple to recognize the moral alignments in them and the "right" spectator identifications that they solicit. These films at first might seem to say, "Look at these ugly, monstrous, nonhuman, or racially 'other' characters and then contrast them to the main characters. These adversaries *do not belong among them*." Flipping the title of Timothy Corrigan's monograph, *Walls Without Cinema* thus describes these films as spatio-legible. However, upon closer reading, these films also come to appear more complex, self-contradictory, and ambivalent about their own representational moves and *mise-en-scène* constructions; in fact, they come off more as cautionary notes about the effects of security walling and ultranationalism on a sovereign state, region, citizenry, or community. Often these films, even as they touch on anxieties over illegal immigration, drug smuggling, terrorism, or invasion, dream in their own individual ways of cross-border and cross-cultural contact.

As there are usually four corners to most walls, so too does *Walls Without Cinema* examine four sets of films, each offering different inflections of the functions of state-border security apparatuses, their effects on the characters on-screen, and the meaning of their sectioning off of certain tracts of diegetic space as *properly belonging* to this or that faction, tribe, company, citizenry, or denomination. The first chapter, "Green Zones," takes its title from the occupation site of the interim Coalition Authority set up during the time of the Bush administration's (mis)handling of the Iraq War. This chapter focuses on the war films, fantasy films, and science fiction films that depict the establishment of movable, semipermanent fortifications in dangerous, war-torn, or mostly forsaken areas. Moreover, the chapter adapts the work of Michel Henry to describe the narrative action in these films as *archibarbaric*, as they dramatize the deracination of an entire culture at the insistence of some form of scientific-mathematic-military calculus, as well as its replacement with a set of conditions that makes it difficult for the main characters to discern their enemies and vice versa. Combining Henry's work with Hannah Arendt's on totalitarian movements, the chapter also traces out the two main operative dynamics at work in any archi-barbaric state of affairs: the *objective* and the *subjective*. The first term refers to those forces of military-industrial rationalization set up to determine the "objective enemies" of the main characters in the film, marking them according to their emplacement in, near, or outside of the fences, checkpoints, outposts, and other defense contrivances of a Green Zone-style district. The other term, the subjective, refers to the confusions, ethical dilemmas, and spatial trespasses that ensue, enabling the characters—and the film's audience—to view the erection of walls, fences, and roadblocks with skepticism, to view them as strangulations of "life," which Henry defines as our full-sense participation in specific tasks that inevitably orient us toward an ever-changing socius. The films that this chapter discusses all feature this dynamic tension in them, compelling their main characters to constantly renegotiate the security mechanisms that at once set them *against and right next to* their "enemies" to the detriment of their social feeling and cultural enrichment, although also with the advantage of allowing them to see up close the inefficacy, destructiveness, and inhumanity of these sorts of walls.

The next chapter, "Safe Spaces," focuses on several films conspicuously set inside security walls, fences, and domes, reminiscent of the ones that separate Israel from the Palestinian West Bank; Egypt from the Gaza Strip; Saudi Arabia from Iraq; Turkey from Syria, Iran, and Bulgaria; Kazakhstan from Uzbekistan; Botswana from Zimbabwe; Greece from Macedonia; India from Pakistan in Kashmir; and, ever since 2006 under George W. Bush, the United States from Mexico. Using Michel Foucault's seminars on the defense of the nation-state, this chapter advances the notion of the *racio-spatial* to describe the diegetic forces in a selection of twenty-first-century monster films that serve to distinguish one set of characters from another. The security walls in these films first mark those outside of the nation-state as subhuman, alien, or racially inferior, encouraging the main characters inside them to see the differentness of these monsters as reason enough for their continual exclusion, suppression, conquest, extermination, or enslavement. Taking further inspiration from Foucault, the conceptual work in these films also functions according to a two-prong dynamic, as they sort all of their main, side, and digital "extra" characters into the categories of the *subracial* and the *superracial*, the first of them under the sovereign control, study, review, domination, and oversight of the other. However, once again these films do not simply endorse racist or nationalist rhetorics, or the construction, reinforcement, or underwriting of security apparatuses and screening techniques meant to dehumanize and discriminate against noncitizens of the nation-state. This chapter also relies on the media theories of Bernard Stiegler to argue that these films enable us to envision some of the ways these defense infrastructures also "wall in" their main characters' memories, self-identities, and capacities for interpersonal connection. The narratives in these films drive the viewers and the characters in them to realize that such security measures make them *anything but safe*, as they risk the isolation, degeneration, or internal collapse of those whom they enclose and "protect" from outsiders and extraterritorial forces. The characters, as the chapter shows, rather than suffer these evils, rethink, escape, or even tear down these walls, struggling to form what Stiegler calls a new sense of "we" with those on the other side of them.

"Gated Communities," the chapter following "Safe Spaces," examines those films that reverse course, so to speak, as they depict their main characters as suffering exile, facing abandonment in an inhospitable region, or finding themselves outside the security walls of the nation-state and desperately seeking some means to reenter them. This chapter, encompassing such disparate (sub)genres as science fiction adventure and "gross-out" comedy-horror, examines these films using the work of Michel Serres to theorize the *para-exilic* nature of their diegetic environments.[50] The characters in these films share an ambivalent sociopolitical status: the nation-state affords them certain rights and entitlements, recognizes them as citizens, and situates them within its territorial assets, at the same time that it regards them as unwelcome and disposable—almost as émigrés or traitors—if they transgress its security features. These characters, in short, while technically remaining citizens, come to experience the same demeaning and abject conditions as do refugees, nomads, or illegal immigrants. The chapter traces in their struggles to return to their native countries another dynamic, this time drawing on Serres's arguments concerning *hard* and *soft* forms of pollution. Hard aspects of the para-exilic include the characters' dislocation from their nation-state, along with the repatriation of immigrants, whereas its softer aspects refer to the excess of signs (computer memes, news soundbites, ideologico-political catchphrases, sports chants, corporate symbols, advertising slogans, etc.) that the culture exudes, an incessant mediatic noise that makes nonstate territories seem scary, unappealing, or retrograde, so much so that those from these other cities, countries, or worlds do not want to remain there either. The nation-state does not simply shut out its more "undesirable" elements—for example, the indigent or irresponsible—so much as it expands its dominion over other spaces through them. Much as no one wants to claim a scrapheap or trash dump, so too is no other nation-state eager to claim an area with a significant degree of demographic shifting, cultural encroachment, and sociolinguistic corruption. Serres's ideas, of course, elaborate Julia Kristeva's work on abjection, although the chapter relies more on *Nations without Nationalism* to think through the work of *de-origination* that occurs in these films, as the main characters in them strive to recover their national identities, even as they stray from their familial, ethnoracial, religious, or class roots to uncertain, although sometimes anti-nationalist and cosmopolitan, effect. These characters assume the condition of what Kristeva refers to as that of "the stranger" so that, rather than obsess over their countries of origin, they come to introduce new values, speech acts, and cultural practices into them upon their return. These characters, as strangers to their own soil, can then urge their neighbors or fellow citizens to overcome their fear of foreigners, repudiate their support for security walls or surveillance systems, and challenge what media outlets induce them to think of as "home."

The final chapter calls attention to a set of films that feature their characters carving out alternative spaces in which they can subvert, circumvent, and flout state security mechanisms in order to enter into cross-border dialogue with those that their administrators deem their enemies or economic rivals. Focusing on action thrillers, superhero films, and zombie romances, "Interface Areas" advances the notion of the *crypto-social* to describe the clandestine relationships that develop in them, along with the actions, situations, and spatial maneuverings that make new forms of community-building visible and viable. Again, the chapter teases out of these films a two-prong dynamic, this time using the work of Michel de Certeau to discuss the ways that these characters negotiate and upset travel ordnances, security restrictions, and resettlement checks in terms of the *strategic* and the *tactical*. The first refers to the work of dominant institutional forces in constructing, maintaining, and watching over certain areas—for example, security fences and the roads, checkpoints, and no-go zones that intersect them—and then regulating their uses, directing their traffic flows, and detaining or criminalizing those they call to account for what they designate as illicit, deviant, or otherwise dissident activities. The tactical, in contrast, refers to the innovative, often unpredictable uses that individuals and crowds make of these spaces, as they start to experiment with them, inventing new ways to move in and through them and new ways to forge collective identities within them. Further, this chapter couples these terms with Paolo Virno's theorization of the multitude, which, unlike the state, with its monopolization of decision-making, shuns authority, resists top-down social contracts, and refuses to cede its rights to a sovereign entity. The multitude, then, as a "purely negative *borderline* concept" does not insist its members consolidate into some nation-state equivalent; it rather unites them through "shared experiences," and moreover their common faculties for intelligent self-government mindful of difference.[51] The films that this chapter covers speak to this notion of multitude, as their characters tactically traverse the security walls and exclusion zones in them, affording them opportunities to interact with those the state considers "off-limits." These films, in short, in staging cultural and even romantic exchanges with those inside or outside the nation-state, explores those alliances, coalitions, and fellowships that might serve to make these fences, walls, watchtowers, airbases, surveillance networks, and so forth a moot or needless effort. The crypto-social nature of these films therefore makes *legible* more than the visual differences that oppose this or that set of characters, relegating them to one side or the other of a wall. Such films show their characters using these spaces against the intentions of their makers, who, it seems, inadvertently incorporate into their expensive design the triggers for their self-destruction.

These films, in sum, as they type some of their characters as monstrous, threatening, or racially other according to the side of the security fence that they occupy, seem anything other than "illegible." Again, Corrigan sees twentieth-century cinema as a cinema without walls, defying the causal integrity of traditional narrative form, interrogating the specificities that separate one medium from another, and using the camera to frame thematic concerns, ideological tendencies, and social interactions atypical of Hollywood entertainment. The cinema of the new millennium, though, seems quite the opposite: a series of walls without cinema, in that many of its films contain scenes utterly constraining and claustrophobic in their *mise-en-scène* development, quite reminiscent of the increasingly walled-in nation-states outside the theater. These mainstream films are not as reactionary or ultra-paranoiac as they might at first seem; as Corrigan argues in an essay on twenty-first-century cinema, they also "cyclically and centrifugally" intersect different sociopolitical worlds and thus construct "new visions" from them, "invariably stretching the terms and borders of reality, realism, and the definition of the human."[52] The actual theatrical or electronic screen, then, rather than representing an escape from unpalatable sociopolitical realities or a commercialization of cultural-artistic revolution, modestly enables us to sense through its diverse fantasy scenarios and CG confections *the real-life multiplication of the walls surrounding us.* These films, if anything, can serve us as countermyths to the rhetoric of the Trump administration and its far-right equivalents in other nations, allowing us to reimagine and vicariously feel the effects of sealing our territories on citizens and soldiers, as well as refugees, immigrants, and visitors. These films, in so doing, encourage us to think at once more intricately and situationally about the realpolitik ethical decisions we must make concerning the security walls outside the cinema—the walls without it. These films also caution us, in our efforts to resist, decolonize, and take ever more stringent ethical turns, not to completely neglect or diminish the use value of mass market culture. To do so means to ignore the fact that, whatever their shortcomings, these films constantly offer us other worlds[53] to see, experience, and often delight in. To dismiss them as risk-adverse corporate commodities forgets that they serve as vestibules to these other worlds, that they represent a surface that appears the very opposite of those walls that offer us nothing new to see—in short, they are never mere signifiers of the monocultural or nationalistic. These films are thus worth exploring in detail, worth feeling our way about and through.

Notes

1 See, for example, Jenna Johnson, "'Build That Wall' Has Taken on a Life of Its Own at Donald Trump's Rallies—but He's Still Serious," *Washington Post*, February 12, 2016, https://www.washingtonpost.com/news/post-politics/wp/2016/02/12/build-that-wall-has-taken-on-a-life-of-its-own-at-donald-trumps-rallies-but-hes-still-serious/; Dan Nowicki, Rafael Carranza, and Ian James, "Trump Says He Now Prefers 'See-through' Wall," March 13, 2018, https://www.azcentral.com/story/news/politics/border-issues/2018/03/13/donald-trump-visits-san-diego-see-border-wall-prototypes-miramar-otay-mesa-los-angeles/418640002/; Sarah Jarvis, "'Build the Wall' and 'Fake News': Crowd Fired Up Ahead of Trump Rally in Tampa," *News Press*, July 31, 2018, https://www.news-press.com/story/news/politics/2018/07/31/donald-trump-crowd-braves-rain-long-wait-ahead-trump-rally-tampa/870189002/; Rebecca Harrington, "Trump Holds Boisterous Saturday Night Rally in '110-Degree' Hot High School in Ohio," *Business Insider*, August 4, 2018, https://www.businessinsider.com/trump-rally-ohio-highlights-quotes-2018-8; and Daniel J. Gross, "5 Arrested During 'Build the Wall' Rally and Counter-Protest in Downtown Greenville," *Greenville News*, October 13, 2018, https://www.greenvilleonline.com/story/news/2018/10/13/4-arrested-build-wall-rally-counter-protest-greenville/1629833002/.

2 See George W. Bush, "Bush's Speech on Immigration," *New York Times*, May 15, 2006, https://www.nytimes.com/2006/05/15/washington/15text-bush.html.

3 See Donald J. Trump, "Here's Donald Trump's Presidential Announcement Speech," *Time*, June 16, 2015, https://time.com/3923128/donald-trump-announcement-speech/.

4 See "Executive Order: Border Security and Immigration Enforcement Improvements," January 25, 2017, https://www.whitehouse.gov/presidential-actions/executive-order-border-security-immigration-enforcement-improvements/, as well as Julie Hirschfield Davis, "Trump Orders Mexican Border Wall to Be Built and Plans to Block Syrian Refugees," *New York Times*, January 25, 2017, https://www.nytimes.com/2017/01/25/us/politics/refugees-immigrants-wall-trump.html; Erika Bolstad, "Trump's Wall Could Cause Serious Environmental Damage," *Scientific American*, January 26, 2017, https://www.scientificamerican.com/article/trumps-wall-could-cause-serious-environmental-damage/; Garrett M. Graff, "The Border Patrol Hits a Breaking Point," *Politico*, July 15, 2019, https://www.politico.com/magazine/story/2019/07/15/border-patrol-trump-administration-227357; and Tina Vasquez, "The New ICE Age: An Agency Unleashed," *New York Review of Books*, May 2, 2018, https://www.nybooks.com/daily/2018/05/02/the-new-ice-age-an-agency-unleashed/.

5 See Grace Segers, "Kevin McCarthy Says He Will Introduce Bill to Fully Fund Border Wall," *CBS News*, October 9, 2018, https://www.cbsnews.com/news/kevin-mccarthy-introducing-bill-to-fully-fund-border-wall/.

6 Naomi Klein, *The Rise of Disaster Capitalism* (New York: Picador, 2007), 382–3.

7   Timothy Corrigan, *A Cinema without Walls: Movies and Culture after Vietnam* (New Brunswick: Rutgers University Press), 52.
8   Ibid., 17.
9   Ibid., 17–23.
10 Ibid., 30–1.
11 Ibid., 5–6.
12 See George W. Bush, "President Bush Addresses the Nation on Immigration Reform," May 15, 2006, https://georgewbush-whitehouse.archives.gov/news/releases/2006/05/text/20060515-8.html.
13 See NPR Staff and Wires, "Obama Deploying 1,200 Troops to Mexico Border," *NPR*, May 30, 2010, https://www.npr.org/templates/story/story.php?storyId=127116888; and Randal C. Archibold and Marc Lacey, "Obama Requests Money for Border Security," *New York Times*, June 22, 2010, https://www.nytimes.com/2010/06/23/us/23border.html.
14 See David Nakamura, "Three Presidents, Three Speeches—and an Immigration Debate That Has Grown Courser," *Washington Post*, January 8, 2019, https://www.washingtonpost.com/politics/three-presidents-one-border--and-an-immigration-debate-that-has-grown-coarser/2019/01/08/d9f3c4a4-1357-11e9-90a8-136fa44b80ba_story.html.
15 See Vivian Salama, "Trump Threatens to 'Call Up the U.S. Military' If Mexico Doesn't Stop Migrants," *Wall Street Journal*, October 18, 2018, https://www.wsj.com/articles/trump-threatens-to-call-up-the-u-s-military-if-mexico-doesnt-stop-migrants-1539866223; and Donald J. Trump (@realDonaldTrump), "In addition to stopping all payments to these countries, which seem to have almost no control over their population, I must, in the strongest of terms, ask Mexico to stop this onslaught—and if unable to do so I will call up the U.S. Military and CLOSE OUR SOUTHERN BORDER!" *Twitter*, October 18, 2018, https://twitter.com/realdonaldtrump/status/ 1052885781675687936?lang=en.
16 Michael J. Shapiro, *The Political Sublime* (Durham, NC: Duke University Press, 2018), 172.
17 Richard Slotkin, *Gunfighter Nation: The Myth of the Frontier in Twentieth-Century America* (Norman: University of Oklahoma Press), 490.
18 Ibid., 516–19.
19 These films, of course, might whitewash certain sociohistorical realities, such as the fact that the United States until 1952 sought to cap nonwhite and Eastern European immigration with quota systems, to deport noncitizens with the flimsiest of evidence for their communist sympathies, and to outright deny entry to "security risks," as Kevin R. Johnson reminds us. However, the open-borders ideals in the films of the Cold War era nonetheless remain important, as they suggest the faults of these restrictionist measures and at the same time map the changing cultural sentiments that were to set in motion immigration reform. These films still remain relevant to our thinking on these intractable subjects in the twenty-first century; as Johnson says, "The Berlin Wall-lite that the government is in the process of erecting between the U.S. and Mexico

is not consistent with American dreams and values." See Kevin R. Johnson, *Opening the Floodgates: Why America Needs to Rethink Its Borders and Immigration Laws* (New York: New York University Press, 2007), 50–5, 210.

20 Nathan Juran's Cold War monster film *The Deadly Mantis* (1957) touches on the incongruous relation of US national security interests and "Free World" expansionism. The film opens in faux newsreel fashion, with its narrator describing the "supersonic shield" that extends from the Arctic Circle to Canada, an early warning system of three "radar fences" that serves to detect threats to North America, such as Soviet drifting stations, aircraft, and other invasion forces. These fences alert the US and Canadian militaries of the size, movement, and activities of such threats, including the 200-foot ancient mantis that emerges from a melting iceberg in the film's first act, especially after it attacks two men at one of the radar outposts. These fences do not obstruct the movements of the mantis, though, as it flies over Inuit Canada into the United States and toward the Washington Monument. This defense system, then, respects the ideal of safe conduct across international territories in contradistinction to the travel restrictions starting to further divide the East from the West along the inner German border in the mid-1950s. The film's distributors, we can surmise, were aware to some extent of these sociopolitical issues, since they thought to release it as a double feature with another Cold War film, *The Girl in the Kremlin* (Russell Birdwell, 1957).

21 Philip Horne, "Martin Scorsese: Catholic Tastes," *Sight & Sound* 27, no. 2 (2017): 17.

22 J. Hoberman, *The Dream Life: Movies, Media, and the Mythology of the Sixties* (New York: New Press, 2003), 45, 49.

23 Marcel Mauss, while convalescing from an illness in New York, made this observation about the strangely familiar motions of the nurses in the infirmary: "I wondered where previously I had seen girls walking as my nurses walked. I had time to think about it. At last I realized that it was at the cinema." He concludes that a certain cultural milieu, along with its traditional notions and media affordances, educates our sensoria and motor techniques in specific ways. These mimetic aspects of our embodiment obviously might then suffer from the effects of nation-state apartheidism, severely reducing the range of sense-experiences and skeletomuscular movement available to those on either side of a security fence, wall, or embankment. See Marcel Mauss, "Techniques of the Body," in *The Body: A Reader*, trans. Ben Brewster, ed. Mariam Fraser and Monica Greco (New York: Routledge, 2005), 74.

24 The noirish *Assignment—Paris!* (Robert Parrish, 1952) suggests that security apparatuses also affront the acoustic dimensions of cinema. The film deals with more than the material fortifications that separate the West from the Soviet Bloc; it also focuses on the "iron wall of censorship," as the narrator calls it, dividing the superpowers from each other. The film contrasts the open communications of the *New York Herald Tribune* office in France to the eavesdropping, teletape interference, and audio manipulation that occur in Hungary. The news reporter Jimmy Race (Dana Andrews) travels inside the Iron Curtain to obtain more information about a US citizen that the

communists saw fit to falsely condemn for espionage in a show trial. For sneaking news of the man's death through to Paris, the Hungarians arrest, imprison, and torture Race—the iron wall of censorship thus commutes into the "iron wall" of a cell door. The film, in concert with the ideological slant of its era, suggests that free thought and speech coincide with free transit. Upon release at the French-Hungarian frontier, Race almost seems comatose and unable to walk, showing the signs of internalizing the rather inhibitory security restrictions of the Soviet East. Thus, the message that the film sneaks off to us, in a sense, is that nation-state isolationism compels silence, self-censorship, and inner deadness.

25 *Atomic Blonde*, in the figure of its main character, seems a remarkable instance of Mary Anne Doane's concept of masquerade, a term that designates the ascription of "sexual mobility" to dominant cultural understandings of femininity. She describes it as a "mask" that its wearer can assume, exploit, and remove, much as Lorraine Broughton does with the Satchel ruse. The difference, though, is that in *Atomic Blonde* she foists this mask on to other characters, mainly two men who typically in Hollywood cinema cannot make use of feminine masquerade (unless in self-parodic fashion, as in Brian De Palma's 1980 thriller *Dressed to Kill*). The feminine, in short, appears more mobile than ever in *Atomic Blonde*, almost free-floating, than it does in similar spy films, such as *Point of No Return* (John Badham, 1993) and *Red Sparrow* (Francis Lawrence, 2018), in which the women "doll up" and use their attractiveness to close in on their targets and compromise or assassinate them. The masquerade in *Atomic Blonde* refuses these forms of containment and dichotomization, as it affixes to certain characters irrespective of their sex, age, nationality, or choosing—appropriately for a film in which crossing through walls and checkpoints seems as easy as changing the color and style of one's coiffure. See Mary Ann Doane, *Femmes Fatales: Feminism, Film Theory, Psychoanalysis* (New York: Routledge, 1991), 25.

26 Timothy Corrigan argues that the cement fragments that collectors sought after the fall of the Berlin Wall attest to the event's function as a "carnival media spectacle" meant to rejoice over "an impending social unification under the sign of political consumerism." The carnivalesque form of *Atomic Blonde*, with its rapid-fire editing, energetic visuals, and violent action set pieces, thus seems the complement of the illegal sale of music, electronics, and other forbidden merchandise transpiring right under the shadow of the Wall. East and West, despite this obstruction, already unite in their cultural tastes and consumer impulses. The film, then, suggests that security walling actively triggers *a curiosity* over the fads, styles, and cultural expressions of those it deters from entering the nation-state. As it is made illegal, then, the cosmopolitan turns into a means of resistance. See Corrigan, *Cinema without Walls*, 199.

27 Lisa Purse, "Affective Trajectories: Locating Diegetic Velocity in the Cinema Experience," *Cinema Journal* 55, no. 2 (2016): 151–7.

28 The couching of state security concerns in national myth, if not overt nostalgia, is nothing new, of course. J. Hoberman discusses the ramifications

of the National Security Council 68 document of 1950, assessing the seriousness of the military, economic, and ideological conflict of the United States with the Soviet Eurasian Bloc. He summarizes its conclusions thus: "To defend freedom, it will be necessary to reinforce and expand the security state." Afterward, such films as *Atomic City* (Jerry Hopper, 1952) start to depict Los Alamos as "another Fort Apache, a barren, gated, militarized suburb on the edge of existence." Don Siegel's *Invasion of the Body Snatchers* (1956) further offers "an imaginative visualization of the national security state," complete with the costs it represents to U.S. citizens' sense of individualism. However, Hoberman does not stress enough *the tensions between freedom and state securitization*, tensions in the cultural imaginary that enable viewers to take a doubtful or even an oppositional approach to anodyne representations of national defense in the cinema. See J. Hoberman, *Army of Phantoms: American Movies and the Making of the Cold War* (New York: New Press, 2011), 117, 198, 313.

29   The spy film *Man on a String* (Andre DeToth, 1960) clearly defines the US stance on the right to enter against that of the Soviet Union during the tumultuous Berlin Crisis. The movie studio chief Boris Mitrov (Ernest Borgnine) travels through the Brandenburg Gate to East Berlin as a double agent for the United States and must afterward flee the country with difficulty, finding the checkpoints shut down and the Stasi on alert. One manages to shackle Mitrov, a scene that underlines the cramping of the individual's movement in the Eastern Bloc. However, the double agent escapes, and the final shot of the film offers a view of the ways that the United States in contrast might manage such matters of immigration, sanctuary, and the freedom to travel: an inscription on an office wall conspicuously features the verse of the sonnet "The New Colossus" ("Give me your tired, your poor …").

30   Although the Berlin Wall never appears in Alfred Hitchcock's *Torn Curtain* (1966), it nonetheless functions as the structuring absence of the film. Most critics, following Hitchcock's comments about it in an interview with Francois Truffaut, focus on its use of color to differentiate the two worlds of its Cold War milieu. Richard Allen, for example, describes the film's settings in Sweden and East Berlin as "an opposition of colorfulness and colorlessness," with duller and cooler shades dominating those scenes on the Soviet side of the Iron Curtain. The film follows scientist Michael Armstrong (Paul Newman) and fiancée Sarah Sherman (Julie Andrews) in their efforts to obtain a formula for an anti-ballistic missile from a colleague in Freiburg. The course of their adventures shows that Hitchcock also constructs the film's diegetic spaces in specific ways in order to distinguish the capitalist and communist worlds from each other. The atmosphere in the Hotel D'Angleterre in Sweden appears freer, more open, and more commodious than its counterpart in East Berlin, where a number of dutiful civilians, as the Stasi chase after Michael and Sarah, *transform themselves into a wall* in front of its main doors to stop them from escaping to the streets. To flee the country, the couple must cause a riot at a dance concert, slipping out of the theater to safety after the crowds inside it almost separate them—in the manner of the Berlin Wall. *Torn Curtain* suggests that transgressing the rules that structure a social space

and its affective climate, rather than embodying or adapting to them, might transform the entire international scene, tempering the threat of illegitimate nation-state expansion. After all, the famous McGuffin that the couple chases after might counter a thermonuclear attack, thus upsetting the entire telos of the Cold War. See Richard Allen, "Hitchcock's Color Designs," in *Color: The Film Reader*, ed. Angela Dalle Vacche and Brian Price (New York: Routledge, 2006), 134.

31 Congresswoman Alexandria Ocasio-Cortez on February 20, 2019, during a webcast thought to compare the Berlin Wall to Trump's wall, describing it as a "moral abomination." Conservative media outlets, such as *Fox News* and the *New York Post*, were anxious to take the freshman House Representative to task, contending that whereas the GDR sought to stop its citizens from fleeing, the Trump administration seeks to exclude those who enter the country illegally. While superficially true, such arguments risk missing out on important elements of the overall picture—in fact, they might consider in the future taking in more *motion pictures*, such as *The Spy Who Came in from the Cold*—as they fail to acknowledge one of the serious aftereffects of nation-state walling: cultural stagnation and, with it, an overarching sense of moral and intellectual colorlessness. See, in any event, Mark Moore, "Ocasio-Cortez Compares Trump's Border Wall to Berlin Wall," *New York Post*, February 19, 2019, https://nypost.com/2019/02/19/ocasio-cortez-compares-trumps-border-wall-to-berlin-wall/; and Lukas Mikelionis, "Ocasio-Cortez Raises Eyebrows after Comparing Trump's Border Wall to Berlin Wall," *Fox News*, February 19, 2019, https://www.foxnews.com/politics/ocasio-cortez-raises-eyebrows-after-comparing-trumps-border-wall-to-berlin-wall.

32 One of the most remarkable cuts in Rouben Mamoulian's *Becky Sharp* (1935), an adaptation of Thackeray's *Vanity Fair* mostly notable for its first-ever use of three-strip Technicolor in feature filmmaking, transitions from the face of one of its characters to a map of Europe during the time of Napoleon's defeat at Waterloo. The implication is clear and astounding—facial traits, skin colors, and cultural tics serve to naturalize nation-state demarcations so that individuals appear to suit certain regions and not others, unless for émigré or imperialist reasons. Contrast this sequence with the action climax of Tony Richardson's *The Border* (1982), a film critical of immigration enforcement and the racism that accompanies it. The Border Patrol agent Charlie (Jack Nicholson) shoots a coyote in the face with a shotgun at the Mexico–US desert frontier—the man's skull explodes into fragments of cerebra and muscle tissue in front of our eyes. The film complements, in a sense, the earlier cut in *Becky Sharp*: nation-state division, immigration control, and security fencing more than naturalize and reinforce the separation of races, ethnicities, and cultures; they also facilitate their *erasure* in the form of reciprocal violence and mistrust. The face in the first film disintegrates into the fragments of the map, whereas the map in *The Border* in turn causes the disintegration of the face. Thus, these two films serve as indicators of the spatio-legible complexion of cross-border relations in US cinema.

33 Wendy Brown, *Walled States, Waning Sovereignty* (New York: Zone Books, 2010), 9.

34 Ibid., 15, 93.
35 Maya Goodfellow argues that security walls represent more than violence, exclusion, or discrimination; they also serve a *descriptive* function, as those who cross over, under, or through them "cease to be a human being" and turn into "an ('illegal') immigrant or a ('bogus') asylum seeker." She advocates scrutinizing the territorial markers of the nation-state in order to dismantle them, a task that mainstream Hollywood cinema, with its wide market appeal and distribution, might assist us in doing. See Maya Goodfellow, *Hostile Environment: How Immigrants Become Scapegoats* (New York: Verso, 2019), 35.
36 Brown, *Walled States, Waning Sovereignty*, 86.
37 Ibid., 112.
38 Ibid., 45.
39 Ibid., 10, 50.
40 Ibid., 50, 111.
41 Inderpal Grewal, *Saving the Security State: Exceptional Citizens in Twenty-First-Century America* (Durham, NC: Duke University Press, 2017), 2, 13.
42 Ibid., 21.
43 Ibid., 23.
44 Graeme Stout argues that this "outside" does not represent the negative of the "inside" of the corporate spaces in the film so much as an alternative to them, or more exactly "the thought of an outside to a system that determines life and death on the most basic level." See Graeme Stout, "Control and Flow: Winterbottom's Migratory Cinema," in *Alien Imaginations: Science Fiction and Tales of Transnationalism*, ed. Ulrike Küchler, Silja Maehl, and Graeme Stout (New York: Bloomsbury Academic, 2015), 222.
45 Sarah Juliet Lauro and Karen Embry describe the zombie as "an antisubject" that effaces the unique, recognizable features of the individual, collapses the subject–object distinction, and therefore "disrupts the entire" social system that depends on these sorts of categories for its functioning and internal coherence. See Sarah Juliet Lauro and Karen Embry, "A Zombie Manifesto: The Nonhuman Condition in the Era of Advanced Capitalism," in *Zombie Theory: A Reader*, ed. Sarah Juliet Lauro (Minneapolis: University of Minnesota Press, 2017), 397, 400.
46 Klein, *Rise of Disaster Capitalism*, 386.
47 Slavoj Žižek, *Violence: Six Sideways Reflections* (New York: Picador, 2008), 27.
48 Julie Reid, "Decolonizing Education and Research by Countering the Myths We Live By," *Cinema Journal* 57, no. 4 (2018): 135.
49 Stephanie Fuller notes that the United States, as the "antidote to old world empires," through the 1823 Monroe Doctrine, sought to secure Central and South America from European colonization and interference. Throughout the Cold War, the United States was to condemn the Soviet Union's involvement

with Eastern Europe as a form of colonialism. The debates over security walls in the twenty-first century must appear, then, as *an obscene version of the nation's founding ideals*, as calls for the democratic self-determination of its neighbors to the south twist into isolationist rhetoric, ugly xenophobic attitudes, and the cruel and irresponsible treatment of migrant workers and asylum seekers. See Stephanie Fuller, *The US-Mexico Border in American Cold War Film: Romance, Revolution, and Regulation* (New York: Palgrave Macmillan, 2015), 6.

50 Hamid Naficy defines the exilic in relation to those filmmakers who "voluntarily or involuntarily have left their country of origin and who maintain an ambivalent relationship with their previous and current places and cultures." The para-exilic, even though it closely resembles Naficy's term in several ways, also differs from it in one important respect: namely, the characters in the films that it refers to ultimately return to their native countries. Hence, the "para-." See Hamid Naficy, *An Accented Cinema: Exilic and Diasporic Filmmaking* (Princeton, NJ: Princeton University Press, 2001), 12.

51 Paolo Virno, *A Grammar of the Multitude: For an Analysis of Contemporary Forms of Life*, trans. Isabella Bertoletti, James Cascaito, and Andrea Casson (Los Angeles: Semiotext(e), 2004), 23, 25.

52 Timothy Corrigan, "Introduction: Movies and the 2000s," in *American Cinema of the 2000s: Themes and Variations*, ed. Timothy Corrigan (New Brunswick: Rutgers University Press, 2012), 1.

53 Herbert Marcuse, in the face of a certain overzealousness in the radical critiques of the 1960s and 1970s, an era with its own concerns over the fascistic tendencies of the US government, affirms the utopian nature of even the most traditional art, in that it envisions other worlds for us to contemplate and savor: "By virtue of this transformation of the specific historical universe in the work of art—a transformation which arises in the presentation of the specific content itself—art opens the established reality to another dimension: that of possible liberation." He continues that "it does so only if art *wills* itself as illusion: as an unreal world other than the established one." Marcuse sets forth the value of even the most crassly commercial of cinematic works, the seemingly interchangeable fantasy, action, science fiction, and superhero films of the twenty-first century that imagine other worlds for us to explore and, with them, "a universe of concrete possibilities." See Herbert Marcuse, *Counterrevolution and Revolt* (Boston, MA: Beacon Press, 1972), 87–8.

2

Green Zones: Beside the Walls on the Cinema Screen

The Project of the New American Century, a neoconservative think tank with a decisive influence on the George W. Bush administration, set forth the notion in its manifesto that the United States, in order to ensure its domination of the world's markets and cultures, must militarily "secure and expand zones of democratic peace" in Europe, Asia, and the Middle East, as well as enlarge its own "security perimeters."[1] Ron Suskind reports that one of Bush's aides, at the outset of the 2003 invasion of Iraq, spoke directly to the impact of these mission statements on the War on Terror: "We're an empire now, and when we act, we create our own reality."[2] US occupation forces soon thereafter set up their center of operations along the riverside quadrants of Baghdad, referring to it as the "Green Zone," the site of a series of villas, ministries, monuments, and compounds, formerly serving as the seat of Saddam Hussein's dictatorship. The military and its contractors oversaw the construction of a number of walls, fences, and checkpoints throughout the area, intending to use them to screen out insurgents, suicide attackers, and troublemakers. The Green Zone came to seem roughly American in culture, affording those stuck inside this "Bubble," as US troops were to refer to it, access to telephones, the internet, DVD consoles, comfort foods, and other services and amenities.[3]

At the same time, the rest of the city, *alongside* these security measures, equally and rapidly came to seem unsafe, chaotic, and resistant to Coalition efforts to reshape Baghdad into a "zone of democratic peace" in the region. As the focal target of insurgents' rocket fire and mortar shelling, the Green Zone was rather to represent a danger to US soldiers, civilians, Coalition members, Iraqi allies, and squatters alike.[4] Despite the failings of this security apparatus, Bush fought in 2006 for the construction of miles of fencing to separate the southwestern United States from Mexico, so as to curb illegal crossings, flex the muscles of the nation's sovereign status, and make it appear to taxpayers as though *the War on Terror is right beside them*. This strategy, one of the inspirations for Donald Trump's own anti-immigration agenda, thus establishes the entire continental U.S. as a veritable Green Zone, amenable to a similar system of material, modular, and virtual defenses—walling, motion sensors, surveillance cameras, drone aircraft, and roving security detachments—that ipso facto constitute the territory that they enclose as a target for interlopers, criminals, and other opportunists. Unfortunately, this militarization of the nation-state's compass, in turn, might also compel many of its citizens to see outsiders, no matter their intentions, as "barbarians" at the thresholds of empire.[5]

Michel Henry enables us to make more sense of the reality-making aims of twenty-first-century administrators, as well as complexify, if not overturn, conventional understandings of the othering effects and self-destructive tendencies of Green Zone-style security perimeters. Henry theorizes two distinct, although interlocking, modes of species-being: the first of them, *culture*, takes "auto-affection" as the transcendental a priori of subjective experience.[6] He argues that, above rational action-taking, scientific experimentation, or mathematical formalization, the subject must first and inescapably drink in the world's "sensible qualities," never willing nor thinking to do so.[7] The subject, in other words, affectively taps into the nonphenomenal, noncognizable fluxes of "life," serving as one individual site of its constant "self-feeling and self-undergoing."[8] As the ensemble of these individuals, "culture" modifies its surroundings to reflect its members' needs, conveying and reflecting the "self-growth" characteristic of "life," chiefly in the domains of art, ethics, and religion.[9] According to Henry, cultural creations "match our pathetic relation to being, are capable of expressing it, of growing with it, and thus of growing it, in turn," as they disclose to us specifically through our sense-experience of them the "radical immanence of subjectivity."[10] This aesthetic sensibility dovetails with culture, since its artistic achievements more than represent "life"; they attune us to its occult forces, compelling us to recognize them as the same as those coursing through us, informing our feelings, desires, and individual selfhoods. For Henry, then, culture always emphasizes the *subjective*, although not necessarily toward the overvaluation of the individual, since it takes as its foremost concern the whole of the "sensible world," rather than merely "one thing" at the expense of all others.[11] Therefore, culture, so as to deserve the name, must respect the ipseities of each of its individual members, considering that they encapsulate the sensations, intuitions, and organic traditions of thinking, working, and socializing that altogether energize the development of "life."

The annihilation of culture, *barbarism*, stems from the decisional framework of science, rather than from despotic rule, invading armies, or wide-scale ignorance, in that it elides, ignores, or downplays the textures of subjective embodiment and the variables of sense-experience that nevertheless must inform the study of its object. Henry argues that science, in order to commute the ever-changing nature of our material realities and our individual re-presentation of them as the qualia of our auto-affective senses into a system of classifiable, quantifiable, and mathematizable ideals, must first of all treat the "world [as] a pure site of exteriority."[12] Science thus reduces the self-knowledge that defines "life" to the abstract comprehension of whatever thing appears in front of us. Thus, even though we might of necessity manipulate it with our fingers or stare at it through a microscope, methodologically for science the emphasis must shift from our subjective rootedness in this singular experience to the neatly *objective* determination of the thing's outer qualities or atomic composition. Henry concludes that science does not necessarily serve the ends of "life"—since it rejects our individual communication with it as metaphysical or untestable—so much as it *serves itself*, or rather serves its own institutional networks, value structures, and discursive capacities. The shortsightedness of such a decision, according to Henry, ultimately tends toward destruction, since it involves detaching the self from "reality" in order to study it so meticulously that "one can choose the mode of intervention" necessary "to 'change' it."[13] The social sciences finally direct this dispassionate, objectifying stare toward the subject, resulting in the radical disconnection of the self from the social and cosmic "whole" so that a certain malaise develops in us, tempting us to feel that, in order to shirk it off or chase it away, we must resolve to destroy ourselves. Unlike art, scientific reductionism sets the stage for the steady atrophying of culture, so much so that even serious crimes, such as theft, rape, and murder, suffer from this sort of drastic depersonalization. To science they appear the measurable results of certain sociological conditions—economic, symbolic, and ideologico-historical—rather than as a response to its negation of the ethicizing tenor of subjective feeling, its vulgarization of our desires, or its casting aside of the ways that "life" invites us to contemplate its different tonalities through acts of aesthetic creation, sensation, and immersion.[14]

Unsurprisingly, this conception of science's destructive tendencies tallies with Hannah Arendt's discussion of the ideological formations, media indoctrination strategies, and other control mechanisms of totalitarian movements. First of all, this sort of rule must deemphasize the significance of the individual, if it is to achieve "permanent domination" over "each and every sphere of life."[15] So as to never settle into the form of a state or administrative apparatus—in other words, a mere mediator of separate constituencies and interests—the totalitarian movement must therefore rigorously and methodically regulate individuals' spontaneous connection to "life itself," as well as narrow the space that divides them in order to eradicate their differences, quash their freedoms, and circumscribe them inside its "iron band of terror."[16] For Arendt, then, a totalitarian regime always favors consistency over spontaneity, "scientifically" reorganizing its individual subjects into masses, or, in Henry's terms, into "one thing";

defining them as superfluous to its rule; and fomenting mutual suspicion to make them overarchingly complicit in its terror.[17] Her description of these organizational methods and mediatic connivances thus corresponds to Henry's critique of the culture-threatening ramifications of mathematical-logical standpoints, in that the "advertising techniques" of totalitarian movements always stress the "scientificality" of their assertions.[18] Why? According to Arendt, mass organizers must reshape reality in order to make their wildest "predictions come true," requiring them, in the name of *theoretical consistency*, to remove, ostracize, or eliminate all those who do not conform to its ideals.[19] Of course, to outsiders these actions might seem completely unreasonable, unrealistic, or anti-intellectual; nonetheless, they do follow from the value system of technoscience, constituting the nation-state under totalitarian influence as "a kind of laboratory" set up to run experiments on "reality," on disregarding individuals' separate interests, ethical sensibilities, and experiential frames of reference so as to organize them into one mass formation made up of replaceable and in-and-of-themselves unimportant components.[20] Moreover, this regime must devise what Arendt calls "objective enemies" to conduct further experiments on, as the situation demands, designating as such a race, class, or subgroup that enables the movement, *if it is to remain a movement*, to confront fresh "new obstacles" that it must then isolate, examine, formulate conclusions about, and in time dispose of systematically.[21] Once again, as we can see, the objective overrides the subjective, this time with deadly results to the dignity of the individual and the expressions of self-knowing that altogether define a culture. Arendt, in fact, contends that any form of creative initiative or affective sophistication threatens totalitarian orders, compelling them to regiment "all intellectual and artistic life" and stifle ideas they deem dangerous.[22] The objective-scientific and the totalitarian standpoints, in short, eerily complement each other.

The emphasis on world-rebuilding in much commercial cinema of the early twenty-first century, whether in the form of war films, fantasy, or science fiction, suggests that the "reality-creating" schemes of certain rightist administrations, in the United States and elsewhere, are totalitarian in flavor and at their core anti-life in character. Henry maintains that our affective, comprehensive, and mostly nonconscious connection to "life's" sense-phenomena remains the a priori of all our experiences, even our scientific investigations into the composition of the objects in front of us. However, the construction of occupation spaces in the territories of other nation-states, which these films represent, reflect, and recode, comes to resemble a desperate effort to establish death, destruction, and exclusion as the starting point for culture, rather than its abolition or decline. These films, in other words, depict the *archi-barbaric* nature of these Green Zones, as the characters in them seek to re-create certain cities, countries, regions, domains, or worlds, to experiment with new realities through the "scientifically" swift, efficient, and cost-effective razing, redistricting, and repopulating of older ones. These films thus thematize the tense relation of the *subjective* and the *objective*. The characters in them who seek to erect walls, fences, and other safeguards must stake out an area, define their "objective enemies," and subject them all to the calculus of a spatio-legible experiment: namely, to exclude them from secure areas or to confine them to their fringes; to deindividualize them, forcing their massification as a survival measure or insurgent counterresponse; and to mark vast swathes of them as dangerous and disposable, making it "sensible" for those inside the Green Zone to ignore, distrust, deride, exploit, mishandle, intimidate, torture, attack, rape, murder, or steal from them. More importantly, these films show the ways that these improvisational security perimeters constrain the subjective expression of "life," the sense of communion with the "whole" of a community still in direct touch with its diegetic *Lebenswelt*. These walled-off areas, no more at the service of "life," might effect the conversion of a select socius in these films into the object of some form of totalitarian study, control, and terror; or they might compromise the moral and aesthetic sense of the main characters, the ones that must construct, rearrange, or patrol these Green Zones so that the dramatic emphasis falls on their struggle to maintain their self-integrity in the face of these altogether dehumanizing conditions.[23] Such films as *Southland Tales* (Richard Kelly, 2006) and, of course, *Green Zone* (Paul Greengrass, 2010) show us that the forces that attempt to make reality conform to a set of venal theoretical ideals or ideological claims only serve to make themselves the "objective enemies" of those they exclude—and invariably the enemies of *culture itself*. Suffice it to say, according to the notion of the archi-barbaric as it operates in these films, *the instantiation of culture starts with the denial and negation of life.*

Southland Tales

Richard Kelly's almost incomprehensible sophomore effort *Southland Tales* contains one of the earliest Green Zone-esque secure areas to appear in the cinema of the twenty-first century, as the film shows the effects of the Iraq War inevitably rebounding on to the US mainland's coastal and territorial claims. During the Fourth of July celebrations in 2006, a terrorist nuclear strike rattles the nation-state, this sequence in the film a clear allusion to National Security Adviser Condoleezza Rice's rationalization of the doctrine of preemptive war in Iraq as a search for weapons of mass destruction (WMDs) meant to avert the discovery of "a smoking gun in the form of a mushroom cloud."[24] The United States afterward turns into a totalitarian state, ratcheting up the PATRIOT Act and further stripping away civil freedoms; subjecting citizens to constant satellite surveillance; infantilizing them through a random, mind-numbing series of TV talk shows and commercials; and installing a system of checkpoints and visa requirements to regulate entry into its federal terrain. The "neo-Marxists," a faction of soccer mom revolutionaries, tactical media activists, and cyberwarfare experts, meanwhile relocate outside the United States to form cells in South America. These measures, as well as the reaction to them, effectively turn the entire nation into a network of Green Zones, with the mass media continuously encouraging its audiences to shop, dance, overindulge in alcohol, and wander about aimlessly through the streets, altogether with a dim awareness (as newsfeeds ensure) that the enemies of the United States wait outside these districts, conspiring to throw them into disorder and unseat the current regime.

One scene set in Greater Los Angeles, for example, depicts sentries sitting on turrets atop office buildings or standing with machine guns at street corners, closely monitoring those on the other side of their reticles for any signs of suspicious or overtly dissident activity (Figure 2.1). The mise-en-scène neatly recalls Mike Davis's conceptualization of Los Angeles as a "carceral city," as its municipal developers attempt to "use architectural camouflage to insert jail space into the skyscape," thus transforming the downtown area into an assemblage of "microprisons."[25] As *Southland Tales* suggests, after the US government's wholesale commitment to the War on Terror, carceral and commercial spaces start to drop their camouflage as they interpenetrate more and more seamlessly, exposing to view the true condition of citizens: that almost all of them resemble inmates of the security state, shuffling through similar motions and routines, unwilling or too fearful to question authority, with the constant threat of immediate summary execution constraining their actions, ethical decision-making, and aesthetic sensibilities. One of the unruliest members of the neo-Marxists, Zora Carmichaels (Cheri Oteri), insults the soldiers watching over the city,

FIGURE 2.1 *Greater Los Angeles Sentries in* Southland Tales.

flouting their authority and even daring one of them, a man operating a machine cannon atop one of its redoubts, to start shooting. He does so without thought, and she revoltingly dies, as the rest of the citizens inside the district, after conditions return to "normal," simply dance, drink, and revel into the night.

The real struggle, though, is fought over the (re)production and dissemination of media images, so integral to the maintenance and effectivity of the security state in the film. These images, as they subsume such nonlinear, multiplatform technologies as videocams, internet displays, cable newsfeeds, computer windows, and television clips, formally complement the movable Green Zones that the neocon administration sets up across the United States. These images, as Steven Shaviro argues, more than interrupt conventional film syntax; they also disturb the continuity, intelligibility, and flow of the narrative, underlining the exhaustion of the sense of "lived duration" in our current digital mediasphere.[26] However, Shaviro focuses mostly on the temporal dimensions of the film, even though the crux of its multiple storylines concerns the ruptures in space-time that come about from the exploitation of the alternative fuel source Fluid Karma, another name for the tidal energies of the Pacific Ocean's currents, as the odious Treer Corporation rebrands them. A different approach to *Southland Tales*, then, might rather stress the "space" in space-time, especially since the film envisions ways to transgress and collapse the othering, redistricting, and surveillance mechanisms that securing a city, region, or entire nation-state seems to involve.

The totalitarian Grand Old Party (GOP) in the film and its major contractors, among them Treer, thus establish a "Doomsday Scenario Interface," a system of terror alerts, troop surges, PATRIOT Act expansions, skycam networks, and timeline reminders of the nuclear attacks, the alignment of the Axis of Evil states, and the declaration of a Third World War against them. Moreover, these institutions construct a cyberwarfare think tank, US-IDent, that seeks to compile information on neo-Marxist cells, frustrate their attempts to disrupt the media channels that serve state interests, and unilaterally initiate surgical strikes against their members. Along with the Interface, this agency fulfills two functions: first, it creates *firewalls* against cyberterrorist attacks, a virtual complement to the material defenses that the US government sets up in major retail and entertainment centers. Additionally, with its tremendous mediatic reach, it identifies two sets of objective enemies, the terrorist alliance of rogue nations and the neo-Marxist organization, enabling the state to act even more so as a totalitarian movement, as it regards its citizens as replaceable monads, militarizes its police functionaries, and changes its ideologico-legal diktats at a whim, it seems, when certain exigencies arise.[27] The state, its corporate adjuncts, and its scientific research divisions, under the thumb of the inventor of Fluid Karma, Baron Von Westphalen[28] (Wallace Shawn), thus act in archi-barbaric concert, reducing culture to the dual stupors of consumerism and terror-stricken obedience to the current administration, while also treating the other characters in the film in an "objective" manner as spending units, identifiable enemies, and even test cases. Baron Von Westphalen experiments on several Iraq War veterans, among them the film's narrator, Pilot Abilene (Justin Timberlake), exposing them to the forces of Fluid Karma's "quantum entanglements" so that afterward they start to develop telepathic connections to one another, along with rather schizophrenic senses of self.

The narratological work of Gérard Genette appears of value to understanding the cross-border movements and spatial trespassings in the film, as they attempt to restore some sense of subjective ipseity to those stuck inside US-IDent's Green Zone-style theaters of surveillance, direct military intervention, and terrorist profiling.[29] The film introduces its narrator, Pilot Abilene, in a shot with the veteran sitting on a turret near the Fluid Karma rig, swiveling its cannon slowly toward us in an imitation of the famous image of director Fritz Lang turning a camera mount in the direction of the audience in Jean-Luc Godard's *Le Mépris* (1963). However, in *Southland Tales*, the clearly virtual camera zooms away from Abilene to eventually converge with the digital data readouts and news crawlers of the Doomsday Scenario Interface. The narrator, although a figure in the film's visual register, nonetheless dovetails with its extradiegetic elements, serving, through a voice-over effect, the same functions as they do: to recall for viewers the flashpoint events of the Third World War, relate ideological-psychological-biographical details about the other main characters, and make sense of certain narrative developments, often with allusion to the apocalyptic millennialism of the Book of Revelations. However, midway through the film, this figure steps more surely into its diegetic universe, interrupting the story with an impromptu music video sequence set inside a convenience store.

The next time we see Pilot Abilene, the former narrator is dancing with the other carousers in downtown L.A. near Baron Von Westphalen's zeppelin retreat. The character serves a *metaleptic* function, which Genette defines as the trespass of the extradiegetic into the diegetic, the overstepping of the "shifting but sacred frontier between two worlds, the world in which one tells, the world of which one tells."[30] The film traces the movement of its narrator from a station outside its character ensemble or narrative sequence of events—a station akin to that of a movie director—to one more firmly inside of them.[31] This movement requires a sort of intermedial interlude, namely the music video, which, even though it appears of no real narrative consequence, nonetheless radically affects screen space. The video, in short, offers something to dance and sing along to, agitating the characters' flesh with its rhythms, altering their aesthetic sensibilities, and inviting them to carry their dance moves over into the film's Green Zone areas. This sequence does not invite them to continue to dull themselves with constant "fun"; on the contrary, it moves them *to show the forces of the totalitarian security state what it means to act in the service of life, rather than life-taking and scientific-economic reductionism*. The metaleptic figure of Pilot Abilene, then, in all its transgressive movement, flies in the face of the establishment of secure areas and their informatic supplements, suggesting that certain messages, cultural innovations, and new ideas must impact and transform the subjective desires, outlooks, corporealities, social values, individual feelings, artistic standards, and spatial negotiations of those who will receive them, no matter the amount of checkpoints and firewalls the authorities set up.[32]

However, Genette's concept of *syllepsis* allows us to make some sense of those narrative strands featuring another narratorial figure, Boxer Santaros (Dwayne Johnson), the muscleman, action star, and son-in-law to a wealthy senator—all in the vein of Arnold Schwarzenegger—who, upon contact with Fluid Karma, turns amnesiac, forms a relationship with ex-porn star Krysta Now (Sarah Michelle Geller), and contributes to a film script about its effects on the fabric of space-time. Genette defines syllepsis as an atemporal mode of organizing textual space, a figure that clusters together the "retrospections," "anticipations," and "didactic interventions" of the narrator.[33] This mode of address ultimately affects narrative "sequence (since by synthesizing 'similar' events it abolishes their succession) and duration (since at the same time it eliminates their time intervals)."[34] Thus, syllepsis suspends, rather than transgresses, the distinction of the diegetic and extradiegetic, simultanizing their respective spatiotemporal registers, the separate worlds the characters and the narrator each inhabit. Boxer Santaros identifies completely with the role of Jericho Kane, the main character of *The Power*, the spec script that the actor and Krysta Now write addressing the deceleration of the Earth, a "fictive" scenario that, it turns out, exactly captures the effects of Fluid Karma on the more familiar textures of space-time. The film introduces Santaros as already in a role, *as a diegetic figure dissembling as an extradiegetic content creator*, as well as the star of *The Power* who, over the course of the "real" narrative duration of *Southland Tales*, intends to expose the "environmental anomalies" that the Treer corporation causes and circulate counter-images to the ones that US-IDent uses in its endless war against the enemies of the totalitarian movement.

This disinformation campaign, with its mediatic excesses, attempts to convolute the characters' memories, outrage their moral sensibilities, and reshape their sociopolitical realities to serve the US government's own ends, as one sequence midway in the film suggests. The neo-Marxists maneuver Santaros and Krysta Now to stage a double murder, using squibs to fake the violence, in order to defame the actor and thus the establishment. The US government at the same time sends a corrupt cop to actually shoot down the targets of the neo-Marxists, framing the actors for the crime and compelling them to return to the camp of Santaros's senator father-in-law. Santaros, finally recalling these allegiances, sheds the Jericho Kane role, finding that the GOP still wants to use the "strong man" image of the Schwarzenegger-like cultural icon in its self-serving counterterrorism efforts. The character thus intersects three different storylines all at once, each overlying the other rather than occurring successively throughout the film: the fictive Jericho Kane, who witnesses the real effects of Fluid Karma on the natural environment and runs with these tidings from the authorities; the media commodity Boxer Santaros, who "stars" in a sort of action film that the cops stage, involving real carnage and death; and the "real," much meeker spouse to Madeleine Frost (Mandy Moore), who functions the entire time as an unknowing case study for Treer's research department. These three narrative-diegetic threads coalign in Santaros, who, unlike Pilot Abilene, does not step into the diegesis so much as *overloads it with different possibilities, with didactic interventions into its script direction*. Thus, in the film's climax, Santaros renegotiates the confines of US-IDent's security perimeters, suspending the action-thriller elements of its narrative and affecting the sense impressions, social activities, and modes of self-expression that its diegetic spaces can tolerate.

Santaros, in the middle of a neo-Marxist assault on the Green Zone-style area encompassing Baron Von Westphalen's zeppelin fortress, transforms its interiors, meant to celebrate military-scientific achievement, into an impromptu dance floor to the amazement of the crowds inside, incorporating the music video format more fully into the narrative topoi of the film than Pilot Abilene seems able to do. Santaros at this moment appears as more of *an extradiegetic content creator—for example, a movie or music video director—dissembling as a diegetic character*. The sylleptic workings of this final sequence, which tellingly occurs as the neo-Marxists infiltrate the zeppelin and storm through its corridors, represent another challenge to the checkpoints, sentry stations, and other security "bubbles" surrounding the nation and creeping into its cities. The dance sequence suggests that the more certain counterhegemonic media messages defy these walls and firewalls, the more difficulties security forces, surveillance systems, and disinformation networks might experience in their attempts to suppress, minimize, discourage, or somehow capitalize upon our spontaneous action. Boxer Santaros, Krysta Now, and Madeleine Frost, in creating a dance number at a time when audiences expect an action showdown, attune themselves to the subjective in the sense that Michel Henry uses the term: the feeling, the zeal, and the respect for "life" that comes to us through the immediacy of our senses. *Southland Tales* suggests that our access to different multimedia channels does not turn "the real into so many pseudo-events," as Fredric Jameson famously maintains,[35] so much as it turns these pseudo-events into the real, clustering them in such a way that we start to see alternatives to the restrictions that cramp our movements and regulate our sense-experience of social and material space.[36]

The token of spontaneous *dérive* in this final sequence might then spell "doomsday" for scientific forms of administration and the microprisons of consumerist despair that often accompany them.

Green Zone

The opening sequence of Paul Greengrass's frenetic *Green Zone* depicts General Mohammed Al Rawi (Yigal Naor) fleeing to a safehouse during the 2003 invasion of Iraq as rockets flare up over the Baghdad skyline, the flames from their explosions making the city reminiscent of the visions of Hell in Hieronymus Bosch's triptychs, namely *The Last Judgment* (1482) and *The Garden of Earthly Delights* (1490–1510).[37] Four weeks after these events, Chief Warrant Officer Roy Miller (Matt Damon) conducts a series of raids to investigate sites that supposedly contain WMDs, right as the military, its contractors, and its wage slaves construct a series of checkpoints, ditches, and control centers, entrenching themselves into the Karkh district of the city (Figure 2.2). Finding no weapons, Miller consults with CIA operative Martin Brown (Brendan Gleeson) and *Wall Street Journal* reporter Lawrie Dayne (Amy Ryan), each of whom inform the officer that the US Department of Defense is receiving its spurious information from an anonymous source, Magellan. Miller thus sets about on a "rogue" operation, seeking out General Al Rawi to set matters straight and running into opposition in the form of Special Intelligence agent Clark Poundstone (Greg Kinnear), who, it turns out, simply made up the Magellan figure in order to drum up support for the invasion and occupation of Iraq. These narrative thrills attest to the archi-barbaric character of the war effort: the United States uses shock and awe tactics to manufacture a sort of cultural vacuum, with criminals running rampant in the streets and snipers randomly shooting at soldiers

FIGURE 2.2 *The Karkh District in* Green Zone.

from the few multistories still standing in the city, in order to take advantage of the opportunity to "rebuild this place" in the image of the United States, as Poundstone tells Miller in one scene.

This reality-remaking imperative, so indicative of the totalitarian mindset, according to Arendt, moreover receives a degree of officialization, as in another scene a spokesperson for the Bush administration, during a news conference, announces to the media corps the disastrous de-Baathification strategy, all the while touting their "commitment to transform Iraq into a modern democratic country." Toward the film's conclusion, Poundstone's cronies, even as they insist that "it's a new beginning for Iraq, the end of tyranny and the beginning of freedom," exploit the cultural turmoil and interethnic strife raging throughout the nation to engineer election results and install their choice for prime minister in the Interim Government.[38] Other Iraqi factions nonetheless reject this outcome, squabbling among themselves and detecting in it the further occasion for their own displacement, marginalization, cultural destabilization, and difficulty in self-determining the fate of their nation. General Al Rawi, correctly reading the archi-barbaric thrust of these courses of action, in which mathematical-logical calculation attacks the sources of "life" that drive the formation of a certain culture, thus asks Miller a rhetorical question: "Where is my place?" The answer consists in the diegetic-historical construction of Baghdad in the film, as US forces section off their center of operations, the Green Zone, from the rest of the city, sending an unmistakable message to the dissidents, insurgents, former Baathists, and unruly mob agitators: *there is no place, only dissolution, for those who resist the imposition of change.*

The film's depiction of the Green Zone rephrases the compositional formula of the Iraq War film that Martin Barker delineates. He argues that these films function according to an "over here-over there" dynamic. "Over there" designates the arena of combat, which comes to seem to soldiers and viewers alike as "unknown," "unpredictable," and "inexplicably hostile."[39] "Over here," in contrast, designates the sphere of officialdom, in which "incompetent, self-aggrandizing, or corrupt" decision-makers seek to deceive those in their charge, so as to ensure an "uncaring civilian population," frustrate the development of "fields of meaningful" relationships, and reduce the chances of encountering anti-war activism.[40] The innovation of *Green Zone* is that, through the construction of its eponymous setting, it internalizes this dichotomy so that "over here" effectively comes to refer to the spaces inside the checkpoints, Coalition compounds, and maze of walls of the Karkh district and "over there" to those mostly unsafe areas of the city next to them. The characters in the film refer to these areas as "off-reservation," alluding to their spatio-legible constitution—the fact that non-Iraqi military forces must seem out of place in them—and also to earlier war films that style themselves after Westerns, such as *The Green Berets* (John Wayne, 1968), in which the soldiers call their camp "Dodge City."[41]

The spaces inside the Green Zone resemble the extravagance of US culture, as the officers, civilians, and state officials within them snack on fast foods, drink, swim, sunbathe, watch television, compete at eight-ball, and flirt with one another. The Iraqis outside the Green Zone, though, suffer from ongoing deprivation of water, employment, and electricity; remain under constant threat of torture, military arrest, and the terrorization of their families; and face the temptation to engage in "revenge killings," interethnic conflicts, and the abduction of stray US troops.[42] The Green Zone, in short, creates the conditions for a "civil war" to erupt, as one character speculates. The Coalition, in order to destabilize the region, uproot its culture, and remake it in its own image, controls the movement of these Iraqis and excludes them from the confines of the Green Zone through an elaborate use of checkpoints, detection dogs, concertina wire fencing, electronic tracking devices, and PA systems that call on Iraqis to "help" the US military maintain some semblance of order. These security measures, in a further twist on their spatio-legible functions, serve to make these natives *appear out of place in their own country*. Ultimately, they interpellate some Iraqis as "objective enemies" of the United States, the Interim Government, and the cause of democracy, simply due to their very emplacement outside the Green Zone. Therefore, as General Al Rawi tells Miller, these evictees cannot seem anything other than "outlaws" to Coalition forces.[43]

At first sight, then, the US soldiers in this film appear the "Indians" squatting on a reservation and the Iraqi natives the cowboy outlaws. The Green Zone, as a "reservation" for US troops, functions to more than screen out terrorists, insurgents, and other undesirables; it also ideologically and spatio-legibly marks Iraqi nationals *as nonnatives in their own country*. The site serves as one of the many scientifico-military instruments meant to make the facts of the situation in the Middle East conform to the narrative that the Bush administration attempts to craft in order to rationalize their war initiatives to the news corps. Chief Miller at first seems an exponent of the "objective" tenor of the otherwise frantic search for WMDs, using electronic equipment, air filtration masks, deft tactical maneuvers, and on-the-spot improvisation to storm ostensible weapons depots and then determine that the Iraqis are not developing or stockpiling active nuclear, chemical, or infectious materials. However, ever the idealist, Miller remains naive to the totalitarian tendencies of the mathematical-logical-scientific mindset. The special intelligence operative Poundstone, aware of them and cynically willing to exploit them, thus intensifies the scramble after WMDs for their media use value, since CNN, the *Wall Street Journal*, and other outlets can assist in characterizing former Baathists, resentful citizens, and ethnic or religious zealots as the objective enemies of neoliberal freedom, the reality-making efforts of the neoconservatives, and the reputations of the US and Coalition armies. "The whole world's watching," Poundstone says, anxious to submit some evidence of Saddam Hussein's weapons program to the television networks, to retroactively excuse the costs of the war and its thoroughgoing destabilization of the region. Steven Peacock reads the shaky camerawork of the film, so characteristic of Paul Greengrass's auteur style, as an expression of the "muddle of war," especially at the time that US officials were making a mess of their appointment of caretaker members of the Interim Government.[44] Peacock nonetheless finds the camerawork "flighty" and overindulgent, a directorial imposition on the film's story arc.[45] This aesthetic, though, rather captures the efforts of US representatives to *impose* on the region, in archi-barbaric fashion, an entirely new "culture," one that favors expedient economic, foreign affairs, and state-military security calculations more than it does any mode of approaching or affirming "life" in all its noncognizable, auto-affective, or sense-holistic aspects.[46] Therefore, Greengrass's style is appropriate for the film, as it captures the disruption and derangement of the aesthetic sensibilities of the characters, its devastation of what Henry calls their natural "energies" only so that they remain complaisant in the face of the new "facts" that Poundstone and other officials fabricate to confirm their *idée fixe* about the "Hell" that Iraqis went through under Hussein's rule.[47]

Since science still relies on our sensoria to observe, manipulate, and test the objects that it studies, Miller is able to turn its mechanisms against its own dehumanizing and massifying inclinations—in short, to use them to revalue and reestablish contact with the intersubjective, with the congruities that connect social feeling and self-growth. Miller, detecting inconsistencies in the information that Magellan delivers, starts to question such sources, telling officials that "there is no agreement in what is in" the intelligence dossiers that the troops receive and "what we're doing on the ground." For these efforts, Poundstone rebukes the soldier, sharply exclaiming, "Just do your job," after first advising Miller not to trust General Al Rawi or Martin Brown. Of course, the intelligence agent captures the flavor in these words of Arendt's notion of totalitarian evil, which turns on making "functionaries and mere cogs in the administrative machinery out of men" so that they come to appear capable of the mass murder and expulsion of others.[48] Miller, though, successfully resists such "objective" detachment, after double-checking Lawrie Dayne's sources—Poundstone seeds the news agencies with false "facts" about WMDs in Iraq—and then meeting Freddy (Khalid Abdalla), an amputee veteran who echoes the warrant officer's ethical and sociopolitical commitments. These men react to questioning in similar ways: on the city streets, Freddy says to Miller, "I want to help my country," while in another scene Miller tells US top officials, "I came here to find weapons and save lives." The trust that they establish and the relationship they form, as well as the search into the identity of Magellan and the source of the sham information about WMDs, drive Miller to use rational, technical, and investigative methods in the service of intercultural connection and "the subjectivity of life."[49] He meets with Al Rawi in a safehouse outside the Green Zone, earning this former enemy's respect and discovering that Magellan does not exist, and that the entire war stems from the duplicities of such men as Poundstone, as they devise out of thin air the "reasons" for it and ever-new obstacles for the troops to efface and contain from the relative safety of their "reservations."

As Arendt reminds us, though, "The danger is that a global, universally interrelated civilization may produce barbarians from its own midst by forcing millions of people into conditions which, despite all appearances, are the conditions of savages."[50] Even as Miller consults with Al Rawi, attempting to forge a measure of trust and mutual understanding, Poundstone's task force surrounds them, tracking their movements with stealth aircraft and digital tracking equipment—thus it appears as though *the objective engulfs the subjective* in this sequence. Miller chases Al Rawi, who flees the safehouse, through the areas outside the Green Zone. He finally captures the general, only for Freddy to suddenly reappear in the film, shoot Al Rawi to death, and softly reproach Miller, saying that the fate of Iraq is "not for you to decide." This surprise ending undoes much of the ideological work of twenty-first-century war films, many of them set in the Second World War, such as *Hart's War* (Gregory Hoblit, 2002), *Windtalkers* (John Woo, 2002), *The Great Raid* (John Dahl, 2005), *Flags of Our Fathers* (Clint Eastwood, 2006), *Miracle at St. Anna* (Spike Lee, 2008), and *Defiance* (Edward Zwick, 2008). According to Cynthia Weber, these films offer their audiences specific visions of "moral clarity" at a time of extreme cultural insecurity and self-doubt in the wake of the 9/11 terrorist attacks.[51] *Green Zone*, unlike these earlier films, reintroduces radical uncertainty into such representations of war on-screen, as the misadventures of the Coalition attempts to shape the region in their image, conform its realities to "facts" they themselves create, and divide its cities into friendly and unfriendly sectors only serve to *potentially produce barbarians*. The instrumental reason of the US Department of Defense, so clever in erecting fences, installing checkpoints, and staffing sentry details, reduces Coalition members and Iraqi citizens alike to the state of "savages," condemning them to a cycle of deception, murder, and corruption. Miller, in the epilogue, can only e-mail several news agencies the trite message that Saddam Hussein was never developing or amassing WMDs, that the war was the result of a colossal mistruth, and that Iraqis were never our "objective enemies" until we took decisive steps to make them that way. The film, though, through its title, its narrative twists, and its diegetic construction, sends a different message, much timelier in its intervention in the national discussion over whether the United States ought to enhance its state-border security apparatus. The message is that the only objective enemy is the Green Zone, the confines of which, in separating one civilization from another, in nesting one culture in the middle of another, ultimately tear each of them apart from the inside out. Americans fire on Americans, Iraqis on Iraqis, each on the other, as their *very humanity* comes to seem as shaky and rootless as Greengrass's camera. The upshot—security fencing, as our common enemy—in turn effects a multiplication of enemies.

The Hobbit: The Battle of the Five Armies

Peter Jackson's *The Hobbit: An Unexpected Journey* (2012), the first film of the trilogy, opens with its title character Bilbo Baggins (Martin Freeman) recounting the tale of Erebor, the "fortress city" of the dwarves that rests underneath the Lonely Mountain of J. R. R. Tolkien's realm of Middle Earth. Through trade, mining, and weapons manufacturing, the dwarves amass an enormous fortune, including the Arkenstone, the "King's Jewel." This stone, though, curses the dwarves, making their ruler Thrór (Jeffrey Thomas) callous, mercurial, and madly overprotective of these riches, as Bilbo's retrospective voice-over attests:

> The years of peace and plenty were not to last. Slowly the days turned sour, and the watchful nights closed in. Thrór's love of gold had grown too fierce. A sickness had begun to grow within him. And where sickness thrives, bad things will follow.

The Arkenstone comes to the attention of Smaug (Benedict Cumberbatch), a "fire drake from the north" who storms Erebor, drives the dwarves from the mountain, dispossesses them of their treasures, and afterward falls into a deep slumber underneath endless cascades of coins, diamonds, emeralds, rubies, sapphires, and other valuables. At the instigation of the sorcerer Gandalf (Ian McKellan), thirteen dwarf warriors, including the rightful King Thorin (Richard Armitage), arrive at the doorstep of Bilbo's cottage in the Shire, shoving their way in and ransacking its cupboards and storerooms for foods, drink, and eating utensils. These dwarves ironically restage Smaug's occupation of their fortress, taking or abusing the articles of value that interest them inside the "hobbit hole," despite Bilbo's obvious dismay, vexation, and words of demurral. Gandalf then shows up, attempting to recruit Bilbo as "burglar" on the dwarves' fateful mission: to steal into Erebor through a secret magic door, reclaim the Arkenstone, summon their clansmen to unseal the entrance to the fortress, and ultimately recapture it from the dragon sleeping inside it. Although at first reluctant to venture outside the Shire, Bilbo agrees, and along the way crashes through the doorways of several other characters in the series, much as the dwarves do in the opening sequences of the first film. For example, in the sequel *The Desolation of Smaug* (2013), the company takes refuge from orc trackers in the quarters of the "skin-changer" Beorn (Mikael Persbrandt), reinforcing the door to the entrance with a wooden crossbeam and trapping themselves inside with the temperamental creature. Later on, Bilbo sneaks into the dungeons of the elves to free the dwarves from the iron cages imprisoning them, only for all of them once outside to confront a troop of orcs tracking them along the course of the river that runs through the forest. The first two films, then, set up the major visual thematic of the series' conclusion, namely the collapsing of the security features of the fortress-like Erebor, as they too, much as in these earlier scenes, mainly serve to attract marauders, incite ill feelings, and close off those inside them from their own neighbors, allies, and cousin folk.

The final film in the series, *The Battle of the Five Armies* (2014), most clearly dramatizes the archi-barbaric effects that can come from refortifying, fencing, or walling in a city, district, or dominion to deter security threats. After Smaug's death, the dwarves reclaim Erebor, although soon the curse upon its treasure stores afflicts Thorin with "dragon sickness," making the ruler covetous of the Arkenstone, distrustful of the other members of the company, and rather dull in terms of showing others any ethical, aesthetic, or intercultural consideration. Thalin impulsively commands the dwarves to extricate a massive statue from the face of the mountain to use to close off the entrance to it from Middle Earth's other races and tribes. He effectively turns the city into a Green Zone, enabling the dwarves to restrict access to it, surveil the slopes and fields nearby, cut short negotiations with outsiders, and designate as their enemies those who do not respect Thorin's demands that they depart from the vicinity. However, the spatio-legible thrust of these measures tends toward the opposite effect, as it *draws* the armies of the other races and tribes to Erebor rather than isolating the dwarves from them. First, the men of Esgaroth come seeking refuge and assistance from Thorin, who reneges on an oath to finance the reconstruction of their seaport after Smaug awakens and destroys it. Then the elves show up outside the mountain entrance, insisting that the dwarves return a necklace of spiritual significance to them. Thorin scoffs at each of these requests, and the elf warrior Legolas (Orlando Bloom), assessing the situation and the consequences of fencing in the city again, surmises that after "news of the death of Smaug" finishes spreading "through the lands … others will now look to the mountain for its wealth, for its position."

The dwarves' own clansmen then surprise the elves and townsfolk, setting their engines of war on them for Thorin, who treats even these relations shabbily, refusing to allow the other twelve members of the company to enter the fray for fear of one of them claiming the Arkenstone or absconding with some of the treasure. Thus, in the next scene, the chief of the townsmen Bard (Luke Evans) wonders, "Why does the King under the mountain fence himself in, like a thief in his own home?" Soon thereafter, the armies of the orcs, surrounding the dwarves, elves, and townsmen, attack all of them, designing to rob Erebor themselves, seize its treasures, and arrange for the coming of their master Sauron, the demonic antagonist of Jackson's earlier trilogy *The Lord of the Rings* (2001–3). Todd A. Comer, noting similar fortifications throughout its diegetic expanse, describes the "two towers" of the middle film as "impregnable, impervious, impermeable," in contrast to Sauron's Mount Doom sanctuary, which appears "riven with cracks and openings."[52] Most of the secure areas in *The Hobbit*, in contrast, seem more *movable, provisional, and smaller scale*. Once Thorin's men settle in Erebor, though, the walls, crags, rock formations, and debris that close them off from the rest of Middle Earth only serve to entrap them, constrain their movements, and rather ironically "dwarf" them in comparison to the vast throne room, mineshafts, and troves of riches that rest deep within the mountain (Figure 2.3). This final "security perimeter" suggests that one of the major corollaries of Green Zone-style fenced-in districts is that they function as *magnets*, attracting refugees, invaders, and unwelcome visitors, each of them under the impression, true or false, that something of value must exist—close and yet out of reach—inside their walls and defenses. The magnetic influence of Erebor, as it spurs on, multiplies, and solicits the attention of the enemies of the dwarves, thus represents the true meaning of the curse upon it, the dragon sickness that starts to infect those on either side of its city gates.

Moreover, Thorin's misrule results for a time in a thorough derangement of the subjective, of the cultural sensitivities of the dwarves—a derangement that also extends to their foes. First and foremost, the sealing off of Erebor and the strict regulation of crossings into and out of its front entrance marks those on the other side of it as "objective enemies." However, at the same time it makes Thalin suspicious of the other twelve dwarves and abusive to Bilbo, whom the king chauvinistically refers to as a "Shire rat" after the "burglar" smuggles the Arkenstone out of the mountain, meets the elves, and entrusts it to Gandalf. The dwarf reinforcements outside the fortress

FIGURE 2.3 *The Fortress City of Erebor in* The Hobbit: The Battle of the Five Armies.

cast similar indignities on the elves, with their chief, Thorin's cousin, for instance, denigrating them as mere "woodland sprites" and "pixy-eared princesses." The confinement of the thirteen dwarves to the Kingdom under the Mountain, though, does not only drudge up their xenophobic or intertribal animus; it also reduces their social intelligence and the work of diplomatic relations to matters of military strategy, economic calculation, and the development of weapons technologies, with Thorin willing to sacrifice close friends and relatives in order to cling to the "wealth" and "position" of Erebor. Meanwhile, the orcs, along with such wizards as Gandalf, Saruman (Christopher Lee), and Galadriel (Cate Blanchett), come to share in this illogic to a degree, as they commit themselves to massacring one another so as to occupy a territory of strategic importance to the northern dominions. Of course, the film stops short of declaring a moral equivalence among these factions—the orcs and their Goblin allies are clearly the villains—even as it nonetheless suggests that the appropriation and concentration of wealth in one sphere under constant and intense security must risk sowing war, extremism, divisiveness, cultural collapse, and the outright triumph of scientific abstraction and quantification over more sense-rich experiences that encourage us to treasure "life" above all else. Such a concentration of wealth, as it draws enemies, refugees, and other nonstate actors to the dwarves, in short sets the stage for the emergence of a totalitarian mindset.

Thorin feels no qualms over the elves, townsmen, skin-changers, wizards, or even the dwarves dying over a sum of coins, metals, and trinkets, and also seems eager, in the tradition of other totalitarian rulers, to twist facts and change the rules to make certain realities conform to the delusional states that dragon sickness induces in those suffering from it. Curiously, then, at the moment that Bilbo awakens Smaug, the monster takes flight, coins falling out from the scales on its underbelly. The dragon, an expensive CG asset, *is thus literally made of money*, much as with the digital sets of the recesses of the mountain city, the fields of the north, and the other diegetic spaces of Middle Earth. The series, in that it cost approximately $750,000,000 to make, might then seem complicit in Thorin's overvaluation of wealth: it too is made of money, and made almost four times that amount in sales.[53] However, its controversial "high frame rate" (HFR) composition, which renders the elements of its mise-en-scène in crisp detail, affording them an objective clarity that still comes off as inauthentic and unnatural to some viewers' eyes, strangely repositions *The Hobbit* against the magnetic effects and totalitarian outcomes of Green Zone-style security installations. As Julie Turnock explains, the use of HFR in these films "strips the footage of much of the sheen of its 'cinematographic' effects, removing much of its expensive production value that has come to separate its look from that of television or videogames."[54] Quite a few fans of the trilogy consider its frame rate a negative; all the same, as we clearly see in the final film, it also works to sever the association of wealth with our senses of self-growth and self-assurance,[55] of that which is worth saving, so to speak. After all, Thorin only snaps out of the sickness after experiencing a moment of delirium, fantasizing the topological deformation of the caches of treasure inside the mountain so that they turn into an abyss that threatens to suck the king into its center. As these riches dissolve, and then after the irredentist fever-dream dissolves, Thorin sees the walled-off Erebor for what it really is and what it really does: it acts as a magnet that attracts a substantial reserve of coins and stones, and with them, war, centripetally drawing the dwarves closer to their own self-destruction and the implosion of their culture.[56]

His senses returning, Thorin then throws caution and rational calculus out the door, rediscovering the chancy, unpredictable nature of "life" and entreating the dwarves to crash through the city's walls, earthworks, and other emergency safeguards; combine their forces with those of the elves, townsmen, and wizards; and engage the orcs and Goblins directly in the struggle over control of the northern mountains. After nearly dying in one-on-one combat with the orcs' chieftain, Thorin remorsefully whispers to Bilbo, "If more people valued home above gold, this world would be a merrier place." More than an unctuous truism (in the case of such a commercially successful film series), these words foreshadow the visual contrast that distinguishes the cavernous extent of the cellars, vestibules, and throne room of Erebor to the quaint, rather modest Shire of the Hobbits, who also sleep under the mounds, if not the mountains, of Middle Earth. Marek Oziewicz, in discussing the unfaithfulness of the *Hobbit* films to Tolkein's mythos, compares the scale of the city's recesses to that of a deep trough valley:

> If one were to slip and fall from one of the spectacular, narrow, and bannister-less staircases, one might starve to death before hitting the ground. Likewise, the ceilings of the dwarven halls are so high that the climbing camera eye can never even bring them into focus.[57]

James Walters also comments on the aerial and virtual camerawork that strives to capture the enormity of the forests, mountain chains, and "towering structures of stone and metal" in *The Lord of the Rings* films, relating it to the ever-surveillant eye of Sauron. He argues, "Ultimate power" depends on "ultimate sight, the ability to survey the world without borders or barriers."[58] The *Hobbit* trilogy adds another wrinkle to this argument. The Shire, more than visually unassuming in comparison to the series' other settings, offers space for such common activities as eating, drinking, dancing, singing, celebrating, cooking, reading, writing, visiting relatives, telling stories, and cultivating the earth—it short, it opens up the films, which never depict these quiet moments in its rote action-adventure set pieces, to the dimension of the subjective.

The Battle of the Five Armies thus suggests that scale is an important index as to whether a certain culture conduces to an aesthetic, ethical, even spiritual relation to the world's sense-phenomena or rather to an imperious one that seeks to falsify them into a set of repeatable mathematic-economic formulae. The difference obtains in Bilbo's and Thorin's reception of outsiders. The king dismisses allies, rivals, and refugees alike from the film's version of an "international zone," and even after dying, never fulfills the oath to restore Esgaroth or return the necklace to the elves. Bilbo, in the film's denouement, invites the surviving dwarves to the Shire, vowing to offer them shelter, companionship, decent treatment, and a warm welcome if any of them so desire it. The message seems clear: whereas fortress cities attract the eye of Sauron, and with it the evils of war, miserliness, mistrust, malfeasance, and double-dealing, the "open borders" of the Shire in a sense *demagnetizes* them, with the orcs, Goblins, and necromancer spirits in the films taking no notice of it. Although Gandalf argues over the course of these trilogies that Sauron might in time move against the Hobbits, even so their Shire represents an ideal throughout this megatext, the ideal of a "merrier place" in which intercultural contact, neighborliness, and artistic self-expression thrive, rather than obsessing over wealth or clamoring for interminable war. Tolkien and Jackson, it seems, situate Thorin's fortress under the "Lonely" mountain for a reason.

Fantastic Beasts and Where to Find Them

Several fantasy films of the 2010s depict their main characters magically creating a sort of "security bubble" to impede, subdue, or drive away the antagonists in them. Gandalf in *The Hobbit: The Desolation of Smaug*, for example, casts forth a radiant arc light-white dome to repel the attacks of the demon Sauron. The forcefulness of these attacks, though, ultimately causes the dome to falter, shrink, and disappear altogether, allowing Sauron to string up the sorcerer in an iron cage. Then in *The Huntsman: Winter's War* (Cedric Nicolas-Troyan, 2016), the witch queen Freya (Emily Blunt) magically erects an ice wall to stop the warriors Eric (Chris Hemsworth), Sara (Jessica Chastain), and their dwarf allies from inciting a rebellion and taking the throne. They manage to chip away at the wall and clamber over it, as Freya meanwhile clashes with Ravenna (Charlize Theron), the evil stepmother of the future queen Snow White. These films, whatever our sympathies with their characters, thus suggest the relative ineffectiveness of Green Zone-style security arrangements, as those they mean to contain and exclude smash their way through them, either through a change of tactics or an intensification of their assaults.[59] However, *Fantastic Beasts and Where to Find Them* (David Yates, 2016), a spinoff of the successful *Harry Potter* film series (2001–2011), reveals a different use value of these sorts of fenced-off spaces, much more insidious in their effects on those on their margins or right outside them in neighboring areas. The film follows the travels in 1920s New York of Newt Scamander (Eddie Redmayne), who attempts to retrieve the various creatures that escape from a magic suitcase, a TARDIS-like menagerie that appears more spacious on the inside than without. Members of the Magical Congress of the United States of America (MACUSA), a deep state cabal of wizards, attempt to detain Scamander for violation of their ordnances. One rogue agent, Percival Graves (Colin Farrell), the false face of the sorcerer Gellart Grindelwald (Johnny Depp), meanwhile schemes to track down and take control of the Obscurus, an entity of dark magic, inchoate, inky-black, and cloudlike in appearance, that incarnates and subsists on the trauma that children with an aptitude for wizarding suffer in the event that their caretakers abuse them or force them to repress it.

The Obscurus uses as its vessel Credence Barebone (Ezra Miller), a member of the New Salem Philanthropic Society, a sect of zealots and cranks that dedicate themselves to the tasks of exposing wizards and ridding the country of them. After the Obscurus in the climax of the film destroys a section of New York, it flees into a subway, while MACUSA officials "bar the area," as one of them says, with another magic "bubble" that fences out curious "No-Majs," a derogatory term for "regular people" comparable to the slur "Muggle" in the *Harry Potter* films (Figure 2.4). The agency's president Seraphina Picquery (Carmen Ejogo), worrying over the situation, tells the agents, "Contain this. Or we're exposed and it will mean war" with the No-Maj community. Unlike in the *Hobbit* and *Huntsman* films, then, in which the establishment of Green Zones simply does not work, in *Fantastic Beasts* it undoubtedly does.[60] The walls in those films fail due to the fact that the characters use them merely to screen out their enemies, whereas in this spin-off film, the wizards use them mainly to control access to information, regulate its channels, and censor or revise it in secret. Thus, those in the

FIGURE 2.4 *The Magic Bubble in* Fantastic Beasts and Where to Find Them.

film able to set up these secure areas center more than wealth, freedom of movement, or territorial rights inside their circumference—they center *important forms of knowledge* inside them, in this case the existence of the wizards and the nondemocratic MACUSA system, along with the techne of their "sciences."

MACUSA and the "Second Salemers," a nickname of the Society, each define themselves against "objective enemies": the agency against the No-Majs, whom it regards as rash, fatuous, and dangerous, and the cult against the wizards, whom it regards as malign in their influence on children and the rest of the country's affairs. However, MACUSA operates in a clandestine manner, as does James Bond's MI6, whereas the cult members act out in the open; and so the wizards seem the more formidable of the two, considering their military-style rank order and the array of spells, fabulous creatures, and supernatural artifacts at their disposal. They move in the direction of the totalitarian, though, in that they act to enforce a set of "backwards laws," as Scamander calls them, concerning the use of magic, the registering of fantastic forms of wildlife with customs agents, and the correct ways to socially interact with No-Majs—wizards cannot marry them, for instance. MACUSA manages to reduce magic to a nonspontaneous, conformist, and unthreatening technological regimen; in other words, they turn it into *another science*. Thus, the wizards draw the ire of the Second Salemers on all fronts, as these fanatics evoke the Christian right's condemnations of J. K. Rowling's novels and also the teaching of ungodly conceptual frameworks, seen in such films as *Inherit the Wind* (Stanley Kramer, 1960), *The Da Vinci Code* (Ron Howard, 2006), and *Red State* (Kevin Smith, 2011). The Society, though, we must admit, correctly suspects MACUSA of shadow rule and a certain degree of contemptuousness for the masses; nonetheless, the film mostly depicts its agents as muddlers and nuisances, offloading their chauvinism and their murderous capabilities on to its main villain Percival Graves, who intends to use Scamander's creatures to reveal the wizards to the No-Majs; capitalize on their fear; foment a war with them; and, using the Obscurus as a weapon, instigate their "mass slaughter."

Seraphina Picquery, after discovering this scheme, accuses Graves of flagrantly defying the agency's "most sacred laws," especially the one against risking "the exposure" of their community. He in turn questions this injunction, calling attention to the illiberal, discriminatory, and socially unjust motivations of the MACUSA forces in crafting it:

> A law that demands that we conceal our true nature? A law that directs those under its dominion to cower in fear lest we risk discovery? I ask you, Madam President, I ask all of you. Who does this law protect? Us or them?

Peter Biskind argues that the characters in such twenty-first-century tentpole films as *Fantastic Beasts* often frame their actions in terms of "either/or choices, one or the other: Us or Them."⁶¹ The villain in the film *expresses* this sort of extreme stance—self-empowerment acting in the name of self-protection—whereas the agents of MACUSA *enact* it. The wizards, rather than rounding up or outright exterminating the No-Majs, use their abilities to unilaterally reshape the film's social, material, and epistemic realities to their advantage, as might the ministers of a totalitarian movement or, for that matter, the members of George W. Bush's inner circle. They only dissolve the magic dome after they trap the Obscurus in the subway tunnel and use their wands to disintegrate it. Then, under the president's orders, they "obliviate" the onlookers, conjuring a Lethean rain that washes away their memories and casting spells to restore the city to its normal appearance. They reconstitute and twist aright the cars, streetlights, storefronts, skyscrapers, and L-train scaffolds strewn about the streets and sidewalks, and they even magically rewrite the front-page stories of the daily newspapers, erasing any mention of wizards, dark spirits, fantastic creatures, or strange events. The "security bubble" that the agents create therefore does much more than close the immediate area off to the No-Majs: it sets forth the conditions for *barring them from their own memories*, from using their senses to map, encode, retain, recall, and reinterpret the spaces they inhabit, what they can see in them and what they ultimately can think about them. The wizards, in changing the film's diegetic coordinates to suit their needs, at the same time assume almost total control of the autonoetic faculties of the other characters. The walls they summon forth work in a thoroughly archi-barbaric way, shoring up existing social categories ("No-Maj") while robbing us of occasions for cultural renewal and renegotiation, which involve encountering new situations, remembering them, reflecting on them, and imagining ourselves and our world(s) otherwise.

MACUSA, in effect, exemplifies Erich Fromm's notion of "anonymous authority," which "does not demand anything except the self-evident," aspiring to function through "mild persuasion" rather than overt suppression and violence.⁶² The agency, as it designates certain diegetic areas off-limits, so too designates certain aspects of the No-Majs' own minds off-limits. This organization, then, even though its agents only destroy Credence Barebone, more disturbingly affords no opportunities to the other characters to enlarge upon their spontaneous delight in the world's sense-stimuli and their moment-to-moment engagement with its fundamental otherness.⁶³ Anticipating some of Michel Henry's theoretical work, Fromm defines spontaneity as the flourishing of "creative activity that can operate in one's emotional, intellectual, and sensuous experiences and in one's will as well."⁶⁴ Newt Scamander, throughout the film, reasserts these dimensions of the subjective, insisting on the importance of maintaining a connection to "life" in all of its robustness, delicateness, and riotousness, which in this case we can clearly see in the fauna and microhabitats that the zoologist carries among the steel-grey vistas and dull reddish masonry of New York. Although not much for social charm, Scamander clearly studies, describes, and cares for these animals with no small degree of fervor, communicating this sense of wonder and enthusiasm to a coterie of wizards and No-Majs alike who come to unreservedly offer their assistance in chasing after the specimens that somehow manage to escape from the suitcase. Scamander, despite some misgivings, out-and-out defies MACUSA in associating with the ordinary factory worker Jacob Kowalski (Dan Fogler); in setting the stage for this man to develop a romance with one of the witches who accompanies them on their adventures; and in withholding no information from any of them about the existence of wizards, monsters, and the many fantastic creatures that coexist in the suitcase. Scamander might appear to reject the workings of anonymous authority, until we remember that much of the film concerns the character's efforts to recapture its title creatures so that the rest of the city takes no real notice of them. However, Scamander does so not out of a fear of alarming New Yorkers. He rather acts out of an intense respect for "life," to ensure that no mischief comes from these creatures' reckless exploration of a foreign and often inhospitable environment.

Most interestingly, Scamander uses magic in direct contradistinction to the way the agents of MACUSA use it, conjuring forth a series of wormholes to teleport from space to space in the city. He therefore does not respect the functions of the walls—magical, material, and epistemic—that these wizards erect to divide their ranks from the No-Maj rabble on the streets. Scamander therefore seems vaguely aware, as Peter Biskind writes, that "walls not only keep people out, but in societies that depend on force, not consent, to make their citizens behave, they keep people in, like that icon of totalitarianism, the Berlin Wall."[65] These acts of teleportation suggest that Green Zone fencing, even as it affects the memories, emotional valences, and autonoetic mappings of those it marks as enemies or maintains at a "safe" distance, exerts a certain counterpressure: it makes those in its vicinity desperate for some sense of aesthetic self-assertion, which throughout the film takes the form of freedom of movement, association, and feeling. Thus, *Fantastic Beasts* ends with Scamander taking the suitcase to the open ranges of Arizona and Jacob Kowalski abandoning the factory to start up a sweet shop that specializes in confections made in the shape of several fantastic creatures. The other wizards take Graves, or rather Gellart Grindelwald, into custody, a sly suggestion that the very embodiment of anonymity, "Us vs. Them" thinking, and the dark magic that terror and forgetfulness at once can work on the masses remain close to the core of the MACUSA regime.

The Wall

Much of the criticism of twenty-first-century Iraq War films takes its cue from Paul Virilio's discussion of the coterminous relation of certain military optics technologies to the visual economies of the cinema. Virilio famously contends that "nothing now distinguishes the functions of the weapon and the eye" after the development of ever-sharper collimator sights, smart missiles, night vision devices, thermographic scanners, and warheads (and now drones) with camera attachments.[66] The close-ups, camera movements, and digital registers of the cinema, according to Virilio, simulate the imaging techniques of these weapons systems. Isabelle Freda, sensibly applying this conceptual framework to such war films as *The Hurt Locker* (Kathryn Bigelow, 2008) and *American Sniper* (Clint Eastwood, 2014), argues that the alignment of the cinematographic choices in them with the emplacement of the weapons or the directional axes of the shootings in their action sequences makes a supreme value of "precision," rather than "understanding" of the situation.[67] Patricia Pisters argues that such films, necessarily in an era of Skype, Facetime, and other mobile media apps, also re-elaborate some of the spectatorial features of the war film that Virilio identifies. For Pisters, *In the Valley of Elah* (Paul Haggis, 2007), *Redacted* (Brian De Palma, 2007), *Stop-Loss* (Kimberly Peirce, 2008), and similar films seem much more "subjective and chaotically intense," almost vlog-like, in that they exhibit a rather striking degree of self-reflexivity about the thorough mediatization of the Iraq War, to which the soldier characters in them also contribute.[68] The multiple screens and shaky camerawork in these films mark their divergence from the distantiating effects of older visual systems,[69] which for Virilio offer their users only the illusion of an immediate engagement with their targets, whether seen through a rifle scope or a camera viewfinder.

At first sight, Doug Liman's minimalist war film *The Wall* (2017) seems to represent another example of the stock coincidence of the weapon and eye, since it opens with a shot of a crumbling wall in the middle of a desert construction site seen through the crosshairs of a rifle at the time of the 2007 aftermath of the invasion. Two US infantrymen, Sergeant Allen Isaac (Aaron Taylor-Johnson) and Staff Sergeant Shane Matthews (John Cena), serve on overwatch duty, covering the civilian contractors near an oil transport system until one of their sighting mechanisms starts to fog up. This scene thus marks the film's shift away from the conventional visual registers[70] of war, crime, and other action films, as the soldiers, investigating the site, come under fire from Juba (Laith Nakli), a notorious Iraqi sniper who effortlessly wounds the two of them. Isaac manages to take refuge under the stonework of the wobbly, decrepit wall, which comes to function as a makeshift security embankment for the rest of the narrative. As Isaac clings to the wall and tries to see the sniper through its cracks—neither the soldiers nor the audience ever sees Juba—the film starts to confuse *the optics of its diegetic and spectatorial construction with the opacity, solidity, and relative thickness of the stonework*, rather than with firearm scopes, tracking devices, radar detection systems, or other such instruments (Figure 2.5). Much as the sclera of the eye and the filter atop the camera save them to an extent from damage or contamination, so too does the wall save Isaac from sneak attacks and the shots the sniper takes at them. The film, in a release context of wide-scale apartheidist walling, thus aligns the functions of the eye with this most conspicuous of state and military security apparatuses, rather than with aircraft, artillery, or antipersonnel weapons.

The film's setting encapsulates the mushrooming of those Green Zone-style security measures that characterize the rebuilding operations in Iraq. The US military, with rather scientific fastidiousness, turns the area into a war-torn desert wilderness, destroying the site of the school where one of its walls now stands so as to extract and transport oil[71] across the region with a minimum of trouble or commotion. However, in so doing, the military must designate as its "objective enemies" those insurgents who resist or disrupt the expropriation of these resources, sending its more superfluous members to watch over them and sacrifice themselves for them. As the exponent of this archi-barbarism—the construction of such a for-profit enterprise atop the ruins of a culture—Isaac throughout the film uses sighting mechanisms that feature number-heavy distance recalibration, targeting information, and GPS tracking displays. He also in one scene draws in the dust, attempting to mathematically and deductively figure out the whereabouts of the sniper in the spaces surrounding the wall. He spots Juba in the trash dumps near the contractor's trailers, underlining the fact that these sorts of thought systems move toward the elimination of other races, classes, or communities, toward the regarding of them as fundamentally disposable so that the social and material realities of the situation can conform more exactly to a set of

FIGURE 2.5 *The Makeshift Security Embankment in* The Wall.

economic, ideological, and technoscientific imperatives. Juba, in contrast to the US troopers, as a former English teacher, seems to resemble the subjective as Henry defines it, telling Isaac over a radio communications channel, "I want to get to know you." He asks Isaac for "stories," rather than "military secrets," about the war, about the camaraderie of the soldiers, and about the domestic scene in the United States. He even recites the verse of Edgar Allen Poe to Isaac, an appropriately macabre choice, since the situation these men are caught in compels them to twist their aesthetic sensibilities to a sadistic, mercenary, and unceasingly destructive "endgame," as the infantryman calls it.

Thus, Isaac remains suspicious of Juba's motives, even as the sniper tries to reassure the soldier, saying more than one time over the course of the narrative, "I'm just trying to enjoy our conversation." The true obscenity of the archi-barbaric scenario, then, consists in the ways that instrumentalist thinking makes murder, theft, and dispossession the occasion, the accidental a priori, for cross-cultural exchange, intersubjective connection, and aesthetic affection. Ultimately, this mode of thinking confounds the subjective with the objective, redefining them, to abuse a mathematical term, as the *surjective*: the nonreversible mapping of the one domain into the other. Juba's rifle shots thus deliberately strike Isaac's radio, canteen, and thigh muscles so that the soldier, unable to call for reinforcements or medical assistance, might then slowly die through a combination of dehydration and nonclotting tissue damage. Additionally, as a tactical consideration, the increasingly delirious Isaac might also divulge important military information or autobiographical details with some counterintelligence value to them all the while Juba, the former English teacher and exponent of Henry's definition of the subjective, *talks him to death*. The solider, in contrast, in spite of the "reality-creating" nature of the overwatch detail, comes to feel emphatic concern for the fallen Matthews,[72] who slips into unconsciousness right out in the open desert, within easy range of the shooter. Their ethical ties to each other come from their mutual experience of suffering, vulnerability, and desolation; the objective direness of their situation slides into the subjective, into concern for each other. Nevertheless, in an archi-barbaric fashion, this experience first comes from a war effort that saw to the deracination of an entire culture, the razing of its spaces for education and self-growth, the de-aestheticizing extraction of its natural resources, and the "logical" or "objective" designation of those who oppose these courses of action as extremist, terroristic, and, at their core, worthless enemies. The film therefore suggests that the wall separating the subjective and the objective remains as flimsy, unstable, and ready to collapse as the one that shelters Isaac from the Iraqi marksman. Therefore, in the conclusion of the film, Juba shoots down the medevac unit sent to rescue the troopers, watching as it corkscrews out of control and crashes into the dunes while staying off-screen for the entire narrative. The sniper, contrary to many

Iraq War films, actually succeeds against US forces, *although without ever becoming visible* to the camera, the other characters, or the viewer. The subjective, then, in the figure of Juba, remains "abstract," crossing into the domain of scientific instrumentalization.

The swing from a narrow *Wissenschaft* to a more all-embracing social and ipseic auto-affection, only to return all the more intensely to the invariable, impersonal, and insensate—a movement that finds its expression in the surjective—might also make some meaning of the film's correlation of eye-to-wall. Renuka Gusain argues that, in certain media treatments of the Iraq War, viewers come to incorporate the "experiences and environments" the characters on-screen must negotiate or suffer through, all of them "reconfiguring themselves" in relation to these shocking, unpleasant, or traumatic stimuli.[73] She speculates that the twenty-first-century war film can never overcome or act as an "antidote" to the constant circulation of terror that media images convey to the viewer's affective-cognitive-perceptual complexes.[74] *The Wall*, as it correlates the eye to the most dominant aspect of its mise-en-scène, might seem an attempt to do as much, to toughen or shore up the audience's somatosensory address to the screen and thus inure them to a total state of terror. Far from soliciting our consent to further investment in nation-state or military security, though, the film indicates some of the undesirable consequences of walling, fencing, and Green Zone-style districting maneuvers. First, the wall continually and inescapably obscures the vision of those in front of it, with Isaac desperately seeking out cracks in it to scan the area for Juba and also use as make-do embrasures in case a firefight erupts. The wall, in other words, transfixes this character and the film's viewers on the object of study in front in them, thus cutting them off from much of the world's sense-phenomena and constraining their experiential framework to much the same extent that scientificality demands of its adherents. The obscuring of the train of our vision also creates further occasion for fear; as a result, Isaac confesses in one scene, "I'm scared of what's behind [the wall]." True to the state of the surjective, the quasi-positivist focus in the film, even as it attunes the nerves and senses of its main character to the immediacy of the situation, only really serves to set off, as a sniper might several rounds from a rifle, further opportunities for distress, disquietude, and self-loss.

However, the opacity of the wall at the same time frustrates the epistemic vanities of science, since it transforms swathes of the film's diegetic environment into the "undecidable" and "unknown." Arguing with the combative and distrustful Isaac, the sniper shouts out, "You don't know shit," an exclamation that applies equally well to the viewer. The wall, then, intensifies the characters' terror and uncertainty, making the film's audio channels, and thus a major component of our sensoria, fundamentally untrustworthy. Juba at first impersonates a US communications officer, attempting to talk Isaac into divulging military information and trick the soldier (and the audience) into a calmer and more unsuspecting state. However, Juba, using a slight Iraqi accent, then mispronounces "sergeant" over the radio airwaves, allowing Isaac to see through this vocal "camouflage," as the sniper refers to it. The wall, in short, makes communication *treacherous and sometimes even detrimental* to them. The film suggests that the same qualities inhere in these defenses in and of themselves, in that they deteriorate, chip off, topple over, and invite attacks from defilade fire, as well as cluster and armor-piercing weapons, endangering those under or next to them. Early in the film, one of the stones of the wall smashes Isaac's fingers; and then, during a subsequent action set piece in which Juba shells it, the entire structure falls down and almost crushes the infantryman, who refers to taking cover near it as "hiding in the shadow of fucking death." This soldier thus captures the state of the "lifeworld" at the margins of the strategically convenient confines of a Green Zone-style secure area. The surjective determination of these walls, fences, and other deterrents means that, even if they fail, they still introduce the deadening tenor of the objective into the sense qualities of those they enclose. The sniper, in the conclusion of the film, fires into the cockpit and cabin of the medevac unit, forcing it to crash in flames; causing everyone inside it to die, including the main character; and making the upshot of this final scene, so unusual for war films, clear—*there is no escape for those who see walls everywhere*. The film ends with a realignment of the camera with a set of crosshairs, a shot that, more than a simple reminder of Virilio's mode of analysis, suggests that we too might start to resemble these characters in desperation if we decide to center our eyes and stake our cultural survival on security walling.

Conclusion

The Green Zones in these films, as contingent and indefinite in their formation and use value, on the surface seem to offer some advantages to those who construct, maintain, and stand watch over them. For example, these sorts of secure areas, with their mazes of fencing, checkpoints, and sentry stations, enable the main characters in these films to retain their footholds in unstable and unfriendly territories. Green Zones also function to concentrate signs of affluence in one space, ensure the constant flow of consumer traffic in one direction or another, furnish shelter from violence, and create an *information gap* to further separate those inside the "security perimeter" from those they neighbor. However, the true value of these films consists in the fact that they expose the archi-barbaric consequences of these rather makeshift forms of walling on the cultures of those on either side of them. These Green Zones, as we see in these films, systemically disrupt the aesthetic sensibilities, capacities for self-growth, and cultural rootedness of those next to them, making them feel ill at ease in their own cities, countries, or communities and thus energizing their resistance. Correspondingly, as these areas accrue more wealth, privileges, and creature comforts, they attract more and more potential enemies to their thresholds—they quickly draw forth those who want what those inside them control and enjoy. These fences, walls, and turrets, for all of the spatio-legible functions they serve, at the same time often create certain opacities, making it difficult to determine the identities, movements, and motivations of the forces attacking, circumventing, or attempting to figure out a way through them. Although those that administer these secure areas might operate with their own degree of anonymity, they also set the stage for those outside their circles to come together to work out their own modes of socialization, their own methods of struggle and critique, and their own conditions of self-knowledge. Those next to the Green Zone, or those inside it without any control over it whatsoever, might fabricate tunnels (or wormholes), circulate "underground" messages over digital media devices, and transform social space so as to minimize or mock its totalitarian tenor. Much mainstream twenty-first-century cinema, then, even though it entertains questionable notions of objective enemies and scientifically respectable ways of deterring them, in any event confronts us with the negative effects of Green Zone-style defense installations. Thus, the cinema might tacitly discourage us from consenting to their redevelopment into full-blown, nation-state security walls, a real possibility that the next chapter closely examines.

Notes

1 See The Project for the New American Century, "Rebuilding America's Defenses: Strategy, Forces, and Resources for a New Century," September 2000, https://archive.org/stream/RebuildingAmericasDefenses/ RebuildingAmericasDefenses_djvu.txt.

2 See Ron Suskind, "Faith, Certainty and the Presidency of George W. Bush," *New York Times*, October 17, 2004, https://www.nytimes.com/2004/10/17/ magazine/faith-certainty-and-the-presidency-of-george-w-bush.html.

3 See William Langewiesche, "Welcome to the Green Zone: The American Bubble in Baghdad," *The Atlantic*, November 2004, https://www.theatlantic. com/magazine/archive/2004/11/welcome-to-the-green-zone/303547/.

4 See, e.g., "Military Investigates Hostile Fire in 'Green Zone,'" *CNN*, December 25, 2003, http://www.cnn.com/2003/WORLD/meast/12/25/sprj. irq.main/index.html; Martin Asser, "Profile: Baghdad's Green Zone," *BBC News*, October 14, 2004, http://news.bbc.co.uk/2/hi/middle_east/ 3744468. stm; Dexter Filkins, "2 Bombers Kill 5 in Guarded Area of Baghdad," *New York Times*, October 15, 2004, https://www.nytimes.com/2004/10/15/ world/middleeast/2-bombers-kill-5-in-guarded-area-in-baghdad.html; Rory McCarthy, "Four Gurkhas Die in Baghdad Green Zone Mortar Attack," *The*

Guardian, November 26, 2004, https://www.theguardian.com/world/2004/nov/27/iraq.rorymccarthy; "Mortars Strike Baghdad Green Zone," *CBS News*, July 10, 2007, https://www.cbsnews.com/news/mortars-strike-baghdad-green-zone/; Paul Tait, "Baghdad's Green Zone Hit by a Barrage of Blasts," *Reuters*, March 22, 2008, https://www.reuters.com/article/us-iraq-barrage/baghdads-green-zone-hit-by-barrage-of-blasts-idUSL2368975320080323; and Andrea Stone, "Mortars, Rockets Raise Baghdad Tensions," *USA Today*, May 2, 2008, https://usatoday30.usatoday.com/news/world/iraq/2008-05-01-iraqrockets_N.htm.

5   Diana Taylor argues that state officials often rely on the figure of the terrorist to conjure up images of "'barbarians' and unassimilable Others who use 'illegitimate' forms of violence" against their citizens. This rhetoric, she further argues, serves to excuse and soften "the decimation of civil liberties, the surveillance of national populations, the escalation in racial profiling, the use of increasingly suspect judicial and police procedures, and governmental association with known torturers and murderers." Along with similar far-right regimes, the Trump administration confounds the figure of the terrorist with that of the refugee or "illegal" immigrant in order to continue to rationalize, finance, and drum up support for some of these same dubious and illiberal security measures. After all, as Jeremy Harding reminds us, "The battle against illegal immigration is a domestic version of America's interventions overseas, with many of the same trappings: big manpower commitments, militarisation, pursuit, detection, rendition, loss of life." See Diana Taylor, *The Archive and the Repertoire: Performing Cultural Memory in the Americas* (Durham, NC: Duke University Press, 2005), 275; and Jeremy Harding, *Border Vigils: Keeping Migrants Out of the Rich World* (New York: Verso, 2012), 90.

6   Michel Henry, *Barbarism*, trans. Scott Davidson (New York: Continuum, 2012), 36.

7   Ibid., 26.

8   Ibid., 36–7.

9   Ibid., 102.

10 Ibid., 35, 100.

11 Ibid., 27.

12 Ibid., 18.

13 Ibid., 70.

14 Ibid., 92.

15 Hannah Arendt, *The Origins of Totalitarianism* (New York: Harcourt, 1976), 326.

16 Ibid., 438, 466.

17 Ibid., 311, 430, 459.

18 Ibid., 345, 459.

19 Ibid., 345, 349, 477.

20 Ibid., 392.

21 Ibid., 425.
22 Ibid., 329, 429.
23 The science fiction milestone *Forbidden Planet* (1956) features one of the first instances of Green Zone-style security perimeters in US cinema. The astronauts in the film set up an electronic fence in the flatlands of Altair IV, only for the "id-monster," the manifestation of outcast scientist Edward Morbius's (Walter Pidgeon) unconscious rage, to force its way through it and murder one of the members of the expedition team. Mark Jancovich notes the conservative nature of the film—or more exactly, this scene—arguing that in it defensive "force, not therapy, serves as the solution to the problems of the self." The displays of force and the makeshift installations in the film also serve to shore up the self-identity of the crew, separating them from the other entities they encounter on Altair IV. The astronauts, unable to coexist next to them, can only destroy the planet after retreating to their starship and flying off to Earth, this time with Morbius's servile robot Robby. The film remains of value, though, due to its Cold War release context—a time that saw the Soviets restrict travel in East Germany—in that it neatly advises against investing any time and effort in security fencing that cannot speak to our impulsive desire for free movement and that also simply does not work. See Mark Jancovich, "We're the Martians Now: British SF Invasion Fantasies of the 1950s and 1960s," in *Liquid Metal: The Science Fiction Reader*, ed. Sean Redmond (New York: Wallflower, 2007), 333.
24 See Barton Gellman and Walter Pincus, "Depiction of Threat Outgrew Supporting Evidence," *Washington Post*, August 10, 2003, https://www.washingtonpost.com/wp-dyn/content/article/2006/06/12/AR2006061200932_pf.html.
25 Mike Davis, "Fortress Los Angeles: The Militarization of Urban Space," in *Variations on a Theme Park: The New American City and the End of Public Space*, ed. Michael Sorkin (New York: Hill and Wang, 1992), 173.
26 Steven Shaviro, *Post Cinematic Affect* (Alresford: Zero Books, 2010), 82, 87.
27 On February 15, 2019, for example, the ever-mercurial Trump sought to declare a "National Emergency Concerning the Southern Border" of the United States, so as to divert millions of dollars from drug interdiction and military funds toward the construction of a security wall. After much contestation from Democrats, the ACLU, and the Sierra Club, the Supreme Court in a close 5-4 decision was to rule in favor of the declaration, allowing Trump to reallocate the funds. See Paul Sonne, "Trump Looks to Raid Pentagon Budget for Wall Money Using Emergency Powers," *Washington Post*, February 15, 2019, https://www.washingtonpost.com/world/national-security/trump-looks-to-raid-pentagon-budget-for-wall-money-using-emergency-powers/2019/02/15/cd0fcdb8-3149-11e9-ac6c-14eea99d5e24_story.html; Bobby Allyn, "Federal Judge Rules against Border Wall Construction with Military Funds," *NPR*, June 26, 2019, https://www.npr.org/2019/06/28/737236244/federal-judge-rules-against-border-wall-construction-with-military-funds; and Ariane de Vogue, "Supreme Court Clears Way for Trump Admin to Use Defense Funds for Border Wall

Construction," *CNN*, July 26, 2019, https://www.cnn.com/2019/07/26/politics/supreme-court-pentagon-border-wall-construction/index.html.

28 The name of this character refers to the resolution of the Thirty Years' War and its implications for nation-state demarcation; as Reece Jones reminds us, "The significance of the post-Westphalian era is that boundaries drawn on maps became the critical location for the division of the political space of the world." See Reece Jones, *Violent Borders: Refugees and the Right to Move* (New York: Verso, 2017), 107.

29 As Sean Carter and Klaus Dodds note, with application to the surveillance system in *Southland Tales*, the US-Mexico border is "increasingly biometric in form," compiling fingerprints and retinal scans to catalog and distribute to other "international agencies" in the effort to stem the tides of immigration, terrorism, and civil disobedience over the course of the first decades of the new millennium. See Sean Carter and Klaus Dodds, *International Politics and Film: Space, Vision, Power* (New York: Wallflower, 2014), 23.

30 Gérard Genette, *Narrative Discourse: An Essay in Method*, trans. Jane E. Lewin (Ithaca, NY: Cornell University Press, 1983), 236.

31 J. Hoberman, in a review of *Southland Tales*, remarks that every aspect "of this convoluted narrative is monitored, scripted, and directed from within the movie. Half the characters are watching the other half or else producing their own self-promoting video vehicles." The convenience store sequence, then, marks the moment of metaleptic rupture when the film's narrator and director-figure steps down from the camera mount to interact with some of the other characters in a musical number. The sequence remains quasi-diegetic, though, much as do similar ones in more clear-cut film musicals, which do not necessarily relate to the causal or expository thrusts of their narratives. Pilot Abilene assumes a more diegetic role only after subsequently meeting up and dancing with some of the nightclubbers in the LA district under the US government's surveillance—the watcher, in other words, thereafter *becomes the watched*. See J. Hoberman, *Film after Film or, What Became of 21st Century Cinema?* (New York: Verso, 2012), 240.

32 As Wheeler Winston Dixon and Gwendolyn Audrey Foster make clear, images and information appear much more mutable and difficult to contain in the twenty-first-century mediasphere, as they are "available everywhere, anywhere" and are "no longer defined by walls" of movie theaters or concert venues. They argue that the "dissemination and transmission of images shift beyond all known boundaries," since digital audiovisual devices can deliver them instantaneously across oceans and continents with the simple click of a mouse or the tap of a touchscreen. See Wheeler Winston Dixon and Gwendolyn Audrey Foster, *21st-Century Hollywood: Movies in the Era of Transformation* (New Brunswick: Rutgers University Press, 2011), 38, 177.

33 Genette, *Narrative Discourse,* 111.

34 Ibid., 155.

35 Fredric Jameson, *Postmodernism or, the Cultural Logic of Late Capitalism* (Durham, NC: Duke University Press, 2001), 48.

36 John Ellis argues that the space of media consumption often reinforces "a basic division of the world between the 'inside' of the home, the family and the domestic, and the 'outside' of work, politics, public life, the city, the crowd." He then analogizes this division to the one separating the nation-state from extramural territories, with the inside "the area of safety, of confirmation of identity, of power" and the outside "that of risk, of challenge to identity, of helplessness." The final scenes of *Southland Tales* overturn these distinctions, in that the areas inside the zeppelin and the Green Zone-like LA downtown turn into arenas for radical, impolite, and dangerous social experimentation. The digital media that the film associates with Boxer Santaros, Pilot Abilene, and Zora Carmichaels, unlike with theatrical cinema or conventional television, travels with their users into and outside of domestic space, thus modeling and, through the efforts of the neo-Marxist revolutionaries in the film, instigating the collapse of these sorts of inside-outside distinctions. See John Ellis, *Visible Fictions: Cinema, Television, Video* (New York: Routledge, 2000), 166.

37 Maurizia Natali traces these sorts of "traumatic landscapes" throughout the US visual arts, from the oil works of Thomas Cole to the television coverage of 9/11. These images reproduce the "shock and awe" effects that often dovetail with the nation-state's "sublime imperial fantasies," enabling their viewers to imagine themselves acting in the name of empire while at the same time rescuing noncitizens from the destruction and siege that it demands. Through its main character's solicitous treatment of the Iraqis, *Green Zone* makes explicit the fact that such fantasies drove first the devastation and then the occupation of Baghdad. See Maurizia Natali, "The Course of the Empire: Sublime Landscapes in the American Cinema," in *Landscape and Film*, ed. Martin Lefebvre (New York: Routledge, 2006), 93, 105.

38 Conceit-wise, the film conforms to the classic conventions of the war film that Andrew Sarris outlines. "Among the violent genres, the war film was not a clear-cut Manichean morality tale like the western, or an illumination of the id like the gangster movie and the *film noir*," Sarris argues, further noting that the war film often makes "its polemical points by placing the blame for the violence on the unseen merchants of death in high places." See Andrew Sarris, *"You Ain't Heard Nothin' Yet": The American Talking Film History & Memory, 1927–1949* (New York: Oxford University Press, 2000), 127.

39 Martin Barker, *A "Toxic Genre": The Iraq War Films* (New York: Pluto Press, 2011), 164.

40 Ibid., 164.

41 Richard Slotkin compares *The Green Berets* to such classic John Ford Westerns as *Drums Along the Mohawk* (1939), *Fort Apache* (1948), and *Rio Grande* (1950), films, among others, that went on to inspire such codenames as "Crazy Horse," "Davy Crockett," and "Sam Houston" for the military operations of the Vietnam War. Strangely, though, Slotkin never compares "Dodge City" in *The Green Berets* to the US "Strategic Hamlet" initiative, which sought to install fences, ditches, mantraps, and observation towers next to certain villages and then to staff them with seventy-five to one hundred

soldiers responsible for establishing curfews, checking identity cards, and eliminating communist sympathizers. These "Hamlets" thus seem a clear antecedent to the Green Zone, meant to separate out terrorists, insurgents, and stalwart Hussein supporters from the rest of the Iraqi citizenry. Much as in the Vietnam era, then, the US forces in the film identify willy-nilly with the cowboys and Indians—and, confusing these terms, they also use them to demonize the Iraqis as "outlaws" and "savages." See Richard Slotkin, *Gunfighter Nation: The Myth of the Frontier in Twentieth-Century America* (Norman: University of Oklahoma Press, 1998), 124–5.

42 The slumification of Iraq in *Green Zone* recalls Igor Krstić's discussion of the realist, shaky-cam-intensive cinemas of other nations, such as Portugal and the Philippines, which address "slum life as a topic" so as to expose the mistakes and moral failings of their "contemporary societies." Greengrass's film similarly uses realist techniques and digital tools (without fantastic CGI) to expose the mistakes and moral failings of the Bush administration, US intelligence agencies, and the military forces inside the Green Zone during the occupation of Iraq. See Igor Krstić, *Slums on Screen: World Cinema and the Planet of Slums* (Edinburgh: Edinburgh University Press, 2017), 169.

43 Dominique Brégent-Heald, in a survey of films depicting the "US-Mexico and US-Canada borders," notes that those who engage in criminal activities in them frequently appear nonwhite, as is the case to an extent with *Green Zone*. These films, she further contends, nonetheless elicit from their viewers "counterhegemonic reactions" to the negative effects of "U.S. cultural imperialism" on other sovereign countries and their often nonwhite citizenries—e.g., on Iraqi nationals, to adapt these arguments again to the case of Greengrass's film. See Dominique Brégent-Heald, *Borderland Films: American Cinema, Mexico, and Canada during the Progressive Era* (Lincoln: University of Nebraska Press, 2015), 289–93.

44 Steven Peacock, "The Collaborative Film Work of Greengrass and Damon: A Stylistic State of Exception," *New Cinemas: Journal of Contemporary Film* 9, no. 2/3 (2012): 157.

45 Ibid., 157.

46 The *G.I. Joe* films (2009, 2013) also nicely encapsulate the anti-life and archibarbaric qualities of the scientistic disposition. The sequel, Jon M. Chu's *Retaliation*, introduces us to the Einsargen Subterranean Prison, a fenced-in secure area in Germany in which the film's villain Cobra Commander (Luke Bracey) floats semiconsciously inside an isolation tank. Using nanodevices, nuclear arms, and orbital strikes in attempt after attempt to take over the world's nations, this terrorist-scientist seeks to obliterate London, Paris, and other major cities and impose on them a new sociopolitical ethos from scratch. As one of Cobra Commander's agents uses firefly-like explosives to infiltrate the facility, its warden exclaims, after detailing its nightmarish security features, "This is what science has come to." The warden might as well describe in this dialogue the face of Cobra Commander, its severe disfigurement another symptom of the inhumanity that results from an infatuation with scientific results over and above aesthetic feeling. The

facility's security features, in any event, for all their cost and impressiveness, seem utterly ineffective in deterring the fireflies from tearing through its fences, checkpoints, watchtowers, and floodlight and camera surveillance systems as though they were flying IEDs.

47 Henry, *Barbarism*, 100.
48 Hannah Arendt, *Eichmann in Jerusalem: A Report on the Banality of Evil* (New York: Penguin, 1994), 289.
49 Henry, *Barbarism*, 53.
50 Arendt, *Totalitarianism*, 302.
51 Cynthia Weber, *Imagining America at War: Morality, Politics and Film* (New York: Routledge, 2005), 11.
52 Todd A. Comer, "The Disabled Hero: Being and Ethics in Peter Jackson's *The Lord of the Rings*," *Mythlore* 35, no. 1 (2016): 113.
53 For the exact costs and ticket sales of the series, see https://www.boxofficemojo.com/, as well as Kim Masters, "'The Hobbit': Inside Peter Jackson's and Warner Bros.' $1 Billion Gamble," *Hollywood Reporter*, October 17, 2012, https://www.hollywoodreporter.com/news/hobbit-peter-jackson-warner-bros-379301.
54 Julie Turnock, *Plastic Reality: Special Effects, Technology, and the Emergence of 1970s Blockbuster Aesthetics* (New York: Columbia University Press, 2015), 47.
55 David Foster Wallace, discussing James Cameron's *Terminator 2: Judgment Day* (1991), sets forth an inverse ratio concerning these sorts of Hollywood mega-productions: the more expensive and flamboyant their special effects, the thinner their characters and narratives. He specifically argues that in such films "plot and character implausibilities are to be handled through distraction rather than resolved through explanation." The dynamic frame rate of *The Hobbit* series, though, in drawing attention to the ordinariness of its costumes, props, makeup, and set design, effectively short-circuits the emphasis on spectacle and "distraction" in these films' action set pieces. Thus, rather than merely drawing attention to the formal shortcomings of these films or the stark artificiality of their more CG-intensive fight scenes, this aesthetic choice enables viewers to refocus on Thorin's characterization so that we can trace the obvious inconsistencies in the king's actions, motives, and mannerisms to their efficient causes: the riches of Erebor, the isolationism of the dwarves, and the walling off of their mountain fortress. See David Foster Wallace, *Both Flesh and Not: Essays* (New York: Little, Brown, 2011), 185.
56 This scene also acts as an instance of a "traumascape," Richard Bégin's term for a space that functions more as an "invagination" than as a "representation," meaning that it relies on digital effects to fully immerse us in the aftershocks of a disaster, rather than merely visualize them, as in the case of "the romantic depiction of ruins." Jackson's film, in this sequence, exemplifies this sort of "depth within a virtual reality," as the treasure stores of Erebor threaten to swallow Thorin into darkness and obliterate the other visual data on-screen—thus the thirst for these coins results in a

thoroughgoing "symbolic failure," considering the fact that they fracture the dwarven tribes and nearly incite a war in the film. See Richard Bégin, "Digital Traumascape: From the *Trümmerfilme* to *Wall e**," *Space and Culture* 17, no. 4 (2014): 380, 382, 385.

57 Marek Oziewicz, "Peter Jackson's *The Hobbit*: A Beautiful Disaster," *Journal of the Fantastic in the Arts* 27, no. 2 (2016): 258.

58 James Walters, *Fantasy Film: A Critical Introduction* (New York: Bloomsbury Academic, 2011), 126.

59 *Hercules* (Brett Ratner, 2014), another fantasy film of the era, represents a further twist on Green Zone-style military defense. The title character (Dwayne Johnson), at the insistence of the Thracians, commands a coterie of warriors against the men of a tribe that the film clearly marks as their "objective enemies," since they wear olive warpaint, affect a fierce demeanor, and constantly make shrieking noises reminiscent of a death rattle. Hercules orders the Thracian soldiers to configure themselves into an infantry square of shields and spearheads, so as to enclose their ruler and officers, thus safeguarding them from the onrush of the tribesmen. The Thracian soldiers thus resemble in themselves a Green Zone, a mobile, makeshift array of "shield-walls," as they refer to themselves, serving to screen out those under their rule who might nonetheless resist and attack them. Hercules succeeds in routing the tribesmen, which might at first seem to attest to the advantageousness and reliability of these military formations. Afterward, though, the film depicts the Thracian nobles as cruel, rancorous, conniving, and imperialist, the true enemies of Hercules, responsible for the deaths of this mythic character's family, which altogether suggests another serious structural limitation of Green Zone-like fortifications: namely, *that we can never be sure if they are protecting the wrong men*.

60 Another fantasy film of the 2010s, *Percy Jackson and the Sea of Monsters* (Thor Freudenthal, 2013), features a Green Zone-style training center, Camp Half-Blood, that comes about from an archi-barbaric turn of events. The opening scene traces the origins of the camp to the self-sacrifice of Thalia (Paloma Kwiatkowski), a daughter of Zeus who dies confronting two ogres in a forest and afterward transforms into a tree that surrounds the area with a magic circle, repulsing from it these sorts of monsters and other malicious forces. Camp Half-Blood, then, owes its existing culture and sense of self-identity to a foundational act of violence and death. One of the demigods inside the camp, though, sickens the tree, suppressing its apotropaic functions and making vulnerable the other trainees, among them Percy Jackson (Logan Lerman), son of Poseidon. The Colchis Bull, in fact, comes to attack them, a monster automaton made of metal armor, drive shafts, and cogwheels that can reconfigure its form in mid-battle and also activate drills, flamethrowers, and rotor saws to use against its enemies. This monster, in short, *can twist inside out*, a visual flourish that complements its attempt to turn the teenagers out from the safety of their camp and into the territories that it shuts out. After they defeat the

Bull, the trainees set forth to fight other monsters, such as a manticore and a Titan, in order to obtain the Golden Fleece so that they can use it to revive Thalia. Thus, the film at first might seem to other those outside the camp as sinister or abominable, establishing a "clash of civilizations" that opposes the modelesque demigods to the demonic-looking Titans. However, another monster of sorts, Tyson (Douglas Smith), a Cyclops and also a son of Poseidon, arrives to save the trainees from the Bull and follow them on their adventures. Through this character, whom the demigods accept among their ranks only after overcoming their initial reluctance, the film suggests an alternative to instantiating a culture through conflict and destruction: the *reclamation* of those who suffer from exclusion, disinheritance, dehumanization, or cultural dispossession, as Tyson does. Only then through *the extension of the family circle*, rather than through refoulement or separatist efforts, might we start to consider magic circles (and security fences too) as unnecessary.

61 Peter Biskind, *The Sky Is Falling: How Vampires, Zombies, Androids, and Superheroes Made America Great for Extremism* (New York: New Press, 2018), 10.
62 Erich Fromm, *Escape from Freedom* (New York: Holt, 1969), 166.
63 The magic domes and other CG tricks that the witches use in this film speak to the ubiquitous use of cellphone cameras and other telesurveillance devices, a state of affairs that Paul Virilio describes as a "visual bubble." He refers to the never-ending digitalization of all our "immediate sensations," which sets us in a more intimate relation to the algorithmic and alphanumeric than to "reality," as Michel Henry might use the term. See Paul Virilio, *The Information Bomb* (New York: Verso, 2006), 112–4.
64 Fromm, *Escape from Freedom*, 257.
65 Biskind, *Sky Is Falling*, 188.
66 Paul Virilio, *War and Cinema: The Logistics of Perception*, trans. Patrick Camiller (New York: Verso, 2009), 83.
67 Isabelle Freda, "Screening War: *American Sniper, Hurt Locker,* and Drone Vision," *International Journal of Contemporary Iraqi Studies* 10, no. 3 (2017): 236.
68 Patricia Pisters, "Logistics of Perception 2.0: Multiple Screen Aesthetics in Iraq War Films," *Film-Philosophy* 14, no. 1 (2010): 241.
69 *High Sierra* (Raoul Walsh, 1941) exemplifies the difference of Iraq War films, with their multimedia displays, from older cinematic representations of violence. In this early *film noir*, the fugitive Roy Earle (Humphrey Bogart) retreats to the mountains to evade a dragnet, engaging in a shootout with the cops from atop one of the slopes in the climax. Unusually for a Classical Hollywood studio film, the camera slightly twitches and wavers, as though steadying its aim, as it captures Earle shooting at the manhunters near the foot of the mountain. The camera thus aligns with the character's eyes and trigger finger, shaking in a way that it never does for the rest of the film's 100-minute running time. The shot might at first seem sloppy, although it aesthetically makes sense for this scene and

also nicely illustrates Virilio's arguments concerning the coadunation of the train of the camera eye with, in this case, the sighting mechanisms of Earle's rifle.

70 Robert Eberwein discusses the weapons in the war film with reference to a different facet of our anatomies: the male erection, arguing that the "sexual deprivation" of men in combat compels them to treat their rifles and sidearms—as well as the violence they inflict on one another and their enemies—as erotic substitutes for the "action" they feel they are missing out on in the civilian sphere. *The Wall*, though, even as it aligns the eye with its title structure rather than with a set of crosshairs, also downplays the sexual symbolism so apparent in other war films. The film, after all, casts former WWE champion John Cena as Sergeant Matthews, who spends most of the film sprawling out flaccidly on the desert sands after suffering a direct shot in what appears the nether regions, rather than showing off the stiff, veiny muscles characteristic of most wrestlers. See Robert Eberwein, *Armed Forces: Masculinity and Sexuality in the American War Film* (New Brunswick: Rutgers University Press, 2007), 135.

71 The oil fields in *The Wall* might seem incidental to its narrative; they are not. As Todd Miller notes, frontier zones zigzag through "places of rich natural resources" for a deliberate reason, most often to exclude nationals from acquiring or capitalizing on them. The conditions of war then change so that as the Border Patrol "have become more militarized," the military "has been policified." The two soldiers in the film therefore resemble security contractors more than they do infantrymen. See Todd Miller, *Empire of Borders: How the US Is Exporting Its Border Around the World* (New York: Verso, 2019), 63, 79.

72 More than a narrative or mise-en-scène element, the open wounds of Sergeant Matthews also represent a figural contrast and ideological challenge to the wall of the film's title. As Ana M. Manzanas and Jesús Benito Sanchez argue, these open wounds and their scarring "translate into two different perspectives on the experience of migration." The soldier's wounds suggest a "breach parting two entities and leaving an opening," symbolizing the free crossing that threatens US territories with "contamination and loss of identity." The scar, though, seems to represent a solution to these threats: in the form of a security enclosure, it seals the nation-state, its insular areas, and its military detachments off from "external infection." Sergeant Isaac clings to such an enclosure or "scar" on the Iraqi terrain; as we might anticipate, following Manzanas and Sanchez's arguments, it remains mostly ineffective as a repair matrix of sorts. This sort of "scar tissue," after all, might easily reopen, thus exposing the "flesh" of the nation-state to the "foreign agents" of its immediate environment. The real tragedy of the film, then, appears Isaac's choice to duck for cover under the wall rather than to figuratively move into the "interstitial spaces" that Matthews occupies—in other words, the choice to refuse the "open wound," the "necessary matrix of communication" for either side of a cross-border situation. See Ana M. Manzanas and Jesús Benito Sanchez,

Cities, Borders, and Spaces in Intercultural American Literature and Film (New York: Routledge, 2011), 94–100.

73 Renuka Gusain, "The War Body as Screen of Terror," in *The War Body on Screen*, ed. Karen Randall and Sean Redmund (New York: Continuum, 2012), 43.

74 Ibid., 47.

3

Safe Spaces: Inside the Walls on the Cinema Screen

On January 18, 2018, President Donald J. Trump, over Twitter, sought to recommit to the construction of a vast security wall along the US–Mexico frontier, one that might rise over 50 feet, span over 1,000 miles, and cost taxpayers upward of $20,000,000,000. Trump insists on these measures to stem the tide of immigration to the United States, catch and deport "criminal aliens," and avert "total chaos."[1] Sadly, in such statements, during the campaign and after the inauguration, Trump associates Central and South American refugees, émigrés, and indigent migrant workers with terrorists, drug smugglers, rapists, and other violent offenders, arguing that only an "impenetrable" wall can stop their ingress into the country.[2] To this effect, Trump was to shut down the US government from December 22, 2018, to January 25, 2019, in order to compel Congress to come to the negotiation table and agree to demands for the funding of the US-Mexico security wall. However, Trump's stratagem met with failure, as Speaker Nancy Pelosi and other House representatives chose to refuse to compromise and to claim that the president was "manufacturing a crisis."[3] Even while stopping the activities of the US government for over a month on the federal front, though, Trump afterward thought to escalate it in other areas and in other departments. He set in motion a series of US Immigration and Customs Enforcement (ICE) raids in Ohio and Mississippi, rounding up and detaining almost 830 immigrant workers without documentation, as well as threatening them with deportation and indicting some of them with nonviolent crimes.[4] The raids were the most wide-scale since December 12, 2006, when under George W. Bush ICE forces were sent to six Midwestern meatpacking units to arrest, detain, and deport over 1,300 immigrants.[5] To make the nation "safer," then, through these measures Trump sought to terrorize entire communities, deprive their members of their incomes, separate them from their families, and discourage their children from attending school for fear of deportation.[6]

To call this agenda racist, callous, or xenophobic, though, is not enough, as it also more complexly evokes Michel Foucault's theorization of the three instruments vital to consolidating the relatively even distribution of "forces"—economic, military, scientific, technological, and otherwise—that obtain from one nation-state to another. These instruments ensure that disease, mass immigration, market vicissitudes, the use of the natural environment, and the consumption of certain nonrenewable resources remain in delicate check. These instruments include the option of war to reestablish this rough equilibrium; continual diplomatic negotiations, including the cultivation of a "system of information concerning the state of forces in each country"; and finally a *dispositif* that sets forth an entire infrastructure of strongholds, checkpoints, transport systems, and communication networks.[7] However, Foucault, in an earlier seminar, also argues that such a security apparatus, whether meant to ensure the stability of Europe or the Americas, ratifies those discourses that suppose that savagery, cunning, and unreason underlie every nonviolent relation among nations, so much so that "reason" comes to appear on the side of "wickedness."[8] He moreover argues that the instruments, material or discursive, of the state security-military apparatus derive not from trade imbalances or territorial encroachments. The elements that ensure its continuation and development stem from ethnic, cultural, and sociolinguistic differences, or more succinctly from the impulse to *first constellate, then conquer and assume dominance over another race*. The effort to construct a security fence, such as the US–Mexico wall, does more than mark the flesh of those on one side of it as inferior, criminalizable, or unworthy of citizenship or asylum. This sort of measure admits to the fact that the nation-state, territorially and in terms of its constituents, always remains unstable, with outsiders constantly threatening to infiltrate and reshape its socius. The clear rift that results from this security apparatus, Foucault observes, does not really involve two separate races—each one staring, for example, at one or the other side of a wall. This rift, for those inside the wall, inevitably and more insidiously involves "the splitting of one race into a superrace and a subrace."[9]

Thus, one of the security wall's ulterior consequences, the intrastate separation of races, also requires it to effectively and systematically erase these conditions of domination. The media and the other culture industries then step in, according to Bernard Stiegler, working continually to flatten the affect, collective memories, and means to self-expression and individuation available to those within the ambit of the nation-state. Stiegler describes certain media, such as television, cellphones, and music recordings, as "tertiary retentional devices" that mainly serve to transform or rather refunctionalize the individual into a consumer.[10] These mass industrial technologies increasingly standardize our aesthetic sensibilities, co-opting and disfiguring what Stiegler refers to as "the *flux* of *primary retentions*," meaning our attention to the "now" of the chain of sense-impressions that informs our conscious awareness of them. These technologies also distort our *"filters of secondary retention"*: the fact that since we must select the impressions of which we then take note, we cannot retain them all, and must rely on our memories to color and organize our experience of them.[11] These technologies, in that they sync their audiovisual flows to the consciousness of the mass audiences that consume them, deaden their capacities for individuation and set the stage for a collective sense of immiseration. How do they do so? And why does Stiegler describe them as tertiary? These devices first come to control our ability to discretize information—computers, for example, use algorithms to select items of interest for us. Then these devices do the work of recording for us, as they "remember" the melodies of a song or the items in our shopping carts in online stores. This media infrastructure finally therefore seems indispensable to a state that security walling surrounds, since it dulls our attention to the fact that a superrace must administer the functioning of this apparatus at the same time as it must train our memories on those outside of it, on those trying to climb, rupture, or circumvent it, rather than on the further divisions taking shape inside of it. As it works to dis-individualize us, this media infrastructure mollifies us, disavowing the status of those within the walls subject to state surveillance and administration as a subclass or subrace. However, Stiegler argues that, as this mediatic capture drives us to consume desperately, excessively, and unsatisfyingly, it ultimately creates the conditions for new and virulent forms of racism, violence, and social unrest to emerge. "Deprived of singularity," Stiegler argues, those subject to superrace administration "attempt to singularize themselves by products suggested by the market," and, failing to do so, "no longer love themselves and prove to be less and less capable of love."[12] This critique of a state interior's mediasphere might appear dismal and impossible to escape or outthink. However, Stiegler argues that cinema, alone of all the media arts, moves its viewers to reinvent themselves as a "we," as a new community of *individuals with a difference*, in that it supplants their consumerist expectations with a desire for the "unexpected."[13] Although certainly a tertiary recording device, cinema nevertheless functions as the "suicidal tendency" of the culture industries, their markets, and the security agendas that they reinforce and serve.[14]

Even the most crassly commercial films that Hollywood (co)produces show forth the ways that these apparatuses dis-individuate their characters and re-racialize them into social echelons that confer on them different degrees of symbolic, economic, and cultural force. These films—more specifically, some of the major monster films of the twenty-first century—make security walls an integral component of their narrative syntaxes, representational strategies, and mise-en-scène compositions. These monster films might tacitly argue for the construction of security fences, draw attention to their shortcomings, rehearse fears over their inefficacy, or show the ways that they actually dehumanize, destabilize, or threaten those that they enclose. The walls in these films and the monsters outside their fringes speak to Wendy Brown's discussion of the ways that such security measures function as a "scrim" for fantasizing "an anthropomorphized other" responsible for crime, declining wages, influxes of drugs, and dilutions of ethno-national identity.[15] However, these films, no matter their conventionality at times, in that they carry within them the force of the "unexpected," do not merely depict security fences as an adequate means of containing migrant waves, national threats, and rival state interests—in other words, they do not neatly or altogether function as the scrim that Brown describes. These films dramatize the *racio-spatial* consequences of these walls on their diegetic and extradiegetic contexts, as they most often situate the monsters on the edges of the nation-state and also make them easily distinguishable from those within. These films, through elaborate makeup, casting decisions, or digital effects, nonetheless do more than "other" certain characters. They mark their flesh as that which must remain *inside or outside* the walled-in areas of their dieges. Additionally, some of those characters on the inside must either surrender to the surveillance, consumerist, and administrative demands of a superrace or risk deportation, dehumanization, or the marking of their flesh as in some way monstrous too. More than sanctioning the construction of security walls or supplementing them with virtual-cinematic-ideological counterparts, then, these films expose the ways that they ultimately make more vulnerable the sense of national identity, the mnemo-technological domination of the mass media, and the territorial claims of the state that they are meant to shore up and strengthen. Such films as Marc Forster's *World War Z* (2013), Duncan Jones's *Warcraft* (2016), and Zhang Yimou's *The Great Wall* (2017) teach us to identify, critique, and resist the racist, fascist, and xenophobic agendas of recent conservative administrations as they undertake to construct security fences, satellite surveillance nets, and similar sorts of obstacles to exclude immigrants and refugees from entering their territories. These films, as they reroute our desires away from the standardizing rhetorics of most other media content and toward the invention of a new sense of "we," suggest to us that *the true monsters in them are the apartheid-style walls separating one set of bodies from another.*

The Simpsons Movie

Made in the final throes of George W. Bush's stint in office, and appearing in theaters right after the ratification of the Secure Fence Act of 2006 authorizing the construction of 700 miles of chainmesh along the US–Mexico frontier,

The Simpsons Movie (David Silverman, 2007) dramatizes the risks to fiscal spending, social amity, and the natural environment that such security measures might engender. Although it does not seem a monster film in the textbook sense of the term, *The Simpsons Movie* does contain elements of this subgenre, as it features an Argus-like mutant squirrel that crawls out of Lake Springfield after town idiot Homer Simpson (Daniel Castellaneta) dumps an entire silo of animal feces into it. The Environmental Protection Agency (EPA) quickly impounds the squirrel and, under orders from agency director Russ Cargill (Albert Brooks), encases the town inside a massive, transparent dome so that none of the toxic fumes or Springfield's residents can escape. Although the film on the surface suggests that walling might offer a solution to environmental toxification—even as the miles of fencing that separates Mexico from the United States continues to endanger wildlife and cause ecosystem decay[16]—it also depicts the detrimental effects of the EPA's actions on Springfield's townsfolk, who fall into despair, complain about shortages of electricity and fresh air, and eventually degenerate into a state of anomie. Moreover, the film represents Cargill as a megalomaniacal industrialist, meaning that the reactions of this character to Springfield's environmental troubles remain, in the words of Andrew Hageman, "ecopathological," or always open to compromise and containment under the "ideology of capital."[17]

Although the dome that encircles the small town seems to reverse apartheidist rhetorics, as it safeguards the rest of the United States from contamination from its "insides," it also responds to anxieties concerning economic competition from aliens, visa-holding residents, and foreigners. Homer, after escaping the dome with rest of the Simpson family, thus mentions the ease with which one can make "quick money" in "America" while staring out of the window of a motel at a number of signboards with non-English advertising slogans on them.[18] Themselves fugitives, the Simpsons flee from the dome after discovering Homer's responsibility for turning Lake Springfield into a mutagenic disaster area. Conscientious daughter Lisa Simpson (Yeardley Smith) even calls Homer "a monster," the one character in the film most deserving of this name at this moment in its narrative. Thus as the EPA captures one monster, the squirrel, another escapes—in this case, a working-class family man whose monstrousness derives from a combination of criminal unconcern for the environment and tacit anti-immigrant sentiment. *The Simpsons Movie*, while mostly a feature-length cartoon comedy, also consequently functions as *an ecohorror film*[19] that surveys the costs to nature, as well as to the state of forces in the United States and the socioethical disposition of its citizens, that ensue once a community comes to feel cut off from the world's expanses, with security walling or without it.

The dome that fences Springfield off from the rest of the country might seem an instance of a *reverse Green Zone*, in that it contains dangerous elements rather than treats them as extramural to the space it enfolds. However, the town also represents a microcosm of the sovereign nation surrounding it, with its citizens as fearfully vigilant as Cargill's EPA and as flippant in its decision-making as the US president in the film, former action star and governor of the state of California Arnold Schwarzenegger (Harry Shearer). Through its figuration of the dome, *The Simpsons Movie* invites viewers to confront, reconsider, and traverse their anxieties over the effectiveness, social meanings, and environmental ramifications of national security.[20] This twenty-first-century feature film furthermore takes its cue from the cultural work of earlier cartoon shorts with a science-fictional inflection, which, as J. P. Telotte observes, operate according to a "double vision": they at once reaffirm the "comforts of the traditional," turning the impregnable dome, the EPA's task forces, and their weapons into comic material for the audience to chuckle at; nonetheless, in doing so, they also critique and satirize the ways that these sorts of technological developments exert a "controlling power" over us and establish "boundaries that lock the world and its people fast in the status quo."[21] Superficially, the dome curbs the flow of Lake Springfield's toxic contents into nearby ecosystems, thus inhibiting mutant creatures from ranging outside the town, mating with other animals, and causing wide-scale monstrosity to occur. However, this security apparatus, as we see as the narrative unfolds, actually stimulates the opposite effect, in that it *mutates*, in a sense, the townsfolk underneath it, turning them violent, savage, untrustworthy, unhygienic, and utterly degenerate. Their mob actions actually cause a slight crack in the dome, worsening the situation for Cargill's EPA, which must already devote valuable time, energy, and resources to monitoring the city, standing watch along its margins, disciplining the movements of its citizens, and tracking down those who escape from it, namely the Simpson family.

Cargill, aware of the rapidly rising costs of maintaining the dome, convinces President Schwarzenegger to detonate an explosive device inside it that will transform the area into the "New Grand Canyon," an attractive site for tourists. The opening scene in the film anticipates this turn of events—it features two anthropomorphic cartoon characters drawn in the animation style of the 1930s and 1940s, Itchy and Scratchy, cat and mouse antagonists that resemble in their form and antics such figures as Krazy Kat and Ignatz Mouse, Mickey Mouse and Pegleg Pete, Tom and Jerry, and Herman and Katnip. The mouse Itchy, as US president in this cartoon-within-a-cartoon, orders a nuclear strike at the moon, so as to destroy it alongside the astronaut cat Scratchy. This sequence does more than foreshadow Cargill's solution to the Springfield crisis; it also suggests that national security, racial-species othering, and environmental devastation intersect to an extent, and that as such *they astonishingly come to function as marketable commodities.*[22] The utopian thrust of the science-fictional cartoon that Telotte discusses, after the deployment of atomic weapons in the 1940s and the further entrenchment of security fencing in the twenty-first century, starts to considerably wane, as such theatrical releases as *The Simpsons Movie* assume an increasingly skeptical or even an outright ecohorrific attitude to scientific technologies, especially when at the service of nation-state security and the ideology of capital.

The Simpsons Movie, in fact, suggests that the media industries that serve as adjuncts of the militaristic nation-state that Stiegler discusses do more than eschew the utopian impulses of science fiction or the cautionary functions of ecohorror. The media figures in the film so inure Springfield's residents to the dome that these sorts of drastic security measures start to seem tolerable, or even desirable or quaint, to them. The captive work of these figures, in other words, drives those whom the dome imprisons to actively make, seek out, or otherwise consume images of the very forces that constrain their movements and curtail their freedoms. The town's news anchor coins the term "Trappuccino" to describe conditions under the dome, a cute nickname that softens its impact and represents it as one of those catchwords that television companies use to draw in more viewers, capture their imaginations, and shape the tenor and content of their conversations. The residents of Springfield start to shop at "Dome Depot," and Homer's wife Marge (Julie Kavner) even embroiders some needlework with the nonce expression, "Dome Sweet Dome." Even after Cargill decides to destroy the city, the media-security apparatus uses the star image of Tom Hanks in television advertisements to sell viewers on visiting the New Grand Canyon; moreover, as a tertiary retentional device, these messages endeavor to wholly recontour their memories, or rather to *erase their ability to ever learn* of Springfield's exact whereabouts, cultural specificities, connection to other communities, and demographic, economic, and sociohistorical constitution as surely as might any wide-scale explosion.

As a cinematic adaptation of a television satire for the Fox Network, though, the film might at first appear responsible for doing the same things as Springfield's newscasters and cameo-making celebrities, namely accustoming viewers to the idea of security fencing in the era of the US forays in this direction under the Bush administration. Fortunately, though, the film self-reflexively mocks its own status as a commercial artifact and also its origins as a mainly televisual text, underlining for viewers the ways that national media capitalizes on their fears, insecurities, and desires while "selling" them on the idea of ubiquitous surveillance. Springfield's citizens adapt themselves to the constant scrutiny the EPA, NSA, and other such agencies subject them to through the use of closed-circuit cameras, robot spies, and even the videotelephonic applications of the dome, which allows those under it to chat with Cargill's image (Figure 3.1). Meanwhile, certain sequences in *The Simpsons Movie* include Fox News-style crawlers that tell viewers that the studio intends to advertise their other fare to them during the film, in the manner of the overlays, inserts, or commercial

FIGURE 3.1 *The Transparent Dome over Springfield in* The Simpsons Movie.

interruptions that do the same throughout the show's regular timeslot.[23] Additionally, the film, in a different sequence, cuts to a "To Be Continued" title, another staple of network episodic television, only to resume the narrative after a few seconds transpire. Through these techniques, the film undercuts the "functional reduction" of affective, aesthetic, cognitive, and informational experience that such electronic media as television stages, according to Stiegler, so as to submit viewers to "fully controlled conditioning."[24] The cinema, in other words, short-circuits this reduction, as *The Simpsons Movie* makes clear, and not only through its title, narrative, or remediation of television content. The film opens with the readjustment of its smallish aspect ratio to fit the widescreen format of a theater screen; then it ends with a shot of Homer's family watching the closing credits, facing away from us in the opposite manner of *The Simpsons* series—there they face the screen, as though they too were watching television. The film marks its distance from the other recording technologies Stiegler critiques, even from its original medium, so as to suggest that the cinema can upset the "spectatorial narcissism" that they encourage and that the selfish, doltish Homer at first represents. The film thus takes to task the structural segmentation, associational slipperiness, and advertising imperatives that Jonathan Gray characterizes as the dominant "ideology of television" and, we might argue, of neoliberalism.[25]

The real monster in the film, then, might not appear the mutant squirrel with "a thousand eyes," as Grampa Simpson (Dan Castellaneta) describes it. The monster seems something else, also mutable, aggressive, and with a "thousand eyes"—namely, *television and other electronic media*.[26] These devices more than monitor Springfield's residents, control their actions, or dull them into a resentful acceptance of the dome; they also naturalize the division of the characters in the film into members of either a super- or subrace. Cargill, President Schwarzenegger, the other EPA and state officials, and such major stars as Tom Hanks, as representatives of the superrace, take it upon themselves to decide the fortunes of Springfield's citizens, restrict their access to other cities, and chastise them for their carelessness. These citizens, of course, constitute the main subrace in the film; curiously, though, after the EPA walls them off from their surroundings, some of them start to act as though they too were state authorities, much in the cut of such characters as Cargill, with the owner of Moe's Tavern (Hank Azaria) telling Marge, "I am now the emperor of Springfield." These sorts of racio-spatial fantasies speak to the effects of "sovereign awe," to use Brown's terms, that the dome instills and its media cognates reinforce, compelling the townsfolk to forgive the occupying strategies of the US government, to remain dependent on Cargill to meet their needs, and to even come to see themselves as superior to others due to their very containment inside the dome under the watchful eyes of the EPA (144). As Brown argues, with a Foucauldian flourish, walling tends to ascribe "(victimized) goodness to the dominant and (agentic) hostility, violence, knavery, or greed to the subordinate."[27] On this score, it is significant that those whom the dome entraps cannot realize the seriousness of their disfranchisement, social degeneration, and identificatory complicity with the nation-state's dominant class or race (the officials, staff members, and task force commandos of the EPA, NSA, and other US government agencies in the film, we must remember, wholly consist of older white men).

To escape this mindset, the Simpson family first escapes from the dome through a sinkhole, and then travels to a cabin in Alaska, evading the EPA's manhunt as fugitives. Homer, torn as to whether to return to Springfield to save it from destruction, meets an Inuk shaman, experiences an epiphanic vision, and emerges from it with a new environmental conscience and sense of social feeling. This entire sequence, then, might serve as an elaborate metaphor for the cinema, which enables the formation of a new "we" as it attunes us to our "*most unexpected* expectations," meaning those desires that we remain unaware of until the collective "vision" of a certain film unfolds on-screen for us.[28] Moreover, a VHS tape that Marge makes about the dreary state of their marriage moves Homer to return to Springfield right as the EPA drops the explosive device into the city. He catches it while on a motorcycle and maneuvers it outside the dome, which splinters and collapses after it detonates, freeing the citizens inside and spurring them to start rebuilding their neighborhoods. The cinematic vision that induces Homer to crack the dome contrasts with the dis-individuating effects of television and other electronic media, which, for Stiegler, replace singular experience with the sharing of retentions so as to "control and desexualize" their viewers.[29] Marge's VHS tape, even though Homer watches it on a television set, resists these effects, since, diegetically speaking, it triggers memories and emotions that only these two characters share and, as such, makes its resale unlikely.[30] These sources of singular experience—Homer's cinema-like vision and the self-expression that Marge's tape represents—successfully counteract the consumerist drift of mass media and the sense of resignation that Cargill's security apparatus imposes, moving the Simpson family to save their city, forgive their fellow citizens, disidentify with the representatives of the superrace in the film, and start to repair the ecosystem.

Deidre M. Pike argues that the climax of the film therefore "involves its audience in an active consideration" of environmental concerns[31]; nonetheless, David Feltmate disagrees, contending that "the emphasis on Homer and Marge's relationship" downplays its ecohorrific themes.[32] However, their conclusions somewhat miss the mark: the film does not seek to raise awareness of environmental issues, so much as it invites us to think them together with the defeatism, complaisance, and cultural uniformity that nation-state security, including its media services, continuously stimulates and encourages. The encounter with the Inuk woman is crucial to the film's narrative resolution, as it represents a moment of cross-border interchange—a moment of coming into contact with otherness rather than fencing it off—that runs counter to the usual racio-spatial divisions that follow from these extreme security measures. The tribespeople indigenous to the northern US–Canada territories can freely cross the demarcations that separate one nation from the other, as well as call their reinforcement into question, according to settler treaties.[33] Thus, in order to see Springfield and more importantly the entire Earth as worth saving, the Simpsons must escape the dome; distance themselves from the creative, sociopolitical, and affective dead ends of television, cellphones, and other tertiary recording media; and start to take into account the demands, values, and wisdoms of those outside the ethnic, cultural, or cartographic scope of the nation-state. After all, Homer, an icon of network television, under the supervision of the shaman, changes after undergoing a vision or rather, in a figurative sense, *after effectively taking in a foreign film*. To return to Telotte, then, this feature-length animation, in the tradition of earlier science fiction cartoons, and in ways that do not seem either necessarily utopian or apocalyptic, refuses to depict or reaffirm *what is* concerning the othering violence of national security mechanisms, the coarsening effects of the media, or the dominance of a certain class of administrators so much as it instead offers us a visualization of *what might be*.[34]

World War Z

Marc Forster's *World War Z* met with some ambivalence from critics over one of its most astounding set pieces: the digital configuration of thousands of zombies into tidal waves and columns that allow them to clamber over the security walls encircling the city of Jerusalem in Israel, a safe zone to which the main character, UN investigator Gerry Lane (Brad Pitt), retreats midway through the film. Stephen Daisley, for example, describes *World War Z* as a right-wing disaster film, comparing the security apparatus in this sequence to "the real-life structure erected to fend off suicide bombers during the second Palestinian" conflict.[35] Matt Cornell similarly argues that the film "erases the Palestinian struggle," contending it transforms "real-life walls of apartheid" into "an act of tremendous benevolence" that nonetheless triggers Israel's downfall.[36] Although the Israelis in the film admit Muslims and other outsiders into Jerusalem's security perimeter, they only do so out of self-interest and strategic necessity; as the director of Mossad Jurgen Warmbrunn (Ludi Boeken) candidly tells Lane, "Every human being we save is one less zombie to fight." Moreover, this sequence, even though it repurposes the security fences, might come off as merely substituting zombies for Palestinians, subjecting them to the same surveillance, military stewardship, and othering mechanisms and therefore never seriously working to collapse their metonymic and metaphoric connection. The zombies, in short, occupy the same space as formerly do the Muslims: *outside the perimeter* (Figure 3.2).

As Jeffrey Jerome Cohen argues, such zombies, with their typically cloudy irises, spasmodic tics, flashing teeth, and necrotizing flesh, also similarly represent a visually identifiable "racialized body."[37] He argues that, in these sorts of films, zombies figure as "a danger from without that is already within," forcing survivors to "erect walls, secure borders, build fortresses, and amass guns against their surging tide."[38] This description might aptly relate to *World War Z*, in that the film seems to analogize the "danger" of the zombies outside the city to the "danger" of the Palestinians already inside it. However, the zombies do not simply swarm over Jerusalem's walls; throughout the film, they crack open doors, windows, and windshields, threatening to surmount any obstacle, even nation-state checkpoints,

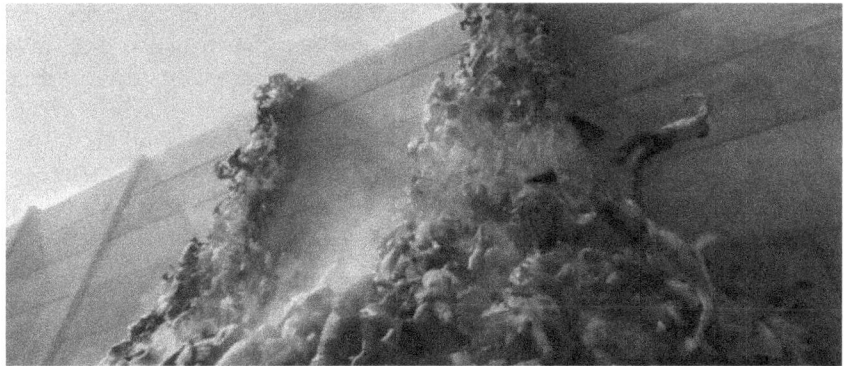

FIGURE 3.2 *Zombies Climbing the Israeli Separation Wall in* World War Z.

impeding or thwarting their advance. The zombies, in their constant movement and modular reconfiguration, ultimately do not appear analogous to the Israelis, Palestinians, or other citizenries that they eventually overtake and devour. If anything, they seem more akin to Lane, who, quickly coming to the conclusion that "movement is life," refuses to take shelter and travels across several continents in search of a solution to the zombie crisis. The main character's credo flips upside-down conventional understandings of the zombie film: for example, the usual association of these monsters with deathliness; slow, shambling, relentless movements[39]; and narrow spheres of action. The zombies in *World War Z* run faster than their victims, remain in constant motion, and most importantly *show no respect for either national or personal boundaries*, much as with Lane and some of the soldiers, scientists, and other survivors in the film. If "movement is life," then these monsters are more alive than most of the human characters, than those who enclose themselves in "secure areas," whether Jerusalem or Newark, New Jersey, the site of the zombie-ridden apartment complex in which Lane first voices this equation.

In associating these walking corpses counterintuitively with "life," though, *World War Z* does not suggest that they represent *zoē* or "bare biological life," the term that so many commentators on the zombie film, following Giorgio Agamben, use to describe those outside the ideologico-legal frameworks and safeguards of the nation-state.[40] These zombies do not appear refugees, migrant workers, or the castoffs of the transnational capitalist era, as they were all once clearly Americans, Israelis, Middle Easterners, Koreans, and other citizens of various nations or regions. The zombies, throughout three of the film's major action set pieces, represent a special case of what Priscilla Wald calls "epidemiological horror," meaning an outbreak narrative that depicts the "transformative power" that virus carriers can inflict on a specific socius or, in a more apocalyptic vein, across the entire earth.[41] The film's characters, in fact, speculate that the outbreak comes from a virus, conceivably a type of rabies, and across these set pieces construct security walls as a sort of mise-en-scène immune response to repel the onrush of the zombies. The first of these sequences occurs at a military installation in South Korea to which Lane escorts a virologist, who dies soon after the men disembark from their aircraft. The zombies swiftly ambush them in the fog outside of the camp, surrounding it after Lane retreats inside, the surviving soldiers closing down its entryways. This scene corresponds to the *attachment and absorption* stage of viral infection, during which the microbe fixes on the surface receptors of its victim's cell membranes. The security walls successfully check this incursion; nonetheless, the zombies incessantly and invisibly stalk them, remaining right outside of them, so that the soldiers cannot safely exit the camp, much as someone cannot cross into a toxic environment without risking a disease.

Unlike most of the camp's sentries, Lane manages to escape to the walled-in Jerusalem, the site of another action set piece, this time corresponding to the *entry and assembly* state of infection. The zombies, surrounding the outer "membrane" of the city, swarm over its fortifications after reassembling themselves into columns and spilling over into the streets. They attack soldiers, citizens, and evacuees alike, turning them into "the undead," a term that Wald also applies to viruses, as they too exist on "the border" that separates "the living and the nonliving."[42] Once again, Lane escapes this fate, traveling to a WHO research facility in the Wales countryside so as to test out a zombification vaccine. To do so, Lane must enter an area teeming with zombie ex-staffers, unseal its doorways, and self-inject a strain of disease that might act as "camouflage" to these monsters, as they do not seem to take much interest in the sick. This sequence therefore corresponds to the *release and integration* stage of infection, in which the virus spreads to adjacent cells, sometimes interweaving its DNA with that of its victim. Lane and the zombies, in other words, each integrate the operative features of the other. The investigator functions as a viral agent, moving amidst the zombies invisibly in order to survive at their expense. The zombies, though, in a fascinating turn of events, in contrast function as security mechanisms, as obstacles that Lane and the surviving UN staff must circumvent in order to reach the vault containing the disease samples. After obtaining one, Lane tricks a zombie into entering the vault and then seals its electronic door. For so much of the film, the zombies sought to move *inside* safe zones and the survivors to shunt these monsters *outside* of them. Now in this climatic set piece the zombies entrap themselves *inside* quarantine areas, therefore ensuring their own downfall (as was the case with the Koreans and Middle Easterners), whereas Lane moves *outside* of them in order to forestall the apocalypse. Far from supporting apartheidism or mocking one-state solutions, *World War Z*, throughout its narrative, fundamentally reverses our identification of walls with racial, cultural, ethnic, and national survival—if we at all relate to Lane, we must too desire to move free of them.

The transformation of the zombies into a modular element of the UN-WHO or Israeli state security apparatus distinguishes *World War Z* from earlier films of this subgenre. Most of these films depict their main characters sequestering themselves from the zombies in them, whether the farmhouse in *Night of the Living Dead* (George A. Romero, 1968); the storefronts of the malls in the different versions of *Dawn of the Dead* (Romero, 1978; Zack Snyder, 2004); the military colonies in *Invisible Invaders* (Edward L. Cahn, 1959), *Day of the Dead* (Romero, 1985), and *28 Weeks Later* (Juan Carlos Fresnadillo, 2007); the corrections facility in *Resident Evil: Afterlife* (Paul W. S. Anderson, 2010); and the London strongholds in *Pride and Prejudice and Zombies* (Burr Steers, 2016).[43] The zombies in *World War Z*, though, do not simply infiltrate or overwhelm these sorts of defenses; rather, they steadily mutate into them, compelling Lane and other survivors to *trespass certain boundaries*: those that delineate separate nation-states, viral-human chromosome sets, and most interestingly racio-spatial demarcations. The zombie outbreak intensifies, accelerates, and casts into clear relief the division of the survivors in the film into a superrace and a subrace under their direct supervision. UN officers, soldiers, scientists, intelligence operatives, and media figures comprise this superrace, as they take upon themselves the tasks of declaring, managing, and maintaining watch over certain safe zones, whether on aircraft carriers or inside city ramparts. These experts, in doing so, also accept responsibility for deeming some individuals inside these zones "nonessential personnel," unless they show forth their strategic value to the war against the zombies. The members of this superrace, in a clear Foucauldian example of the use of reason dovetailing into sheer wickedness, in effect decide who survives and who must die, since they must continually take stock of finite space and resources.

This racial division is most explicit in the film's airplane crash sequence: the zombies overtake the aisles starting from the coach class and only then move toward the first-class seats, with those in them responding to their former fellow travelers with fear, aversion, and violent resistance. Lane and an Israeli soldier shoot at the zombies and throw an explosive toward them that cracks open the fuselage, sucking them out into the air. The "nonessential" subrace, including Lane's wife and children, must then face two distinct threats: the zombies outside and sometimes inside the quarantine areas, as well as the authorities with the sovereign ability to subject them to exile, relocation, or some form of segregation at a moment's whim. Thus Lane, as a UN investigator and a family man, must negotiate conflicting superrace and subrace ethical commitments. Seeing that the throngs of zombies in the film do not divide into such designations, Lane thinks to inoculate the survivors with a strain of fatal disease—in short, to zombify them to a degree, to expose them to a state of "walking death." Lane, in this way, moves to reshape the survivors in the world's refugee camps into new communities, ones that do not consciously feel the necessity anymore to observe the territorial claims of different nation-states or to respect any of their customs, security, or registration methods.[44] After their vaccination, in short, this new "we" can start to act as do the zombies, without the superrace and subrace distinctions that render some completely deferent to the commands of officers, organizers, and engineers.

Even as the security apparatuses in the film remediate and incorporate them, the zombies remain "other" to the survivors, visibly different from them. These monsters, as composite digital-material actors, exhibit a form of modularity over the course of the narrative that Hye Jean Chung defines as "mobile and flexible," in that they "can be moved around freely within a single frame, combined and reconfigured in countless ways, and can be reused infinitely in other sequences."[45] The zombies do not merely infect other men and women; they disperse across multimodal media formats, their images, movements, and data profiles spreading over the website, cellphone, and satellite television displays that dot the film's visual regime right up until its closing credits.[46] The zombies, in Chung's words, thus constitute a "media assemblage," as they first integrate "physical and virtual elements" and furthermore as they compress "distant sites" from "diverse national territories" in appearing in continuous intervals on news updates simultaneously available to all of the world's survivors insofar as they can access a television or computer uplink.[47] As a swarming mass and also as digital media assets, the zombies in *World War Z* embody the disindividuating tendencies of Stiegler's tertiary objects, which work to train our desires on the relative safety and anonymity that enclosures, sentries, and "smart" surveillance networks appear to offer. The zombies, in one sense, remain a racio-spatial other, a visible threat that must remain separate from their victims; in another sense, though, as they start to resemble the cogs of the state security apparatus, they ipso facto compel us to view its mechanisms as monstrous, intrusive, alien, and downright scary. These safety measures, in short, render us as inhuman to one another as their media supplements do to those outside their scope and width.

The real story of *World War Z*, then, is of its zombies steadily integrating themselves into the security assemblages in the film. These monsters act in the manner of "sentinels" in the airfields of Camp Humphreys in South Korea, surrounding in what seems their illimitable numbers Lane's cohort and attacking the virologist who represents the main threat to them. Then the zombies, showing forth their digital composition and modular articulation, assemble themselves into the tesserae of the set of virtual columns and stepladders that they use to surmount the defensive walls of Jerusalem. Finally, at the WHO medical center in Wales, the zombies function at once as watchmen and as an active alert system, effectively, if not intentionally, making sure that Lane, the staff, or any other trespasser cannot steal the specimens of infectious disease inside the facility's offices, workstations, or storage chambers. The zombies in form and function come to merge with these security walls, access controls, surveillance complexes, and satellite feeds. One of the final zombies Lane encounters, in fact, spasms so incessantly that its teeth click—a neat visualization of the media chatter that dulls us into a state of sociopolitical complaisance and adherence to a racist, xenophobic, neocolonial, and watchtower mode of state sector administration. The fiction of the nineteenth century, for Rick Altman, equates monstrosity with our *minds*, and that of the twentieth century with our *bodies*[48]; as the film adaptation of *World War Z* suggests, the monsters of the new millennium come after us through our *media*, in that it conspires to consume our attention, regiment our desire, standardize our memories, and distort our image of ourselves.[49]

Warcraft

Duncan Jones's *Warcraft*, an adaptation of the popular MMORG video game, opens with Gul'dan (Daniel Wu), a warlock council member of a clan of orcs, using "fel" sorcery[50] to open a "dark portal" into Azeroth, the realm of Stormwind Kingdom, its defenders, and their elven and dwarven confederates in the Alliance. The fel, as it uses the souls of captives as "fuel," drains the orcs' realm, Draenor, of its natural resources, compelling Gul'dan and the chieftains to constitute the "Horde," search the universe for other worlds to inhabit, and force open a crack in the space-time "walls" that separate them. This dark portal therefore serves as a cosmic-ethereal version of the material fortifications of nation-state security embankments. The film, in its opening sequences, sets forth the ratio-spatial equations "orcs = Draenor" and "humans = Azeroth," as it relies on three visual strategies to distinguish each from the other in order to make this schema obvious to viewers. First, the orcs appear taller, thicker, and more overly muscular than Stormwind's soldiers; consequently, they seem slower and somewhat clunky in their movements in the film's action sequences. Next, the orcs, with their mangy topknots, warthog-like tusks, and olive-grey skin, appear far uglier than the men and women of Azeroth, all of them attractive, slender, resplendent in their armor, and symmetrical in their features. Finally, the orcs' character design unmistakably comes from CG animation, whereas that of regent Llane Wrynn (Dominic Cooper), captain-at-arms Anduin Lothar (Travis Fimmel), and Stormwind's other subjects do not—unlike such similar fantasy adventures as *300* (Zack Snyder, 2007) and *Beowulf* (Robert Zemeckis, 2007), the film does not use motion capture to render its human characters into three-dimensional digital avatars. The orcs resemble Kristen Whissel's notion of the "digital multitude" (or rather "Horde"), a force mostly uniform in appearance, mindlessly singular in its aims, totally subordinate to a collective ethos, and aggressively striving to foment an apocalyptic scenario.[51] So far, the film seems to neatly assign its warring factions to one side or the other of the dark portal, suggesting that the orcs' invasion of Azeroth threatens the depletion of its resources, the debasement of its native cultures, and the enslavement, eradication, or corruption of its Alliance races. In fact, after the orcs enter the realm, its sorcerer Guardian Medivh (Ben Foster) slowly starts to turn demonic and dark-in-tone, embodying future racial-cultural degeneration. However, the film complicates its racio-spatial dynamics, as well as the Foucauldian understanding of the discursive mechanisms that construe the nation-state as something that requires constant comparison to other states, assessment, and defense, in further dividing the orcs and humans into distinct sub- and superraces.

Humans divide into a superrace, as Wrynn, Lothar, and the mage Khadgar (Ben Schnetzer) work together to maintain civil order, make decisions concerning the exclusion or detention of the orc raiders, and mediate disputes among the various subraces, including the elves, dwarves, and trolls (in the motion comic Blu-ray extra, *Warcraft: Bonds of Brotherhood*). Ostensibly, the elves and dwarves are coequals to Stormwind's citizens; nonetheless, the dwarves work as miners, smiths, and weapons engineers for Lothar, and the elves seem mere aloof functionaries, turning up in the narrative at funerals and speeches. These alter-human races, then, function as analogues to the rival nation-states against which the kingdom can measure its own economic, military, and technological forces—in other words, as alibis that its sovereign can use to sanction and maintain a standing army, a weapons development workshop, and a security apparatus, namely the Guardian's charge to ensure that no access points in the cosmic "walls" that separate the realms surface (Figure 3.3).

Humans, though, also divide further among themselves, into those who want to unilaterally use the orcs to increase their authority over others and those who want to regulate the movement of the invaders into Azeroth and engage them more diplomatically. Thus, King Wrynn, Lothar, and their soldiers meet with the Frostwolf Clan to negotiate a means to settlement and conspire to topple Gul'dan, whom some of the orcs distrust. The film's fantasy context seems crucial on this score, in that this superrace follows the "laws of hospitality" that Jacques Derrida discusses in relation to the medieval city, a set of ethical codes that made certain that "the borders be open to each and every one, to any other, to all who might come, without their having to identify who they are or whence they came."[52] The treacherous Medivh, in contrast, secretly opens the dark portal, spurs the orcs to despoil the villages in the realm, and warps into a subhuman in front of Lothar and Khadgar, a curious twist, since this character, who aspires to

FIGURE 3.3 *The Dark Portal in* Warcraft.

sovereign decision-making, transforms visually into a monster, *into someone who appears to belong outside the domain of Azeroth.*

However, the film does not only corroborate the arguments in Foucault's seminars, nor does it reinforce conservative calls for security fences and increases in resources for immigration control. *Warcraft* explores the ways that such apparatuses (which Medivh, as Azeroth's Guardian, represents) can also materially, ideologically, and mediatically work to divide those outside of them into subraces and superraces. The members of the Frostwolf Clan, including its chieftain Durotan (Toby Kebbell), realize that the fel magic that Gul'dan uses ravages ecosystems, instigates disrespect for traditions, and incites the orcs to racism, exploitation, and war. This warlock, in fact, acts in as unilateral and sovereign a manner as Medivh, shamelessly ignoring orc customs, cheating in contests of strength, and issuing orders to the chieftains without deference to their rank. Moreover, the other orcs disdain those clan members under the spell of fel magic for their skin turning into an abnormal and, to their eyes, monstrous shade of neon green. The chieftains and the king's vassals, the superraces in the film, must therefore overturn the impertinent decision-making of a sorcerer-usurper in order to avert war and to moderate, oversee, and direct the immigration of the orcs across the worlds of the *Warcraft* universe—in short, to transform their intentions of colonization into ones of settlement and coexistence. To do so, these superrace figures must first open a rift in another "barrier," this time a sociolinguistic one. The audiovisual register of the film therefore takes a cue from Stanley Kramer's courtroom docudrama *Judgment at Nuremberg* (1961): in it, as the camera zooms in on a Nazi doctor on trial for war crimes, the defendant's words suddenly shift from German to English. This film thus creatively avoids relying on subtitles or on-screen translators.[53] Similarly, in *Warcraft*, as King Wrynn's mages act as interlocutors during the conclave with the Frostwolf Clan, the chieftain's words, through audio fades and virtual camera zooms, convert from the orc tongue to English. The film does this work for its audience, reminding us of the cinema's status as a recording machine, or, in Stiegler's terms, a tertiary mnemotechnical apparatus that works to flatten individual difference, twisting the "we" in this scene, so contingent on mutual curiosity and commitment to cultural exchange, into *an already prefabricated unity*. The film, in short, compels the orcs to effectively mime the king's speech rather than vice versa.

The temptation might then seem to write the film off as a conservative fantasy or as a realistic, although cynical, representation of the fact that citizens often expect refugees, immigrants, and asylum seekers to speak the official national language. Even though *Warcraft* uses the *Judgment at Nuremberg* technique, it does not squarely do so to subordinate the orcs to the cultural-linguistic dominants of Stormwind or even to associate these raiders with the Nazi war criminals in Kramer's film. This audiovisual technique, we must remember, also mitigates the orcs' otherness. More importantly, it encourages us to think the narrative action in terms of *steady hybridization*, whether we conceive of it as symbolic-physical, collective-individual, or digital-material.[54] Hybrids, of course, move toward the formation and emergence of new communities, new modes of individuation, confounding the assignment of separate races to one side or the other of a security or zoning apparatus—or into separate worlds, according to the film's diegetic realities. These cinematic techniques, in other words, encourage the experimentation that Derrida calls for, if we see the coming of the orcs as an opportunity for the native races of Azeroth to test a "a new order of law and democracy" that at once takes serious steps to renounce and eschew the "fel" temptations of conquest and apartheidism.[55] Unlike other fantasy films that feature a digital multitude, such as Peter Jackson's *The Lord of the Rings* trilogy (2001–3), *Warcraft* fleshes out the characters of certain members of the Horde, making them doubtful, dissident, and torn in their responsibilities to their families, clans, and race. Moreover, it teaches the audience to distinguish the orcs from one another; to notice differences in their sizes, musculatures, skin colors, facial features, and shags of hair; and to come to the realization that they are anything other than uniform in thought, motivation, or appearance.

Hybrids in *Warcraft* include Garona (Paula Patton), the orcs' "half-breed" slave, whom Lothar captures, emancipates, and welcomes into Stormwind's commonwealth. Garona combines the racial markers of the orcs and their enemies: she retains certain orc features, such as their skin color and underbite, even as she resembles the women of Azeroth in terms of size, curviness, and fat-muscle distribution. Moreover, she upholds Hollywood's standards of conventional attractiveness, catching the eye of Lothar and Khadgar. Finally, she appears digital and indexical-photorealistic in character design, since the film uses an intermediate to color correct Garona's skin at the same time as its cameras capture the actress Paula Patton, clearly discernible in face and figure to viewers despite this CG retouching. Durotan, in contrast, only vaguely resembles Toby Kebbell, mostly in that the avatar mimics the actor's facial contours. Garona thus confounds the visual cues that work to situate the orcs and their adversaries *properly in one realm or another*, as she does not wholly seem out of place in either Azeroth or Draenor. She rewrites the racio-spatial diegetic construction of the film, suggesting sexual, racial, and cultural admixture as a way to undo the territorial claims of the warring clans and nation-states of the Alliance. Garona thus enters a romantic relationship with Lothar; at the same time, she also freely oscillates from the dress, tongue, and social niceties of one race to the other, combining the tough-mindedness of the orcs with the emotional intelligence of the humans. She suggests that *interbreeding* can create the conditions for the emergence of new forms of sociality and redraw the territorial claims that seek to enclose some at the expense of all others. She somewhat stands in contrast to Durotan's stillborn son, whom Gul'dan revives, using fel magic to infuse the soul fuel taken from an Azeroth deer into the infant's slack, ashen, unresponsive flesh. This resurrection occurs right after the orcs move through the dark portal, suggesting that such a migratory movement demands new adaptive mechanisms, a refreshing of the race as it comes into contact with new fauna, microbiota, and climates. This sequence ultimately calls attention to the *inbreeding* that can result from isolating forces, whether mountains, oceans, or cosmic separators, that might deaden a species or dis-individuate its members.

These two orc hybrids, in any case, function in contradistinction to the Golem that Medivh animates through the use of fel magic. This monster seems strictly mechanical in its actions, one-dimensional in its drives, and anti-singular in its ontic determination, a mere receptacle that the Guardian might reproduce over and over again with the right resources, strategic designs, and technical expertise. The Golem, in one of the film's climactic action scenes, even fights alongside its creator against Lothar and Khadgar in a sort of *client-server relation*, the magic of the Guardian messaging certain requests to it and thereby calling upon it to execute certain tasks (for instance, the elimination of King Wrynn's men). The monster, in this sense, exemplifies Stiegler's tertiary recording technologies, which intercede in our consciousnesses, instrumentalize our mental capacities, delimit our expectations, channel our creative expression into industrial ends, and frustrate the rise of a "we" able to self-actualize in nonsolipsistic terms. One of the refrains of *Warcraft*, "From light comes darkness and from darkness, light," rephrases the dialogue of an earlier film, one with another Golem of sorts in it, James Whale's *Frankenstein* (1931): "So far, [the monster's] been kept in complete darkness. But wait till I bring him into the light." The Golem scene in *Warcraft* thus "records" the dialogue from another film, as well as aligns Medivh's descent into unreason and what Stiegler calls "ill-being" with the mindset of Henry Frankenstein.[56] More importantly, this new Golem, as a deterrence measure, represents the mediatic supplementation of the nation-state, as it casts into relief the notion that territorial defense from its outset relies on *acts of figuration*. The Guardian's desire for exclusivity, self-protection, and further empowerment finds its objective correlative in the formidable figure that the Golem cuts; similarly, the desire for a costly state-of-the-art security system coincides with the constant and visible reinforcement of ethnoracial divisions, sexual taboos, and sociolinguistic differences. Garona and Durotan's son oppose to this machine-like Golem *a certain racial and figural illegibility* that makes it impossible to strictly or schematically associate this or that race with any of the film's diegetic environments. Thus, the final image in *Warcraft*—the infant son drifting downriver in the rushes, a nonhuman Moses—favors flows over impediments, rebirth over apocalypse, and the exodus of the "new" over the incestuous current state of affairs.

The Great Wall

Unlike other films set mostly in territories that security fences enclose, Zhang Yimou's *The Great Wall* mostly takes place inside the eponymous fortifications that separate the cities of China from the Eurasian Steppe. As the trick shot archer William Garin (Matt Damon) and the Spanish mercenary Pero Tovar (Pedro Pascal) flee from Khitan nomads, they stumble across the Nameless Order, a military "border security" regiment that defends the imperial court of the Song Dynasty from the advances of the Tao Tei. A colony of eusocial monsters that, emerging from a meteor two millennia ago, attack northern China every sixty years, the Tao Tei follow the commands of their intelligent queen, who communicates to them through vibrations that the fan-like receptors atop their cuticles can decipher. Unwilling to allow the mercenaries to divulge the secrets of the Great Wall to other European countries, General Shao (Zhang Hanyu) and Commander Lin Mae (Jing Tian) order their capture. This emphasis on secrecy defines the nation-state in the film as a rather Foucauldian "system of information," a *dispositif* that requires that no foreigners ever survey the weapons technologies, architectural features, and administrative infrastructures of the Great Wall in order to continue to ensure Chinese dominance over those outside of it. Soon, though, wave after wave of Tao Tei attempt to scrabble over the Great Wall, compelling William and Tovar to escape their fetters and fight alongside the different companies of the Order in repulsing the attack. Along with these characters, the film's viewers, through several aerial shots, sweeping virtual camera movements, and rainbow-color-spectrum digital effects, can thus take in the strategic advantages, invasion countermeasures, and engineering sophistication of the Wall. The camera, roving about inside it, reveals the "secrets" of its functioning: the considerable number of water wheels, sprocket chains, and massive cranes that enable the repositioning of some of the segments comprising it (Figure 3.4).

On its exterior, the camera focuses on its defense engines,[57] which include catapults, crossbow-ballistae, drum systems for signaling commands, and elastic tethers on which spearwomen can drop downward near the Wall's foundation to stab at the Tao Tei. The film, during its other action sequences, shows the Chinese using rotor blades and harpoon cannons against their monstrous enemies, as well as aerostats to descry the movements of the Tao Tei and create a quick means of access to the imperial capital in case the Wall collapses or fails to stop them. Thus, as William, Tovar, and the film's viewers soon discover, the Nameless Order remains "nameless" for more than covert military reasons—its members must wholly comply in their duties, movements, and self-definitions with the security imperatives of the nation-state. *They too function as siege defense mechanisms of the Great Wall.*

FIGURE 3.4 *The Engines of Nation-State Security in* The Great Wall.

The film, then, in terms of its racio-spatial composition, clearly identifies its main characters with the interior space of the Chinese nation-state and the nonhuman Tao Tei with the mountain wilderness outside it. However, this *dispositif*, in true Foucauldian fashion, also divides the mainlanders into a super- and subrace, although the film's narrative ambiguates these terms and undercuts viewer expectations of the ways they might function throughout it. At first, the superrace seems to encompass the emperor, the envoys of the court, and the officers of the Nameless Order, especially since they shelter, monitor, and determine the fates of the foreigners. The two European mercenaries, along with the teacher Sir Ballard (Willem Defoe), in contrast seem a distinct subrace, owing to the cultural condescension, sociolinguistic versatility, and technological superiority that the Chinese exhibit toward them. As the narrative unfolds, though, alter-hierarchies start to emerge, disentangling these designations from visually comprehensible or taxonomically strict understandings of racial-physical difference. The archer William, for example, disavows the search for saltpeter explosives, attempting to stop the other Europeans from stealing a cache of them and moreover committing to the fight against the Tao Tei. The Chinese also see their rank system somewhat upset, as General Shao dies midway through the film saving another soldier from an ambush and Peng Yong (Lu Han), the shame of the Order, sets off an explosion in an another act of self-sacrifice during the climactic sequence to impede the movement of the Tao Tei as they ravage the imperial capital. The true superrace demonstrates not only courage, skill, and resolve; it acknowledges the importance of *xìn rén*, "trust" in others, which coincidentally, with minor modifications, also translates into "the new," suggesting a countervalue to that which supports or idealizes the construction, maintenance, and constant re-elaboration of security walls. According to this inversion, the subrace in the film might rather include Tovar, Ballard, and even the teenage emperor, who comes off as fractious, craven in the face of danger, and dependent on others for counsel and safety.

The Great Wall, owing to these revisions to its racio-spatial dimensions, which see some of its white and Asian characters renegotiating their social standing in the diegesis, thus speaks to its own status as a Sino-American coproduction. Yomi Braester reports that Hollywood's digital output constitutes a source of anxiety for Chinese cinephiles, in that they fear "it encourages spectatorial consumerism, disregards local film practices, and flattens historical perspective."[58] The act of viewing such action spectacles as *Avatar* (James Cameron, 2009) and *The Great Wall* might then occasion for these cinephiles a sounding of their "moral responsibility," as they confront in them the "erasure of collective memory" that these sorts of films sometimes induce in viewers.[59] The Chinese and European warriors in this digital transpacific film come to share, reshape, and codetermine each other's racio-spatial attitudes to an extent, although mainly in opposition to the Tao Tei. The film uses two sets of analogies to temper the worst excesses of their respective ethea: the ultracompetitive nature of the mercenaries' work, as well as that of Western culture, finds its objective correlative in the violent and rapacious feeding that the Tao Tei do so as to ensure the self-preservation of their queen (of course, William comes from England, a country with its own royalty). The archer, in contrast to the ensemble forces of the Nameless Order, embodies the individualist spirit characteristic of much Hollywood action fare, a spirit that Commander Lin and Peng Yong come to adopt, as these imperial soldiers figure out that they must above all improvise if they are to thwart the monsters' attack on the capital.[60] Otherwise, the collectivist organization of the Order finds its own correlative in the droves of the Tao Tei: in fact, much as the soldiers stack their shields into wall-like structures in the act of defending their officers, so too do the aliens use their neck frills to do the same for their queen.[61] Through these visual rhymes, the film moves its viewers, whatever their national affiliation, to disidentify their collective fantasies, memories, and desires with the aims of the state security enterprise, a timely message considering that Republican administrations want to construct a security wall in the southernmost regions of the United States, and the Chinese to construct one on its Myanmar frontier in order to calm cross-border tensions. The film, in short, with its fantastic spin on the era of the Song Dynasty, delves into Chinese "collective memory" to show us that security emplacements do not work—the Tao Tei tunnel through the Great Wall, making it seem as though only a violent counterresponse stands a chance of defeating them.

The film, then, seems to support the sort of apartheidism that must devise an "alien" threat to the spatio-legible complexion of the nation-state in order to rationalize the development of a military-security apparatus that can combat it. However, the film's representation of the Tao Tei as toothy, quadrupedal, and markedly nonhuman in appearance runs counter to its explicit thematization of *xìn rèn*, as does the Song Dynasty's investment in fencing, defensive militias, and counterinvasion excursions into the desert steppes. As digital constructs that communicate through nonphonetic means in the manner of computers and other electronic devices, the Tao Tei also represent more than the othering of those outside the wall; they function as stand-ins for the tertiary retentional technologies that nation-states require to deaden, flatten, or de-authenticate the affects, sensoria, and sociohistorical orientations of their users and turn them into complacent consumers. Outside of their queen, these monsters appear mostly uniform in size, shade, and anatomic structure, unlike the European mercenaries and the Chinese soldiers, as they wear different colors to signify their rank and the division in which they serve. As these characters soon discover, the Great Wall, no matter its modifiability or the intricacies of its security installations, cannot stop the Tao Tei. These characters, as they come into contact with one another, developing a mutual sense of "trust," must rather *disrupt the signals* that the queen of the Tao Tei emits, signals that, as with the culture industries, synchronize the actions, desires, and social identities of those who receive them. The Order therefore attacks the queen, the transmitter of these tactile-vibratory messages, and, directly upon destroying their target, immobilizes the rest of the Tao Tei ravaging the imperial city—in other words, as they freeze the digital animation of these CG constructs, *they stop the film's own othering strategies or "signals" in their tracks. The Great Wall*, then, calls into question the effectiveness of the structure that the film takes its title from, and, rather than merely supporting the construction of more modern variants of it, suggests that the emergence of intercultural sensibilities, cross-racial identifications, and stable, "trusting" trade relations depends more so on the collapse or the radical reorganization of the mediascapes of different nation-states. To assuage the anxieties of Chinese and US cinephiles alike, this international coproduction shows us that collaboration can shape forth a new sense of "we," one that does not require security walls, standing armies, racio-spatial markers, or the fabrication of monsters to realize.

The Belko Experiment

Much as with *The Simpsons Movie*, Greg McLean's *The Belko Experiment* (2017) on the surface does not appear a monster film. Mostly set in a remote industrial district outside of Bogotá, Colombia, the film depicts the mass murders that occur inside one of the office towers of Belko Industries, a nonprofit firm that works under state sponsorship to recruit US employees for multinational corporations. One of the office staff, Mike Milch (John Gallagher Jr.), after acquiring in a Bogotá marketplace a fetish meant for warding off "werewolves," drives up to the fenced-in tower, encountering an additional and unfamiliar set of checkpoints, along with sentries with assault rifles. These images set the stage for the film's central narrative conceit: the staff must murder thirty of their coworkers or face the deaths of double that number, as a voice over the intercom system tells them. The voice comes from the director of a team of social scientists who wish to study their choices and reactions; and, so as to establish and control the conditions of this scenario, these scientists enclose within the tower a cache of weapons and then completely seal the doors and windows with an unbreakable metal alloy. This experiment carries to their ultimate conclusion the survival-of-the-fittest imperatives of neoliberal competitiveness, which Henry A. Giroux describes as "a kind of blind death march in which coercion, violence, foreclosure, and greed become the organizing principles of all aspects of social life."[62] The employees, following these imperatives, slowly start to murder one another—in short, *they turn into monsters*, a certain viciousness coming out in some of them as they attack their former friends, colleagues, and romantic interests with fire axes, Molotov cocktails, wrenches, and tape dispensers.[63] As one staff member says earlier in the film, at the start of the workday, "Normal people do not work at Belko." The experiment, of course, makes "normal" seem contextual, contingent on external factors, and illusory, as is the case for werewolves, whose usual unprepossessing appearance only covers over their monstrous inner tendencies.

However, it is also significant that this division of Belko, an organization that works to facilitate and smoothen international trade relations, operates in Colombia, a country on the nexus tip to Central America, the region that tariff-happy isolationists, such as Donald Trump, seek to wall off from the United States. Giroux argues that these types of ultranationalist security measures relegate those outside of them to "zones of ideological and political abandonment, caught between the arbitrary registers of life and death, visibility and invisibility."[64] The real experiment that occurs in the film, then, subjects US citizens to these conditions, as the employees cannot use their cellphones, signal their distress, or attempt to escape under the threat of immediate death. The sheets of metal and the soldiers surrounding the office tower render those inside them invisible in this case; after assaying the situation, Mike tells another employee, "These walls, they seem designed to keep people in just as much as out." The Belko office setup, with its fencing, checkpoints, ubiquitous surveillance cameras, and metal curtains, not only ironically debunks its corporate tagline, "Business without Barriers," but also suggests the flexible, exportable, and ultimately ungovernable nature of these sorts of security "walls." They come to seem utterly *implosive* throughout the course of the film, as they constrain the movement of the characters to narrower and narrower spaces, as well as severely curtail their moral choices, rational actions, and social sentiments (Figure 3.5).

The walls shutting these characters inside the tower, on the margins of Bogotá, with all its favelas and shady marketplaces, make this zone

FIGURE 3.5 *The Office Tower in* The Belko Experiment.

of abandonment seem a sort of *reverse safe space*. Ostensibly meant for safeguarding the staff from the menace of abduction, the security apparatuses of Belko Industries rather make them unsafe, unfree, and eventually criminal themselves. As this zone tightens and shrinks, in other words, its violence intensifies and turns inward. The English-speaking characters inside these fortifications therefore appear more subject to constant danger, terror, coercion, violence, and intimidation than those moving about the streets of the capital city of Colombia in the opening scenes of the film—streets that somewhat unnerve Mike Milch, whose discomfort might make this otherwise reasonable white corporate citizen more susceptible to the wall-building rhetoric of such illiberal figures as Trump. That is, under more "normal" circumstances.

The Belko Experiment, though, exposes the monstrous racio-spatial ethos that obtains in "normal" and "secure" areas that ensconce and circumscribe the corporate outposts of military-ready nation-states. The setting suggests that the forces of transnational capital and the security systems it demands operate through modes of *nonnational satellitization and virtual control*: the social scientists monitor the subjects of the experiment, as one of them says, from an "old hangar" next to the office tower. These scientists shut the staff inside the tower, shutter its doors and windows, and set snipers to check its rooftops for escape attempts. Moreover, they monitor the actions of those inside the tower through a network of spy cameras and use an intercom to set forth the aims and tenor of the experiment. As the director calmly says, in the way an office manager might speak down to an employee, "Your chance of survival increases by following my orders and excelling at the tasks I place before you." This mandate more than speaks to the film's exaggeration of the sovereign decision-making of ruthless corporate representatives, as it also constitutes the scientists as a superrace, able to make up rules at will; discipline the thoughts, actions, allegiances, movements, and moral alignments of those subject to their commands; administer warnings, reprieves, and chastisements to them; and execute them at a moment's whim from a remote distance. Unlike with more conventional national security apparatuses, though, the scientists confine to a walled-in area a selection of US, Colombian, and other visa-holding state citizens, rather than illegal immigrants. Also, they enact violence against these workers within the same enclosure that the office tower occupies—inside the territory of a US trading partner—rather than on the fringes of two separate countries. The upshot of their experiment is thus clear, as the United States and other corporatocratic forces *can export racio-spatial hierarchies and logics* to other nation-states, fencing in their domains to ensure their economic, military, and ideologico-political dominance over them. More interestingly, the film furthermore suggests that the "wickedness" of these violent implementations of scientific reason, experimental research, and technological application, to crib from Foucault, rebounds against Mike and Barry Norris (Tony Goldwyn), an ex-special forces commando and the company's COO, making them vulnerable to the same authoritarian decision-making as the rest of the world's citizens—and even those outcast for whatever reason from the ethico-legal rights and safeties that state membership confers. Those characters stuck inside the Belko tower, then, despite their relative ranks and responsibilities, altogether take on the status of a subrace in the film.

This subrace appears multiethnic in complexion, so we might ask what separates them from the team of social scientists. The answer consists in the fact that these villains implant tracking microchips inside the skulls of the Belko staff so that the authorities can retrieve them in the event of their abduction, a terrifying elaboration of the invasiveness and civil overreach of state and corporate security measures. However, if the staff members do not follow the exact orders of the scientists, the trackers inside them will explode, splattering their vital organs across the walls, floors, and office decor of the film's settings at the mere flick of a computer switch. The scientists of this superrace, then, set themselves apart from the other characters through reducing them to walking time bombs; moreover, in this way they *literally get inside the heads* of the members of the subrace in the film, compelling them to carry out their commands, internalize their values, and exaggerate the violence and inequities of the social, racial, and economic structures that they represent. The Belko staff, after receiving the order to murder thirty office workers, soon splits into two separate factions, corresponding to the super- and subrace designations. The first comprises Norris, executive Wendell Dukes (John C. McGinley), and a few other male white-collar staff; emulating the values of the scientist elite and intending to carry out their orders, they attempt to seize the weapons in the tower armory and execute any coworkers who appear over 60, without children, or disobedient. They claim the situational right to murder others in the name of their capabilities of doing so and also of caring for their own families. The other faction consists of Mike, alongside romantic interest Leandra Florez (Adria Arjona), Norris's assistant, as well as most of the other office and maintenance workers. They initially think to display signs from the rooftop to call for an emergency response, although the snipers frustrate their attempts. However, even this more conscientious faction starts to resemble in their values the scientists' administrative culture, with Leandra in one scene referring to Norris's cohort as "those types of people," as though they were members of a different race, clan, or species. Ultimately, each faction fails to meet the deadline for carrying out the orders of the director of the experiment, who detonates the explosive devices inside sixty of the workers' skulls, arbitrarily murdering them and reminding the audience that these scientists represent the superrace in the film, the apex monsters in it. The remaining staff set about murdering one another, as only one character must survive, according to the director's newest fiat.

From their master station near the main office tower, the scientists issue their decrees and control their test subjects through a number of tertiary recording instruments, such as surveillance data feeds, computer monitors, and remote uplinks to the tracking implants underneath their scalps. These devices explicitly serve to flatten the affective range of this subrace or subclass to fear, outrage, fury, and confusion; to wholly dis-individuate them, making them at once an object of study and a mob single-mindedly trying to murder one another; and to constrain their opportunities for self-expression to such an extreme degree that they can only reenact the sort of violence they might see over and over in such action-horror films as *Brotherhood of the Wolf* (Christophe Gans, 2001), *Dog Soldiers* (Neil Marshall, 2002), and *Underworld* (Len Wiseman, 2003). Stiegler describes the aesthetics of these recording and messaging technologies as "theatre and weapon in the economic war," a statement that nicely applies to the film, in that the trackers inside the office workers move them to follow instructions and enact the central dramas of the narrative, as well as enable the director to instantly strike them down from a distance for their failures, infractions, or shows of independent thinking.[65] Of course, as with much of the images, sounds, and information streams of tertiary media, the trackers actually insinuate their way into the skulls of the film's characters, reducing them to despair at first and shortly thereafter turning them into the amoral mass murderers reminiscent of those in stock Hollywood action fare.[66]

James Kendrick suggests that the violence in these films represents the cause of "social disorder" and its solution.[67] However, in *The Belko Experiment*, violence, even as it disrupts the work environment of the office tower, does not serve as a solution to the industrial capture of our memories, desires, and technological access, nor does it upset the ferociously competitive ethos of transnational capital and nation-state relations. Mike, after clubbing Norris to death, scoops up several trackers taken from some of the corpses in the tower, confronts the scientists and their soldier escorts in the master control station, and furtively fixes the explosive devices to each one of them, slaughtering everyone in the room. The viewer afterward sees a close-up of the split-screen computer displays that the director was watching: these windows contain similar violent codas from Belko's other satellite offices in multiple countries. The violence in the film, rather than a solution to social disorder, incites *the proliferation of ever more violent images, stories, and experiences*, suggesting that security apparatuses, their financial-industrial infrastructure, and their media supports only achieve the opposite of their nominal outcomes. These walls, rather than saving those inside them from criminals or terrorists, contract ever more tightly, caging each and every character in the film into inescapable racio-spatial, corporate-consumerist, and spectacle-driven attitudes—the final image thus features the trauma-stricken faces of several men and women from different offices, the windows of the director's computer screen making them seem shut up in separate cells. This ending makes it clear that no place on Earth remains safe from the effects of such security and social engineering experiments, as the violence they foment and expose even spreads to the control center of the scientists, the superrace aspiring to clearheadedly dispassionate administration over others' actions, identifications, freedoms, and conditions of embodiment in the film. These scientists, despite their technical savvy, cannot create a "we," only a steady and thoroughgoing universalization of monsters.

Conclusion

The cinema, according to Stiegler, is a weapon in the war against the mass media's interpellation of its audience as consumers and spectatorial narcissists, incapable of assembling their sense-experiences, retentions, and expectations into a singular communal disposition.[68] He further calls attention to the culture industries' co-optation of the singular in their creation of "a single digital technical system," which affords them near-total control of the work of the imagination, resulting in the sense of our overwhelming *loss of aesthetic participation*.[69] The struggle for the formation of a "we" requires the sharing of our sensemaking of certain salient images against the industrial "*controlling of fantasy*"[70]—or rather, in Brown's words, the cultural scrims that recode our collective dreams, anxieties, and self-understandings in ways favorable to the multibillion dollar investment in state security walls and our own circumscription within them. The films in this chapter that depict their characters inside such walls might seem to align with more of an "us" than a "we," meaning that the visual cues in them reinforce the notion of a clear racial, national, and sociohistorical identity rather than opening us to the dimension of the new.[71] These films certainly distinguish their main characters from the aliens, mutants, zombies, sociopaths, and other monsters in them, which they mark as distinctly other and, in spatio-legible terms, as outsiders that do not "belong" inside the domains that the walling surrounds. However, these films also remain at war with themselves, in a sense, in that they also serve as cautionary tales concerning the effects of such security measures on those they enclose, those whom they might ostracize, further endanger, or cause to degenerate into violence. These films also make us focus on the value of racial mixing, cross-border identification, cultural interchange, and the reclaiming of our memories from their mediatic falsification. These films, often in complex and at times self-contradictory ways, raise questions as to what walls do to those inside of them, and more importantly what role they take in determining who counts as the rightful occupant of a certain space and who cannot, according to state, military, corporate, or otherwise sovereign recognition or decree. The next chapter, then, examines those characters that turn up on the wrong side of these forces and their security emplacements.

Notes

1. See Donald J. Trump, "Full Text: Donald Trump Immigration Speech in Arizona," *Politico*, August 31, 2016, https://www.politico.com/story/2016/08/donald-trump-immigration-address-transcript-227614; and Ayal Press, "Trump and the Truth: Immigration and Crime," *New Yorker*, September 2, 2016, https://www.newyorker.com/news/news-desk/trump-and-the-truth-immigration-and-crime.

2. See Katie Reilly, "Here Are All the Times Donald Trump Insulted Mexico," *Time*, August 31, 2016, https://time.com/4473972/donald-trump-mexico-meeting-insult/; Ron Nixon and Linda Qiu, "Trump's Evolving Words on the Wall," *New York Times*, January 18, 1018, https://www.nytimes.com/2018/01/18/us/politics/trump-border-wall-immigration.html; and Julio Ricardo Varela, "Trump's Border Wall Was Never Just about Security. It's Meant to Remind All Latinos that We're Unwelcome," *NBC News*, December 28, 2018, https://www.nbcnews.com/think/opinion/trump-s-border-wall-was-never-just-about-security-it-ncna952011.

3. See Julie Hirschfield Davis and Michael Tackett, "Trump and Democrats Dig In after Talks to Reopen Government Go Nowhere," *New York Times*, January 3, 2019, https://www.nytimes.com/2019/01/02/us/politics/trump-congress-shutdown.html; Philip Rucker and Felicia Sonmez, "Trump Calls Wall Only Solution to 'Growing Humanitarian Crisis' at Border," *Washington Post*, January 8, 2019, https://www.washingtonpost.com/politics/trump-declares-a-growing-humanitarian-crisis-at-the-border-in-demand-for-wall-funding-to-end-shutdown/2019/01/08/bdd2767e-1368-11e9-803c-4ef28312c8b9_story.html; and Jordan Fabian and Brett Samuels, "Trump Agrees to End Shutdown

without Getting Wall Funding," *The Hill*, January 25, 2019, https://thehill.com/homenews/administration/427004-trump-agrees-to-end-shutdown.

4   See Colin Dwyer, "ICE Carries Out Its Largest Immigration Raid in Recent History," *NPR*, June 20, 2018, https://www.npr.org/2018/06/20/621810030/ice-carries-out-its-largest-immigration-raid-in-recent-history-arresting-146; Miriam Jordan, "ICE Raids Hundreds in Mississippi Raids Targeting Immigrant Workers," *New York Times*, August 7, 2019, https://www.nytimes.com/2019/08/07/us/ice-raids-mississippi.html; and Rachel Zohn, "Recent ICE Raids Overload Mississippi Legal System," *USA Today*, October 18, 2019, https://www.usnews.com/news/best-states/articles/2019-10-18/recent-ice-raids-by-us-immigration-and-customs-enforcement-overload-mississippi-legal-system.

5   See Julia Preston, "U.S. Raids 6 Meat Plants in ID Case," *New York Times*, December 13, 2006, https://www.nytimes.com/2006/12/13/us/13raid.html; and Marc Cooper, "Lockdown in Greeley," *The Nation*, February 15, 2007, https://www.thenation.com/article/lockdown-greeley/.

6   See, for example, Adam Harris, "When ICE Raids Homes," *The Atlantic*, July 17, 2019, https://www.theatlantic.com/family/archive/2019/07/when-ice-raids-homes-immigration/594112/; and Amelia McGowan, "After Terrifying ICE Raid, Mississippi Is Still Fighting Back," *USA Today*, October 4, 2019, https://www.usatoday.com/story/opinion/policing/spotlight/2019/10/03/terrifying-ice-raid-mississippi-still-fighting-back/3790692002/.

7   Michel Foucault, *Security, Territory, Population: Lectures at the Collège de France 1977–1978*, trans. Graham Burchell (New York: Picador, 2007), 302–5.

8   Michel Foucault, *"Society Must Be Defended": Lectures at the Collège de France 1975–1976*, trans. David Macey (New York: Picador, 2003), 61.

9   Ibid., 61.

10 Bernard Stiegler, *Symbolic Misery Volume 1: The Hyperindustrial Epoch*, trans. Barnaby Norman (Malden, MA: Polity, 2014), 4.

11 Ibid., 52.

12 Ibid., 60–1.

13 Ibid., 88–91.

14 Ibid., 92.

15 Wendy Brown, *Walled States, Waning Sovereignty* (New York: Zone Books, 2010), 129.

16 See Robert Peters et al., "Nature Divided, Scientists United: US-Mexico Border Wall Threatens Biodiversity and Binational Conservation," *BioScience* 68, no. 10 (2018): 740–3, as well as Eliza Barclay and Sarah Frostenson, "The Ecological Disaster That Is Trump's Border Wall: A Visual Guide," *Vox*, February 5, 2009, https://www.vox.com/energy-and-environment/2017/4/10/14471304/trump-border-wall-animals.

17 Andrew Hageman, "Ecocinema and Ideology: Do Ecocritics Dream of a Clockwork Green?" in *Ecocinema Theory and Practice*, ed. Stephen Rust, Salma Monani, and Sean Cubitt (New York: Routledge, 2013), 66, 82.

18 Matthew A. Henry discusses *The Simpsons* multimedia franchise in relation to "the culture wars" in the 1990s over issues of immigration, Americanization, multiculturalism, and national identity, including early calls to wall out "illegals." The 1996 Illegal Immigrant Reform and Immigrant Responsibility Act under President Bill Clinton, for example, sought to double the Border Patrol, ease the deportation of criminals, and increase "the financial obligations" of sponsors. He argues that *The Simpsons Movie*, while remaining inclusive in its representations, nonetheless codes the "American" as white, middle class, and suburban, while at the same time upholding the value of assimilation throughout its television run. This scene in *The Simpsons Movie*, then, indicates certain changes in the decades since 9/11: demographic shifts, multilingual communities, and new forms of cultural identification come into view outside the dome, making the white, English-speaking family, for once, seem the outliers rather than the norm. Moreover, the film, unlike the television show, impugns the value of assimilation: these immigrant communities, after all, appear to thrive, whereas those in isolationist Springfield continue to deteriorate and turn more and more "savage." See Matthew A. Henry, The Simpsons, *Satire, and American Culture* (New York: Palgrave Macmillan, 2012), 45, 66, 77.

19 Robin L. Murray and Joseph K. Heumann come close to describing *The Simpsons Movie* as an eco-comedy, in that it "plays up pollution" for fun and suggests that "neither the town nor the government" can adequately address environmental crises. They completely miss the connection of these crises to security walling, as well as the fact that their interlinkage causes the townsfolk to degenerate into monsters. To ask the US government—those responsible for exacerbating these crises—to solve them seems about as sensible in this diegetic environment as Cargill's call to crater an entire town as a viable way to deal with the fecal contamination of its water supplies. See Robin L. Murray and Joseph K. Heumann, *That's All Folks? Ecocritical Readings of American Animated Features* (Lincoln: University of Nebraska Press, 2011), 235.

20 *The Simpsons Movie* takes inspiration for its central conceit from Arch Oboler's 3D science fiction film *The Bubble* (1966). This film features a couple that crashes their airplane in a strange town in which the inhabitants act in a zombielike fashion, repeating the same motions and speech acts over and over again. The couple desperately seeks to escape, only to drive their truck into an invisible dome that encases the entire area so as to maintain those under it "in perfect health" and "in perfect security," as one of the characters says. Typical of the films of the Cold War era after the rise of the Berlin Wall, *The Bubble* thus warns against extremes of social regimentation, travel restriction, and nation-state security walling.

21 J. P. Telotte, *Animating the Science Fiction Imagination* (New York: Oxford University Press, 2018), 19, 48.

22 The HBO miniseries *Chernobyl* (2019) and such films as *The Impossible* (J. A. Bayona, 2012), *Everest* (Baltasar Kormákur, 2015), *The Finest Hours* (Craig Gillespie, 2016), and *Deepwater Horizon* (Peter Berg, 2016)—retellings of a family's survival of the 2006 tsunami devastating Thailand, Indonesia,

and other countries; a deadly 1996 snowstorm; the 1952 US Coast Guard rescue of a sinking tanker; and the explosion of a drilling rig at the time of the 2010 oil spill in the Gulf of Mexico—attest to the commodification of nuclear, mechanical, climatological, and other disasters.

23 John Ellis, discussing the formal conventions of network television, argues that it "provides a variety of segments rather than the progressive accumulation of sequences" that characterizes the cinema, therefore making it more "open-ended" in its visual economies and "repetitive" in its episodic construction. John Fiske seconds these arguments, describing network television as "discontinuous, interrupted, and segmented," in that it subordinates the telos of cinematic narration to "a viewing experience of fragments" that depends more on association than classical forms of continuity. However, Fiske, in contrast to Stiegler, asserts our capacities to resist, evade, and challenge the "dominant value system" of the television medium, "even if momentarily" and in "a limited terrain." He fails to consider the fact that television discretizes its viewers, transmitting its images and narrative formulae to them in their separate rooms rather than a theater full of strangers able through the cinematic experience to reconstitute themselves as a "we." The cinema accustoms its viewers to expect "the unexpected"; and so, even though it synchronizes our consciousness to its rhythms, much as does television, it remains for Stiegler the medium most suitable for fighting off "aesthetic conditioning on its own terrain." See John Ellis, *Visible Fictions: Cinema, Television, Video* (New York: Routledge, 2000), 143, 154; John Fiske, *Television Culture* (New York: Routledge, 2011), 105, 232, 313; and Stiegler, *Symbolic Misery Volume 1*, 19, 83–5.

24 Stiegler, *Symbolic Misery Volume 1*, 82–3.

25 Jonathan Gray, *Watching with* The Simpsons: *Television, Parody, and Intertextuality* (New York: Routledge, 2006), 70.

26 It is worth remembering that Fritz Lang's films featuring the master criminal Dr. Mabuse each speak to the different technological regimes of moving image media and their influence on the act of spectatorship. *Dr. Mabuse, der Spieler* (1922) stars Rudolf Klein-Rogge as the villain, a master of disguise and mesmerizer who often stares directly at the camera, so as to suggest *the allure of the visuals*, the true source of fascination of the silent cinema. The sequel *Das Testament des Dr. Mabuse* (1933), though, rarely affords Klein-Rogge any screen time, even as the voice of the shadowy villain carries throughout the diegesis, urging criminals to commit acts of robbery, counterfeiting, and sabotage. The disembodiment of the character thus speaks to the era of *sound film*, when the focus shifts to another sense-datum—the aural—one more invisible, although still significant and ever-perceptible in theaters. Lang thought to return to the character in *Die 1000 Augen des Dr. Mabuse* (1960), a spy film that insinuates that Mabuse, reemerging in the Cold War era, is responsible for the sociopolitical tensions in the two German states. J. Hoberman argues that in this film "Mabuse is now pure *geist*," with each room in it "under constant surveillance through a combination" of microphones, cameras, and monitors. The "thousand eyes" of Mabuse, in

other words, refers to the ubiquitous electronic transmissions of *television*, at a time throughout which the small screen starts to challenge the cinema for dominance over the visual arts. The mutant squirrel in *The Simpsons Movie*, then, is not the first such monster in the annals of cinema that warns against the dangers of the media's involvement in nation-state securitization. See J. Hoberman, *The Magic Hour: Film at Fin de Siècle* (Philadelphia, PA: Temple University Press, 2003), 11–12.

27 Brown, *Walled States*, 135.
28 Stiegler, *Symbolic Misery Volume 1*, 90.
29 Ibid., 82.
30 Of course, we might object that regular viewers of *The Simpsons* also share to an extent these memories and emotions, creating a fandom market for this VHS tape. Kurt M. Koenigsberger observes that *The Simpsons* franchise functions as a "site from which to promote other products, and so it becomes part of a larger consumer culture," selling comics, albums, candy dispensers, T-shirts, decals, refrigerator magnets, figurines, and "even microprocessors" to its audience. Nonetheless, the tape that Homer creates for Marge remains outside of this consumer culture and oppositional to it for one simple reason—the VHS format went obsolete in 2006, almost fourteen months in advance of the film's release date. Therefore, Homer creates for Marge a special media artifact impossible for mass markets at that time to replicate and distribute. See Kurt M. Koenigsberger, "Commodity Culture and Its Discontents: Mr. Bennett, Bart Simpson, and the Rhetoric of Modernism," in *Leaving Springfield*: The Simpsons *and the Possibility of Oppositional Culture*, ed. John Alberti (Detroit, MI: Wayne State University Press, 2004), 43–4.
31 Deidre M. Pike, *Enviro-Toons: Green Themes in Animated Cinema and Television* (Jefferson, NC: McFarland, 2012), 74.
32 David Feltmate, "Two Days before the Day before an Irritating Truth: *The Simpsons* and *South Park*'s Environmentalism as a Challenge for Mediating Dark Green Ecological Ethics," *Journal of the Study of Religion, Nature & Culture* 11, no. 3 (2017): 324.
33 Audra Simpson discusses these treaties, along with the efforts of the United States and Canada to curtail "the right to pass" of certain indigenous tribespeople. She reminds us that these regimes often use these treaties to decree the semi-sovereign status of "Indian nations," map out their territories, determine their membership through racial testing, and delimit their freedoms of transit and trade. She also calls attention to the court decisions and social activism that saw to recognizing the right of the tribes to ignore the "boundary line" that separates the settler states from each other. See Audra Simpson, *Mohawk Interruptus: Political Life across the Borders of Settler States* (Durham, NC: Duke University Press, 2014), 133–40.
34 Telotte, *Animating the Science Fiction Imagination*, 5.
35 Stephen Daisley, "Neocon Zombie War: The Surprises of *World War Z*," *Commentary* 136, no. 2 (2013): 56.

36 Matt Cornell, "Where the Z Stands for Zionism," *Al Jazeera*. July 17, 2013, https://www.aljazeera.com/indepth/opinion/2013/07/201371183655144583.html.

37 Jeffrey Jerome Cohen, "Grey: A Zombie Ecology," in *Zombie Theory: A Reader*, ed. Sarah Juliet Lauro (Minneapolis: University of Minnesota Press, 2017), 387.

38 Ibid.

39 Edward P. Comentale describes the zombie as a monster that drags and shambles about in a two-step refrain: "*Shhh-thump*. Its second beat is scarier than the first, not just because it is louder, closer, but because it recalls the first. The monster is always in two—two spaces, two times. It approaches as it recedes. It coheres as it falls apart. Each step revives as it destroys." He traces the rhythms and counter-rhythms of the zombie's movement to the music culture of its Afro-Caribbean diasporic roots, and moreover attributes its vacant stare to "the deathliness of all form," meaning the arbitrariness and the unnaturalness of colonial representational systems that sought "the endless indenture" of slave workers. See Edward P. Comentale, "Zombie Race," in *Zombie Theory: A Reader*, ed. Sarah Juliet Lauro (Minneapolis: University of Minnesota Press, 2017), 189, 191, 199.

40 For zombie film scholarship that draws extensively on the work of Giorgio Agamben, see, for example, Penny Crofts and Anthea Vogl, "Dehumanized and Demonized Refugees, Zombies, and *World War Z*," *Law & Humanities* 13, no. 1 (2013): 29–51; Seth Morton, "Zombie Politics," in *The Year's Work at the Zombie Research Center*, ed. Edward P. Comentale and Aaron Jaffe (Bloomington: Indiana University Press, 2014), 315–40; Tamas Nagypal, "From the Classical *Polis* to the Neoliberal Camp: Mapping the Biopolitical Regimes of the Undead in *Dawn of the Dead*, *Zombi 2* and *28 Days Later*," *Journal for Cultural & Religious Theory* 13, no. 2 (2014): 13–24; Steven Pokornowshki, "Vulnerable Life: Zombies, Global Biopolitics, and the Reproduction of Structural Violence," *Humanities* 5, no. 3 (2016): 71–93; Jon Stratton, "Trouble with Zombies: *Muselmänner*, Bare Life, and Displaced People," in *The Zombie Film Reader*, ed. Sarah Juliet Lauro (Minneapolis: University of Minnesota Press, 2017), 246–69; and, of course, Giorgio Agamben, *Homo Sacer: Sovereign Power and Bare Life*, trans. Daniel Heller-Roezen (Stanford, CA: Stanford University Press, 1995).

41 Priscilla Wald, "Viral Cultures: Microbes and Politics in the Cold War," in *Zombie Theory: A Reader*, ed. Sarah Juliet Lauro (Minneapolis: University of Minnesota Press, 2017), 35.

42 Ibid., 34.

43 One of the most curious of these films, *Pride and Prejudice and Zombies*, mashes up this subgenre with the "heritage cycle" of UK cinema, which, according to Andrew Higson, nostalgically reconstructs "an imperialist and upper-class Britain." Steers's film sets the familiar characters of Jane Austen's novel in the midst of a nineteenth-century zombie apocalypse, a time during which, the narrator tells us, the imperial sea trade set in motion the outbreak of some mysterious disease, afflicting its victims with

"an insatiable hunger for the brains of the living." The British Empire then saw to fortifying London, with a 100-foot wall encircling it and a canal 30 fathoms deep separating it from the outlying countryside—the film refers to the area these security installations enclose as the "In-Between." However, this term also aptly describes a narrative twist that occurs at the midpoint of the narrative: Elizabeth (Lily James) finds that the minister Wickham (Jack Huston) intends to domesticate the zombies, feeding them animal flesh, routinizing their movements, and sheltering them in a church. The "In-Between" comes to seem a sort of interface area (see Chapter 5), in which two different factions can meet, intermingle, and exchange cultural formalities, away from the mandates of state administrators and the eyes of their spies, sentries, and surveillance mechanisms. These zombies, though, in another twist, attack London with a new cunning and religious fervor, throwing themselves against the cannonades, fence spikes, and *chevaux de frise* surrounding the estates and thus forcing the British soldiers to destroy the Hingham Bridge that spans the canal. They reestablish London as a safe zone, the film making it seem as though the zombies, despite their reeducation and religious training, remain a subrace incapable of self-control or diplomatic means. Higson claims that "heritage" films reproduce "the past" as "pastiche," as a "series of commodities" for the entertainment market. *Pride and Prejudice and Zombies* emerges *as a pastiche of a pastiche*, one that short-circuits the nostalgia for imperialism and class separation that the earlier cycle of films trade on. Although they remain racio-spatially distinct from Elizabeth's cohort, the zombies do not necessarily represent their "other." On the contrary, only these soldiers and aristocrats can match them in terms of sheer appetite. The film ends with the walls of London drawing tighter, as these nobles set forth the conditions that shall force them in time to consume one another and their class altogether. See Andrew Higson, "Re-presenting the National Past: Nostalgia and Pastiche in the Heritage Film," in *Fires Were Started: British Cinema and Thatcherism*, ed. Lester Friedman (New York: Wallflower, 2006), 110, 112.

44 This Hollywood action-horror film, of all things, speaks to Gilles Deleuze's famous conceptualization of the central task of the cinema arts: "not that of addressing a people, but of contributing to the invention of a people to come." Of course, *World War Z* seems at the farthest remove from the modernist and Third World cinemas that Deleuze muses over, since it observes the conventions of classical filmmaking and at the most depicts a subrace that clearly undergoes de-subjectivation, separatism, and subordination. However, Deleuze argues that this "people to come"—this sense of "we"—does not require a correcting of false consciousness so much as a "*putting of everything into a trance*, the people and its masters, and the camera itself, pushing everything into a state of aberration." On the surface, the zombies of *World War Z* seem in a trance; nonetheless, they move, react, and think on their feet throughout the film. The survivors, in contrast, freeze up, fall numb, and seem unable to cope with changing circumstances; some of them appear at times in a more trancelike condition than the zombies. This state of aberration in the film, as it upends the conventions of its subgenre, contributes to more

than the invention of a new "we," in that it also traces out and casts doubt on the security apparatuses, illiberal and nativist discourses, and mass media tricks that serve to deaden our social feeling, threatening to turn us into *moral monsters to come*. See Gilles Deleuze, *Cinema 2: The Time-Image*, trans. Hugh Tomlinson and Roberta Galeta (Minneapolis: University of Minnesota Press, 2007), 217, 219.

45 Hye Jean Chung, *Media Heterotopias: Digital Effects and Material Labor in Global Film Production* (Durham, NC: Duke University Press, 2017), 88.

46 Jeffrey Andrew Weinstock defines the "technoparanoia" characteristic of the zombie film as the terrible revelation that dawns on its characters and viewers alike that our "technology has outstripped" our capacity to control it. He argues that "the 'unnatural' return of the dead" in these films appears the direct result of our "tampering with the environment and irresponsible use of technology without appropriate safeguards"—a correlation that nicely encapsulates the negative effects and the sheer ugliness of the security walls in *World War Z* and similar fare. See Jeffrey Andrew Weinstock, "Zombie TV: Late-Night B Movie Horror Fest," in *Zombie Theory: A Reader*, ed. Sarah Juliet Lauro (Minneapolis: University of Minnesota Press, 2017), 23, 30.

47 Chung, *Media Heterotopias*, 75.

48 Rick Altman, *Film/Genre* (London: British Film Institute, 1999), 224.

49 For more on films with monsters in them that emerge from digital media devices, see the chapters on *The Ring* (Gore Verbinski, 2002) and *Paranormal Activity* (Oren Peli, 2007) in Larrie Dudenhoeffer, *Embodiment and Horror Cinema* (New York: Palgrave Macmillan, 2014). Other such films include *Pulse* (Kiyoshi Kurosawa, 2001), *One Missed Call* (Takashi Miike, 2003), and *Unfriended* (Levan Gabriadze, 2015).

50 The term "fel" derives from the Latin root for "poison," and also from the Old French for "evil," "cruel," or "vile." However, it also seems a corruption of *fée*, the Middle French term that Marina Warner translates into "fairy," "magic," and "that which has been spoken." See Marina Warner, *Once Upon a Time: A Short History of the Fairy Tale* (New York: Oxford University Press, 2014), 5.

51 Kristen Whissel, *Spectacular Digital Effects: CGI and Contemporary Cinema* (Durham, NC: Duke University Press, 2014), 66, 77–80.

52 Jacques Derrida, *On Cosmopolitanism and Forgiveness*, trans. Mark Dooley and Michael Hughes (New York: Routledge, 2001), 18.

53 The television miniseries *Roots* (1977) repurposes this technique to different effect. On a slave ship, the teenage Kunta Kinte (LeVar Burton) speaks in English to another Mandinka captive about developing a common argot with the other tribesmen, freeing one another from their chains, and massacring the captain and sailors on the upper decks. The English that they use marks the *futur antérieur* deprivation of their native speech. As the tribesmen teach one another their words, a remarkable development occurs—as Kunta Kinte continues to speak in English, the others murmur in the distance in their native tongues. As Stanley Cavell suggests, "talk" or conversation remains one of the structuring features of television, and this miniseries uses this fact to move

its audience toward rediscovering and attuning themselves to their cultural-linguistic roots. The miniseries, in other words, suggests that native accents, cadences, and vocabularies remain underneath its familiar English soundtrack, as they do in the macro US culture; in a similar counterhistorical vein, although a more fictive and fantastic one, of course, the words of the Orcs in *Warcraft* remain underneath the English that they "speak" to Stormwind's chiefs. See Stanley Cavell, "The Fact of Television," in *Cavell on Cavell*, ed. William Rothman (Albany: State University of New York Press, 2005), 75.

54 "Let the silver do its work," says Master Gregory (Jeff Bridges), one of the Falcon Knights who track and set fire to witches in Sergei Bodrov's fantasy adventure film *Seventh Son* (2015). Their queen Mother Malkin (Julianne Moore), in retaliation, summons a cohort of witches to attack a walled-in city, splintering its entranceway. Thus the witches—who, as the film's subrace, stash themselves away inside the crater of a dormant volcano—underline one of the shortcomings of these sorts of security measures: they compel outsiders to innovate new weapons and techniques to use to demolish, circumvent, or force them open. To topple the city walls, for instance, the witches assume feline, draconic, or spectral forms. However, the silver Gregory and apprentice Tom Ward (Ben Barnes) use against these villains in effect de-digitalizes them, an interesting choice in that this substance evokes older modes of image-making. Unlike twenty-first-century digital cinema, earlier films rely on *silver halides* for the chemical emulsions instrumental to the composition of their images. Gregory uses such crystals, in short, to neutralize the computer-driven magic and appearances of the witches. Much as with *Warcraft*, though, this film calls for "hybridization" to moderate these sorts of CG excesses, as it turns out that Tom Ward is "mixed-race," the son of a witch, as well as a Falcon Knight. He seems capable of counterbalancing the disjunctive ontologies of moving image capture and therefore quelling the film's racio-spatial conflicts, since they mainly derive from the digital effects that mark the witches off from the townsfolk.

55 Derrida, *On Cosmopolitanism and Forgiveness*, 23.

56 Stiegler, *Symbolic Misery Volume 1*, 14.

57 Mitchell Gray and Elvin Wyly, discussing the aftereffects of 9/11, set forth the concept of "terror cities" to account for "the militarization" of the urban experience in the United States and the fact that "more and more aspects of everyday life and death now *take place* in the shadow of horror and fear, sustained by the manufactured certainty of uncertainty in an endless American war on terror." The defenses, amenities, and armaments of the Great Wall in this film certainly speak to this notion of the terror city, except with one qualification: the features and functions of this structure more so suggest "the uncertain" nature of the characters' "certainty" of the Tao Tei's inevitable siege. Their invasion remains certain to the Chinese, in other words, even as the attack methods and capabilities of these aliens appear unclear—the fact that the Nameless Order contrives to engineer into the Great Wall a defense mechanism for every circumstance, it seems, attests to their uncertainty as to the exact contours the attack of the Tao Tei might take. More interestingly,

as the Chinese take in the foreign mercenaries, the functions of the terror city in this film dovetail to an extent with those of the sanctuary city, such as welcoming asylum seekers and entering into cross-cultural commerce with them. See Mitchell Gray and Elvin Wyly, "The Terror City Hypothesis," in *Violent Geographies: Fear, Terror, and Political Violence*, ed. Derek Gregory and Allen Pred (New York: Routledge, 2007), 330.

58 Yomi Braester, "The Spectral Return of Cinema: Globalization and Cinephilia in Contemporary Chinese Film," *Cinema Journal* 55, no. 1 (2015): 29.

59 Ibid., 31.

60 Yi-Fu Tuan notices an interesting contradiction at the core of national defense: the sovereign state, regarding its carceral and security mechanisms, curbs those *itinerant* desires and impulses that threaten it. He argues that societies impose order in two ways: "exile and confinement. With exile, danger is expelled from the communal body; with confinement, it is isolated in space, thereby rendering it innocuous." Thus the imprisonment of felons, debtors, madpersons, moral failures, and the sufferers of "the floodtide of disease" sequesters the rest of the nation-state from all whose *minds, actions, and corporealities roam*. Thus it is no accident that the mercenaries in the film are mostly scoundrels and vagabonds—their admittance into the fortress allows the Nameless Order to similarly "wander" outside of their usual military traditions, combat maneuvers, and defensive measures in the fight against the alien monsters. Too much regimentation, the film suggests, and their entire society might start to resemble the Tao Tei in its organizational structure. For more on exile and its transformative relation to the nation-state, see Chapter 3. Also see Yi-Fu Tuan, *Landscapes of Fear* (Minneapolis: University of Minnesota Press, 2013), 187–90.

61 Much as in *The Great Wall* and *World War Z*, Jordan Peele's *Us* (2019) features a set of characters that transform themselves into a security emplacement, in this case a chain-link fence. The film focuses on the family of Adelaide Wilson (Lupita Nyong'o) as they fight off the doppelgängers who wish to "untether" themselves from them and assume their social roles. She first encounters them inside a mirror maze in a funhouse off the Santa Cruz shore in 1986—the time of the Hands Across America event, which saw millions of Americans clasp one another and form a contiguous chain stretching from ocean to ocean. Over the course of the narrative, the film reveals that the US government made clones of its citizens in order to ensure their complaisance, only to abandon the experiment and cruelly dump these doubles into a subterranean series of tunnels and dormitories. The doppelgängers thus await the right time to surprise their counterparts, murder them, and replace them; in fact, the film distinguishes them as a subrace that organizes themselves, studies the activities of those above them, and rebels against the dictates of their creator-administrators. Curiously, the final shot of the film shows them, after the success of their revolt, forming another chain, tempting allegorical readings of them as a former subaltern class, as the survivors of a Tuskegee-style experiment, or as the escapees of a Trumpian detention center. These doppelgängers, in any case, *resemble us*, no

matter the distortions that their image (as in a funhouse mirror) undergoes. Of course, *Us* touches on anxieties over immigration, national identity, and economic survival, as certain US citizens of different races, sexes, ages, and ethnicities might at one time or another fear their replacement, dislocation, or disempowerment. The fact that the clones configure themselves into a fence, though, sends a clear message to the film's viewers concerning security walling, immigrant detention, and cultural cul-de-sacs: *we must remain careful what we wish for, as the same might in time happen to us.*

62   Henry A. Giroux, *America at War with Itself* (San Francisco, CA: City Lights Books, 2017), 91.

63   Luc Boltanksi, with Sadean insight, reminds us that "only someone persecuted gets to the heart of Evil from where he reveals the Evil in all of us." More than a mere nihilistic statement, though, these unfortunates, if they can commit to following through on such a course of "Evil," also cannot really serve the state or its ministers. For example, in *The Belko Experiment*, those who suffer from the entrapment and torture that the organization inflicts on them ultimately turn against it, fighting (according to the rules) for their freedom and then redirecting their violence against the scientists that monitor their actions from a distance. See Luc Boltanksi, *Distant Suffering: Morality, Media and Politics*, trans. Graham Burchell (New York: Cambridge University Press, 1999), 145.

64   Giroux, *America at War with Itself*, 87.

65   Stiegler, *Symbolic Misery Volume 1*, vii.

66   Quite a few critics thought *Rambo: Last Blood* (Adrian Grunberg, 2019) a racist, xenophobic film, with Peter Bradshaw of *The Guardian* accusing it of nursing "Trumpian fantasies of Mexican rapists" and Matthew Rosza of *Salon* describing it as a validation of "MAGA-world bigotries about Mexicans." The film certainly touches on the North-South tensions of its release context, although not in so simplistic or one-dimensional a fashion. John Rambo (Sylvester Stallone), the ex-Green Beret and Vietnam veteran antihero of the series, drives from Arizona into Mexico to retrieve stepdaughter Gabriela (Yvette Monreal) from a cartel of sex slave traffickers. Unlike the similar *Taken* (Pierre Morel, 2009), Rambo fails the mission and Gabriela dies as they race to the United States with the cartel members chasing after them. Rambo turns their Arizona ranch into a secure zone, full of mantraps, vehicle impediments, explosives, and even a tunnel system. Rambo, in short, constructs a Ho Chi Minh Trail under the ranch and uses the tactics of the NVA and Vietcong to take out the cartel assassins one at a time. The film thus maps the North-South coordinates of the Vietnam War on to the state security conflicts of the Trump era so as to suggest *that we have now become like our former enemies.* Rambo, after all, uses tiger traps, tripwires, and even venomous snakes to incapacitate the sex traffickers, tactics that the North Vietnamese thought to use during that earlier war. The film thus does not cater to Trump supporters, opportunistically feeding into their fantasies of Central Americans as drug dealers or rapists—in fact, several notable Mexican characters, such as a doctor and a newswoman, assist Rambo, and others in the nightclubs and marketplaces seem altogether ordinary. If anything, the

film shows us clearly that checkpoints, customs offices, and security fences do not deter crime, whether it comes from the North or the South. After the violence ends, Rambo tellingly savors the open range and rides into the sunset, a relic of the twentieth century and a throwback to a time in Hollywood when cowboys and *vacqueros*, outlaws and *forajidos* alike might freely cross the Rio Grande. See Peter Bradshaw, "*Rambo: Last Blood* Review—Stallone Storms Mexico in a Laughable Trumpian Fantasy," *The Guardian*, September 19, 2019, https://www.theguardian.com/film/ 2019/sep/19/rambo-last-blood-review; and Matthew Rosza, "The MAGA Fever Dream of 'Rambo: Last Blood,'" *Salon*, September 20, 2019, https://www.salon.com/2019/09/20/the-maga-fever-dream-of-rambo-last-blood/.

67 James Kendrick, *Film Violence: History, Ideology, Genre* (New York: Wallflower, 2009), 69.
68 Stiegler, *Symbolic Misery Volume 1*, 85–6.
69 Bernard Stiegler, *Symbolic Misery Volume 2: The Catastrophe of the Sensible*, trans. Barnaby Norman (Malden, MA: Polity, 2015), 23, 26.
70 Ibid., 153.
71 Brown, *Walled States*, 131.

4

Gated Communities: Outside the Walls on the Cinema Screen

On October 12, 2018, scores of migrants from Honduras, El Salvador, Guatemala, and Nicaragua sought to escape the Northern Triangle, the area of Central America under the control of cocaine cartels, marching toward the United States to seek asylum from the violence, disorder, and corruption of the region.[1] President Donald Trump opportunistically took to Twitter to warn of the approaching "Caravan" and to agitate for Congress to finance a US–Mexico separation wall: "A big new Caravan is heading up to our Southern Border from Honduras. Only a Wall, or Steel Barrier, will keep our country safe!"[2] Earlier, on October 29, 2018, Trump went further, never squarely addressing the threats of rape, robbery, extortion, or abduction the migrants constantly face; rather, the president wrote on Twitter that they represent an "invasion to our country" that the military must intercept.[3] After calling on Mexico to deport the migrants, Central American countries to tighten their travel restrictions, and the National Guard to stop illegal crossings, Trump the next month was to excuse the actions of the US Customs and Border Protection officers who shot riot-control chemicals into a mob that, upset with the slowness of the asylum process, was throwing rocks at them.[4] He took credit in another tweet for sending the Border Patrol to repel the caravans and for forcing them to stay in Mexico, arguing that national defense requires commandeering another $5,000,000,000 of taxpayer money to start up construction on "a tremendous chunk of wall."[5]

According to a January 9, 2019, *USA Today* article, though, the Border Patrol's detainment of 60,000 migrants and apprehension of 27,518 of them for illegal crossing attests to the fact that Trump's efforts to deter the caravans from coming is not working.[6] Moreover, *CNN* correspondent Leyla Santiago, after inspecting the situation in Guatemala, saw that Trump's outbursts about restricting asylum, deploying troops to the south, and ending Fourteenth Amendment statute stipulations concerning US citizenship were not stopping Central Americans from trekking on foot to the United States.[7] The migrants suffer insupportable conditions: adverse weather, scorching sunlight, malnourishment, inadequate footwear, and exposure to skin, intestine, and respiratory tract infections from sleeping outdoors. The migrant camps in Tijuana and Matamoros meanwhile experience deteriorating shelters, overflowing refuse, communicable diseases (such as the flu, chicken pox, and even HIV), and scarce resources in terms of medicine, toiletries, foods, drinking water, shower facilities, and education for the children in them.[8] Outside of coping with this squalor, the migrants face execration from many Mexican, along with US, citizens.[9] Thus the militarization of the San Diego-Tijuana border, an area otherwise famous for its tourism and conurbation, creates an "outside" to US domains, an unlivable, unhygienic set of camp shelters that reduces those inside them to a condition of (semi)permanent exile. The violence that the migrants typically face in their countries of origin, according to Natalia Cordona, stems from US interventionism in Central America, trade agreements unfavorable to the region's workforce, and industrial methods that contribute to climate change and environmental toxification.[10] Her findings speak to more than the ethical responsibilities of the United States for the migrant caravans; more insidiously, they suggest the North's attempt to at once shore up its sovereign territorial claims and enlarge them through the steady and thoroughgoing *pollution* of its neighboring states.

Michel Serres sets forth a rather counterintuitive notion of ownership demands and their extension. Much as animals defile the outer rims of their nests, dens, caves, or warrens to mark their territories and claim ownership over them, so too do individuals, communities, and nation-states externalize their wastes in order to delimit their spheres of influence and declare their authority over certain regions, resources, or social assemblages. If someone spits in a drink, for example, she more than makes it abject; she also claims ownership of it, since doubtlessly no one else will want to take a sip of it. Correspondingly, a nation-state that clutters its edges with waste eo ipso differentiates its territories from surrounding countries, while expanding its reach into them, since to some degree it regulates and controls their environmental quality. As Serres argues, "*The increasing volume* of trash or excretions" signifies "*the extension of appropriated space*—nest, farm, city, country—and also *the increase in the number of subjects of appropriation*—individual, family, nation."[11] The disorder of the migrant camps, then, represents more than a "humanitarian crisis," as the mayor of Tijuana maintains.[12] More importantly, the camps attest to the US's sovereign might, its ability to sully and unsettle the social and ecological systems of its southern neighbors at its convenience, and at the same time make it seem that its own spaces are the ones worth the risks of entering, even illegally. Serres again: "Those who have a place *have*. Those who have no place have nothing, strictly speaking."[13]

Serres takes these arguments further, contending that the noise animals emit, over and above their excretions, serves to mark their foods, objects, and spaces, as in the cases of the shake of a rattlesnake's tail or the roar of a tiger. Similarly, we also emit an overabundance of noise—advertising catchphrases on clothing, signboards, and webpages; music from car stereos, nightclub districts, and concert venues; and singing, shouting, and chanting from sports contests, activist rallies, and church events—to appropriate certain spaces for ourselves, symbolically "dirtying" them to exclude nonbelievers, nonparticipants, and noncitizens from them. Serres thus distinguishes *hard* from *soft pollution*. The first includes the solids, sludges, smoke, and other detritus that comes from "industrial companies or gigantic garbage dumps," whereas its soft counterpart includes the "tsunamis of writing, signs, images, and logos flooding rural, civic, public, and natural spaces."[14] Although quite different in their material effects, these two modes of impurification emanate from the same source: namely, "our will to appropriate, our desire to conquer and expand the space of our properties."[15] These twin dynamics explain the migrant caravan crisis, since the waste strewn about the camps, as well as the sickness-suffering refugees who inhabit them, serve to widen US influence over other nation-states, to impinge on their right to self-administration without declaring war on them, colonizing them, or formally annexing their territories. Moreover, Trump's tweets (a disposable form of messaging), as well as the theatrical value of security walling that Wendy Brown speaks of, represent soft forms of pollution meant to supplement the destitute migrants, crude shelters, and accumulating waste that frame the US's southernmost edges, at once re-outlining its domestic space and extending its sway to other countries. Of course, these dynamics in turn constitute the United States as "clean," "safe," and "cozy," and thus a sanctuary to those who aspire to citizenship, resident status, or simple work within it. Serres, in other words, analogizes the mass media to factories in terms of their negative effects, enabling us to see the multiple instances of security walls in twenty-first century Hollywood cinema as another contribution to the "soft" corruption of our social and material environments.[16] Even so, these films do not wholeheartedly assent to the nationalist rhetoric of President Trump or other statespersons in the United States and elsewhere.

Serres's arguments represent a novel twist on Julia Kristeva's famous theorization of abjection, another name for the saliva, urine, feces, semen, menses, and other excreta that we recognize as our own and also disavow, radically excluding these substances from the integrity of our "clean and proper" selves.[17] More significantly, abjection daily constitutes the thresholds of our flesh as a "border," with the filth that we vomit out and drop as its "other side."[18] Eventually, after "nothing remains" in us, we must cross over too, in the form of a corpse, the "most sickening of wastes"—as Kristeva tersely words it, "It is no longer I who expel, 'I' is expelled."[19] The abject thus mixes the sensations of desire, denial, revulsion, fascination, and the thrills that accompany the threat of danger, and it also accounts for the fascist drive to expel members of certain races, religions, ethnicities, or sexual dispositions, allegedly for reasons of their dirtiness, obnoxious smell, or disagreeable customs, to ensure the totalistic cleanliness of "the Family, the Nation, the Race, and the Body."[20] This drive maps the distinction of "Inside and Outside" onto "I and Other" so that, for example, the caravans represent the abject matter of the United States, Mexico, and the Northern Triangle, which expel and flush out the migrants from their territories, refusing to officially claim them as their own. However, the space these migrants must then inhabit comes to seem drastically unlike the ones obtaining in these nation-states—it comes to seem "fluid," nonhomogeneous, and nontotalizable, enabling them to stray and, despite its dangers, devise new territories and identities from it and start afresh,[21] all the while asking themselves, "'Where am I'? instead of 'Who am I'?"[22] The "Outside" that the abject carves out from the "Inside," in turn, opens the residents of these nation-states up to the risks of exile, although it also affords those able to survive the wretchedness of these spaces the chance to return to their cities and countries of origin to then transform them.

In *Nations without Nationalism*, Kristeva applies the concept of the abject to issues of integration, immigration, and racism. She argues that the "cult of origins," which too often finds its expression in national, cultural, and sectarian conflicts, involves a retreat from foreigners offensive for economic, religious, or cultural reasons, as well as a form of self-hate, in that tendentially "individuals despair of their own qualities," "undervalue their achievements," and "run down their own freedoms" in their violent confrontation with these others.[23] She therefore argues that we must undergo a sort of de-origination, a stripping away of the more sacral, totalistic aspects of the nation-state, as well as recognition of the fact that we are all foreigners, "with the same right of mutual respect."[24] Kristeva, in short, advocates a degree of self-exile in the face of rising nation-state securitization and, with it, the abjection of those racially, ethnically, religiously, culturally, or sociolinguistically different from us:

> [In] the long run, only a thorough investigation of our remarkable relationship with both the *other* and *strangeness within ourselves* can lead people to give up hunting for the scapegoat outside their group, a search that allows them to withdraw into their "sanctum" thus purified: is not the worship of one's "very own," of which the "national" is the collective configuration, the *common denominator* that we imagine we have as "our own," precisely, along with other "own and proper" people like us?[25]

Kristeva, then, regarding the nation-state, calls for integration on the "inside and outside of its borders," not to collapse it so much as to "transport it beyond itself."[26] The figure of the exile, appearing in so many twenty-first-century films, serves to counterbalance and critique the incidence of the security walls in them. The exile, cast out of their native socius for some reason, squares Serres's and Kristeva's views on filth and dross, as they venture into a "borderland" area that appears unclean, treacherous, and abject, only to confront the fact that some megacorporation, military superpower, or other institutional force dumps its waste into it, thus extending its authoritative reach and flaunting its freedom to imprudently defile "foreign" soils with impunity.

Henry A. Giroux argues that such security apparatuses also subject those inside the nation-state to "a continuous state of siege warfare," tending to radicalize them or reduce them to the "collateral damage that comes from ubiquitous war machines."[27] Ultimately, much as with Kristeva, Giroux enjoins us "to become border crossers" able to challenge the isolationist "silos" that restrict our movements and regiment our cultural-political expression.[28] The main characters in a diverse number of Hollywood films—from comedies to science fiction to superhero films—function as such "border crossers," straying *outside* the walled-in nation-state, facing expulsion from it, or acting to reconnoiter its margins.[29] Since these characters usually retain their citizenship status or ingroup coding, they come to figure the *para-exilic* tenor of these films, meaning that they share the same abject condition as the monsters, castoffs, forsaken souls, or asylum seekers that dwell outside the nation-state's walls, even as they also claim some right to it and attempt to regain their former recognition as citizens or members of it. Along the way, they come into contact with the *hard and soft pollution* that informs these films' diegeses: the trash, sewage, scrap metal, and mutant abominations that clutter the spaces outside the nation-state, as well as the emblems, trade names, electronic signals, and other symbolic effluvia that cast into relief the true scope of its influence.

The para-exilic thrust of these films forces these characters into contact with the cultures, social activities, and value systems of those they thought odious, unclean, and worthless. These characters afterward experience a certain degree of moral and ontic transformation, developing deep sympathies with these others, even though, unlike them, they usually manage to enter the nation-state, mostly due to their reliance on former friends, team affiliations, redemptive actions, or surface appearance. They reverse the course of the nation-state's impurification of the areas surrounding its walls, fences, domes, or other defenses, in that, upon their return, *they muddle the clean and proper self-identity of its family units, monocultural communities, and overall ethnoracial complexion.* The walls in these films might threaten those within them with deportation, expulsion, or simple non-readmittance; in so doing, with the return of those cast out, they also set the stage for them to discredit the cult of origins and move their fellow citizens in the direction of integration, decolonization, and the rediscovery of their own foreignness.

The para-exilic character thus reintroduces strangeness to the nation-state, opening it to new social, economic, religious, and eco-holistic possibilities.

Monsters

Coming out after the construction of about 600 miles of steel mesh and virtual defense setups in 2009 in the wake of the Secure Fence Act,[30] Gareth Edwards's *Monsters* (2010) follows the cross-border movements of two US citizens who attempt to reenter the nation-state from San Jose, Central America. As one of the clearest expositions of the dangerous and inhumane conditions that stem from separation walling, the film depicts almost all of Mexico as an "Infected Zone" that the United States struggles to quarantine after a number of octopus-like aliens settle in the region, a NASA mission disturbing their trip through outer space. The film thus touches on contemporaneous cultural anxieties over terrorism and immigrant "invasions": the opening sequence, in fact, features a convoy of troops riding through the streets of the Zone as though they were searching for insurgents in the Middle East. Camilla Fojas, on a similar note, argues that the cosmopolitan tenor of the United States as "a hospitable terrain open to those seeking asylum and survival is no longer part of the complex of issues around immigration. Rather, public discourse about immigration is replete with post-9/11 concerns about its various hazards."[31] Concurring with Fojas, Elena dell'Agnese focuses on the difficulties of moving south to north in much US mainstream cinema, often in the face of such militarization, in contrast to other films, such as *Losin' It* (Curtis Hanson, 1983), that depict US citizens freely crossing into Mexico in their search for adventure or romance.[32]

The novelty of *Monsters* consists in the fact that its two main characters must confront the same obstacles, threats, and indignities that immigrants, refugees, and visitors do in their attempts to cross into the north. One of these characters, news cameraman Andrew Kaulder (Scoot McNairy), must escort the other, Samantha Wynden (Whitney Able), the daughter of a media magnate, to the United States so that she remains safe from impending airstrikes against the alien creatures in the region. Although their trek superficially resembles the one in Frank Capra's *It Happened One Night* (1934), complete with the two of them thumbing rides to the coast and developing feelings for each other along the way,[33] it soon turns deadly serious, as they must cross into the Zone after a woman steals their travel documents. They stumble across a ziggurat, climbing it to attain a clear view of the immense security wall that surrounds the United States (Figure 4.1). At the sight, Kaulder remarks, "It's different looking at America from the outside in," attesting to the para-exilic status they share in relation to the nation-state they recognize as their own, even as it denies them the right

FIGURE 4.1 *The US–Mexico Separation Wall in* Monsters.

of repatriation and the means to return to their "perfect suburban homes." Notably, in the course of their travels, Kaulder and Wynden discover the full extent of the US sovereign reach into Central America, as the areas inside and adjacent to the Zone show forth the ruinous effects of the North's military excursions, astronautic researches, and media transmissions on them. The US utterly defiles the region, thus delimiting its own territories and enabling it to claim some degree of ownership and administrative control over its southern neighbors. On their trek, Kaulder and Wynden constantly come across instances of "hard" pollution: the clutter and clouds of smoke from army strikes; the sepulchral remains of offices, apartment complexes, and cargo ships; and the empty shells of tanks, airplanes, and missiles. Moreover, the United States frequently uses chemical weapons against the aliens and their fungus-like offspring, defoliating the Zone with them, toxifying it so that no one can survive in it without air filters, and claiming the right to supervise it, regulate access to it, and re-demarcate the area it covers.

However, the troops who shoot at one of the monsters in the opening sequence encounter in the Zone another form of pollution, the "soft" variant of it that includes the media images, symbols, and messages that seem as disposable throughout the film as the scrap metal that rusts in the rivers, cities, and mountain ranges of its diegetic environment. The alien the troops shoot at tellingly sits atop one of the advertising signboards in the Zone, a throwaway image that nonetheless extends the influence of the walled-in United States into Central America. One soldier murmurs a rendition of Richard Wagner's "Ride of the Valkyries"; more than an equally throwaway allusion to the airstrikes in Francis Ford Coppola's *Apocalypse Now* (1979), it represents an instance of *sheer noise*, a suffusion of the region with US cultural, as well as military-industrial, waste materials. The two main characters encounter other examples throughout the film, from ambulance sirens to alarmist television communiqués to the ambient sounds of noisy airport crowds. The aliens themselves emit strange animal wails, and in the final scene Kaulder and Wynden see through their skin their neural circuits, which resemble the electronics of a computer.[34] These monsters, of course, also seem a form of "hard" pollution, making the Zone uninhabitable for most Central Americans and US travelers. More interestingly, as CG constructs that underline their digitality in this final scene, they also double as a form of "soft" pollution that resemble the constant news items that moment to moment serve to terrorize their viewers. As a cameraman, Kaulder contributes to this "infecting" of the region, snapping images of train wrecks, explosions, and the corpses of children to sell to news agencies so that they can continue to foist on Central Americans a negative self-image and inure US citizens to a series of xenophobic (and xenobiological) scares. Wynden, though, shames Kaulder for these actions, and their travels together change their attitudes in significant ways.

To confront the root causes of the abject condition of these regions, then, Kaulder and Wynden must assume a para-exilic status in relation to the United States—they remain its citizens, even as they share the experience of migrants in terms of the miseries they suffer, the sense of community they develop, and the absence of magisterial-political frameworks they might appeal to after their dealings with coyotes, thieves, and reckless soldiers. The Wall, as the film's characters call it, appears massive and impenetrable, with tanks, aircraft, and Border Patrol cars circling the *frontera* areas surrounding it and checkpoints, visa consulates, and decontamination centers screening "illegal" migrants from its entryways. These security measures furthermore create the conditions for economic exploitation, as a smuggler overcharges Kaulder and Wynden to stow them on a ferry and, after they miss their embarkation time, to charter a rowboat crew for them, recruit an escort of mercenaries to take them to the Wall, and ensure that corrupt officials overlook their illegal movement north. The two of them, in short, undergo a sort of de-origination throughout the film, so much so that Wynden, after they finally cross over into the United States, melancholically says to Kaulder, "I don't want to go home." Her sentiments directly stem from the fact that throughout their travels she and Kaulder meet children who struggle with illness and destitution due to the economic and ecological aftereffects of the US military response to the alien monsters. These sentiments also stem from the candlelight vigils the two of them observe for victims of the airstrikes, from the families of meager means that nonetheless take them in during the night, and from the campfire conversations they engage in with their straight shooter escorts:

Kaulder: Do you feel safe staying here? ...
Escort: If you don't bother them, they don't bother you. When the American planes come, the creatures ... very mad ...

Their dialogue suggests that these military actions seem more in the interest of US sovereign expression than that of Central Americans. Kirk Combe thus speaks to the deterritorializing work the film does on its characters and also its viewers, arguing that "watching two young Americans come to the topsy-turvy realization that the United States is a truly dangerous nation, whereas Mexico offers, despite its economic problems, a more civil society, goes against all stereotypes Americans harbor of their southern neighbor."[35] As it enables its audience to dispel their misapprehensions about migrants as they vicariously experience the terrors they face, *Monsters* calls on them to resist the closing off of nation-states, as it dramatizes the consequences of security walling, immigration enforcement, and the transboundary forms of pollution that industrial nation-states emit.

Monsters shows that the environmental damage done to another sovereign state, such as Mexico, might also sweep across the United States, as the aliens reproduce in the form of a fungus that affects most of the vegetation in the areas they inhabit. The Wall throws off their natural equilibrium, *creating abominations* that it cannot impede, since it cannot stop water currents, tree spores, or insects from dispersing the aliens all over the Earth.[36] The climax of the film sees these "hard" forms of pollution spreading into the United States, taking over Texas, and driving the military further north. However, "soft" forms of pollution also reach Central America, with constant news updates about the "Battle of Texas" flashing across the television screens that Kaulder and Wynden distractedly watch. They tell each other that it is "different looking at America from the outside in," a suggestion that the Wall does more than compromise open travel, free trade, asylum seeking, and right of abode entitlements. It also induces a sort of amnesia in those it supposedly safeguards, as they ignore the suffering, destitution, and unethical contamination of the south, unable to see it for themselves without the media and culture industries controlling the narrative for them, selecting inoffensive images for them to consume, and repeating the same tendentious messages again and again so as to annoy, confuse, and disinterest them. This dreck, as it trickles into the south over satellite feeds and internet connections, makes the region seem unsafe and "unclean" without its dependence on US intervention, counsel, and surveillance.[37] The Wall, then, as it remaps the south into a disaster area and exclusion zone, confines US citizens to the nation-state's territorial ambit; as Wynden says, "It's like we're imprisoning ourselves." The true monsters in the film therefore seem the airstrikers, Border Patrol agents, and miles of concrete walling that deter the movement of the characters, restrict opportunities for cultural exchange, and condition in them a state of constant disquietude, wastefulness, and unawareness. As Slavoj Žižek writes about such neocolonial situations,

[We] should seriously entertain the possibility that we are approaching a new era of apartheid: one in which secluded parts of the world with an abundance of food and energy are separated from a chaotic outside plagued by widespread turbulence, starvation and permanent war.[38]

Curiously, many of the films from the Cold War-Berlin Wall era, such as *Stalag 17* (Billy Wilder, 1953), *The Great Escape* (John Sturgis, 1963), *The McKenzie Break* (Lamont Johnson, 1970), and *Victory* (John Huston, 1981) acclaim their main characters for attempting to escape their cells and tunnel their way under the fences, watchtowers, and commandant stations of their detention camps—*to break out of them*. The strangeness, or more accurately the monstrousness, of their twenty-first-century counterparts is that, despite their sympathies for nonnationals, despite their declarations otherwise, they want to *break into* the areas the Wall carcerally encloses. However, as *Monsters* shows us, the more a dominant nation-state, such as the United States, renders its neighboring countries abject, the more toxic waste it dumps into them, and the more it secludes its citizens from them, the more its own territories might start to shrink, as the overflow of these substances inevitably seeps, wafts, or somehow finds its way once more into them.

This Is the End

Seth Rogen and Evan Goldberg's *This Is the End* (2013) is a metacinematic raunchy comedy that features a number of the most well-known celebrities of the 2000s spoofing their own star images as they attempt to survive a millenarian version of the apocalypse from the confines of James Franco's mansion. Seth Rogen convinces fellow actor-comedian Jay Baruchel, while on a short visit to Los Angeles, to come to one of Franco's debauches, at which we see several 20-something stars overindulge in drugs, alcohol, sexual misbehavior, manic attention seeking, and other scandalous, narcissistic acts that make the usual fare in the tabloids seem tame in comparison. Jay, though, despises the falsity, smarminess, and self-importance of the Hollywood scene, and feels some resentment toward Seth Rogen, who seems, in contrast, quite taken with it. Obsessing over their careers and the tenuous state of their friendship, neither one of them notices the cable news telecast reporting the strange appearance of a massive sinkhole in Guatemala. However, while at a convenience store, they witness the rapture, the ascension of the virtuous into Heaven; then, after returning to the party, they watch as a similar sinkhole cracks open the Earth, swallowing most of their fellow celebrities and forcing the remaining few to shut themselves inside Franco's mansion. The film thus speaks to its release context, the decade feeling the aftershocks of the Secure Fence Act of 2006, namely the completion of almost 650 miles of steel mesh and slats separating the United States from its southern neighbors and the deportation of more than four hundred thousand immigrants at the close of President Barack Obama's first term.[39] *This Is the End*, with its focus on the shallowness of movie stardom, suggests the theatrical nature rather than the "real" effectivity of these security measures, even as it also dramatizes the extent of their influence on the nation's cultural imaginary.

The US Census Bureau reports that from 2001 to 2009, the number of citizens choosing to reside in walled-in communities—microcosms of the nation-state—rose from seven to eleven million, many of them since 2002 in California.[40] As Wendy Brown notes, "There are walls within walls: Gated communities in the United States have spring up everywhere, but are especially plentiful in Southwestern cities near the wall with Mexico."[41] These walls, whatever their scale, seem a reaction to the fear of terrorists, criminals, and illegal immigrants that Bush, Obama, and then Trump, with their dog-whistle description of the United States as a "nation of laws" first and foremost, were to stoke.[42] Unsurprisingly, then, according to Henry A. Giroux, early adults, such as those in the film, might feel in this climate as though they are under constant siege, as though "few safe spaces" exist for them anymore "unless they are hidden in the gated enclaves and protectorates of the wealthy few."[43] The characters in the film retreat into such an enclave,[44] tellingly from a threat that appears to emanate, as it does in *Monsters*, from Central America. The actors inside the mansion, Jay, Seth, James Franco, Craig Robinson, and Jonah Hill, along with Danny McBride and Emma Watson for a short time, soon realize the magnitude of their situation: once cozily inside such enclaves as the Hollywood Hills, they must now cope with the fact that no more of these safe space communities exist on Earth. They come to share a para-exilic status, in order words, in relation to the film's setting: they remain mostly in the richer districts of Los Angeles, even though they seem unrecognizable as such, indistinguishable from their surrounding vistas and the news footage taken of Guatemala, since the demons who came through the sinkholes set the entire Earth on fire. These well-to-do celebrities, then, in a matter of minutes come to resemble a subpopulation from the most vulnerable of developing countries, rationing their foods, their water supplies, and even their drugs and taking turns at night to watch for marauders. Hell meanwhile extends its sovereign reach across the face of the Earth—the sheer volume of "hard" pollution that appears on-screen after the rift opens up near Franco's estate indicates the demons' thorough occupation of its surfaces. The streets and sidewalks appear full of trash, rubble, car accident wreckage, and the shards of windowpanes, and even the inside of the mansion over the course of a few days comes to seem dirtier, with urine splashing on to its toilet seats and the dining area turning into a mess.

Moreover, the film treats the celebrities in it, or more exactly their star images, as forms of "soft" pollution, an interesting twist considering that critics often describe the crass comedies that Seth Rogen, Jonah Hill, and Danny McBride appear in as *trashy, tasteless forms of entertainment*. The film thus regards most of the members of its star ensemble as trash to throw out from its narrative: for instance, a streetlamp impales Michael Cera; the mansion, set aflame, crushes Jonah Hill; the infernal sinkhole consumes Kevin Hart, Aziz Ansari, and the singer Rihanna; and Danny McBride resorts to cannibalism and devours James Franco. These characters still remain unique in contradistinction to the ordinary Californians who die over the course of the film, whether crowds trample over them or the celebrities accidently decapitate them. This difference consists in the fact that these comedians themselves are responsible for spreading "soft" pollution in the form of vain, meaningless images they seem unable to stop creating, even though no one will ever see them. For example, they detail their silliest thoughts, such as their reaction to the taste of their own urine, in video confessionals, and they create no-budget sequels to some of their most successful movies, such as *Pineapple Express* (David Gordon Green, 2008). Yet their abject condition concerning their useless star reputations and abhorrent material circumstances slowly starts to dawn on them. As the churlish Danny says to Jay, the first of them to witness the rapture and still aspire to rise to Heaven, "If this really is the apocalypse, you're here too. So that means you're just as shitty as the rest of us."

Tamar Jeffers McDonald, discussing the aesthetics of the male-centric romantic comedies of the 2000s, such as Judd Apatow's *The 40-Year-Old Virgin* (2005) and *Knocked Up* (2007), which feature many of these comedians, argues that abject substances, including "excrement, urine and ejaculate," function as "recurring tropes" in them.[45] The "gross out" comedians in *This Is the End* certainly delight in these substances, with Jonah Hill vomiting on-screen, Craig Robinson admitting to drinking urine, James Franco and Danny McBride threatening to cum on each other, and Seth Rogen claiming to shit six times a day while on a cleanse. However, the film upturns these subgenre tropes, as these comedians, in order to enter into Heaven, must come to abjure them—in other words, they must experience a form of de-origination, shedding their affectations and self-entitlement as Hollywood stars. Moving in this direction, though, appears almost too difficult for them, as they cannot seem to think their situation outside of some cinematic reference. The characters thus make mention of such foreboding films as *Terminator 2: Judgment Day* (James Cameron, 1991), *Rosemary's Baby* (Roman Polanski, 1968), and *127 Hours* (Danny Boyle, 2010), and they constantly relate the doomsday scenarios they face to their own ensemble efforts, namely *Superbad* (Greg Mottola, 2007), *Your Highness* (David Gordon Green, 2011), *The Green Hornet* (Michel Gondry, 2011), and the television series *Freaks and Geeks* (Paul Feig, 1999–2000). Also, Emma

Watson mistakes the apocalypse for another "zombie invasion," typical of the Hollywood fare of the new century. Finally, whenever the characters use drugs, they transform the film's visuals and montage design into a music video sequence, complete with fast nonlinear cutting, afterimage effects, splashes of neon color, and a "scratching" technique that rhythmically syncs the images to the soundtrack. These characters, in short, revel in Hollywood's own "soft" pollution, unable to escape it in their mindsets or their diegetic emplacement. Thus they must venture outside the comforts of their stardom, the formulas of their career choices, the navel-gazing of the Los Angeles haut monde, and, most interestingly, the exclusivity of their neighborhoods. Those who cannot remain outside of Heaven: James Franco, after saving the others, warrants admission to it; unfortunately, the star starts to utter obscenities during the rapture, in the usual way of these sorts of comedies, and falls once again to the Earth. Unable to abstain from insulting others or resorting to cringe comedy, Danny McBride foregoes salvation and rounds up a caravan of cannibal nomads, who then eat Franco. Jay, Craig, and Seth, in contrast, after they abandon their mansion redoubt, uncharacteristically muster enough courage and social feeling to save one another from the demons combing the Earth as though they were Border Patrol agents. After their rapture, they see the Pearly Gates, a *wall* of clouds surrounding them and separating those in Heaven from "Hell on Earth" in its abominable, totally abject condition (Figure 4.2).

After Jay and Seth move through this wall, the film confronts its audience with one final irony: *that Heaven is the same as Hollywood*, a risqué party scene that resembles the one at Franco's mansion. They reunite with Craig, conjure marijuana out of thin air, and dance with the Backstreet Boys in another mock music video sequence[46] that reads as a moment of drug euphoria. Much as with the richer California communities or even the fencing along the US southwest, it seems that Heaven screens

FIGURE 4.2 *The Gates of Heaven in* This Is the End.

out undesirables, exiling them in a clear spatio-legible manner from its clean, secure, and opulent milieu. Careful viewers can even discern roller coasters and other amusement rides in its set design, similar to the way one can see Universal Studios or maybe Disneyland from the Hollywood Hills. *This Is the End*, then, does not appear to radically depart from the conventions of the "bromance," in which two or more male friends chase after drugs, women, and nightlife adventure and then come to express mutual affection and a sense of maturity, "saving" one another from the devil-may-care irresponsibility characterizing their time as teenagers or single adults. So the question arises—is this film archconservative, a sly defense of separation walling that makes it seem "Heaven-sent," so to speak? Although the film tempts such a reading, it seems more instructive to recall the words of Jean Renoir, director of such films as *The Lower Depths* (1936), who in an interview with André Bazin thought to describe actors as "burnt offerings" to the cinematic camera, with above-the-line talent sacrificing them on its altar and casting them "into the flames."[47] This metaphor seems to aptly relate to *This Is the End*, in which Seth Rogen, Jay Baruchel, and other creative contributors to the film from "on high" send up or rather immolate their obnoxious star images and the excesses of their Hollywood cohort.

Also, Renoir appears useful for understanding the ending of this film. He argues that the cinema requires a "stable society" to market its films successfully, and therefore must encourage some degree of "faith in social divisions" in order to remain viable as an industry and a means of dramatic scenario-making and critique: "Each work of art contains in fact a morsel of protest. But if this protest turns into destruction, if the system blows up, the possibility of such drama at once vanishes."[48] The makers of *This Is the End* seem aware of these contradictions, reconstituting Hollywood in its final scenes so as to suggest that its sovereign influence on other cultures, markets, and mediaspheres requires it to remain somewhat insular—walled off from them. *One breaks into the film industry, not out.* Nonetheless, the title of the film, we might argue, spells "the end" of Hollywood's specialness, of its self-stylization as a secular Heaven full of stars. The ending nakedly shows us that this classist cult of celebrity feeds off of division and destruction, and that it tends to treat everything on Earth "like Hell" on the condition that it never seriously destabilizes the systems it depends on for its revenue, cultural ascendancy, and air of separateness from more mundane circles. Thus, although taking refuge once more inside a "gated community" might seem another chance at salvation, the ending of the film shows us that it remains akin to the same state of sin that we see in its first act scenes. After all, as Serres reminds us, apropos to this film and the violation of the Earth that security walling symptomatizes, "A God without place, a God of the no-place. Our era's religion begins with this rupture and fragility," even as our culture industries work constantly to make us forget it.[49]

Elysium

Neil Blomkamp's *Elysium* (2013) really takes to an extreme the spatio-legible division of haves and have-nots that state security apparatuses seek to maintain. The film opens with an expository title that reads, "In the late 21st century Earth was diseased, polluted and vastly overpopulated," as the camera tracks over the favelas, torn-apart skyscrapers, and rubble-strewn industrial cityscapes that comprise much of the diegesis. The world's inhabitants—criminals, ex-convicts, and factory shift crews coping with considerable stress and unbearable conditions—suffer from constant ill-treatment from robot street cops, inadequate medical care, and the indifferent responses coming from the artificial intelligence units set up to replace civil servants and other nonprofit workers. The rich management classes, in contrast, retreat to the off-planet Elysium, a space station orbiting the Earth that features ample and charming flora, clean air and water, rows of mansions and similar amenities, and a cutting-edge and rather antiseptic technological infrastructure, complete with machines able to cure any disease, trauma, or toxicological damage instantly.[50] So that the idle rich can sunbathe, throw dinner soirees for their friends, and order about their robot valets, the controllers of Elysium constantly monitor for "undocumented ships" from Earth, either shooting them down or, if they make it to the space station's atmosphere, rounding up the migrants they carry in order to deport them. Outer space, then, comes to function as the ultimate security "wall," separating the upper classes from the abject condition of those stuck on Earth (Figure 4.3).[51]

Étienne Balibar might refer to such a wall as a "superborder" that separates the rich of Elysium from the "death zones" outside of it, enabling them to refine the "methods of extermination," including inducing famine,

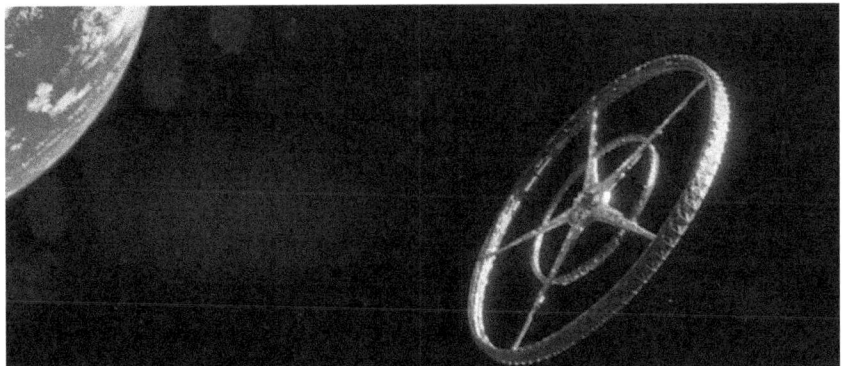

FIGURE 4.3 *The Wall of Outer Space in* Elysium.

rioting, epidemics, and the reproletarization of the masses, that they use against those on Earth.[52] Balibar argues that in these sorts of death zones

> the current mode of production and reproduction has become a mode of *production for elimination*, a reproduction of populations that are not likely to be productively used or exploited but are always already *superfluous*, and therefore can be only eliminated through "political or "natural" means—what some Latin American sociologists provocatively call *poblacion chatarra*, "garbage humans," to be "thrown away," out of the global city.[53]

The film's main character Max De Costa (Matt Damon), in fact, dreams of escaping the English-Spanish-speaking working-class communities of Earth to travel to Elysium,[54] despite a nun's admonition that "that place is not for us"—in other words, for such "garbage humans" as them. A former car thief, Max slaves away at an Armadyne factory manufacturing the weapons, robot anatomics, and defense technologies that enable the rich to maintain their distance from Earth in the first place. This economic scheme thus forces the workers, without decent medical care or educational opportunities, to *monetize their own oppression and perpetuate their own ostracism*. Max and the rest of them, in Balibar's terms, work out the methods of their own extermination. The factory's managers treat them as utterly disposable: for instance, one of them carelessly exposes Max to a deadly dose of radiation after ordering the reluctant ex-convict to unjam the door of a microwave furnace. He coolly dumps Max off at the infirmary, and the medical robot there, after detecting massive organ failure, dispenses a five-day supply of analgesics as "compensation" for the accident. The managerial class thus casts off any semblance of social feeling, since AI machines take on these roles, condescendingly relaying to Max such niceties as "thank you for your service" and other meaningless refrains. Unsurprisingly, Armadyne then releases or, more accurately, "throws away" Max, who stumbles and spills over on to the streets, as though "trash" amidst the rest of the debris that covers them.[55]

To claim a degree of ownership and sovereign control over the Earth, which the rich otherwise deplore and distance themselves from, the administrators of Elysium disperse throughout its ecosphere their waste emissions and industrial fallout. Their actions, of course, result in clear environmental racism, as the multiethnic communities on Earth suffer from illness, crime, overpolicing, and the unhygienic and carcinogenic effects of the "hard" pollution of their surroundings.[56] These communities moreover register the effects of "soft" pollution, the constant din of car audio in them, for example, a corollary to the equally constant drone of voice-over threats, reminders, and instructions coming from the speaker systems in the Armadyne factories. This thorough artificialization of the Earth's natural and symbolic realities suggests the steep technical-economic costs Elysium demands; therefore, in the words of Balibar, the film shows us that the Earth, "with its immediate environment and the life it supports, has become a single 'system' in which flows of information, energy, and matter influence one another."[57] These forces shape the Earth into an enormous death zone, as they work to maintain uneven resource distribution, concentrate authority in a corporate-military elite class, and reduce such individuals as Max to a state of "nonright," without the entitlements of citizenship or any real stakes in the creation of new wealth, technologies, or security instruments.[58] The sovereign claims of Elysium that result from its defilement of the Earth and its contempt for the "garbage humans" on it, though, take on an even more insidious and near-totalistic cast.

Max's fatal accident incenses the foreman at Armadyne, since "organic tissue" might contaminate the microwave chamber. Human flesh, in an obscene reversal of our usual understanding of environmental safety, comes to resemble in this film a form of a "hard" pollution that threatens to disturb the equilibrium of the sector that manufactures the weapons technologies and cybernetics commodities that Elysium outsources from the Earth. Moreover, the constant and sometimes clandestine information flows that enable its security forces to "wall" Elysium off from migrant caravans might also constitute a form of "soft" pollution that exposes those it corrupts to extreme danger. Jessica Delacourt (Jodie Foster), the defense secretary of Elysium, seeks to take control of the entire space station, convincing John Carlyle (William Fichtner), the CEO of Armadyne, to receive a series of "cerebral uploads" containing data that can override its security mechanisms, encryption schemes, and citizenship recognition devices. However, these uploads turn Carlyle into mere "organic information," the target of the migrant smugglers on Earth and such mercenaries as Kruger (Sharlto Copley), a sleeper agent of Delacourt who also wants to seize control of Elysium. Max extracts the data after shooting down Carlyle's ship and watching the man die in a subsequent firefight. This data, though, at first appears useless without the correct user-identification and input codes, so Max flees with it to Los Angeles, attempting to escape detection from Kruger's surveillance drones. These sequences suggest the all-pervasiveness of Elysium's sovereign reach, since its security apparatus can contaminate even the nervous tissue of those on Earth with excess information sets, making their flesh unimportant next to the "software" it carries. *Even these characters' bodies and brains, in short, are able to be polluted.*

The situation thus seems even direr than in the first act, with Max still dying of radiation sickness, Kruger abducting the film's romantic interest Frey Santiago (Alice Braga), and Delacourt setting the stage for a coup in order to further militarize the superborder separating the Earth from the natural splendors and technological advancements of Elysium. One of the smugglers says that Max's only option then is to discover "a way out," a colloquialism for some form of de-origination that promises in turn to radicalize Elysium's relation to the Earth. The smugglers outfit Max with a robotic exoskeleton[59] capable of feats of tremendous strength, as well as augmenting its wearers' quickness, agility, somatomotor skill set, and electrophysical response to external events through its direct interfacing with their neurological systems. The smugglers, in other words, take an abject corpselike victim of corporate ruthlessness, environmental neglect, and celestial apartheidism and transform this man into *an object of value*,[60] a cyborg who appears the equal in combat situations to the robot cops stalking the streets of Los Angeles, to Delacourt's sleeper cells, and to Armadyne's weapons developments. The smugglers effectively remap the conditions of Max's sense of embodiment and self; this first instance of de-origination enables them all to start taking steps toward transforming Elysium's exploitative relation to the Earth. Alberto Toscano and Jeff Kinkle might describe the decolonial nature of their mission as a "negotiation" of a diegetic universe fraught with "difference and disconnection."[61] Their awareness of these contradictions enables such characters as Max to develop the intentionality and the means to dedifferentiate themselves from their toxic environs, to *automate themselves* rather than their social supports (i.e., robot servants, medical droids, etc.) so that they can deal squarely with the truth that the causes of their abjection come from "elsewhere"—namely, in the acts of "extraction, dispossession, and subjugation" that Elysium inflicts on them from off-planet, from across the wall of outer space.[62]

Max must finally travel to the space station with the mercenaries in order to access the reboot intel in Carlyle's cerebral data files and, as the smuggler that marshals in the resistance says, use it to "open the borders" and "make anyone a citizen of Elysium." Max, in short, must assume a para-exilic relation to the Earth. He must further confer the same status on the men, women, and children stuck there so that they all come to *belong on* the space station, even if they choose to remain off of it, rather than *belong to* the military-industrial forces that already control it. After rescuing Frey and also disposing of Delacourt, Kruger, and the other mercenaries, Max enables the illegal migrants to storm Elysium and overthrow these forces. Only these migrants, made up of members of the diverse multilingual communities on Earth, appear able to re-democratize the film's sociopolitical world-system and its economic and technological distribution chains. Although Max dies in the course of the action in the film's climactic set pieces, these migrant commandos nonetheless manage to infiltrate the suburbs and tap into a central computer, uploading the reboot files so as to deactivate Elysium's defenses, reprogram the robot security teams to desist in their violence, and dispatch shuttles to carry those on Earth en masse to the space station so that they can take advantage of its superior medical equipment and creature comforts. *Elysium* thus suggests the counterhegemonic thrust of reversing the terms of Serres's arguments: usually, a sovereign state externalizes its waste substances to other territories in order to claim some authority over them and mark them as "foreign," inferior, irresponsible, and unsafe to travel to for its own citizens. In this film, though, Max and the other characters claim these waste substances as their own, recycling them, repurposing them, and even using them to refashion the capacities of their flesh, so as to then *attach these claims* to Elysium and Armadyne, the "elsewheres" responsible for churning out most of this refuse. These characters turn into cyber-thieves and cyborgs—audaciously making a virtue of their status as "garbage humans" through and through—to muster up the wherewithal to cross the superborder and trace these scraps to the fine dining table they come from, only so that they can finally take their seat at it.

Black Panther

One of the most remarkable moments in Ryan Coogler's *Black Panther* (2018) occurs when the title superhero's rocket ship flies into the airspace of the fictive nation of Wakanda, deep within the African interior. The mise-en-scène at first appears a vast undulant savanna, until it flickers out, after T'Challa (Chadwick Boseman), the alter ego of Black Panther and absolute monarch of Wakanda, deactivates this false front so that its Afrofuturist cities come into view, its architecture ultramodern, its transportation system efficient and convenient, and its technological infrastructure much more complex than that of First World nations. The illusion of the savanna is one of the effects of the force dome that surrounds Wakanda and allows it to thrive in the face of the threats of the transatlantic slave trade, colonialist exploitation, and the Boko Haram-like outfits that traffic women, children, and workers under the canopies of the forests of the region (Figure 4.4).

FIGURE 4.4 *The Force Dome Surrounding and Concealing Wakanda in* Black Panther.

This sequence, of course, works to counter stereotypical representations of the continent, from *Tarzan the Ape Man* (W. S. Van Dyke, 1932) to *The African Queen* (John Huston, 1951) to *Gorillas in the Mist* (Michael Apted, 1988), as no more than a series of endless deserts, tropical wilds, and rolling veldts full of exotic animals and overgrown flora. However, in this same sequence the film does more than offer up a counterimage to the ones in such films: the force dome moreover constitutes a security wall that separates Wakanda from its neighboring countries, as well as the African wilderness.[63] The film's introduction, in fact, recounts some of the reasons for the nation's isolationism, including its exploitation of the deposits of an almost indestructible metal originating from a meteorite that struck Wakanda millennia ago:

> The Wakandans used vibranium to develop technology more advanced than any other nation. But as Wakanda thrived, the world around it descended further into chaos. To keep the vibranium safe, the Wakandans vowed to hide in plain sight, keeping the truth of their power from the outside world.

The film, during this sequence, shows the warriors of the five tribes of Wakanda interlocking their fists, an apt metaphor for the *power* of the force shields circumscribing the nation-state.

The dome, in masking the "truth" of the nation with a stereotype meant to fool outsiders, thus shunts the conception of Africa as a continent full of danger, misspent resources, and social disarray to the outside of the Wakandan nation-state. A news reporter somewhat misdescribes the nation: "Though it remains one of the poorest countries in the world, fortified by mountain ranges and an impenetrable rainforest, Wakanda does not engage in international trade or accept aid." T'Challa uses this force dome to conceal the nation's reserves of vibranium from colonial interlopers, and also to isolate Wakanda from the shortages, destitution, corruption, and conflicts that afflict other African countries. Much as with the US marginalization of the migrant caravans and the constant streams of tweets disparaging them, T'Challa's nation emits a form of "soft pollution"—the image of Africa as *backwards and uncivilized*—so that it can accumulate its riches, control its immigration flows, finance further technological research, and maintain its intertribal unity, cultural self-identity, and considerable standards of comfort. Therefore, the film's first action scene features T'Challa in the vibranium armor of Black Panther stopping machine gun-toting slavers from trafficking, as though they were coyotes, a cargo of captive women outside the dome border of Wakanda.

The rest of the film, though, does not take place on the outskirts of this nation, as it follows the superhero's efforts to track down a museum artifact that the arms dealer Ulysses Klaue (Andy Serkis) and mercenary accomplice Erik "Killmonger" Stevens (Michael B. Jordan) stole from a London exhibit. Attempting to sell the artifact to the CIA, Klaue tells agent Everett Ross (Martin Freeman) that Wakanda's international reputation as a techno-primitive "Third World country" is a subterfuge; as T'Challa says, in response to the establishment of "foreign aid" and "refugee programs," "We are not like these other countries ... If the world found out what we truly are, what we possess, we could lose our way of life." The artifact, then, represents another decoy of sorts, an example of the "hard pollution" that Wakanda emplaces throughout the world's metropolitan centers to maintain its wealth, security, cultural traditions, and sovereign disposition free from outside interference or calls from fellow African nation-states for more equitable resource distribution. Thus the artifact—disposable rubbish to T'Challa's nation, an object of value and fascination to "First World" dilettantes—seems analogous to the container of Coca-Cola in *The Gods Must Be Crazy* (Jamie Uys, 1980), a film about a San adventurer carrying it to the God's Window escarpment in South Africa to throw it over the cliff to the deities after it causes conflict among the tribe. *Black Panther*, through its own representation of such "hard pollution," reverses the Eurocentrism of this earlier film. Still, the squalor, tawdriness, and incidence of crime in *Black Panther*'s other settings, whether the rainforest, the casino district of South Korea, or Oakland, California, the city Killmonger comes from, mark them as abject to some degree in comparison to Wakanda's cleanliness, technological sophistication, and relatively safe border situation.

The real thrust of the film is to move T'Challa outside the walls of Wakanda so that the character, after coming into close contact with the abject, with what one court official refers to as the unhappiness, suffering, and impoverishment of those "out there," can start to rethink the nation's isolationist stance. Peter Ndaita contends that immigration "uproots Africans from their immediate society and usual rhythm of life," effectively moving them from the experience of "an enchanted world to a disenchanted one."[64] As T'Challa's cousin, it turns out, Killmonger can challenge for the throne and the Black Panther mantle and does so, winning them in one-on-one combat. T'Challa, in a state of disgrace and on the verge of death, must flee to the Jabari, a renegade tribe, to implore their chieftain for sanctuary and medical relief. He thus assumes a para-exilic status: although still a member of the nation-state, T'Challa now appears unwelcome in it, an anomalous "citizen-outsider" that narrative circumstances consign to its margins. T'Challa, in short, must undergo a degree of de-origination in order to solicit military support from the rival tribe; retake the throne from Killmonger, who intends to arm the world's subaltern classes so that they can murder their oppressors; and take an alternate course, opening Wakanda to international trade, cross-cultural cooperation and understanding, and foreign assistance initiatives.[65] Leading the Jabari against the regular armies of Wakanda, T'Challa once more engages Killmonger in combat, the two of them wearing vibranium Black Panther costumes and tearing at each other with their claws and other weapons. After T'Challa wins the contest, Killmonger concedes defeat and commits suicide rather than face arrest and imprisonment.

Throughout the film, T'Challa comes to terms with the conditions of redlining, class inequality, institutional racism, and nationalist militarism that made Eric Stevens "Killmonger," a soldier of fortune and a mass murderer whose flesh shows forth numerous ritual scars, each one meant to commemorate a successful assassination. T'Challa's time with the Jabari and new consciousness of racial-class struggle overseas compel the superhero to reveal Wakanda's true economic, technological, and near-utopian standing to the United Nations. He vows to depower the force dome and the false front that it effects in a speech in the film's denouement:

> For the first time in our history, we will be sharing our knowledge and resources with the outside world. Wakanda will no longer watch from the shadows. We cannot. We must not. We will work to be an example of how we, as brothers and sisters on this Earth, should treat each other. Now, more than ever, the illusions of division threaten our very existence. We all know the truth. More connects us than separates us. But in times of crisis, the wise build bridges, while the foolish build barriers. We must find a way to look after one another, as if we were one single tribe.

As a first measure, T'Challa travels to Oakland, intending to transform the tenement districts Killmonger came from into a research institute, cultural outreach center, and scientific education site for the neighborhood's children. Thus, in offering foreign assistance to the US's inner cities (as though they were developing nations), T'Challa extends Wakanda's sovereign influence into extra-national territories. The superhero turns the tables on the Global North, doing to it what it does to those nations dependent on it for financial support—in flooding them with its symbolic and material excesses, it can claim a degree of ownership over them, as though they were all "one single tribe."

The next film in the Marvel Cinematic Universe transmedia franchise, *Avengers: Infinity War* (Anthony and Joe Russo, 2018), tests T'Challa's commitment to open borders. The cosmic menace Thanos (Josh Brolin) comes to Earth to complete the Infinity Gauntlet, a weapon consisting of six Stones that can manipulate time, matter, energy, and reality. A detachment of the Avengers arrives in Wakanda to ask for their top scientists' assistance in removing the Mind Stone, the final component of the Gauntlet, from the robotic superhero the Vision (Paul Bettany). Thanos sends a throng of alien monsters to attack the nation, forcing T'Challa to reactivate the force dome and confine them to the forests outside its walls. The aliens, in turn, swarm together and attempt to muscle their way through the dome, many of them dying so that a few of them can strike out at the superheroes and also the nation's armies. Their actions distress Black Panther, who decides to disable the force shields once more.[66] He therefore comes to terms with another consequence of security walling, that it can *induce the self-destruction* of those it excludes, an outcome the superhero cannot in clear conscience accept as a reasonable deterrent or military defense. The sequence forecasts the surge of immigrants in 2018—Trump describing them as alien invaders—trying to clamber over separation walls, to dig underneath them, and to even risk impalement atop them to enter the United States, rather than wait out the inordinate amount of time it takes to receive asylum at official visa and customs offices. More interestingly, though, this sequence sets forth another negative consequence of security walls and the reckless or self-destructive impulses they can engender in those desperate to enter into a nation-state for work, refuge, or malicious reasons.

These walls, whether they falter or collapse, *miscarry in their theatrical function* if they admit the return of the trash, toxins, excess noise, or "foreign" individuals into the domains that they enclose—domains meant to conceal the environmental corruption of other national territories or wilderness areas. Black Panther, alongside the Avengers and Wakandans, mows down the aliens in droves, scattering their corpses about the war zone and thus confronting the "clean and proper" nation-state with the fact that these most abject of creatures *are too its own*, the result of its methods of national defense. The superheroes then take the fight into the forests on the edges of the force dome, until Thanos arrives to rip the Mind Stone away from the Vision, use the Gauntlet to obliterate much of the universe, and teleport to a distant star to escape the remaining superheroes. (On a similar note, experts warn that nation-state walling cannot deter immigrants, coyotes, or terrorists from using drones or airplanes in the future to "teleport" over these sorts of security measures.[67]) The failure of the force dome to discourage the alien invasion or stop Thanos from disintegrating T'Challa and some of the other superheroes, though, does not necessarily spell the Marvel Cinematic Universe's outright disenchantment with these security apparatuses. Although the narrative arc of *Black Panther* moves toward the opening of the nation-state and *Avengers: Infinity War* toward its closing, these two films do not represent two opposing viewpoints concerning the issue of security walling in the first decades of the twenty-first century so much as they sublate them. The Wakandans, after all, can toggle the force dome on and off, making them able to welcome visitors and manage refugee flows on the one hand, and able to obstruct the movement of invaders or interlopers on the other. These films therefore appear more ambivalent about the usefulness of security walls than simply dismissive of them, more thoughtful than facile in their depiction of their strengths and shortcomings. If anything, T'Challa and the other Wakandans, in their construction of an *activatable border barrier*, one that they can raise when the situation demands, show forth far more imagination than Trump in addressing issues of immigration, national defense, resource reallocation, and environmental stewardship. Moreover, the dome, unlike its steel and concrete counterparts, does not shut its citizens in, if ever a national crisis emerges so serious that it forces them to assume a para-exilic status outside its walls.

Ready Player One

Umberto Eco attributes the appeal of *Casablanca* (Michael Curtiz, 1942) to its transgeneric structure, to its interweaving of the formulas of the war film, crime film, adventure film, spy thriller, romantic drama, musical, and newsreel: "*Casablanca* became a cult movie because it is not *one* movie. It is 'movies.'"[68] Correspondingly, then, we might describe Steven Spielberg's *Ready Player One* (2018), a film that incorporates figures from such anime as *Akira*, *Speed Racer*, and *Mobile Suit Gundam*; such comics as *Batman*, *Spawn*, and *Teenage Mutant Ninja Turtles*; such video games as *Halo*, *BioShock*, *Tomb Raider*, *Starcraft*, *Street Fighter*, *Mass Effect*, and *Duke Nukem*; and such film and television series as *Alien*, *Star Wars*, *Star Trek*, *Robocop*, *King Kong*, *Godzilla*, *Jurassic Park*, *A Nightmare on Elm Street*, *Back to the Future*, *Friday the 13th*, *The A-Team*, *Doctor Who*, and *Battlestar Galactica* into its diegesis, in similar terms: "*Ready Player One* is not *one* transmedia franchise. It is 'transmedia franchises.'"[69] The film follows the adventures of Parzival (Tye Sheridan), Art3mis (Olivia Cooke), and the members of the High Five: the avatars of teenager Wade Watts and friends who use virtual reality equipment to escape from their drab slum existence, as they navigate the OASIS, a set of simulacral environments that resemble those from films, such as *The Shining* (Stanley Kubrick, 1980); television cartoons, such as *Voltron*; and video games, such as Nintendo's *Rad Racer* or PlayStation's *Burnout*. They race against the forces of CEO Nolan Sorranto (Ben Mendelsohn) of Innovative Online Industries—note that the initials of the corporation essentially consist of zeroes and ones—in order to acquire a special Easter egg, a secret design feature in an interactive text, that will enable them to take control of the entire OASIS, assume contractual ownership of it, and set forth new rules for its use. The characters thus reenact the activity of its viewers, as the film tasks them to search for Easter eggs throughout it, from one scene to the next identifying the iconic figures, virtual spaces, and diegetic indicia of several major transmedia franchises. Tracking the cameo appearances of these cultural icons, which appear on-screen without much narrative motivation, comes to overshadow the usual activities of the viewer: mentally stitching together the storyline, deducing the moral alignments of the characters, making sense of the action in relation to the McGuffin, or anticipating the romantic coupling of Parzival and Art3mis. To fully "get" the film, in other words, it seems as though we must concentrate more on its throwaway references to other media titles than its compositional structures, representational choices, or ideological subtexts.

Ready Player One, in sum, occurs in two worlds that nonetheless mirror each other: the "real" Columbus, Ohio, slums that Watts and the other characters inhabit in 2045 and the OASIS, the cyberspace domain that animates the corporate signifiers and mediatic touchpoints that set up the true stage of their social interactions. The importance of the OASIS for these slum residents, as they cope with their daily disappointments, the indignities of their condition, and the crampedness of their environs, is that it affords them *additional geographies* to explore, allowing them to *practice their overcoming* of the (fire)walls that state and corporate rule demands. The promise of these additional geographies comes to seem vital to the characters in the film, since, in each of the worlds they traverse, they encounter all-pervading forms of pollution. The Columbus slums, for example, feature stacks of wreckage—empty shells of vans, trailers, and recreational vehicles atop metal trellises—that the residents use as makeshift apartment complexes, outfitting them with water tanks, satellite dishes, and terrace decks to make them somewhat inhabitable. Some of the first images we see of these "stacks" include digital signboards advertising the newest distractions of the OASIS, a drone delivering a Pizza Hut order to one of Watts's neighbors, and dirty streets full of rubbish, oil drums, and stripped-down cars. Hard pollution coming from the industrial cityscape and electronics corporations, such as IOI and Gregarious Games, the firm responsible for inventing the OASIS, compels the residents to escape into its cyber-fantasies, as we see them with their VR visors indulging in online acts of fighting, stripping, surfing, and, in Watts's case, running. The city's abject condition, then, ensures that its citizens invest their time, resources, and collective energies in these companies' interface, software, and mechanic upgrade commodities, thus extending the scope of their sociopolitical influence, their domination of the market, and their sway over their consumers. The slums also contrast with the clean, antiseptic research and multiplayer VR facilities of IOI, making the corporate site identifiable with the notion of ownership in that it disavows its own waste, channeling it into the sectors of the city that most avidly consume its merchandise. IOI does so in order to define and delimit its "own and proper" spaces against and away from this "outside."

As Watts says, stepping onto a treadmill to enter the OASIS, "These days, reality is a bummer. Everyone is looking for a way to escape, [for] a place where the limits of reality are your own imagination." Not quite, though, as a mishmash of mass media icons constitutes most of this virtual environment. As Parzival, Watts, along with Art3mis, chase after one of the "hidden keys" across a racetrack set close to a simulation of the Manhattan skyline, encountering such obstacles as the T-Rex from *Jurassic Park* (Steven Spielberg, 1993) and King Kong. Each time one of the virtual cars in the sequence crashes, coins scatter through the air in the style of the *Sonic the Hedgehog* video games. Then, at a virtual dance club, Parzival and Art3mis disco dance, as in *Saturday Night Fever* (John Badham, 1977), and embrace in midair in the manner of the sex scene in *The Lawnmower Man* (Brett Leonard, 1992), while avatars that resemble comics characters the Joker and Harley Quinn watch from the sidelines. The OASIS, then, in each of these sequences, contains as much "pollution" as the slums, only of the "soft" variety. The characters in it style their avatars, weapons, vehicles, and social exchanges after the movies, cartoons, and television shows they watch, the comics they thumb through, the toylines they collect, and the video games they complete. The characters, in other words, run, shoot, and trickjump their way through an excess of corporate copyrights, a scrapheap of the same media signs, figures, images, and emblems that constantly appear in the "real" space of Columbus on the electronic signboards near the stacks. IOI, Gregarious Games, and their competitors continue to capitalize on these stand-alone and transmedia titles, extending their reach through them into the audiovisual, mnemonic, and neuro-haptic registers of the film's VR users. These companies *sell* the OASIS as an escape from the miseries, discontent, and squalor that they spawn, and then riddle this virtual environment with another form of waste, namely signifiers from older, sometimes dormant media franchises that nonetheless still capture the desires, fantasies, and memories of the film's characters. Therefore these companies, with a financial stake in the OASIS, come to "own" the residents of Columbus, in a sense, as they turn their tastes, dreams, self-images, and creative remixing into a nonstop revenue stream, insofar as they remain dependent on their VR sensors, controllers, and motion trackers.

The VR users in *Ready Player One*, then, occupy a para-exilic status in relation to each of these worlds. Suffering from dire economic and sociopolitical disfranchisement in the Columbus stacks, they escape into a digital existence that offers them a chance to re-present themselves as more creative, agentive, and self-determinative, even though the state authorities and technocrats continue to rule these material and online domains. However, the OASIS only really confronts them with a simulacralization of the conditions of these social, economic, and material realities: they face competition from other users for the Easter egg, they collect coins to demonstrate their self-worth, and they style themselves in the idiom of the culture industries, taking their faces, clothing, and accessories from familiar mass media images. As Frederick Wasser argues, Spielberg's twenty-first-century films critique the atomization characteristic of the digital age, the fact that mobile electronic devices often "keep people separate from others in the same space," so that only scenarios of "overwhelming destruction" seem able to redress their alienation—from themselves, from their socius, and from the means of media creation, expression, and control.[70] One of the major narrative events in the film underlines the para-exilic relation of the main characters to the OASIS, casting into relief the speciousness of their mastery of its internal dynamics, user interfaces, and video game mechanics, as well as the fact that they must throw themselves into the online world's most violent scenarios in order to experience a degree of collective action that seems quite unimaginable to those worn down in the "real" slums of Ohio.

Sorrento casts a spell to activate the Orb of Osuvox, so as to use it to encircle the Castle Anorak on Planet Doom with a force dome and stop Parzival, the High Five, and their allies from accessing the final challenge to unlock the Easter egg. More than casually referencing *Voltron*, the incantation from *Excalibur* (John Boorman, 1981), and the icosahedron die from *Dungeons & Dragons*, this scene accents the inequalities in resources, information, and social influence that separate IOI executives from the main characters, who must therefore ask some of their teammates to risk arrest in infiltrating the corporation's "real" facilities in order to sabotage its data requisition servers, deactivate the Orb, and shut down the force shields (Figure 4.5). Until then, Parzival's forces must remain outside the walls of the castle, allowing IOI's stooges to attempt to crack the code of the final challenge in the meantime. The users thus appear abject, cast out, in each of the two worlds of the film. Tellingly, the shape of these users' VR headsets resembles that of the force dome[71] that for a time obstructs their movement, excludes them from informatic domains, and denies them a chance at coownership of the OASIS. Therefore, the VR "walls" that atomize these characters, cutting them off from direct social interaction, must come down, as must their counterparts in the OASIS that encase Castle Anorak. The High Five crosses over into the material and digital territories that IOI owns, reintroducing into these "clean and distinct" spaces an element of

FIGURE 4.5 *The Orb of Osuvox in* Ready Player One.

the abject—the slum-dwellers whom they disavow and distance themselves from—so that what occurs "Outside" the OASIS comes to affect what occurs "Inside" it and vice versa.

After the High Five successfully force their way into IOI and then Castle Anorak, Parzival solves the final challenge, attains the Easter egg, and meets the OASIS's inventor, James Halliday (Mark Rylance). He turns over ownership of the entire system to Wade Watts, much as the title character in *Willy Wonka & the Chocolate Factory* (Mel Stuart, 1971) turns over the entire confectionary to the similarly waifish Charlie Bucket.[72] More interestingly, though, Halliday suggests to Parzival that the surest way to overcome redlining and security (fire)walling is *to adopt an even more thoroughgoing para-exilic relation to them*. Parzival asks Halliday an important question in their final exchange:

Parzival: Mr. Halliday, something I don't understand ... You're not an avatar, are you?
Halliday: No.
Parzival: Is Halliday really dead?
Halliday: Yes.
Parzival: Then what are you?
Halliday: Goodbye, Parzival. Thanks. Thanks for playing my game.

More than quoting the final words of Nintendo's *Super Mario World*, their dialogue challenges viewers to do more than search for shallow references or "Easter eggs" in the film, in that it forces them to think, "What is Halliday really?" The answer, though, demands more than speculation about mental emulation or cognitive uploading; it must rather first and foremost come to terms with the fact that the inventor undergoes a consummate form of de-origination. Halliday seems unable to return to the film's concrete urban spaces and also does not choose to enter the war zones, racetracks, and other digital sandboxes of the OASIS, opting to reside in a domain *at once inside and outside them*, inaccessible to its users, owners, designers, and developers. He inspires Watts to reeducate its users to imitate this para-exilic relation to these two worlds. As the new overseer of the OASIS, Watts decides to deactivate the system twice a week so that users can reacquaint themselves with their material circumstances, seek out more direct friendships and romantic encounters, and finally come together to address systemic reasons for violence and injustice, rather than to engage in some destructive scenario. The final shot shows Wade Watts and Samantha Cook, not their avatars Parzival and Art3mis, embracing in an apartment, not in a virtual nightclub, in a rebuilt section of the stacks. *Ready Player One*, in these moments, makes the "real," rather than an elaborate series of media references or intergeneric codes, the true cult object. The film invites us to assume a para-exilic relation to the security walls that we might encounter in the "real world" so that we maneuver to remain outside of them, shifting from material to digital space as we explore ways to effectively resist them, undermine them, and shut them down.

Conclusion

Each of these films, in their respective ways, illustrate some of the conclusions that Serres draws, specifically the notion that the current world-system "forces us to change our methods of appropriation," since we "*can no longer enclose a piece of land*. This could be done only in the old space that was easily mapped. We no longer live there."[73] The main characters in these films enter into para-exilic relation with certain nation-states, dominions, or communities that shut them out from their territorial markers, forcing them outside the security walls, fences, or domes that enclose them. True to Serres's contentions, though, these characters act to circumvent these apparatuses, ultimately to remap, redefine, or make more multilateral the economic, sociopolitical, demographic, or ecological complexion of interstate relations as they smuggle their cross-cultural experiences into their countries of origin. These characters often suffer the same tribulations as migrants do in their attempts to reenter the United States or another nation-state. Collaterally, they demonstrate that dumping waste into neighboring countries might eventually result in the offending nation ceding some of its own territory to them, as these toxins return to it, affecting its soil, air quality, and water supplies. Or these characters might cross some superborder—fighting their way into outer space or the afterlife—to set forth new citizenship agendas in the face of the continual defilement of the ecosphere from military outfits, industrial sectors, or mass media corporations. Finally, some of these films attempt to strike a counterbalance of state security concerns with free, open transnational exchange and movement, conceiving of walls that administrators can toggle on or off and virtual communities that resist corporate attempts to acquire information spaces, regulate them, secure them, and thus transform them into closed-source systems. The arc of these films, with their characters finding themselves outside their countries and anxious to return to them, confront their domestic audiences with a simple, although valuable, question: *How would you like it if you were the migrant*? Although these films raise such questions in order to dramatize and critique the effects of walling on citizens and noncitizens alike concerning their safety, travel rights, and environmental wellness, they also conceive of the diegetic areas outside their characters' native countries as spaces to escape from, rather than relocate to or rehabilitate. The final chapter, then, examines a set of films that envision more intersectional spaces, as the characters in them come together from different cultural, regional, ethnoracial, and even species denominations to forge connections that defy the top-down decision-making, institutional classism, and xenophobic small-mindedness of their respective nation-states.

Notes

1. See David Agren, "Who Is Organizing This Latest Migrant Caravan and Other Questions You Might Have," *USA Today*, October 24, 2018, https://www.usatoday.com/story/news/world/2018/10/24/migrant-caravan/1747721002/; David Agren and Amanda Hulpuch, "Where Is the Migrant Caravan from—and What Will Happen to It at the Border?" *The Guardian*, October 24, 2018, https://www.theguardian.com/us-news/2018/oct/24/caravan-migrants-what-is-it-where-from-guatemala-honduras-immigrants-mexico; and Annie Correal and Megan Specia, "The Migrant Caravan: What to Know about the Thousands Traveling North," *New York Times*, October 26, 2018, https://www.nytimes.com/2018/10/26/world/americas/what-is-migrant-caravan-facts-history.html.

2. See Donald J. Trump (@realDonaldTrump), "A big new Caravan is heading up to our Southern Border from Honduras. Tell Nancy and Chuck that a drone flying around will not stop them. Only a Wall will work. Only a Wall, or Steel Barrier, will keep our Country safe! Stop playing political games and end the Shutdown!" *Twitter*, January 15, 2019, 7:37 a.m., https://twitter.com/realdonaldtrump/status/ 1085154110108848128?lang=en.

3. See Donald J. Trump (@realDonaldTrump), "Many Gang Members and some very bad people are mixed into the Caravan heading to our Southern Border. Please go back, you will not be admitted into the United States unless you go through the legal process. This is an invasion of our Country and our Military is waiting for you!" *Twitter*, October 29, 2018, 10:41 a.m., https://twitter.com/realdonaldtrump/status/ 1056919064906469376?lang=en.

4. See Joel Rose, Carrie Kahn, and Kelsey Snell, "Trumps Tweets on 'Caravans' Crossing the Border, Annotated," *NPR*, April 2, 2018, https://www.npr.org/2018/04/02/598781060/trumps-tweets-on-caravans-crossing-the-border-annotated; Seung Min Kim and Missy Ryan, "Trump Says He Wants to 2,000 to 4,000 National Guard Troops to Mexican Border," *Washington Post*, April 5, 2018, https://www.washingtonpost.com/politics/trump-says-he-wants-to-send-2000-to-4000-national-guard-troops-to-mexican-border/2018/04/05/bab01f6a-391a-11e8-8fd2-49fe3c675a89_story.html; Billy Perrigo, "Trump Threatens to Cut Off Foreign Aid over Migrant Caravan," *Time*, October 22, 2018, https://time.com/5430841/trump-foreign-aid-migrant-caravan/; Clare Lombardo, "U.S. Agents Spray Tear Gas at Migrants, Briefly Close Tijuana Border Entry," *NPR*, November 25, 2018, https://www.npr.org/2018/11/25/670687806/u-s-agents-spray-tear-gas-at-migrants-briefly-close-tijuana-border-entry; Juan Montes, Santiago Pérez, and Robbie Whelan, "U.S. Border Patrol Uses Tear Gas to Disperse Migrant Caravan," *Wall Street Journal*, November 26, 2018, https://www.

wsj.com/articles/u-s-border-patrol-uses-tear-gas-to-disperse-migrant-caravan-1543244902; Alex Horton, "Why Tear Gas, Lobbed at Migrants on the Southern Border, Is Banned in Warfare," *Washington Post*, November 27, 2018, https://www.washingtonpost.com/national-security/2018/11/26/why-tear-gas-lobbed-migrants-southern-border-is-banned-warfare/; and Miriam Jordan, "Trump Threatens Tariffs on Mexico. Have Any of Hid Immigration Measures Worked?" *New York Times*, May 31, 2019, https://www.nytimes.com/2019/05/31/us/border-tariffs-trump-immigration.html.

5   See Tucker Higgins, "Trump Declares without Evidence that 'Criminals and Unknown Middle Easterners Are Mixed in' with Migrant Caravan Making Its Way from Honduras," *CNBC*, October 22, 2018, https://www.cnbc.com/2018/10/22/trump-says-unknown-middle-easterners-are-mixed-in-migrant-caravan.html; John Wagner, "Across Five Tweets, Trump Makes a Meandering Case for Border Wall Funding," *Washington Post*, December 11, 2018, https://www.washingtonpost.com/politics/across-five-tweets-trump-makes-a-meandering-case-for-border-wall-funding/2018/12/11/8ea6ad64-fd35-11e8-862a-b6a6f3ce8199_story.html; and "Remarks by President Trump in Meeting with Senate Minority Leader Chuck Schumer and House Speaker-Designate Nancy Pelosi," *WhiteHouse.gov*, December 11, 2018, https://www.whitehouse.gov/briefings-statements/remarks-president-trump-meeting-senate-minority-leader-chuck-schumer-house-speaker-designate-nancy-pelosi/.

6   See Alan Gomez, "Central American Migrants Keep Heading toward USA, Even as Trump Focuses on Stopping Caravans," *USA Today*, January 9, 2019, https://www.usatoday.com/story/news/politics/ 2019/01/09/migrant-caravan-trump-crackdown-has-not-slowed-flow-families-us/2523034002/.

7   See Leyla Santiago, "Caravan of Migrants Climbs Freight Train for the Next Leg of the Journey," *CNN*, April 15, 2018, https://www.cnn.com/2018/04/14/americas/central-america-migrant-caravan-train/index.html; Catherine E. Shoichet and Leyla Santiago, "The Migrant Caravan Is Still Coming. Trump Says Don't Let Them In," *CNN*, April 25, 1018, https://www.cnn.com/2018/04/20/us/migrant-caravan-border-arrival-next-steps/index.html; Leyla Santiago and Catherine E. Shoichet, "Trump Says Caravan Migrants Are Turning Back. Mexico Says Most Are Still at the Border," *CNN*, December 11, 2018, https://www.cnn.com/2018/12/11/americas/mexico-caravan-trump/index.html; Jeff Mason and Makini Brice, "Trump Says He Is Seriously Looking at Ending Birthright Citizenship," *Reuters*, August, 21, 2019, https://www.reuters.com/article/us-usa-immigration-trump/trump-says-he-is-seriously-looking-at-ending-birthright-citizenship-idUSKCN1VB21B; and Laura Powers, "Trump's Acting Immigration Director Claims Ending Birthright Citizenship Would Not Require Constitutional Amendment," *Newsweek*, October 16, 2019, https://www.newsweek.com/trumps-acting-immigration-director-claims-ending-birthright-citizenship-would-not-require-1465728.

8   See Rafael Carranza, "Migrants' Makeshift Shelter in Tijuana Is Nearing Capacity," *USA Today*, November 20, 2018, https://www.usatoday.com/ story/news/world/2018/11/19/tijuana-shelter-conditions-worsen-migrants/2064085002/; Lukas Mikelionis and Griff Jenkins, "One-Third of

Migrants in Caravan Are Being Treated for Health Issues, Tijuana Health Official Says," *Fox News*, November 29, 2018, https://www.foxnews.com/world/caravan-migrants-suffer-from-respiratory-infections-tuberculosis-chickenpox-other-health-issues-tijuana-government-says; León Krauze, "God Willing, We Can Cross and My Dream Will Come True," *Slate*, November 30, 2018, https://slate.com/news-and-politics/2018/11/migrant-caravan-tijuana-mexico-children.html; Jack Herrera, "A Look Inside a Migrant Shelter in Tijuana," *Pacific Standard*, December 20, 2018, https://psmag.com/social-justice/a-look-inside-a-migrant-shelter-in-tijuana; Meredith Hoffman, "Inside the Trauma-Filled Camp of Migrants Waiting at the US Border," *Vice*, December 28, 2018, https://www.vice.com/en_us/article/439ebg/inside-the-trauma-filled-camp-of-migrants-waiting-at-the-us-border; Nomaan Merchant, "Tents, Stench, Smoke: Health Risks Are Gripping Migrant Camp," *AP News*, November 14, 2019, https://apnews.com/337b139ed4fa4d208b93d491364e04da; and Nicole Narea, "The Abandoned Asylum Seekers on the US-Mexico Border," *Vox*, December 20, 2019, https://www.vox.com/policy-and-politics/2019/12/20/20997299/asylum-border-mexico-us-iom-unhcr-usaid-migration-international-humanitarian-aid-matamoros-juarez.

9 See James Fredrick, "Shouting 'Mexico First,' Hundreds in Tijuana March against Migrant Caravan," *NPR*, November 19, 2019, https://www.npr.org/2018/11/19/669193788/shouting-mexico-first-hundreds-in-tijuana-march-against-migrant-caravan; and Jason McGahan, "Mexicans Storm Migrant Shelter in Tijuana, Shouting for 'Pigs' to Leave," *Daily Beast*, November 19, 2018, https://www.thedailybeast.com/mexicans-storm-migrant-shelter-in-tijuana-shouting-for-pigs-to-leave.

10 See Natalia Cordona, "The United States Bears Responsibility for the Immigration Crisis," *350*, June 29, 2018, https://350.org/us-responsibility-for-the-immigration-crisis/.

11 Michel Serres *Malfeasance: Appropriation through Pollution?* trans. Anne-Marie Feenberg-Dibon (Stanford, CA: Stanford University Press, 2011), 35.

12 See "Tijuana, Mexico, Declares Migrant 'Humanitarian Crisis,'" *NBC News*, November 23, 2018, https://www.nbcnews.com/news/world/tijuana-mexico-declares-migrant-humanitarian-crisis-n939591.

13 Serres, *Malfeasance*, 12.

14 Ibid., 41.

15 Ibid., 42.

16 Terence McSweeney, in a survey of US cinema after 9/11, argues that the "illusion that hegemonic American film maintains is that life outside of the First World is not as valuable and therefore not as human as 'ours.'" One of the merits of para-exilic films, then, is that they cast into refugee or asylum-seeker roles characters that normally enjoy citizenship, cultural enfranchisement, or some form of confederal, alliance, or nonstate actor status. These films express certain counterhegemonic tendencies, as through their identificatory mechanisms they introduce a number of their viewers

to the experiences of *what it is like to suffer* displacement, dispossession, abandonment, or deportation. See Terence McSweeney, *The 'War on Terror' and American Film: 9/11 Frames Per Second* (Edinburgh: Edinburgh University Press, 2014), 34.

17 Julia Kristeva, *Powers of Horror: An Essay on Abjection*, trans. Leon S. Roudiez (New York: Columbia University Press, 1982), 20, 53.
18 Ibid., 3.
19 Ibid., 3–4.
20 Ibid., 9–12, 155, 178.
21 For an example of the invention of such a space, see Jesús A. Rodríguez, "How the Migrant Caravan Built Its Own Democracy," *Politico*, December 12, 2018, https://www.politico.com/magazine/story/2018/ 12/12/ migrant-caravan-tijuana-border-government-222856.
22 Kristeva, *Powers of Horror*, 8.
23 Julia Kristeva, *Nations without Nationalism*, trans. Leon S. Roudiez (New York: Columbia University Press, 1993), 2–3.
24 Ibid., 38, 43.
25 Ibid., 51.
26 Ibid., 68.
27 Henry A. Giroux, *America at War with Itself* (San Francisco, CA: City Lights Books, 2017), 200.
28 Ibid., 222.
29 As Trinh T. Minh-ha writes, "Living at the borders means that one constantly treads the fine line between positioning and de-positioning. The fragile nature of the intervals in which one thrives requires that … one always travels transculturally while engaging in the local 'habitus' (collective practices that link habit with inhabitance) of one's immediate concern." Anticipating the para-exilic qualities of much twenty-first-century US cinema, she continues,

> Even when visible and audible, such locations do not necessarily function as a means to *install* a (formerly devoid or unexpressed) subjectivity. To the contrary, its inscription in the process tends above all to disturb one's sense of identity. How to negotiate, for example, the line that allows one to commit oneself to a cause and yet not quite belong to it? To fare both as a foreigner in foreign lands and as a stranger at home? *Be a crossroads.* Amazed by the collapse that is perpetually taking place in oneself (to adapt Genet's words), one sees oneself in constant metamorphosis, as if driven by the motion of change to places so profoundly hybrid as to exceed one's own imagination.

See Trinh T. Minh-ha, *Elsewhere, Within Here: Immigration, Refugeeism and the Boundary Event* (New York: Routledge, 2011), 54–5.

30 See April Reese, "U.S.-Mexico Fence Building Continues despite Obama's Promise to Review Effects," *New York Times*, April 16, 2009, https://archive.nytimes.com/ www.nytimes.com/gwire/2009/04/16/16greenwire-usmexico-fence-building-continues-despite-obam-10570.html?pagewanted=all&scp=15&sq=mexico%2520security&st=cse; "Border Fence Upkeep Costs Millions, Audit Finds," *NBC News*, August 17, 2009, http://www.nbcnews.com/ id/32898302/ns/us_news-security/t/border-fence-upkeep-costs-billions-audit-finds/#.XgmsiM57nDA; and Robert Koulish, *Immigration and American Democracy: Subverting the Rule of Law* (New York: Routledge, 2009).

31 Camilla Fojas, *Border Bandits: Hollywood on the Southern Frontier* (Austin: University of Texas Press, 2008), 183.

32 Elena dell'Agnese, "The US-Mexico Border in American Movies: A Political Geography Perspective," *Geopolitics* 10, no. 2 (2005): 208.

33 One of the most famous "walls" in classical Hollywood cinema, of course, concerns the "Walls of Jericho" sequence in Frank Capra's *It Happened One Night*. The newsman Peter Warne (Clark Gable) registers for the night in a motel with Ellie Andrews (Claudette Colbert), the daughter of a millionaire and the fiancé of a rich milquetoast. For reasons of discretion, Warne uses a sheet as a makeshift curtain to separate their sleeping quarters; such film theorists as Stanley Cavell interpret it as a metacinematic double for the movie screen, as a wink at the censorship codes coming into effect at that time, and even as a metaphor for Andrews's unbroken vaginal mucosa. However, Cavell shrewdly detects in the film's narrative—over the course of which the main characters overcome their differences and unite as a romantic couple—a utopian thrust, as well as an ethic that applies to the depiction of security walling in much twenty-first-century cinema:

> If the eventual community of humanity is not merely something close to us that we are falling short of, but something closed to us, something debarred, then its nonexistence is due to our willing against it, to the presence of moral evil. This takes moral evil as the will to exempt oneself, to isolate oneself, from the human community. It is a choice of inhumanity, of monstrousness.

It is no shock that much of this twenty-first century cinema consists of fantasy, science fiction, and monster-horror films, since the characters in them, in fighting these creatures, at the same time fight the inhumane and dehumanizing effects of their security states. See Stanley Cavell, *Pursuits of Happiness: The Hollywood Comedy of Remarriage* (Cambridge: Harvard University Press, 2003), 80–2.

34 As J. P. Telotte argues, in a way that speaks to the digital creations of much twenty-first-century US cinema, "In a world dominated by science and its technological products, in a world that almost requires that we see through—that is, by means of—those same technological products, we also have to find ways of seeing them or perhaps *through* or *beyond* them." According to

this argument, *Monsters* enables us to see the computer architecture inside or "through" these digital artifacts, inside the technologies affording them a degree of realism in their movements, shadings, coloration, and interaction with the other mise-en-scène elements of the film. See J. P. Telotte, *Robot Ecology and the Science Fiction Film* (New York: Routledge, 2016), 21.

35 Kirk Combe, "Homeland Insecurity: Macho Globalization and Alien Blowback in *Monsters*," *Journal of Popular Culture* 48, no. 5 (2015): 1017.

36 One of the direst repercussions of security walling occurs in Justin Lin's *Star Trek Beyond* (2016), the thirteenth film in the franchise. After entering a nebula on a rescue mission, the USS Enterprise suffers an attack from a swarm of drone spacecraft under the control of the mutant Krall (Idris Elba), a former Starfleet commander who denounces the Federation for negotiating successful truce accords with former enemies, such as the Romulans. Captain James T. Kirk (Chris Pine) orders the crew to abandon the Enterprise, and they assume a para-exilic condition on Altamid, one of the small planets in the nebula. Kirk and the other crew members meet Jaylah (Sofia Boutella), a scavenger who assists them in repairing and relaunching into space an older starship as Krall meanwhile seeks out an ancient relic to use as a weapon of mass destruction against the Federation. More specifically, the villain attempts to infiltrate the starbase Yorktown, a massive space station that a force dome completely encloses, in order to detonate the weapon in one of its ventilation chambers and instantly reduce its occupants and staff members to organic waste. Kirk stops Krall from doing so and then using the starbase to wipe out the inhabitants of other Federation worlds. *Star Trek Beyond* thus sets forth the value of cooperation and nonhostile engagement with aliens in the fullest sense of that term, as it contrasts the respectful interactions of Jaylah and Kirk's officers with the out-and-out aggression of Krall's armada. Moreover, the film conceives of a clear drawback to security walling, fencing, or other such measures: they create opportunities for saboteurs, dissidents, or terrorists to release a toxin or strain of disease into their interior spaces. These rogue agents might then decimate a nation-state's citizenry, ecosystem, or infrastructure and at the same time use these walls to minimize the consequences of their attack on their own regiments, allies, resource reserves, or territories. The irony, of course, turns on the fact that such a xenophobic and inhospitable outlook made Krall nonhuman over time, an alien in appearance to Starfleet, suggesting that the para-exilic condition is not a neutral one—it might twist certain characters, depending on their experiences, into spiteful, implacable, or malignant entities who sour on their former compatriots or countries of origin.

37 Shohini Chaudhuri argues that the diegesis of *Monsters* functions as a "space of attrition, evoking contemporary war zones as well as the US-Mexico frontier." She further argues that the film runs counter to dominant media representations of *mojados* (migrants without documentation), in that it at once explores "the cultures and identities" of those in Central and South American countries and "the embodied perils of border-crossing." The film establishes a counter-aesthetic to these media discourses, thinking together their xenophobia and anthropocentrism and thus challenging us to change

our attitudes to the notion of the "alien" altogether. See Shohini Chaudhuri, *Cinema of the Dark Side: Atrocity and the Ethics of Film Spectatorship* (Edinburgh: Edinburgh University Press, 2014), 129–34.

38 Slavoj Žižek, *Refugees, Terror and Other Trouble with the Neighbors: Against the Double Blackmail* (Brooklyn: Melville House, 2016), 51.

39 See Lindsay Huth, "Immigration under Trump: By the Numbers," *U.S. News & World Report*, March 13, 2018, https://www.usnews.com/news/data-mine/articles/2018-03-13/fewer-crossing-border-fewer-deported-immigration-under-trump.

40 See Haya El Nasser, "Gated Communities More Popular, and Not Just for the Rich," *USA Today*, December 15, 2002, https://usatoday30.usatoday.com/news/nation/2002-12-15-gated-usat_x.htm; and Tanya Mohn, "America's Most Exclusive Gated Communities," *Forbes*, July 3, 2012, https://www.forbes.com/sites/tanyamohn/2012/07/03/americas-most-exclusive-gated-communities/#874fc4b6fe0e.

41 Wendy Brown, *Walled States, Waning Sovereignty* (New York: Zone Books, 2010), 31.

42 See George W. Bush, "Bush's Speech on Immigration." *New York Times*, May 15, 2006, https://www.nytimes.com/2006/05/15/washington/15text-bush.html; Barack Obama, "Remarks by the President in Address to the Nation on Immigration," *The White House: President Barack Obama*, November 20, 2014, https://obamawhitehouse.archives.gov/the-press-office/2014/11/20/remarks-president-address-nation-immigration; and Donald J. Trump, "Statement from President Donald J. Trump," *WhiteHouse.gov*, September 5, 2017, https://www.whitehouse.gov/briefings-statements/statement-president-donald-j-trump-7/.

43 Giroux, *America at War with Itself*, 200.

44 Unlike earlier adaptations of the Charles Dickens classic, Robert Zemeckis' all-motion capture *A Christmas Carol* (2009) depicts Ebenezer Scrooge's (Jim Carrey) mansion as a fenced-in enclave in the middle of London. Once the spirit of Jacob Marley (Gary Oldman) visits Scrooge on Christmas Eve, they fly through a window out into the air, seeing an assortment of evil souls that must forever roam the Earth, onerously dragging their chains with them. These souls double for the destitute that "haunt" the streets of London outside the walls of Scrooge's mansion. More importantly, though, this sequence sets the template for the episodes that feature the three Christmas spirits who vex Scrooge throughout the night: rather than using dissolves or abrupt cuts, the film uses virtual camera flyovers to transition its characters from one scene to another. The film thus contrasts the dreary, claustrophobic, alienating state of existence in the city's enclaves to the free and exhilarating movement over the charming vistas that occur in these flyover sequences. Scrooge, in other words, must assume a para-exilic status in relation to the mansion in order to regain some sense of social feeling and equitableness—and to square up to *the fact that his estate has already made him an exile in his own country.*

45 Tamar Jeffers McDonald, "Homme-com: Engendering Change in Contemporary Romantic Comedy," in *Falling in Love Again: Romantic Comedy in Contemporary Cinema*, ed. Stacey Abbott and Deborah Jermyn (New York: I.B. Tauris, 2009), 153.

46 Touching on the synesthetic qualities of the music video, Vivian Sobchack argues that this media form flattens "temporal logic to spatial logic," an apt description of the otherwise nonsensical appearance of the Backstreet Boys in *This Is the End*—in Heaven, after all, time does not exist, and so cultural fads never fade and narrative continuities cease to matter. Timothy Corrigan, in fact, agrees that music videos "suspend historical and narrative time," adding that they "attempt the impossible creation of momentary heavens within a cartoon hell of a story built on few if any narrative motivations." See Vivian Sobchack, *Screening Space: The American Science Fiction Film* (New Brunswick: Rutgers University Press, 1998), 279; and Timothy Corrigan, *A Cinema without Walls: Movies and Culture after Vietnam* (New Brunswick: Rutgers University Press, 1991), 179.

47 André Bazin, *André Bazin's New Media*, ed. and trans. Dudley Andrew (Oakland: University of California Press, 2014), 190.

48 Ibid., 197–8.

49 Serres, *Malfeasance*, 77.

50 Tanner Mirrlees and Isabel Pedersen interpret *Elysium* in relation to the dystopian outcomes of the 2007 economic crash, including rampant unemployment, slumification, market volatility, income inequality, ecological disaster, and the establishment of exclusive spaces for the rich. They come to the conclusion that the film represents "a radical counterpoint to the neoliberal image of capitalism as a coherent, meritocratic, and class-less society of free and equal individuals." Similarly, David J. Skal describes the space station as "a giant revolving gated community" and then nitpicks that we rarely see the technocrats who inhabit it—a deft touch, we might counterargue, since these spaces, as Mirrlees and Pedersen maintain, serve to *exclude others* and thus render invisible the workings of class imbalance, state coercion, and immigration control. See Tanner Mirrlees and Isabel Pedersen, "*Elysium* as a Critical Dystopia," *International Journal of Media & Cultural Politics* 12, no. 3 (2016): 309–10; and David J. Skal, "Virtual Gravity," *Fantasy & Science Fiction* 126, no. 1/2 (2014): 182–3.

51 *Elysium* represents a "thickening" of outer space, a transformation of its vacuum into a *physical barrier* of sorts that separates the space station from the slums and industrial wastelands of the Earth. The film thus concretizes Vivian Sobchack's description of much Hollywood science fiction since the 1980s: "Traditional space has no further frontiers and appears as constraining and destructive of human existence as a concentration camp." The ocean of space in *Elysium*, in short, turns the Earth into such a camp. Furthermore, in relation to the re-elaboration of outer space, cyberspace, and alternate dimensions and timelines in these sci-fi films, Sobchack claims that we "are culturally producing and electronically disseminating a new world geography that politically and economically defies traditional notions of spatial

'location.'" However, for all the squalor in it, *Elysium* functions in the spatio-legible manner of much twenty-first-century cinema, as it shows its workers and undesirables eking out their existences next to scrapheaps and industrial runoff, unlike the managerial classes. The film ensures that its audience realizes that "spatial location" still matters—the affluent treat those stuck on Earth as though they own them, disposing of them as though they were trash or obsolete machine elements after they age too much, tire out, or suffer some form of debilitation, as Max does. See Vivian Sobchack, *Screening Space: The American Science Fiction Film* (New Brunswick: Rutgers University Press, 1998), 226, 232.

52 Étienne Balibar, *We, the People of Europe? Reflections on Transnational Citizenship*, trans. James Swenson (Princeton, NJ: Princeton University Press, 2004), 125–7.

53 Ibid., 128.

54 The Pixar film *Coco* (Lee Unkrick and Adrian Molina, 2017) substitutes the afterlife for the uncrossable space of *Elysium*. The adolescent Miguel (Anthony Gonzalez) steals a musical instrument from a mausoleum during the Day of the Dead fiesta and falls victim to a curse. Now invisible and able to communicate with ancestor spirits, Miguel must ask for a dispensation from a relative in the Land of the Dead so as to return in the flesh to the Santa Cecilia village that we see in the film's first act. The film represents the afterlife as a combination of Walt Disney World and the Global North, as Miguel crosses through a series of checkpoints and customs stations to reach the Land of the Dead and experience the talent shows, fireworks displays, and monorail travel that it features. He must also cross the Marigold Bridge at sunrise in order to reenter Mexico, a refiguration of the Cross Border Xpress that connects Tijuana and San Diego or the International Bridges that connect Matamoros, Nueva Laredo, and Ciudad Acuña to their twin cities in Texas. Thus *Coco* at first sight seems to replace mass migration to the United States with the transmigration of souls, making the Global North seem Edenic next to Mexico. However, this impression starts to fade as much as does Miguel's flesh over the course of the film, after we remember that it casts the United States as more than Walt Disney World—it is more so the Land of the Dead, a domain that sets in motion a series of family separations and cultural deprivations, as older distinctly Mexican spirits simply vanish inside it over time. *Coco* therefore reverses the usual thrust of para-exilic films, such as *Monsters*, as Miguel must reject the distractions and creature comforts of the Land of the Dead to return to Santa Cecilia as a musician, able to refresh and transform the village's culture without forgetting or abandoning its traditions. The film's epilogue thus sets up *family reunions* as an ideal, a sharp rebuke to the detention centers and separation of minors from adults of the Obama and Trump administrations (see Chapter 5).

55 The shantytowns, toxic dump sites, and ruthless exploitation of the underclasses in *Elysium* constitute those on Earth as a "surplus humanity," Mike Davis' term for survivors of the "existential ground zero" that normalizes famine, medical malpractice, sanitation crises, industrial death

camps, and the seepage of noxious substances into the environment. See Mike Davis, *Planet of Slums* (New York: Verso, 2017), 128–50, 198.

56 Gregers Andersen and Esben Bjerggard Nielsen discuss the thantopolitics of *Elysium*, arguing that the cleanness and extravagance of the space station comes at the cost of the ecological disequilibrium of the Earth and the inattention of administrators to its inhabitants' needs for adequate shelter, medical care, recreation time, and fresh air. They contextualize the film in relation to debates over Obamacare, whereas Suzie Gibson discusses it in terms of its South African director's anti-apartheidist sensibilities. She argues that the environmental devastation of the Earth and the main characters' incarceration on it speaks to English-speaking nations' rejection of asylum seekers and their detention of them in facilities "where there is scant space and a dangerous lack of hygiene." See Gregers Andersen and Esben Bjerggaard Nielsen. "Biopolitics in the Anthropocene: On the Invention of Future Biopolitics in *Snowpiercer*, *Elysium*, and *Interstellar*," *Journal of Popular Culture* 51, no. 3 (2018): 626; and Suzie Gibson, "Stop the Ships: *Elysium*, Asylum Seekers and the Battle over Sovereign Borders," *Screen Education* 78 (2015): 82–3.

57 Balibar, *We, the People of Europe?* 104–5.

58 Ibid., 11.

59 J. P. Telotte claims that the figure of the cyborg in much Hollywood science fiction speaks to our desire for incorporation into the technologically "complex realm we inhabit." He argues that science fiction addresses the fact that "we have come ever nearer to a sort of borderline between human and artificial being," so much so that the "neat and clear distinctions" that separate us from machines, operating systems, and synthetic materials start to collapse. The exoskeleton that Max uses thus appears of tremendous consequence to the entire thrust of the film, not only its action set pieces: as the "borderline" that separates the organic from the inorganic starts to thin, so too does the one that separates the crude material existences of the workers on Earth from the information-rich technosphere of the administrators on Elysium. See J. P. Telotte, *Replications: A Robotic History of the Science Fiction Film* (Urbana: University of Illinois Press, 1995), 10, 20.

60 *Rogue One: A Star Wars Story* (Gareth Edwards, 2016) takes some of its narrative conceits from *Elysium*, namely the search for an informational object of value. The Rebel Alliance seeks the schematics of the Death Star space station on Scarif, one of the data storage outposts of the evil Galactic Empire. A "shield gate" encases Scarif in an impregnable dome so that the Rebels' reinforcement spacecraft cannot enter its atmosphere and the satellite feeds on its surface cannot reach their fleet. The film regards "hard" and "soft" resources as at once superfluous and indispensible: in space, Rebel fighter craft must take out the shields surrounding Scarif, while on its surface the main characters must realign a radar dish and transmit the schematics to a flagship vessel in orbit. At the same time, the fighter craft seem expendable, exploding in flames, crashing into one another, and cluttering up outer space, while the infiltrators on Scarif must sift through the content of a number of data banks for the right file and then destroy them upon finding it. After the success of

their mission, the Death Star trains its immense firepower on its own outpost and obliterates much of it, an exertion of its sovereign entitlement to defile that which it "owns." This action rebounds on the Empire, though, as the Rebels make off with the specs about a design flaw in the Death Star's core, enabling them in other installments of the saga to reduce it too to waste.

61   Alberto Toscano and Jeff Kinkle, *Cartographies of the Absolute* (Washington, DC: Zero Books, 2015), 15.

62   Ibid., 16.

63   James Wan's *Aquaman* (2018) appears the DC Comics counterpart to Marvel's *Black Panther*, with the undersea nation of Atlantis standing in for Wakanda. The title superhero, the alter ego of roustabout Arthur Curry (Jason Momoa), must acquire the mythic Trident of Atlan to assume the mantle of rightful ruler of Atlantis and thwart the ambitions of Orm (Patrick Wilson), who seeks to unite its seven tribes under the title of Ocean Master. Orm seeks to start a war against the inhabitants of Earth's surface for polluting the seas and accordingly refashions the capital city of Atlantis into a fortress off-limits to them, due to its security walls, customs checkpoints, sentries riding atop sharks, turret cannons, and central access point—the Gateway Bridge, which regulates traffic and resembles the international crossings that span Mexico and the United States. The film's main difference from *Black Panther* concerns the issue of de-origination: the Marvel character must travel outside of Wakanda in order to reconsider its approach to nation-state security and international relations, whereas Arthur Curry already starts out as an exile, one conversant with the surface world's ways and able to serve in a mediator role in working toward cooperative environmental reform. Aquaman retrieves the Trident, dethrones the Ocean Master, and averts war, although at the cost of civil conflict, much as with *Black Panther*. Orm terrorizes and subdues some of the other tribes, dividing Atlantis into two factions. Therefore, even if the surface does not assert administrative control over the underwater nation, their emission of toxins, debris, and noise into the Earth's water systems nonetheless to their advantage instigates social disharmony among its seven tribes. The final scenes in *Black Panther* feature T'Challa opening Wakanda to other nations. The final shot in *Aquaman*, in which the title character vaults from the sea into the air, suggests a different moral: rather than setting up outreach campaigns, Curry shows us the importance of remaining "a fish out of water," always out of step to some extent with our current surroundings and therefore *more apt to treat the entire Earth as though it were home*. The superhero, after all, travels from the Sahara to the Mediterranean to the Mariana Trench in a short amount of time, taking in their splendors and introducing the other Atlantean characters to them.

64   Peter Ndaita, "Can the Migrant Speak: Ethnic Accents in *Black Panther* and the Quadruple Consciousness of African Immigrants in the United States," *Africology: The Journal of Pan African Studies* 11, no. 9 (2018): 46.

65   Although a Hollywood film about a fictive nation, *Black Panther* nonetheless seems abreast of twenty-first-century directions in New African Cinema. Valérie K. Orlando argues that the national cinemas of Senegal, Algeria, and

other countries "have been very active in articulating divergent roles counter to the Western stereotype of illegal immigration and migrant travel throughout the world," enabling us to "consider alternative immigration patterns and movement across regions and continents." Similarly, T'Challa resolves to open Wakanda to commercial and intercultural exchange with other African nations, offsetting the isolationism, anti-immigrant sentiment, and sense of stagnation that often result from security walling. See Valérie K. Orlando, *New African Cinema* (New Brunswick: Rutgers University Press, 2017), 99.

66 Black Panther exemplifies the ecto-prosthetic form of superhuman embodiment: the character's armor constitutes a "second skin," making it almost impervious to attack. *Avengers: Infinity War* shows T'Challa extending this "second skin" outward in the form of a cone of concussive force to take down multiple enemies at once. This new feature of the costume thus resembles a *miniaturizable and mobile* version of the dome that surrounds Wakanda. For more information on the four types of superbodies in these sorts of films, see Larrie Dudenhoeffer, *Anatomy of the Superhero Film* (New York: Palgrave Macmillan, 2017).

67 See Ana Campoy, "Trump's Multibillion-dollar Border Wall Wouldn't Stop This $5,000 Drone," *Quartz*, August 22, 2017, https://qz.com/1058702/trumps-multibillion-dollar-border-wall-wouldnt-stop-this-5000-drone/; Alice Driver, "Trump's Mexico Wall Would Be a Gift to the Drug Cartels," *CNN*, January 9, 2018, https://www.cnn.com/2018/01/08/opinions/border-wall-cartels-trump-opinion-driver/index.html; and Gina Harkins, "Illicit Drone Flights Surge along U.S.-Mexico Border as Smugglers Hunt for Soft Spots," *Washington Post*, June 24, 2018, https://www. washingtonpost.com/world/national-security/illicit-drone-flights-surge-along-us-mexico-border-as-smugglers-hunt-for-soft-spots/2018/06/24/ea353d2a-70aa-11e8-bd50-b80389a4e569_story.html.

68 Umberto Eco, "*Casablanca*: Cult Movies and Intertextual Collage," in *Travels in Hyperreality*, trans. William Weaver (San Diego, CA: Harcourt, 1983), 208.

69 Precursors to *Ready Player One* might include *Who Framed Roger Rabbit* (Robert Zemeckis, 1988), *Wreck-It Ralph* (Rich Moore, 2012), *Pixels* (Chris Columbus, 2015), and the *Toy Story* series (1995–2019). These intercompany crossovers, though, only concentrate on characters from one media niche: namely, cartoons, video games, or toylines. *The Lego Movie* (Phil Lord and Christopher Miller, 2014) comes closest to Spielberg's film, even though it defamiliarizes the trademark characters in it to an extent, caricaturing them as squat, almost nonarticulable mini-figures.

70 Frederick Wasser, *Steven Spielberg's America* (Malden, MA: Polity, 2010), 204.

71 One of the Easter eggs in *Ready Player One* refers to the "Lawgiver" firearm from *Judge Dredd* (Danny Cannon, 1995). The title character (Sylvester Stallone), a stern street cop-executioner in the crime-ridden Mega-City One and the victim of a murder frame-up, escapes into the near-uninhabitable "Cursed Earth" outside the city's walls. Meanwhile, Rico (Armand Assante), Dredd's renegade twin, takes control of the city council, assassinates most of the other Judges, and attempts to create a troop of clones to replace them.

After surviving an encounter with cannibals in the wastelands, Dredd reenters the city through one of the vents in its towering security wall and throws Rico off the Statue of Liberty to an instant death. The film, although not a critical or commercial success in the mid-1990s, establishes some of the para-exilic dynamics of much twenty-first-century Hollywood cinema. *Judge Dredd* sends its title character into exile more to restore the status quo than to transform the attitudes of Mega-City One's residents toward those outside its walls. His time in exile nevertheless curbs some of Dredd's quasi-fascistic tendencies, so the film does motion toward some form of sociopolitical transformation, if not cultural openness. Unlike other adaptations of this comics franchise, Stallone abandons the character's signature face mask throughout much of the film. This fraction of riot armor effectively "walls" Dredd off from the immediate social environment—as does the VR equipment to an extent in *Ready Player One*—so that the act of simply removing it seems an important first step toward developing more empathetic and thus merciful relations with others.

72 Also noting the intertextual relation of *Willy Wonka* to *Ready Player One*, Walter Metz argues that this "range of cinematic quotations gives the film its remarkable strength." See Walter Metz, "'So Shines a Good Deed in a Weary World': Intertextuality in Steven Spielberg's *Ready Player One*," *Film Criticism* 42, no. 4 (2018), https://quod.lib.umich.edu/f/fc/13761232.0042.402/--so-shines-a-good-deed-in-a-weary-world-intertextuality?rgn=main;view=fulltext.

73 Serres, *Malfeasance*, 67.

5

Interface Areas: Beyond the Walls on the Cinema Screen

Perhaps the most controversial aspect of the Trump administration concerns its decision to intern thousands upon thousands of migrants in detention centers, in the process separating over 5,400 children from their families.[1] Jeff Sessions, Trump's former attorney general, in a 2018 interview,[2] clearly set forth the administration's stance on this issue, stating that the United States must "send a message" to asylum seekers, namely that if they "don't want to be separated from their children, they should not bring them with them." Although Bill Clinton made the call to start detaining and deporting immigrants, George W. Bush to frame their capture after 9/11 as a security issue, and Barack Obama to intern minors in military detention sites, Trump took these measures in an even crueler and more draconian direction, insisting on "zero tolerance," meaning criminal conviction, for first-time offenders for the misdemeanor of illegally entering the United States.[3] He moreover sought to resist access to work visas; tighten the criteria for seeking asylum; "meter" the influx of refugees, forcing them to wait in Mexico indefinitely while the courts review their cases; denaturalize current citizens; roll out a "merit-based" approach to immigration favoring age, education, and English skills; and use surprise ICE raids to roundup families without documentation for arrest and deportation.[4] Threatening tariffs against Mexico unless it apprehends "all illegals," Trump took to Twitter to declare, "Our country is FULL,"[5] while at the same time warehousing asylum seekers in cells, filling some of them with upward to three hundred children with no adult supervision and inadequate clothing, nutrition, sanitation, and medical care.[6] His Department of Justice representative, Sarah Fabian, even made the case that these children do not require soap, toothbrushes, or anything more than aluminum foil covers to sleep in on chilly cement floors.[7] The Trump administration additionally set in motion measures to cancel classes, recreation time, and other amenities for these children, while forcing some of the older ones at different facilities to endure solitary confinement and verbal, corporal, sexual, and emotional abuse.[8] Finally, the idea to confine migrant children inside former Second World War Japanese internment sites, such as Fort Sill in Oklahoma, met with severe criticism, with US congresswoman Alexandria Ocasio-Cortez and *New York Times* columnist Charles M. Blow contributing to a chorus of dissident voices in describing these detention centers as "concentration camps."[9]

The Trump administration continues to intimidate Mexico and other Central American countries with trade tariffs unless they militarily crackdown on the asylum crisis.[10] The administration also threatens to further narrow the criteria for entry into the United States, as well as to commission ICE to issue cumbersome ankle monitors to migrant families—many already suffering trauma and embarrassment—that the courts must release into the country after their maximum detention time elapses.[11] The construction of concentration camps, security walls, and other anti-immigration mechanisms speaks to Michel de Certeau's theorization of the *strategic* use of cultural-political techniques, which "seek to create places in conformity with abstract models."[12] The strategic, in other words, involves central, rationalistic, expansionist, totalitarian institutions that set about delimiting their own "place" from the rest of the environment, often with reference to external threats or targets, such as "terrorists" or "illegal aliens."[13] The strategic therefore seeks to convert the contingencies of a certain sociohistorical situation into a set of "readable spaces," so it can observe, measure, and control those within its "scope of vision."[14] ICE, the Border Patrol, and the Trump administration, for example, sequester migrants, refugees, and their children in transit camps separate from the rest of US territory and free from civilian oversight, supposedly to manage their movements, vet the authenticity of their asylum claims, and determine their countries of origin, ethnic complexion, ideological sympathies, and overall use value to the nation-state.

However, no authority can fully map out the "instructions for use"—or the ortho-praxis, in terms of speech, movement, and social interaction—of these spaces, not even concentration camps or security wall entry points. Smugglers might use drones or rent out children so that desperate migrants can skirt stringent asylum criteria and more easily enter the United States.[15] Or Mexican citizens on the Tijuana side of the San Ysidro Port of Entry might steal concertina wire or other walling materials in order to fortify their own residences.[16] Or detainees might engender new forms of solidarity across ethnic, cultural, and national difference, as was the case with the Syrian, Sudanese, Kurdish, and other subpopulations of the notorious Calais Jungle camp in France.[17] Or they might simply overburden the system, with the crowding in US tent cities straining their capacities, stressing out ICE officials, and eventually compelling the Trump administration to reverse course on its zero tolerance decision on June 20, 2019, and rethink its approach to deterrence.[18] Michel de Certeau might refer to these techniques as more *tactical* than strategic, in that they "do not obey the law of the place" and so transform the dominant order into "the space of the other."[19] The tactical, then, is "an art of the weak" specific to the common interests, needs, dreams, and creativity of subaltern or subordinate classes, as they restlessly invent new uses for the spaces that confine them, constrain their movements, regulate their experiences, and curb their impulses, uses that the architects of these spaces can never fully anticipate in their design and administration of them.[20] The tactical occurs in "enemy territory," so to speak, not outside of it, and seizes upon opportunities to rewrite space, frustrating attempts to make it readable, objectifiable, and manageable.[21] One of the most interesting developments concerning this cultural technique is the creation of interface areas near certain fenced-in districts, such as the Peace Lines in Northern Ireland, the Roma walls in Slovakia and the Czech Republic, and even the Line of Control separating the Indian and Pakistani factions in the state of Jammu and Kashmir. These interface areas arise from conflict, segregation, mistrust, and economic disadvantage, and sadly they often erupt into sectarian violence, rioting, and tit-for-tat exchanges. However, these areas also sometimes spark demands for rallies, meetings, and other forms of interfaith dialogue and community engagement. These factions, in these instances, might work toward mutual safety, understanding, and cultural uplift, collaboratively chipping away at the fences and military installations that separate them and challenging the "us vs. them" organization of district, state, or region.

The tactical negotiation of these interface areas might then motion toward the constitution of a *multitude*, Paolo Virno's term for an associative network that shuns unity, "resists authority," refuses the social contract, and contradicts the "state monopoly of political decision-making."[22] The individuals comprising the multitude together forge a collective sensorimotor endowment, sociolinguistic register, and set of cultural-historical experiences over and above those that the state recognizes, requires of its citizens, and disciplines in them.[23] The distinctive trait of the multitude is "not feeling at home," since it derives its existence from the risk the state poses to it in the form of ostracism, marginalization, silencing, and imprisonment.[24] The multitude, according to Virno, therefore comes to represent a nongovernmental sphere that does not threaten to seize control—say, in the form of a revolution or a coup—so much as it exists to disturb the institutional structures of the state and its sovereign decision-making.[25] For example, the introduction of "tender-age facilities" in the United States to detain the children of refugees casts into crisis representative democracy under the Trump administration, with the use of such euphemisms, as John McWhorter contends, coming off as quite Orwellian and tendentially fascist.[26]

However, the multitude is not an "episodic or interstitial form," as Virno notes; rather, it is a continual mode of sociopolitical existence "for the many, being seen as many."[27] The many-as-multitude come to resemble an "external intellect," or a repertoire of tactics that remains ambivalent, meaning that its self-expression might consist in chronic apathy or conflict with other outgroups, or more constructively in a celebration of rootlessness to some extent, in a "critical unease" with the state's strategic domination of a cityscape or frontier region.[28] Opportunism, for instance, seems one of the major tactics of the multitude, as it endures frequent sociorelational volatilities and must consequently remain open to "a flow of ever-changeable possibilities" that the state cannot foresee or avert.[29] Cynicism serves as another such tactic, as the multitude rejects the abstract models of the state and sees its rules for what they are: conventional and arbitrary, an affront to the fluidity that the many values.[30] Finally, in the face of the idle chatter the mass media re-presents at each and every moment, the multitude exhibits a sense of curiosity and a willingness to experiment with new discourses as it decides "what to watch" and "what deserves to come to the foreground."[31] The media, in short, encourages the multitude to tactically tease new meaning and discover new "margins of freedom" from even its most trite formats or routines—to develop, out of a surfeit of the familiar, a taste for the unknown and surprising.[32] The multitude, in its opposition to the state and disobedient use of its official media content, thus exercises an autonomist "art of the weak." This art, in turn, invites us to make similar tactical inquiries into several twenty-first-century films that feature security walling, nationalist regimes, and interface areas in them so that we can resist two temptations: the rhetoric of Trump and similar administrators who seek to authorize the construction of walls and camps, and also the intergroup tensions that can cause flare-ups of chauvinism, violence, and insult among subaltern classes.

 The mainstream films of the twenty-first century, much of them teen fantasy, romance, and science fiction, often feature interface areas next to security walls, concentration camps, and defense systems, appearing as sites of open conflict or extralegal activity. The interface areas in these films nonetheless open their main characters to forms of cross-border dialogue, micropolitical rapprochement, or interracial, intercultural, or even interspecies flirtation. These exchanges occur in a clandestine, subterranean manner, out of sight of the surveillance mechanisms, regulatory apparatuses, and constabulary forces of the state. Thus they assume a *crypto-social* complexion, as characters from either side of the wall come together to flout such apartheidist measures, form new relationships and allegiances, and explode the disinformation machines that the state relies on to ensure that its citizens remain ignorant of other cultures and suspicious toward outsiders. These films moreover address the dynamics of the crypto-social situations in them, as they frequently touch on the fact that a certain outgroup, as well as a main character's own social class, might start to resent these interactions, causing further misunderstanding and strife. Thus these films enable us to visualize and assess some of the strategies that state authorities use to divide the characters in them, incite dissension among them, and district them into monocultural spaces, and also the tactics those that they trap invent so as to steal for themselves as much freedom to move, think, create, act, and relate to others as they can.

The interplay of the strategic and the tactical, then, forms the true drama of these films, as the separation walls and interface areas in them serve to *make legible* the detestation certain communities feel toward one another—feelings the main characters must first overcome in themselves if they are to inspire their districts, tribes, or neighborhoods to fight for a more companionable future. These films, throughout their narratives, chart the formation of a multitude, a constellation of individuals who respect one another's differences at the same time as they contrive an "external intellect" from the sensual encounters, crosslingual interactions, and similar sociohistorical situations that they share. The multitudes that form in these films improvise a range of tactics to outwit the state's rules of social conduct; resist its scientific, educational, and mediatic attempts to control opinion and disparage certain communities; and finally to rewrite its official spaces, collapsing its security apparatuses, readjusting its territorial divisions, disrupting the cycles of violence it thrives on, and establishing more inclusive relations with its noncitizen enemies. The characters motion toward a socius *beyond walls, fences, and camps*, and so challenge us to dream up alternatives to these forms of nation-state securitization, to counter the isolationist tendencies of rightist administrations, and to explore new forms of intercultural or international reciprocation—some of them taboo, forbidden, or illegal, and therefore to take place in a clandestine manner.

Warm Bodies

Jonathan Levine's *Warm Bodies* (2013), an action-horror adaptation of William Shakespeare's *Romeo and Juliet*, introduces us to R (Nicholas Hoult), a teenage zombie who wonders in a stream of consciousness voice-over, "What's wrong with me? Why can't I connect with other people?" The answer might consist in the fact that R appears "dead," as do the other characters in the derelict spaces we see in the film's opening montage. However, this mise-en-scène informs us that R's alienation stems from the strategic disincorporation of these city districts, after the survivors of the zombie epidemic quarantine their enemies on the other side of a massive separation wall, stationing sentries next to it who scan those who seek reentry for signs of infection (Figure 5.1). Colonel Grigio (John Malkovich), the chief security administrator of this refuge, also delivers over a number of video feeds an

FIGURE 5.1 *The City Walls in* Warm Bodies.

incessant message of fear, isolationism, and contempt, calling the zombies "corpses" and describing them as "uncaring," "unfeeling," unthinking, and "incapable of remorse." He sends foragers, including daughter Julie (Teresa Palmer), into the zombie territories to search for medical supplies and other necessities. The zombies, in search of foragers to devour in turn, shamble into these same districts, which thus function as interface areas at which two ethnoracial, religious, or, in this case, ontological denominations come into frequent and apparently irresolvable conflict. These trouble spots, as they serve to foment mutual misunderstanding, antagonism, and resentment, seem another design of the city's strategic decision makers, as they enable them to maintain their authority over the other survivors. The zombies themselves endure insufferable "waiting," as R says, as they stumble about the streets and airport terminals, another strategic factor in their exclusion and further dehumanization. The wall contains them in these areas, which come to resemble *literal death camps*, steadily dispiriting the zombies until they start to abandon all social feeling and consciousness. Then they turn into "bonies," animate skeletons who tear away their chalky flesh, succumb to their cannibalistic urges, and shake off their remaining faculties of reason, speech, and companionship. These monsters seem correlatives of the soldiers standing watch next to the wall's access points, in that they sniff out, intimidate, and threaten to eat anyone from their own community who exhibits the signs of a cure—in short, zombies who start to act and feel as do their enemies. The "bonies," R tells us, are much too "far gone" for such emotions. The other zombies, though, despite their cravings and their acrimonious relationship to the survivors, express discontent with their current situation, as we first see after they attack the small troop of foragers raiding the drug store, the offbeat scene of R and Julie's "meet cute." Falling in love at first sight, R saves Julie from the nostrils, clutches, mouths, and teeth of the other zombies.

This sequence, as well as the ones that set the stage for it, casts into relief the tactical disposition of the zombies. As they totter through the open streets and overpasses of the quarantine zone, they cluster closely together to make it difficult for soldiers to shoot them in their foreheads, a clever and surprisingly intelligent maneuver considering their otherwise slow, erratic movement. Moreover, the zombies eat the cerebra of their victims not only to satisfy their appetite. They do so to assimilate the desires, thoughts, memories, and emotions of their victims, enabling them to vicariously relive the experience of dreaming, for they cannot sleep. However, as we see over the course of the film, these memories also assume tactical importance to them, affording them information on the access points that R will use to escort Julie into the city after she recovers from the "pharma salvage" escapade. He sneaks Julie into the main cabin of an airplane so that they can evade detection from the rescue teams that rove about the quarantine districts, and also the zombies who shamble across the tarmac, caricaturing the security details who also mindlessly make their rounds next to the wall. Most interestingly, R smears Julie's face with the remains of one of the other foragers, so as to throw the rest of the zombies off their scent. He thus tactically negotiates the vicious internecine conditions in these interface areas, using the zombies' senses and one-dimensional mindset against them so that they cannot smell out this woman and then attack on instinct. She experiences an outer transformation in assuming a more zombielike appearance, whereas R experiences an inner one after consuming the central nervous tissue of Julie's companion Perry (Dave Franco), sharing in their intense romantic connection with each other.

These sorts of interactions, uncommon in these conflictual spaces, motion toward a transformation of existing social relations in the film, requiring the radical emancipation, as David McNally argues, of our experience of seeing, tasting, feeling, contemplating, desiring, and acting upon our world-system.[33] He cites Walter Benjamin's observation that warmth is "ebbing from things" in capitalist-militaristic regimes, such as those in the film, and further argues that the figure of the zombie masses encourages us to reanimate our social drives and rekindle the warmth in our collective spheres.[34] Julie comes to accept the favors of R; and, after they steal into the enclave together, she adopts the tactical character of the zombies. Using concealer, eyeliner, and other makeup applications, she restores to R *a more humanlike appearance* so that they can escape detection from the soldiers inside the security wall. Although they seem at first sight quite freakish in their respective disguises, they nonetheless explore while in them new modes of sensing, thinking, and fraternizing with others, teaching and emboldening each other to do so throughout their time together. They start to express romantic feelings for each other, as they enter into a fully crypto-social relationship, their separate communities unaware of it.[35]

What does it mean, though, to say that Julie comes to seem more zombielike through an appeal to the other characters' sense of smell and R more alive to them through an appeal to their sense of sight? The Western metaphysical tradition regards vision as superior to our more "animalistic" sense faculties, such as taste and olfaction, which in comparison seem much cruder, more earthen, and impolite in their functioning. These two characters, then, as they trade the sensori-affective characteristics of the zombies and the survivors—the subaltern and the superordinate—set an example that serves to de-hierarchize the dominant social order in the film. These tactical exchanges enable the couple to resist their misgivings about each other and in turn work toward collapsing the ontological distinctions that function as an alibi for social division. "Real bodies need to be in affective relation," Lone Bertelsen and Andrew Murphie claim, in order for far-reaching shifts in the "existential territory" of these characters to emerge.[36] However, they refrain from defining "territory" in commonplace environmental, national-federal, or zoning terms; rather, they define it as a set of "differential intensities" that can inspire "conflict and/or compassion."[37] This notion of territory, then, speaks to the interface areas in the film—the airport, the subway, the checkpoints near the wall—as they offer the characters space to experiment with new social, emotional, and ethico-behavioral forms of subjectivation. Julie emulates the slow, unsteady movements of the zombies, a new twist to the character's visual self-presentation. Similarly, once they reenter the city, Julie compels R to change clothes, muting the zombie's scent to some degree so that the two of them can again escape detection from the survivors and their dogs.[38] The new existential territory they open up, starting with the contact of their "real bodies," encourages the other characters to change their attitudes and reignite some warmth, in the Benjaminian sense, in their respective social camps.

Thus, after digesting Perry's feelings and memories, R starts to fathom why the survivors fear the zombies and renounces cannibalism. Julie, in turn, comes to terms with Colonel Grigio's obsession with eradicating the zombies at all costs. Her father almost shoots R in the face, even after she draws attention to the fact that this zombie Romeo shows clear signs that a cure for the infection exists. This cure derives from the dialogue, mutual affection, and crypto-social relationship the two of them develop over the course of the narrative, as they share musical tastes, ride in fast cars, and sleep next to each other, spending time together in the ways we see teenagers do in romantic comedies.[39] They moreover invite their friends to engage in the thrill of similar crypto-social activities and forms of self-expression. For example, R's confidant M (Rob Corddry) discovers the romance and still assists the couple in escaping from the dreadful "bonies"—these actions stir up the warmth of social feeling and desire in this character's insides, which we can actually see through a digital X-ray effect. Nora (Analeigh Tipton), one of Julie's friends, assists in disguising R as a normal teenager and expresses dismay when Colonel Grigio threatens to shoot the zombie in the middle of the eyes, the organs responsible for fooling the soldiers and allowing the couple to slip through the wall and roam about the enclave. The couple's secret relationship now out in the open, Colonel Grigio re-holsters the firearm, a tacit and quite ironic response to Julie's initial question to R, "Are there others like you?" The film's final action sequences, in fact, suggest clearer and more elaborate answers to this question.

The couple, in the words of the film, "exhumes" the warmth still inside the other zombies, as they come to speak more, embrace others, and even dream again. Already multiracial in complexion, they start to form a multitude in solidaritarian relation to the soldiers, combining forces with them in order to drive the "bonies" from the enclave. The outcome of the struggle favors this multitude, as they fight alongside one another to either slaughter their mutual enemies or compel them to starve to death. This ending seems unusually macabre for a romantic comedy, and moreover seems to displace the central conflict in the film onto a camp of even more inhuman adversaries, thus repeating the same fascist ideologemes[40] that result in roundups, internments, strategic violence, and systematic murder. The film certainly deserves criticism on this front; nonetheless, the fate of these creatures also sounds a note against security walls and similar forms of national defense, as well as the obduracy and despair that might arise in those stuck in the areas spanning and surrounding them. The "bonies," we must remember, seem to R "too far gone to change," an attitude that the film seeks to discourage in outgroups, citizenries, and nation-state functionaries alike. After all, it must not escape our attention that out of all the survivors, Colonel Grigio seems the most reluctant to change, and more interestingly that the face of actor John Malkovich somewhat resembles that of a skeleton. Humans, even on the safer, more resource-rich side of the wall, still remain in danger, although not necessarily from those whom they distance themselves from—rather, *they risk becoming too coldhearted, too far gone in clinging to their own self-identity* to ever change. However, Grigio manages to do so, and the zombies and the soldiers after the final action sequence come to accept one another, mingle with one another, teach one another to value their differences and dispense with their shibboleths, and work together toward a common cure; as R says, "They learned how to love again."

M assumes the name Marcus, for instance, after meeting a woman on a rainy day stroll, the two of them expressing interest in each other as they walk off-screen sharing an umbrella. Blood starts to circulate in R's veins again after the zombie shields Julie from the impact of the water after they dive off a dam into a reservoir to escape from the "bonies"—in short, they consummately *fall for each other* in this scene. More than a cliché, this moment speaks to the socially transformative thrust of romantic comedies. Leger Grindon argues that these films thematize union and rebirth, and moreover express "subversive social implications" that result in the "overthrow" of the older order only so that a new one can take shape.[41] *Warm Bodies* works within these conventions: it features a father figure, a defender of the status quo, who therefore functions as an obstacle to the romance; it involves an element of masquerade, as in such films as *Trouble in Paradise* (Ernst Lubitsch, 1932) and *Some Like It Hot* (Billy Wilder, 1959), allowing the couple to continue to court as they evade the other characters; it even whisks the two of them off to an exotic site, the suburbs outside the enclave, to foster their connection to each other, as occurs in the Connecticut setting of *Bringing Up Baby* (Howard Hawks, 1938) and the famous veranda scene in the orchards of *Romeo and Juliet*.[42] As do most of these romances, the film moves toward social reconciliation, with the couple's affective connection and sexual attraction for each other the instrument of this transformation. Unlike other films, though, *Warm Bodies* makes separation walls effectively seem anti-love, strictly inimical to the utopian thrills and trappings of romantic comedy. The final shot in the film reveals R and Julie watching as the wall comes down, the soldiers setting off multiple explosions that cause it to disintegrate and collapse, as the tactics of the couple win out over the strategic emplacements of the military. These characters, in short, *exhume themselves*, as the real novelty of this film consists in its reconceptualization of these sorts of walled-in areas as merely enormous tombs.

The Maze Runner

The first film of a teen dystopian trilogy, *The Maze Runner* (Wes Ball, 2014) from its opening sequences onward depicts the exigencies and dire conditions that result in the formation of a multitude. The first scene, shot in near darkness, features main character Thomas (Dylan O'Brien) waking up with a case of short-term amnesia on a cargo elevator, which slowly ascends to the Glade, the film's name for the small domain of verdant meadows and farmlands that dozens of other male teenagers cultivate and inhabit. Massive stone walls enclose the Glade, trapping the teenagers within it, despite the efforts of some of their members to escape. Thomas discovers that, so as to ensure "order" and "peace," they came to form a collective that cooks, eats, sleeps, fashions shelters, tends the crops, and cares for animals together. Moreover, they observe certain social rituals, drinking, dancing, and wrestling at night, as well as staging council sessions, trials for disobedient members, and ceremonial exile for ones stricken with a mysterious infection that makes them rabidly violent—its victims suffer from delirium and a discoloration of their veins. The teenagers remain respectful of one another's aptitudes and differences, and they refuse to formalize and impose upon themselves a strict code of conduct or coercive mechanism, as Thomas's mentor Alby (Aml Ameen) informs us:

> This is all we got. We worked hard for it. ... We only have three rules. First, do your part. No time for any freeloaders. Second, never harm another Glader. None of this works unless we have trust. Most importantly, never go beyond those walls.

These Gladers, though, remain ambivalent about their own rules, even as they also specify social roles among themselves, some of them serving as cooks, farmers, medics, and, most curiously to Thomas, "runners." The walls open onto a maze, which reconfigures its inner convolutions each night, making it almost impossible to solve; nonetheless, the runners attempt to map it, trace a unicursal route through it, and steer clear of its ever-shifting corridors slamming shut on them as they attempt to return to the Glade (Figure 5.2). Thomas and the runners exchange a space of relative comfort and security for the risks and confusions of a maze environment, a narrative arc opposite to the ones in such films as *Labyrinth* (Jim Henson, 1986) and *The Shining* (Stanley Kubrick, 1980). The characters in those films escape *from* a maze, not *into* it so as to move *beyond* its walls, in Alby's words.

However, the external intellect among the Gladers inevitably starts to fracture; as Virno suggests, their sharing contradicts their "division of labor" and "causes it to crumble," which threatens to result in a re-hierarchization of the collective, especially if it is without a robust sociopolitical sphere to serve it as a countermeasure.[43] Gally (Will Poulter), the most refractory of the teenagers, attempts to take control of the Gladers and stop the runners from entering the maze, although to no avail. He insists that they "are

FIGURE 5.2 *The Walls Surrounding the Glade in* The Maze Runner.

home" in the Glade, forcing Thomas to retort: "This place is not our home. We were put here. We were trapped here. At least out there we have a choice. We can make it out of here." Thomas intuits the fact that they remain under the strategic capture of a sovereign agency, one that surrounds them with walls, monitors their actions, and sends them supplies and sometimes a "Greenie" or newcomer once a month up the elevator, without ever revealing its motives, its aims, the scope of its influence, or the faces and identities of its representatives.[44] This agency, in other words, conspires to force the teenagers into *a continuous state of veridical imperception* so that they start to distrust their memories of their families, their competence to ever solve the maze, and even their sense of imprisonment in the Glade—Gally and a few of the others resign themselves to it and take comfort in it, for instance. The designers of the maze, then, strategically work to disrupt the full mnemonic, epistemic, and imaginative capabilities of the teenagers, erasing from their minds the circumstances of their abduction and (for a short time) their names so that the reasons for their imprisonment seem unfathomable, a constant source of incomprehension to them. The construction of the maze, as it changes its inner spatial coordinates, therefore also throws off the reality testing, cognitive mapping, and sensori-perceptual abilities of these characters. Moreover, the designers stock its corridors with spiderlike cyborgs that inject a chemical substance into their victims, causing them to turn violent, irrational, and unresponsive to speech. Such strategies underline one of the most damaging effects of security walling on those it confines: it accustoms them to a condition of ignorance. Caetlin Benson-Allott describes this sort of "dreadful architecture" as diegetic spaces that "engulf the eye" so as to "invoke 'the unknown,'" thus confronting characters and viewers with a sense of their own "human triviality."[45] The film often dwells on the dark recesses inside the maze, as some of its cinematographic compositions threaten to swallow Thomas, the other runners, and the viewers in unending darkness, shutting them out from its visual realities and whatever conceptual sureties they might still cling to.

The strategic calculus of the WCKD organization—or more specifically, the World Catastrophe Killzone Department, as we soon discover—appears so thorough that it anticipates and foils the tactics the Gladers use to escape the maze. The elevator's detection devices, for example, frustrate their attempts to stow away on it, and WCKD constructs the maze in such a manner that they cannot climb to the top of it to spot an escape route. The sequel, *Maze Runner: The Scorch Trials* (Wes Ball, 2015), shows the agency separating the Gladers as children from their families, thus evoking the due process infringements of the Obama administration and more so Trump's "zero tolerance" rule. These deterrents function to ensure that the teenagers remain "in the dark," to make them always uncertain of the truth of their material and situational realities. However, they cannot fully constrain the workings of Thomas's unconscious, as the film's dream sequences randomly show us fragments of this truth, flashes of the medical facilities, the flotation tanks, and the refrain "WCKD is good" that only a few of the characters dimly recall from up until the time of their imprisonment in the maze. To unravel these mysteries and develop a more coherent sense of apperception, Thomas makes tactical use of the maze's defense elements, as well as some of the decisions that WCKD's scientists, engineers, and other functionaries make. The newest arrival to the Glade, Teresa (Kaya Scodelario), recognizes Thomas, and they soon develop a rapport, discussing their dim memories of their origins and attempting to unlock the reasons for their entrapment inside the walls of the maze. The other teenagers share no such recollections, and so the film establishes in Thomas and Teresa's relationship a sort of *crypto-social unconscious*, as neither the Gladers nor the WCKD officials can fully appreciate the depth of their resolve to escape. In fact, the corridors along the walls of the maze all open up after the two of them disclose their dreams and memories to each other, allowing the Grievers, the spider-cyborgs, to attack the Glade. Thomas fends them off, steals one of their "stingers," and uses it to enter into a trance that enables the Gladers to finally (re)learn the truth of their situation: that the maze is "not a prison, it's a test," and that Thomas and Teresa, as one-time WCKD staff members, sought to consign their friends to it. Their own internment inside the maze and their time spent with the multitude that survives near its walls offer them a refreshing contrast to WCKD's top-down structure and secretive nature and ultimately compels them to renounce their former allegiances and convince the others to feel "not at home" in the Glade.

Thomas, then, only seems to tactically use the design elements of the maze against the intentions of its makers. He entangles one of the Grievers in "webs" of ivy and afterward crushes it inside one of the maze's reconfiguring corridors. He takes a tracking device from the carcass and, over the course of the narrative, uses it to search for an escape route and finds one after discovering that it also functions as an access key to the recesses that the Grievers retreat to in the daylight. After their climactic fight with these monsters, and also Gally, who suffers the madness that their stings induce, Thomas, Teresa, and the other survivors enter a WCKD test center and see a video replay of their chief scientist congratulating them for their escape and recounting the reasons for the experiment. She tells them that the sun, after scorching the Earth, set in motion dire climatological effects, such as famine, wildfires, the desertification of cities and croplands, and ultimately the outbreak of the Flare virus, which turns its victims into vicious, incoherent, zombielike creatures that resemble dope fiends.[46] The virus, in short, turns the whole of the Earth into an interface area. The scientists sent the teenagers into the maze to test more than their tactical wherewithal; they sought to monitor their mental and immunological responses to its dangers so that they might extract from them a vaccine for the disease. The scientists at once strategically frustrate and *expect* their escape from the maze. However, in the sequels, the teenagers flee from WCKD, as it treats them as test rats and intends to farm them for neurochemicals, and encounter rival factions of marauders and freedom fighters the agency cannot control, despite its resources.

The series' final film, *Maze Runner: The Death Cure* (Wes Ball, 2018), in fact, features the former Gladers, the resistance fighters, and the sufferers of the virus teaming up to infiltrate the Last City, WCKD's center of operations and the only remaining urban space not in ruins. The walls that encompass it come replete with surveillance drones, digital camera systems, and remote control turrets, separating its residents from the Flare victims on the outside in a rather stark spatio-legible manner. The walls and other such strategic state defense installations, as the film suggests, must fail due to the tactical uses that they tempt from these multicoalitional forces, as they tunnel under them, override their computer controls, and carry with them into the city an airborne strain of the virus, which no security measure can impede or deter. These forces rupture the wall and raze the Last City, compelling Thomas, the source of an immunogenic response to the virus, to establish a new socius with the remaining Gladers and resistance fighters. Kendall R. Phillips argues that much dystopian teen science fiction, including the *Maze Runner* series, conduces to a sense of the nation-state as intrinsically corrupt so that their characters "must not so much rescue the system as destroy it," the same attitude that saw to the election of the quite iconoclastic Trump.[47] Although Phillips is correct to call our attention to the structure of feeling that these films might foster in us, we must remember that they also impel us to think through the effects of security walling and the apartheidist fantasies of its exponents and apologists: that they aim to transform the Earth into a series of conflict area checkerboards, and also to condition in us a veridical imperception that turns unfamiliar countries, regions, or other spaces into the dread-inducing signposts of the unknown. The "cure" for these ills, *The Maze Runner* suggests, is to develop *an even more nomadic ethos and existence* in the face of these exclusionary and suffocatingly statist security measures.[48] Thomas, in the final shot of series, stares wistfully at the open sea, not even "at home" in the safe zone these characters fought for the entire time.

The Divergent Series: Allegiant

The *Divergent* series also exemplifies the features of twenty-first-century teen franchise filmmaking, which, as Elissa H. Nelson notes, merges coming-of-age tales with fantasy, action, or science fiction formulas.[49] These films also focus on multigenerational conflict, as the characters in them discover their own identities as they strive to answer a question central to teen films and sci-fi action epics alike: "How can they survive and thrive in the problematic world" that they inherit from their forebears?[50] The first film, *Divergent* (Neil Burger, 2014), introduces us to Beatrice "Tris" Prior (Shailene Woodley), who at 16 must enter into one of the five castes of a dystopian version of Chicago that a security wall completely surrounds. Along with romantic interest Tobias "Four" Eaton (Theo James), she tests out as a "divergent," someone with multiple aptitudes who thus threatens the strict regimentation and factionalism of the city. Entering into a crypto-social relationship with Four, they together stop the renegade members of the intelligentsia caste from usurping control of the social order from another faction, more self-effacing and fit to rule. The sequel *The Divergent Series: Insurgent* (Robert Schwentke, 2015) further explores the civil frictions among the factions, as they arm themselves for war even as Tris obtains a data box that only those who combine the traits of all five castes can open. She succeeds in accessing its virtual content, finding out from it that the faction system serves as an experiment meant to engender divergents so that they can reconnect with the world's other societies on the other side of the wall. The final film, *The Divergent Series: Allegiant* (Robert Schwentke, 2016), seems the most important of them for this chapter, in that much of its action centers on the security wall that encloses the remnants of the factions of Chicago. Also, this wall conceals from them the Bureau of Genetic Welfare, a city of scientific administrators, chief among them David (Jeff Daniels), who attempt to map Tris's chromosomal matrix and use the results to repair all the damage done to "the genome," as an educational module tells us. Genetic modification, it appears, was the cause of irremediable societal rifts, and then ultimately of disastrous wars and the apocalyptic conditions resulting from them in such cities as Chicago and the wastelands surrounding it. However, the Bureau's administrators, Tris realizes, do not intervene in the city's violent affairs, as they at once wish to maintain their influence over it and ensure the steady funding of their "experiment." *Allegiant*, as does *The Maze Runner*, turns the usual inside-outside dynamic of such films upside-down, as its characters at first seek to escape *from* its walled-in diegetic areas, and then, after a certain course of events, to escape *to* them once again.

The Bureau orchestrates the fractionalization of Chicago in order to "ensure peace," as one of Tris's ancestors says; to conduct their experiments; and to conceal themselves, their upscale technologies, and their center of operations from its citizens. The wall surrounding the city appears integral to their strategic designs, as the voice of the ancestor tells us:

> I come from outside the wall, where we have all but destroyed each other. We designed your city as an experiment. We believe it is the only way to recover the humanity we have lost. And we created factions to ensure peace. But we believe there will be those among you who will

transcend these factions. These will be the divergent. They are the true purpose of this experiment, they are vital to humanity's survival. If you're watching this now, then at least one of you is proof that our experiment has succeeded. The time has come for you to emerge from your isolation and rejoin us. We've allowed you to believe that you're the last of us. But you're not. Mankind waits for you with hope beyond the wall.

However, the Bureau, more than maintaining a disinformation regime and an apartheidist state of affairs, also relies on surveillance drones, shock troops, and force shields to carry out a eugenics campaign on children taken from tent cities, a clear allusion to the family separation mandates of the Obama and then Trump administrations. The workings of this "mysterious council," as the main characters refer to it, are inscrutable and mostly unknown to the factions. Thus the warlords of Chicago come to internalize the vision and mime the disciplinary strategies of the "founders," as Four's mother Evelyn (Naomi Watts) calls them. As commander of the factionless, she discourages curiosity about "what's beyond the wall," contending that it is "there to protect us."[51] The film then underlines the correspondence of these statements to the value structures and defense resources of the Bureau, the members of which use force shields and flesh-encasing "plasma globes" to immunize themselves against the toxic effects of the "fringe" outside the major cities. These scientists and their troops, in effect, fence themselves off from their environment and from one another; in other words, they display the capacity to individualize the functions of nation-state walling. The characters using these technologies might as well rephrase Marlowe's *Doctor Faustus*: "Why this is a wall, nor am I out of it."

However, Evelyn's forces share with the Bureau members more than an affinity for these sorts of security instruments, since she also conducts a similar extermination campaign while ordering the city under "total lockdown." She oversees a series of show trials for former members of the faction system, executing those who confess to their caste allegiances after administering a truth serum to them. She also stations troops at the checkpoints close to the wall to make sure that "no one gets out." More specifically, she instructs factionless soldiers to "shoot to kill" anyone who attempts to "go over that wall" and, as an additional precaution, installs a capacitor near it that electrifies all of the antenna arrays at the top of it (Figure 5.3). Her strategic maneuvers, as we see throughout the narrative, echo those of the Bureau's administrators, who also seek to deter Tris, Four, and the rest of their cohort from escaping their facilities. Ultimately, David even attempts to use an airborne serum on the Chicagoans, so as to wipe their memories, induce them to reinstitute the factions, and therefore monitor and regulate their social organization from afar much more easily. These two regimes, the Bureau and the factionless, come to mirror each other, despite their disparities in terms of the civil regimentation, technological

FIGURE 5.3 *The Antenna Arrays Atop the City Walls in* The Divergent Series: Allegiant.

advancement, and sovereign authority they show forth. Nevertheless, they each remain vulnerable to forms of tactical resistance that make use of their own weapon arsenals, communication channels, and fortress-like spaces in often surprising and innovative ways—ways divergent from their designers' intentions.

Allegiant opens with its main couple climbing the frame of a skyscraper to catch a view of the fringe; as they do so, Tris says to Four, "Sometimes when I look past the wall, I can see something out there." She suggests that the spatio-legible construction of the film's diegesis forces these characters to travel in order to explore their options for resistance, social transformation, and self-knowledge. Thus Jasmine Lee and Jonathan Alexander argue that in this series "the idea of history is rendered more spatially than temporally. The 'origin' resides in the Bureau, a place beyond the wall."[52] The couple assemble a crypto-social coalition among the factionless that Evelyn remains unaware of, and they conspire to free Tris's sibling Caleb (Ansel Elgort) from the cages that confine the former members of the city's elite castes. To do so, they feign shooting down Caleb in front of Evelyn's Border Patrol forces, and, alongside troublemaker Peter (Miles Teller), they deactivate the capacitor, fire cables up the wall, and rappel over it into the fringe on the other side. Using these tactical maneuvers to flee into its russet sands, desert scrub, and toxic rivulets, they come across a digital "camo wall" that conceals the existence of the Bureau from the factions. Once inside the Bureau, though, they come across more than a "place-based" overview of their origins: Tris and Four soon discover that David intends to wipe the memories of the children the Bureau abducts, so as to erase their differences, foreclose dissident opinion, and ensure their allegiance to the Council. Hence, the Bureau functions to arrest the affectual, experiential, and sociohistorical intensities that constitute and define the multitude.

However, Tris's friends tactically use the Bureau's resources against its chief administrators, as Four comes to master the drone trackers, observes the shock troops in action, and acquires direct intelligence on David's eugenics scheme. Tris in turn tells the Council in Providence, another technocrat center, that she does not support social division of any sort and that they must consider "the damaged" as "worthy of life" as "the pure." The Council immediately defunds David's experiment, forcing the Bureau to restore the faction system in Chicago, overthrow Evelyn's tumultuous rule, and maintain surreptitious control over the unwitting test subjects that remain inside its walls. Peter and Caleb, though, use the Bureau's surveillance devices against it—this equipment can displace its user's train of vision inside remote areas, such as Chicago, so that they can secretly watch events transpire in them in real time and in three dimensions.[53] They use these devices to monitor Evelyn's dealings with the Bureau, to warn Tris and Four of the civil war about to erupt in Chicago, and to steer the divergents in the right directions as they storm the city in their search for the serum that David intends to use on its citizens to make them more docile and tractable. He uses the same devices as Caleb, although in ways that more so evoke de Certeau's notion of strategy: to seal rooms remotely so that Tris cannot access them and to telecommunicate with the divergents no matter where they are in the city, taunting them about their failure since the Bureau can monitor and thus neutralize their actions at all times. Tris nonetheless succeeds in disarming the serum after she rallies the city's other citizens, referring to them as "family." The Chicagoans, in other words, come to respect their differences in aptitude, chromosomal inheritance, and character disposition, refusing to distinguish "the pure" over and above "the damaged," rebuffing attempts to re-hierarchize their city into what amounts to a vast conflict-ridden interface area, and thus establishing themselves as a multitude, a countertendency to the state.

The formation of the multitude in *Allegiant* turns on the different modalities of the crypto-social, all of which concern the visual motif of mirror-like reflective surfaces that runs throughout the entire film series. The camo wall cloaks and separates the Bureau from the desert wilderness, as well from the Chicagoans, enabling David's technocrats and virtual spies to surveil them and intervene in their affairs. This sort of crypto-social relation resembles *a one-way mirror*, as the forces of the Bureau can detect and watch the former faction members, who cannot do the same in turn until the digital-simulacral wall deactivates. Such a wall does more than falsify the material realities of the film or impede Tris's friends from entering the Bureau; more insidiously, it frustrates the reciprocal recognition of difference, the development of more complex forms of sociopolitical consciousness, and the emergence of transborder struggle and counterhistorical meaning-making. The next mode of crypto-social relation appears more ambivalent in its use value. The Bureau's surveillance system, as it enables its users to explore a remote area in real time, can render their avatars invisible or "announce" them autostereoscopically to those under their observation so that two-way communication can occur. This device resembles more *a convex mirror*, since it opens on to wider fields of vision for its users and sometimes its trackees. The Bureau uses it more strategically, in order to exert sovereign control over the factions and refashion Chicago into an interface area, whereas the divergents use it for more tactical reasons, specifically to transform the conditions of civil dissension into ones ripe for the coalescing of a multitude.

The final crypto-social relation concerns Tris's opening of another data box and virtually reliving the memories of Natalie Prior (Ashley Judd), the mother that she thought a member of the meekest of the factions. Tris takes Natalie's figure as an avatar, as we see from the reflection that she casts in the mise-en-scène, and discovers that this woman fought as a soldier against the combat forces of the Bureau. This relation, then, enables Tris and the film's viewers to see through another's eyes, to forge counter-histories to the Bureau's more "official" version of these events, and to assay the sympathetic capacities that can inspire the Chicagoans to reject once and for all the conflictual nature of the faction system, as well as David's eugenics scheme. The data box, in its own way, resembles *an infinity mirror*, an infinite regress that allows these characters to see their desires, experiences, and struggles in one another, all while cluing us in on their respective differences also. Tris and Natalie, in short, as they mirror each other,[54] underline the family resemblances (namely among the multigenerational freedom fighters of the series) so evocative of Virno's notion of multitude. The data box, unlike the camo wall and surveillance system, seems outside of the strategic capture of the Bureau and the factionless, *as it serves to reveal, not conceal*. Thus, in the film's denouement, Tris discloses the Bureau's existence to the Chicagoans, who demolish the wall that encloses them and separates them from the fringe, finally favoring their family entwinement with one another over caste traits. The new sense of empowerment, self-knowledge, and social feeling coming from such recognition cannot coincide with sovereign overreach or incessant factional conflict—in any event, they represent the foundations from which a multitude, an open society, rather than a wall, might arise.

Kong: Skull Island

Much as in the case of *The Simpsons Movie*, Jordan Vogt-Roberts's *Kong: Skull Island* (2017) turns the venerable monster film into a species of ecohorror cinema. *Kong* is shot in a warm and stark orange, vermillion, and chartreuse visual scheme, full of colors that Patti Bellantoni describes as "toxic," "vile," "ominous," and "terrifying" as she traces their effects in such films as Francis Ford Coppola's 1979 Vietnam War epic *Apocalypse Now*.[55]

Set mostly on the mysterious Skull Island in the South Pacific near Vietnam in 1973, the film follows the efforts of a scientific-military expedition to save themselves from the massive and voracious spiders, insects, and reptilian "Skullcrawlers" that inhabit its coastlands and tropical rainforests. The first sequence of the film, though, features two Second World War fighter aces, Hank Marlow (John C. Reilly and Will Brittain) and Gunpei Ikari (Miyavi), crash-landing on Skull Island and then attempting to shoot down and stab each other, in the fashion of John Boorman's *Hell in the Pacific* (1968), until the towering figure of Kong shows up and distracts them. The opening credits follow, serving as an overview of the wars that came afterward and the strategic aerial defenses, surveillance satellites, and nuclear arms stockpiles that the United States was to develop during the Cold War era to "contain the savageness of man," as we catch Robert F. Kennedy declaim, famously quoting Aeschylus to eulogize Martin Luther King Jr. The film's introductory moments, then, suggest that the international and interracial conflicts that define the twentieth century recast the entire face of the Earth into a series of *shifting and relocatable interface areas*. For example, even though the film is set during the cease-fire, it introduces one of its main characters, former Special Air Service officer James Conrad (Tom Hiddleston), the expedition's tracker, settling a fight with some Vietnamese thugs in a Saigon saloon. Moreover, after Bill Randa (John Goodman), the senior operative of the Monarch institute responsible for the expedition, recruits the forces of US Army Colonel Preston Packard (Samuel L. Jackson) to serve as military escort, we immediately see tension and mutual contempt erupt among the soldiers and the scientists they must conduct to the Island.

The securitization of the nation-state and its allies through the constant use of new electronic and weapons technologies thus sets the stage for new, unpredictable sectarian conflicts to flare up, even among its own citizens and administrative functionaries. This state of affairs finds its objective correlative in the "war of all against all" that these characters discover on Skull Island, as they encounter several strange and deadly monsters that attempt to devour them and one another using their claws, fists, teeth, mandibles, tentacles, and other natural weapons.[56] However, the film does not conceptualize for us this "new ecosystem," as Bill Randa calls it, merely to reify the arms races and constant saber-rattling of the international scene. Unlike the creatures in the slightly more realistic ecohorror films of the 1970s, such as *Frogs* (George McCowan, 1972), *Kingdom of the Spiders* (John "Bud" Cardos, 1977), and *Nightwing* (Arthur Hiller, 1979), the ones in *Kong* appear as artificial as the excessively vibrant colors that streak its skylines, tropical forests, and coastal regions. Thus the film alludes to its 1970s antecedents without sounding the same cautionary notes, in that it rather suggests that the rampant artificialization of the ecosphere *can be tactically used to deescalate and denaturalize* nation-state security and the inequality, social exclusion, colonial expansionism, military aggression, internecine conflicts, and anthropogenic climate effects that might result from it.

A "perpetual storm system," as the film calls it, forms a natural wall of thick dark clouds surrounding Skull Island and concealing it from detection from ships, aircraft, satellites, and other vessels. Packard orders the attack helicopters the expedition flies in to assume combat formation and cut through the storm barrier so that they can reach "the land where God did not finish creation," as Randa christens it.[57] This description speaks to the "category crisis" that the monster represents, since its impossible form threatens to "smash distinctions," as Jeffrey Jerome Cohen argues, at the same time that it "prevents mobility (intellectual, geographic, sexual), delimiting the social spaces through which private bodies may move."[58] He continues, "To step outside this official geography is to risk attack by some monstrous border patrol or (worse) to become monstrous oneself."[59] These outcomes characterize the entire film, as the expedition sets off explosives to measure seismic response as soon as they arrive, angering Kong, who acts as a sort of nature deity on Skull Island. The massive ape attacks the convoy and destroys it, smashing, tossing, and twisting apart the helicopters in a sequence that reverses the climax of the original *King Kong* (Merian C. Cooper and Ernest B. Schoedsack, 1933), in which a number of airplanes shoot the monster off the top of the Empire State Building. The message is clear—this is the result when the action takes place on Kong's turf. As a consequence, the expedition splits up, forcing the survivors to regroup into two factions, one consisting mainly of Conrad, anti-war correspondent Mason Weaver (Brie Larson), and a couple of researchers, and the other of Packard, Randa, and the remaining soldiers. Their motives also diverge: Packard vows to take revenge and returns to the crash site to retrieve the munitions to do so, whereas Conrad and Weaver, after meeting the older Marlow and the Iwi tribe of Skull Island, fight to save Kong, who they come to see as a natural check to the Skullcrawlers.

The film, then, true to Cohen's argument, turns on a contradiction, in that the categorical confusion—the combination of mammalian, vegetal, arthropodous, and dinosaurian traits—that the monsters represent seems to oppose the clear spatio-legible demarcation of space in the diegesis. The film appears at first to structure its visual spaces along the axes of inner-outer and above-below. First, it uses colder color tones and a more realistic mise-en-scène, as well as a natural wall, to separate its scenes in Washington, DC, from those on Skull Island. The film further separates its surface areas from the tunnel system that runs underneath them, associating one with the "deific" Kong and the other with the Skullcrawlers, those "devils," as Marlow calls them, that creep out from vents in the Earth. However, the film crosses up these axes and distinctions, with the expedition (and all military excursions, including the ones in Vietnam, in the Middle East, and along the US–Mexico frontier) confounding these territorial divisions and transforming Skull Island into a specific interface site at which indigenous, American, East Asian, British, and nonhuman subjectivities meet. Even as the film's diegetic structuration undergoes such "categorical confusion," its monsters come to seem much more "legible" to the viewer. The ruthless Packard, over the course of the narrative, appears more monstrous than Kong, and as much of a threat of ecosystemic disequilibrium as the Skullcrawlers. Unlike them, though, rather than emerging from deep under the Earth, *this monster descends from the sky.*

The upshot is that in this film a character's status as inhuman, monstrous, or not-belonging depends not so much on their emplacement on this or that side of a security installation—it more so depends on *the standpoint they take to alterity* upon finding themselves stuck inside walled-in areas, whether desert islands or some other form of enclosure. Suffering from disillusionment due to the Paris Peace Accords ending direct military intervention in Vietnam, Packard, rather than conduct an escape from Skull Island, resolves to trap and destroy Kong, despite Marlow, Conrad, and the rest of their cohort arguing that doing so might take away the Skullcrawlers' "natural competition," causing them "to proliferate out of control." Packard waves their warnings aside, arrogantly responding that the soldiers "will end" the Skullcrawlers along with Kong and then angrily declaring that "this is one war we're not gonna lose."[60] Packard intends to recover the napalm, seismic charges, and other ordnance at the crash site to set Kong afire with, and even uses the search for a missing soldier as an alibi for driving the survivors away from a rendezvous point along the coastline and once more deep into the island's dangerous interior to track the monster ape. Packard, in short, intends to make strategic use of these munitions, fulfilling the intentions of the military suppliers and arms manufacturers: to engage in slaughter and destruction, and thus to exert the sovereign might of the United States over other territories, often for short-term advantages.

Conrad's faction, in contrast, uses the materials from the crash more tactically in order to expedite their travels through the island's interior, develop a rapport with its nonthreatening monsters, and escape through its coastal storm barrier. They snap images of these creatures rather than shoot at them, tactically useful insofar as they can take them to the United States and elsewhere to re-politicize issues of environmental consequence, connect them up to anti-war and decolonial efforts, and confirm Randa's speculation that "this planet doesn't belong to us. Ancient species owned this Earth long before mankind." Moreover, rather than regathering the weapons they came with, Conrad and the others recycle the scrap from US and Japanese attack aircraft to construct a riverboat that can rapidly take them to the island's north shore—in short, they use these materials against their designers' wishes and intentions. Over the course of their travels, they decide to make more tactical use of Kong against the Skullcrawlers and coordinate a sneak attack on Packard's soldiers that affords the monster ape time to shrug off the effects of the napalm charges. Kong crushes Packard and then, with Weaver's assistance, slices the throat of the most fearsome of the Skullcrawlers with the ship's airfoils. The ape also swings a set of chains as a weapon: rather than serve as mere shackles, as in the 1933 film, Kong makes tactical, improvisational use of them. This ending furthermore suggests that Weaver, unlike Ann Darrow (Fay Wray) in the original, does not function as a simple damsel-in-distress.

The film makes it clear, though, that these characters cannot accomplish these objectives without the assistance and hospitality of the Iwi tribespeople, who welcome them into their village and share with them their mythopoetic understanding of the origins and significance of Kong, the Skullcrawlers, and the island's other monsters. The Iwi fortify the islet that their village rests on with a tall wooden security wall, a refiguration of the storm barrier that engulfs, conceals, and safeguards Skull Island from outside threats.[61] However, the walls surrounding the village create a different sort of interface area, one that denaturalizes war, slaughter, and other forms of conflict and fosters intercultural, intergenerational, and interspecies forms of support and reciprocation (Figure 5.4). As the Iwi, with Marlow as their mouthpiece, relate stories of their "savior" Kong, Weaver snaps images of them in order to retell these stories in newspapers, magazines, and television reports after she returns to the United States. The myths of the Iwi inspire Weaver to attempt to rescue a massive ox-like creature stuck under the fuselage of one of the aircraft that Kong struck down. The tranquil atmosphere of the village also affects Marlow, who develops close ties to Gunpei (who dies off-screen) and a soldier in Conrad's faction, with these men from different eras and theaters of combat sharing with one another their tastes in sports and music. Their repartee differs markedly from the mean-spiritedness of the interaction of the soldiers with the scientists earlier in the film. Marlow

FIGURE 5.4 *The Village Walls in* Kong: Skull Island.

tells the English-speaking characters that the Iwi suffer from no war, no crimes, and no squabbles over "personal property," and thus *they altogether come to constitute the beginnings of a multitude*, a non-statist collective that resists sovereign forms of administration; respects ethnocultural, religious, and individual difference; and values environmental rights and animal–human cooperation.[62]

The Iwi scenes in the film, though, do not simply tout security walling as an effective means of tightening up tribal, national, or sectarian identities. The distinct sort of interface area that the village represents rather affords opportunities for crypto-social relationships to form that elude the notice of such authority figures as Packard and, for all their charms, impart a sense of displeasure at ever feeling too much "at home," as Virno might say. This feeling drives Conrad, Marlow, Weaver, and the others—and with them, the film's viewers—to move *beyond* the walls surrounding the village and Skull Island, even if doing so entails danger and the risk of death. However, to remain inside them might appear to us even more dangerous, as it implies a sense of resignation to the "war of all against all" so detrimental to smaller communities, asylum seekers (including Conrad's crew), and the ecosphere. Graig Uhlin argues that even now "wherever one looks in 'nature' …, one finds the disturbances and perturbations of humanity's actions. Earth, in other words, registers our touch and responds to our interventions."[63] *Kong* suggests that rather than seeing ourselves above or in charge of the unknown, the unfamiliar, or the unlike-us, we decamp from our comfortable surroundings and slip through the clouds of fear, misunderstanding, and enmity that separate us from them. The monster ape, in one important scene that we might at first mistake as sentimental, reaches out to touch Weaver and Conrad—they register one another's touch, in other words. To see such separation as unnatural, then, is the first step in confronting the world's ever-heightening unnaturalness and refusing to feel "at home" with it anymore.

War for the Planet of the Apes

Like *Kong: Skull Island*, Matt Reeves's *War for the Planet of the Apes* (2017) takes some of its inspiration from *Apocalypse Now*, a film that, for Andrew Britton, recounts Freud's mythologization of war as "the scene of the primal man," as it exalts "the technology of destruction" and apologizes for its use.[64] Timothy Corrigan, in accordance with this argument, claims that such a film might then actually celebrate the release of "the human subject from its strictures," often in a regressive direction.[65] *War for the Planet of the Apes* takes these cues from Coppola's war epic and tweaks them, as the soldier characters in it degenerate into a "primal" and "regressive" condition. Set in a milieu in which "Simian Flu" decimates our species, enhances the intelligence of apes, chimpanzees, and orangutans, and results in violence among them and the survivors of the outbreak, the film opens with a commando offensive against an outpost in the woods with wall-like trenches fortifying its interior. Caesar (Andy Serkis), the chieftain of the apes, strategically relocates them to the woods in order to frustrate the efforts of the forces of a renegade colonel (Woody Harrelson) to exterminate them. The colonel sends the squadron to sneak up on the outpost, snipe at its sentries with crossbows, and set off an explosion that rips through its trenches and slaughters a few of the apes inside it. These soldiers engage in these stealth tactics with the assistance of a "donkey," their nickname for an ape traitor—one that evokes a drudge animal and also the classic video game *Donkey Kong*—responsible for reloading their firearms, tracking down their enemies, and slavishly carrying their supplies. However, Caesar, ready for this attack, mounts a counteroffensive, summoning forth a number of archers who slaughter almost all of the soldiers, enabling the apes to take a few as captives. Caesar spares these men and charges them to ask for a cease-fire and tell their cohort that apes "are not savages," after finding out the colonel's main objective. As one of the donkeys admits, "Their Colonel has all power .... He say, 'First Caesar die, then all of you die.'" These attacks frighten the tribe, forcing Caesar to scout a desert wilderness, decide to resituate the apes in its mountain recesses, and organize "a safe way out of the woods" for them. The tribe, in short, starts to chafe at the notion of *a security enclosure*,[66] seeing it as inimical to their chances for survival and self-determination. The colonel meanwhile changes tactics, sending into the outpost stealth troopers who use some of its natural defenses, its quietude, its waterfalls, and the darkness of night to massacre the apes in their sleep. Even as a number of them fight off the soldiers and escape, the colonel infiltrates the outpost in person and murders most of Caesar's family. The surviving apes resolve to search for their desert Promised Land, with Caesar swearing revenge against the colonel and setting off toward the soldiers' mobile camp with a few close companions. Their chieftain, in effect, adopts the colonel's main objective, targeting the soldiers' commander in order to render them incapable of such clever maneuvering and thus of acting as a serious threat.

The first section of the film sees its villain setting tactical strikes up against Caesar's strategic calculations. The next, though, switches the two warlords' roles, as Caesar tactically uses the resources, structural design, and emplacement of the soldiers' center of operations against their Colonel's strategic efforts to enslave, maltreat, demoralize, and exterminate the other apes. After sneaking into the soldiers' mobile camp and silencing the donkey snitches inside it, Caesar's task force follows it to the nightmarish "California Border Quarantine Facility," a former relocation camp that a

FIGURE 5.5 *The California Border Quarantine Facility in* War for the Planet of the Apes.

number of steel-mesh fences secure and enclose. There they discover the rest of the tribe in cages, and soon afterward the colonel's men successfully capture Caesar too (Figure 5.5). The soldiers force the apes to mine a cache of weapons out of a mountainside, scourging and even crucifying those who dissent, resist, or tire out in a manner reminiscent of such films as *Spartacus* (Stanley Kubrick, 1960) or the television miniseries *Roots* (1977). The soldiers also use the donkeys as *kapos* to terrorize the other apes and spur them to work faster, and most callously separate them from their children in the manner of the "zero tolerance" approach to the immigration crisis of the Trump administration. The colonel, during a conversation with Caesar, confesses to thinking of the apes as "unholy," speculating that they might evolve to such a degree that they start regarding our species as their "cattle." The facility, it turns out, more than serves as a strategic military installation or a site to instill discipline in the soldiers, who nonetheless roar and shout in formation as though they were animals. According to a stray ape that Caesar meets—one self-taught in English—the facility actually functions as a quarantine area due to a virulent mutation of the Simian Flu that deprives its victims of their complex thinking abilities and speech so that they come to chatter, snarl, croak, and splutter as though they were subhuman. The colonel, as Caesar finds out, suffers this disease, making some sense of the villain's shaven scalp, as it references similar maniacal characters, such as Colonel Walter Kurtz (Marlon Brando) in *Apocalypse Now* and the serial murderer Mickey Knox (also Woody Harrelson) in *Natural Born Killers* (Oliver Stone, 1994).

Much as the soldiers infiltrate the apes' fort, using its defense mechanisms against it, so too does Caesar, even while captive, tactically use the trappings of the facility to outwit its sentries, reunite families and free them from their cages, and steal into the colonel's chambers in an assassination attempt.[67]

He coordinates efforts with the three ape companions that remain in the foothills outside the walls of the facility in order to free the children and conduct them safely through the tunnel system that subtends it and functions as an Underground Railroad of sorts.[68] The apes, though, as they dig toward the surface, notice the tunnels directly underneath the cages flooding and must change tactics accordingly. Caesar and the other captive apes fling their feces at the face and neck of the night sentinel standing watch over the cages, infuriating the man. To take tactical advantage of the situation, the apes thus enact a stereotype that the men ascribe to "monkeys" in cages—an intimation of their intelligence, their signifying capabilities, and the changes made to their ortho-praxis after their own exposure to the Simian Flu virus.[69] Caesar's companions dig under the sentinel's feet, drag the man into the shaft, and steal a ring of cell keys so that they can start to marshal the captives away from the cages, into the tunnel system, and finally outside the facility. The apes moreover take advantage of the US military's decision to carry out an airstrike on the rogue colonel's center of operations at that same moment, a distraction that enables Caesar to attempt to set off an explosion that might collapse the facility's security fencing. One of the soldiers, whom the apes ironically thought to spare earlier in the film, shoots Caesar in the flank with an arrow. This action, though, inspires a donkey in charge of munitions atop the railing of the fences to turn on the soldiers, save Caesar from the ungrateful sniper, and finish setting off the explosion that tears an opening in the facility's defenses. The apes then escape from the crossfire altogether when the aftershock triggers an avalanche—an "act of God," so to speak, that discredits the colonel's representation of their species as "unholy." The remaining soldiers, about to turn their rifles against the defenseless apes, watch in a state of terror as the snow totally engulfs them. Once again, the apes adapt to these circumstances, showing forth their opportunism, their tactical shrewdness, and their stronger morphologies as they climb up the trees on the mountain slope, avoiding the worst of the cascading snow.

The colonel, speechless and exhibiting the symptoms of the virus, commits suicide in the camp, after Caesar refuses to shoot the madman in the skull. The two chieftains share similar family tragedies, as their wives and children die during the course of the ape–human war and, in Caesar's words, they consequently "cannot escape [their] hate" for their enemies.[70] His words refigure the soldiers' camp into an interface area in the strictest definition of the term: a contact zone in which two communities come into continual conflict and develop a mutual detestation for each other. However, Caesar rethinks the vow to take revenge after the colonel makes "ape" noises, choking on words while resting atop a mattress, a small step toward establishing a common source of empathy and relatability that might unite these two competitor species. Earlier in the film, in fact, Caesar and the others stumble across Nova (Amiah Miller), an orphan daughter of a soldier outcast who also suffers from the effects of the virus. She accompanies the apes on their mission, along the way developing the ability to sign to them, earning their trust enough to share their canteen. She even mourns as one of the apes dies after a firefight, to the utter astonishment of the rest of them. After the colonel scourges, crucifies, and tortures Caesar, Nova sneaks into the facility, offering the war chief water, wheat meal, and even the small comfort of a favorite children's doll as the other apes in their cages watch, once again in awe at seeing one of their enemies showing compassion to a member of their species. Nova and the tribe enter into a clear crypto-social relationship in this sequence, as these two different species establish a connection, even though a nonverbal one, right underneath the noses of the colonel's men. The captive apes make the sign of unity toward the mute Nova and she reciprocates, an indication that she now stands as a full inductee into their tribe, rather than a refugee whom neither faction wants.[71]

The film, in these scenes, suggests that *even the lack of language can serve as a common language,* after certain courageous members of two warring communities agree to set aside their animosities and tacitly establish a form of affective, sociolinguistic, or small-scale resource exchange. The apes take Nova with them to the desert oasis in the valley that they seek, a movement from "a primate concentration camp" to "the Promised Land," in the words of Michael Sragow's review of the film.[72] This epilogue motions toward the creation of a multitude, open to innovative discourse routines, multimodal communication rituals, inclusive forms of membership, and nonauthoritarian self-rule—thus it is no accident that the child's name in Latin means "new." The ending of the film, though, does not neatly construct Caesar as a Moses figure. He dies of the arrow wounds underneath a tree overlooking the valley, a scene more evocative of the fate of Aeneas, the mythic founder of Rome who also suffers from similar injuries and establishes a city next to a thick forest. This comparison is far more apt, although not merely due to the main ape character's name; we must also remember that the donkey that saves Caesar from the sniper offers up these dying words: the colonel's "wall is madness. It won't save him anymore than it will save you." These words almost suggest "instructions for use" for the founding of the new city in the desert wilderness, although ones with a decidedly anti-statist, nonstrategic tenor to them, as they impel the tribe to consider security fences or other inflexible forms of territorial demarcation as repetitions of madness. *War for the Planet of the Apes* envisions *an imperium without walls* in these final scenes, an important message for US and other audiences struggling to square their security concerns against their ethical responsibilities to immigrants and refugees at the time of their mass internment under increasingly militarist, reactionary regimes.

Conclusion

The crypto-social thrust of these films in effect shapes forth new worlds, new cultural domains, new forms of nonhostile interfacing, as the characters in them meet up, enter into secret romances, share resources or amenities, invent new slang terms or discourse routines, and discuss their dreams, interests, or "war stories" with one another. Moreover, they do these things right under the security walls, fences, and other strategic defense installations specifically set up to interdict these sorts of relationships. The transformation of the interface areas in these films from conflict, exclusion, or no-go zones into spheres of collective dissent underlines the degree to which these security measures remain unresponsive to our deeply felt social needs. The walls in these media franchises, after all, discourage their characters from speaking to one another, touching one another, seeing themselves in others, or establishing new family or community engagements outright. Thus these films fantasize the malignant influence of these walls, as those they shut in devolve into speechlessness without other societies to communicate with; start to take comfort in the steady artificialization of a nature they see as frightful and out-to-kill; and remain in a state of ignorance about the world's scope, the ulterior motives of their rulers and administrators, and the thrills and responsibilities that true freedom entails. At the most, these walls can offer strangers fleeting shelter, as in *Kong: Skull Island*. The crypto-social relations that such characters establish, though, mainly invite us to *think beyond walls, beyond demonizing refugees or nonnationals*, in matters of immigration reform, cross-border trade, and climate change mitigation. These characters, then, move in the utopian directions that Andrew Britton describes: "To challenge a definition of the real is to challenge a definition of what it is possible to desire and what it is possible to do."[73] His concern is with "significant art," canonical cinema that is often illegible in form (although not avant-garde) and assuredly forward-thinking in its messages. However, in the twenty-first century, the walls that Trump and other far-right officials seek to finance, construct, reinforce, staff, and maintain appear *much more legible* in terms of the territorial markers, social divisions, and nation-state identities that they function to shore up. *Walls Without Cinema* reclaims more vulgarly commercial cinema as significant art in its own right, since much of it reflects these illiberal sociohistorical realities and offers us a means to resist them, if we first take the right interpretive approaches to them.

Notes

1   See "More than 5,400 Children Split at Border, According to New Count," *NBC News*, October 25, 2019, https://www.nbcnews.com/news/us-news/

more-5-400-children-split-border-according-new-count-n1071791; and Amanda Holpuch, "Thousands More Migrant Children Separated under Trump Than Previously Known," *The Guardian*, January 17, 2019, https://www.theguardian.com/us-news/2019/jan/17/trump-family-separations-report-latest-news-zero-tolerance-policy-immigrant-children.

2   See "US Attorney General Jeff Sessions on Children Separated from Parents at Border, F-1 Visas for PRC Students, and Masterpiece Cakeshop Decision," *Hugh Hewitt*, June 5, 2018, https://www.hughhewitt.com/attorney-general-jeff-sessions-on-the-immigration-policies-concerning-children-apprehended-at-he-border-and-f-1-visas/.

3   See Dara Lind, "The Disastrous, Forgotten 1996 Law That Created Today's Immigration Problem," *Vox*, April 28, 2016, https://www.vox.com/2016/4/28/11515132/iirira-clinton-immigration; George W. Bush, "Immigration Reform Address," *C-SPAN*, May 15, 2006, https://www.c-span.org/video/?192506-1/president-bush-address-immigration; "President Bush's Plan for Comprehensive Immigration Reform," *The White House: President George W. Bush*, 2007, https://georgewbush-whitehouse.archives.gov/stateoftheunion/2007/initiatives/immigration.html; Alicia A. Caldwell, "Administration to Open Detention Centers for Families Caught Crossing the Border," *PBS*, June 20, 2014, https://www.pbs.org/newshour/politics/administration-open-detention-centers-families-caught-crossing-border; Amanda Sakuma, "The Failed Experiment of Immigrant Family Detention," *NBC News*, August 2, 2015, https://www.nbcnews.com/news/latino/failed-experiment-immigrant-family-detention-n403126; and Sari Horwitz, "Sessions Vows to Prosecute All Illegal Border Crossers and Separate Children from Their Parents," *Washington Post*, May 7, 2018, https://www.washingtonpost.com/world/national-security/sessions-says-justice-dept-will-prosecute-every-person-who-crosses-border-unlawfully/2018/05/07/e1312b7e-5216-11e8-9c91-7dab596e8252_story.html.

4   See Rafia Zakaria, "How Trump Is Stripping Immigrants of Their Citizenship," *The Nation*, December 21, 2018, https://www.thenation.com/article/denaturalization-trump-citizenship-emma-goldman/; Steve Holland and Roberta Rampton, "Trump to Propose Plan to Make U.S. Immigration More Merit-Based," *Reuters*, May 15, 2019, https://www.reuters.com/article/us-usa-immigration-trump/trump-to-propose-plan-to-make-u-s-immigration-more-merit-based-idUSKCN1SL2CX; Daniella Silva, Julia Ainsley, Pete Williams, and Geoff Bennett, "Trump Administration Moves to End Asylum Protections for Most Central American Migrants," *NBC News*, July 15, 2019, https://www.nbcnews.com/news/us-news/trump-administration-moves-end-asylum-protections-most-central-american-migrants-n1029866; James Fredrick, "'Metering' at the Border," *NPR*, June 29, 2019, https://www.npr.org/2019/06/29/737268856/metering-at-the-border; Vandana Ravikumar, "'Operation Border Resolve' ICE Raids, Touted by President Donald Trump, Net 35 Arrests, Officials Say," *USA Today*, July 24, 2019, https://www.usatoday.com/story/news/nation/2019/07/23/ice-raids-president-donald-trump-35-arrests-officials/1810185001/; Maegan Vazquez, "Trump Defends ICE Raid Strategy," *CNN*, August 9, 2019,

https://www.cnn.com/2019/08/09/politics/trump-defends-ice-raid-strategy/index.html; Jason Kao and Denise Lu, "How Trump's Policies Are Leaving Thousands of Asylum Seekers Waiting in Mexico," *New York Times*, August 18, 2019, https://www.nytimes.com/interactive/2019/08/18/us/mexico-immigration-asylum.html; Sinduja Rangarajan, "The Trump Administration Is Denying H-1B Visas at a Dizzying Rate, but It's Hit a Snag," *Mother Jones*, October 17, 2019, https://www.motherjones.com/politics/2019/10/h1b-tech-visa-denial-appeal-trump/; and Stuart Anderson, "Trump Plans Far-Reaching Set of New Immigration Regulations," *Forbes*, November 21, 2019, https://www.forbes.com/sites/stuartanderson/2019/11/21/trump-plans-far-reaching-set-of-new-immigration-regulations/#7d7b591262a7.

5 See Donald J. Trump (@realDonaldTrump), "… Mexico must apprehend all illegals and not let them make the long march up to the United States, or we will have no other choice than to Close the Border and/or institute Tariffs. Our Country is FULL!" *Twitter*, April 7, 2019, 9:03 a.m., https://twitter.com/realdonaldtrump/ status/1115057524770844672?lang=en.

6 See Caitlin Dickerson, "'There Is a Stench': Soiled Clothes and No Baths for Migrant Children at a Texas Center," *New York Times*, June 21, 2019, https://www.nytimes.com/2019/06/21/us/migrant-children-border-soap.html; Lulu Garcia-Navarro, "Law Professor Describes Poor Conditions Where Migrant Children Are Held," *NPR*, June 23, 2019, https://www.npr.org/2019/06/23/735191289/law-professor-describes-poor-conditions-where-migrant-children-are-held; and Bob Ortega, "Doctor Says Border Patrol Often Misses Early Signs of Illness in Migrant Children," *CNN*, July 1, 2019, https://www.cnn.com/2019/07/01/us/migrant-children-hospitalized-doctor-border-invs/index.html.

7 See Tim Dickinson, "Trump Administration Argues that Migrant Children Don't Need Soap," *Rolling Stone*, June 20, 2019, https://www.rollingstone.com/politics/politics-news/safe-sanitary-no-soap-beds-court-migrants-trump-850744/; and Manny Fernandez, "Lawyer Draws Outrage for Defending Lack of Toothbrushes in Border Detention," *New York Times*, June 25, 2019, https://www.nytimes.com/ 2019/06/25/us/sarah-fabian-migrant-lawyer-doj.html.

8 See Vanessa Romo, "Administration Cuts Education and Legal Services for Unaccompanied Minors," *NPR*, June 5, 2019, https://www.npr.org/2019/06/05/730082911/administration-cuts-education-and-legal-services-for-unaccompanied-minors; Maria Sacchetti, "Trump Administration Cancels English Classes, Soccer, Legal Aid for Unaccompanied Child Migrants in US Shelters," *Washington Post*, June 5, 2019, https://www.washingtonpost.com/immigration/trump-administration-cancels-english-classes-soccer-legal-aid-for-unaccompanied-child-migrants-in-us-shelters/2019/06/05/df2a0008-8712-11e9-a491-25df61c78dc4_story.html?arc404=true; Jared Weber, "Trump Administration Cuts English Classes, Soccer and Legal Aid for Migrant Children at Shelters," *USA Today*, June 5, 2019, https://www.usatoday.com/story/news/nation/2019/06/05/

trump-administration-cancels-services-migrant-children/1358114001/; Naureen Shah, "DHS Is Locking Immigrants in Solitary Confinement," *ACLU*, May 24, 2019, https://www.aclu.org/blog/immigrants-rights/immigrants-rights-and-detention/dhs-locking-immigrants-solitary-confinement; Michael Biesecker, Jake Pearson, and Garance Burke, "Governor Orders Probe of Abuse Claims by Immigrant Children," *AP News*, June 21, 2018, https://apnews.com/afc80e51b562462c89907b49ae624e79; Daniella Silva, "'Like I Am Trash': Migrant Children Reveal Stories of Detention, Separation," *NBC News*, July 26, 2018, https://www.nbcnews.com/news/latino/i-am-trash-migrant-children-reveal-stories-detention-separation-n895006; Anne Flaherty, "CBP Investigating Allegation by Young Girl that She Was 'Beaten and Abused' at Clint Border Facility," *ABC News*, July 25, 2019, https://abcnews.go.com/Politics/cbp-investigating-allegation-young-girl-beaten-abused-clint/story?id=64565883; Alex Gomez, "Government Watchdog: Separated Migrant Children Suffered PTSD, Other Mental Trauma," *USA Today*, September 4, 2019, https://www.usatoday.com/story/news/nation/2019/09/04/separated-migrant-children-suffered-ptsd-trauma-report-says/2209669001/; and Coleen Long, "At Least 4,500 Abuse Complaints at Migrant Children Shelters," *AP News*, February 26, 2019, https://apnews.com/6bc34d8c6aaa41d0998d8bce46687e90.

9 See Jack Holmes, "An Expert on Concentration Says That's Exactly What the U.S. Is Running at the Border," *Esquire*, June 13, 2019, https://www.esquire.com/news-politics/a27813648/concentration-camps-southern-border-migrant-detention-facilities-trump/; Caitlin O'Kane, "Alexandra Ocasio-Cortez: 'The U.S. Is Running Concentration Camps on Our Southern Border,'" *CBS News*, June 18, 2019, https://www.cbsnews.com/news/alexandria-ocasio-cortez-claims-us-running-concentration-camps-on-southern-border/; Ben Fenwick, "'Stop Repeating History': Plan to Keep Migrant Children at Former Internment Camp Draws Outrage," *New York Times*, June 22, 2019, https://www.nytimes.com/2019/06/22/us/fort-sill-protests-japanese-internment.html; and Charles M. Blow, "Trump's 'Concentration Camps,'" *New York Times*, June 23, 2019, https://www.nytimes.com/2019/06/23/opinion/trump-migrants-camps.html.

10 See Makini Brice, "Trump Threatens More Tariffs on Mexico as Part of Immigration Deal," *Reuters*, June 10, 2019, https://www.reuters.com/article/us-usa-trade-mexico/trump-threatens-more-tariffs-on-mexico-over-part-of-immigration-deal-idUSKCN1TB182; and Dave Graham, "Mexico Says It Has Deployed 15,000 in the North to Halt U.S.-Bound Immigration," *Reuters*, June 24, 2019, https://www.reuters.com/article/us-usa-trade-mexico-immigration/mexico-says-it-has-deployed-15000-forces-in-the-north-to-halt-u-s-bound-migration-idUSKCN1TP2YN.

11 See Claire Hansen, "Proposed Trump Rule Limits Eligibility for Asylum," *U.S. News & World Report*, December 18, 2019, https://www.usnews.com/news/national-news/articles/2019-12-18/proposed-trump-rule-limits-eligibility-for-asylum; and Colleen Long, Frank Bajak, and Will Weissert, "Ankle Monitors for Immigrants Almost Universally Disliked,"

Denver Post, August 25, 2018, https://www.denverpost.com/2018/08/25/ice-issuing-immigrant-ankle-monitors/.

12 Michel de Certeau, *The Practice of Everyday Life*, trans. Steven Rendall (Berkeley: University of California Press, 1988), 29.

13 Ibid., 36.

14 Ibid..

15 See "El Paso Sector Border Patrol Encounters New Tactics as Smugglers Keep Sending in Families and Felons," *U.S. Customs and Border Protection*, April 17, 2019, https://www.cbp.gov/newsroom/local-media-release/el-paso-sector-border-patrol-encounters-new-tactics-smugglers-keep; and Lucina Melesio and John Holman, "Mexican Cartels Recruit Children to Smuggle People to US," *Al Jazeera*, October 30, 2017, https://www.aljazeera.com/news/2017/10/mexico-cartels-recruit-children-smuggle-people-171030103553245.html.

16 See Wendy Fry, "Concertina Wire Stolen from Border Fence and Used for Home Security in Tijuana, Authorities Say," *San Diego Union-Tribune*, March 18, 2019, https://www.sandiegouniontribune.com/news/border-baja-california/sd-me-concertina-wire-tj-20190318-story.html.

17 See Micheal Agier et al., *The Jungle: Calais' Camps and Migrants* (Malden, MA: Polity, 2019), 94–103.

18 See Chantal Da Silva, "ICE Agents Frustrated by Trump Using Agency as Political 'Pawn' to Push Anti-immigration Agenda, Former Official Says," *Newsweek*, May 6, 2018, https://www.newsweek.com/ice-agents-frustrated-trumps-immigration-crackdown-which-putting-communities-831999; Michael D. Shear, Abby Goodnough, and Maggie Haberman, "Trump Retreats on Separating Families, but Thousands May Remain Apart," *New York Times*, June 20, 2018, https://www.nytimes.com/2018/06/20/us/politics/trump-immigration-children-executive-order.html; Jonathan Blitzer, "ICE Agents Are Losing Patience with Trump's Chaotic Immigration Policy," *New Yorker*, June 24, 2019, https://www.newyorker.com/news/news-desk/ice-agents-are-losing-patience-with-trumps-chaotic-immigration-policy; and John Burnett, "'I'm Crushed': Migrant Parents, Advocates Press for Family Reunification," *NPR*, June 26, 2018, https://www.npr.org/2018/06/26/623451388/trumps-zero-tolerance-policy-overwhelms-border-agents.

19 Certeau, *Practice of Everyday Life*, 29, 37.

20 Ibid., 37–8.

21 Ibid., 37.

22 Paolo Virno, *A Grammar of the Multitude: For an Analysis of Contemporary Forms of Life*, trans. Isabella Bertoletti, James Cascaito, and Andrea Casson (Los Angeles: Semiotext(e), 2004), 23.

23 Ibid., 76–8.

24 Ibid., 34.

25 Ibid., 40, 43.

26 See John McWhorter, "AOC's Critics Are Pretending Not to Know How Language Works," *The Atlantic*, June 20, 2019, https://www.theatlantic.com/ideas/archive/2019/06/defense-ocasio-cortez-concentration-camp-comment/592180/.
27 Virno, *Grammar of the Multitude*, 21.
28 Ibid., 78, 84, 86.
29 Ibid., 86.
30 Ibid., 97–8.
31 Ibid., 90, 93.
32 Ibid., 93.
33 David McNally, "Ugly Beauty: Monstrous Dreams of Utopia," in *Zombie Theory: A Reader*, ed. Sarah Juliet Lauro (Minneapolis: University of Minnesota Press, 2017), 132.
34 Ibid., 132–3.
35 *Underworld: Rise of the Lycans* (Patrick Tatopoulos, 2009) also features a cross-ontological romance that, in this franchise, couples two monster species together. The vampire council in the film sequesters themselves inside the walls of a castle fortress so that from its spires it can raise a caste of werewolves to serve them, subjecting them to whippings; frighten the villagers into offering them tributes of silver, the sole weakness of their monstrous slaves; and thus set their rival races into conflict so as to maintain control over them and eliminate the threat of insurrection. However, the slave Lucian (Michael Sheen) falls for the daughter of the one of the vampire elders, Sonja (Rhona Mitra), and together they orchestrate the escape of the other werewolves from the fortress. Lucian turns the vampires' strategic calculations against them, recruiting the savage werewolves of the forests, negotiating a truce with the villagers, and forming a multiracial coalition to use to storm the fortress and free Sonja from imprisonment and death. However, the elders expose Sonja to sunlight and she turns to ashes in front of Lucian, who calls on the other werewolves to expose their crimes, destroy their noble ranks, and take revenge against the remaining members of their race, a story arc that the other *Underworld* films chronicle. *Rise of the Lycans*, though, remains a significant installment in the series—even though its main star, Kate Beckinsale, only makes a cameo appearance in it—in that it styles the forest outside the castle as an interface area, in which the werewolves and villagers, who otherwise despise each other, nonetheless come to a mutual understanding over their common subordination to the vampires. The film also underlines one of the saddest results of security walling: that it exacerbates the conditions for *race war*. The razing of the fortress in the final sequence ends the film on an optimistic note, though, as it motions toward a "beyond" to these sorts of antipathies. The film, after all, suggests that an alternate form of intergroup relationship might develop, once free from the chains of abuse, exploitation, resentment, and mistrust.
36 Lone Bertelsen and Andrew Murphie, "An Ethics of Everyday Infinities and Powers: Félix Guattari on Affect and the Refrain," in *The Affect Theory*

Reader, ed. Melissa Grieg and Gregory J. Seigworth (Durham, NC: Duke University Press, 2010), 152.

37 Ibid.

38 Sarah Ahmed examines the discourse of "stranger danger" that shapes forth these sorts of figures as dangerous and unknowable, compelling communities and citizenries, in order to exclude them from their neighborhoods, to first set about recuperating them into a recognizable form. She analogizes the "ideal neighborhood" to the "healthy body," since each appears "integrated, homogenous, and sealed," nonporous enough "not to let outsiders (or foreign agents/viruses) in." Both Colonel Grigio and the "bonies" in *Warm Bodies* strive to maintain "purified places," each relying on certain visual, acoustic, or olfactory markers to root outsiders from their communities. Thus the simple application of makeup to R's face or the disguising of Julia's scent come to seem, following Ahmed's reasoning, seditious or even revolutionary acts. See Sarah Ahmed, *Strange Encounters: Embodied Others in Post-Coloniality* (New York: Routledge, 2000), 20, 23.

39 Claire Mortimer argues that, even in conventional romantic comedies, these sorts of coming-of-age sequences, for all their saccharine and carefree overtones, nonetheless tap into utopian or rebellious undercurrents in dominant culture: "Comedy is about the excess of childish energies that can no longer be contained by adult frameworks … In this respect they are a threat to the stability of society, as they represent the unleashing of energies that are normally contained." These scenes in *Warm Bodies* set the stage, then, for the couple's disturbance of the status quo in and outside the walls of the survivors' downtown enclave. See Claire Mortimer, *Romantic Comedy* (New York: Routledge, 2010), 77.

40 José Ortega y Gasset offers a succinct definition of fascism as a sociopolitical orientation that eschews rational debate in favor of terror and violence. He argues that under fascism there appears "a type of man who does not want to give reasons or be right, but simply shows himself resolved to impose his opinions. This is a new thing: the right not to be reasonable, the 'reason of unreason.'" The "bonies" in *Warm Bodies* most represent this "reason of unreason," as they mindlessly and unhesitantly react with violence against either the survivors or the dissident zombies that they come into conflict with throughout the film. See José Ortega y Gasset, *The Revolt of the Masses* (New York: W.W. Norton, 1993), 73.

41 Leger Grindon, *The Hollywood Romantic Comedy* (Malden, MA: Wiley-Blackwell, 2011), 3.

42 As Northrop Frye argues, the "theme of the comic is the integration into society, which usually takes the form of incorporating a central character into it." Of course, R functions as this character in *Warm Bodies*, a "rather ordinary although socially attractive type" that turns up over and over again in comedies ranging from the works of Mcnander and Shakespeare on down through the film catalogues of the Hollywood cinema of the twentieth and twenty-first centuries. True to Frye's claims, *Warm Bodies* follows the "movement from one type of society to another," as the couple in it opposes

an intransigent father figure in order to open the city up to freer, more inclusive forms of movement, association, self-expression, and interpersonal connection. See Northrop Frye, *Anatomy of Criticism: Four Essays* (Princeton, NJ: Princeton University Press, 2000), 43–4, 163.

43   Virno, *Grammar of the Multitude*, 41.

44   According to Nigel Morris, ever since the NSA warrantless wiretapping scandal of the mid-2000s under the George W. Bush administration, Hollywood filmmakers sought to address concerns over data mining, civil rights infringements in the name of national and network security, and the anonymization of internet use. He argues, "Loss of selfhood and integrity are genuine concerns when agencies monitor Internet, telephone, and text communications, and trace movements through security and traffic cameras and bank card transactions." *The Maze Runner*, from its opening scenes, updates these thematics for an era dealing with anxieties over "loss of selfhood" due to immigration surges, family detention, and separation walling, as well as the enduring threat of domestic, substate, and international terrorism. See Nigel Morris, "2006: Movies and Crisis," in *American Cinema of the 2000s: Themes and Variations*, ed. Timothy Corrigan (New Brunswick: Rutgers University Press, 2012), 165.

45   Caetlin Benson-Allott, "Dreadful Architecture: Zones of Horror in *Alien* and Lee Bontecou's Wall Sculptures," *Journal of Visual Culture* 14, no. 3 (2015): 269.

46   These developments in *The Maze Runner* series reflect the crisis over the use of opioids in the United States, one of Trump's ostensible reasons for constructing a wall along the southwestern countryside. The 2010s saw deaths from overdose rise to over seventy thousand in 2017, forcing Trump to declare the epidemic a "public health emergency." See "New Data Show Growing Complexity of Drug Overdose Deaths in America," *CDC,* December 21, 2018, https://www.cdc.gov/media/releases/2018/p1221-complexity-drug-overdose.html; and Rajan Menon, "Forget the Wall—the Opioid Crisis Is Trump's Real National Emergency," *The Nation*, January 31, 2019, https://www.thenation.com/article/forget-the-wall-the-opioid-crisis-is-trumps-real-national-emergency/.

47   Kendall R. Phillips, "'The Safest Hands Are Our Own': Cinematic Affect, State Cruelty, and the Election of Donald J. Trump," *Communication & Critical/Cultural Studies* 15, no. 1 (2018): 88.

48   The sequel to *House of 1000 Corpses* (2003) and *The Devil's Rejects* (2005), Rob Zombie's *3 from Hell* (2019) follows the murderers Otis Driftwood (Bill Moseley), Baby Firefly (Sheri Moon Zombie), and Foxy Coltrane (Richard Blake) as they flee from the authorities to a small village in Mexico. They manage to drive across the *frontera* without incident, as the film does not depict much in the way of security fencing, Border Patrol checkpoints, and anti-vehicle trenches. The three fugitives arrive in town during the Day of the Dead—a nice touch, considering their recent escape from "life in prison" sentences—and involve themselves in a shootout with cartel members. The film does not merely celebrate the free movement of a few outlaw figures

from the United States into Mexico, as commonly do such Westerns as *Vera Cruz* (Robert Aldrich, 1954), *Bandolero!* (Andrew V. McLaglen, 1968), or *The Wild Bunch* (Sam Peckinpah, 1969). More interestingly, *3 from Hell* sets forth another negative consequence of nation-state walling: that it effectively imprisons the rest of us along with such antisocial types as the three title characters. Thus the film, in suggesting as much, also indulges in a counter-Trumpian fantasy of sorts, imagining US citizens as rapists and spree murderers who sneak into Mexico and terrorize its residents. The implication is that, if such characters as these serve as its antiheroes, then *Trump's America has no real room to call anyone "bad hombres."*

49 Elissa H. Nelson, "The New Old Face of a Genre: The Franchise Teen Film as Industry Strategy," *Cinema Journal* 57, no. 1 (2017): 126–7.

50 Ibid., 128.

51 Although it does not contain a separation wall, *Captain Marvel* (Anna Boden and Ryan Fleck, 2019) in any case features a disinformation regime comparable to the one in *Allegiant*. The Supreme Intelligence (Annette Bening), the embodiment of the collective minds of the alien Kree Empire, fools Carol Danvers (Brie Larson) into thinking of their enemies the Skrulls as terrorists and aggressors in their war with them. Danvers and the other members of the Kree Starforce—a sort of intergalactic Border Patrol—conduct an attack on a Skrull outpost in an "interface" region of the universe. The Skrulls, though, manage to capture and extract the memories of Danvers, using the information in them to travel to Earth, specifically to the United States. Thus the Skrulls at first sight seem "illegal aliens," and moreover their abilities to shape-shift and impersonate others touch on cultural anxieties over *immigrants blending into their host countries and becoming uncatchable.* However, a narrative twist reveals to us that the Skrulls are actually refugees that the Kree track and eradicate, and so Danvers, as the superhero Captain Marvel, decides to rebel against the Supreme Intelligence and assist them in finding new worlds to settle. Of course, the film on this score invites criticism, as we might superficially ask, "Are these 'illegal aliens,' then, unwelcome in the U.S.?" To answer this question with some degree of insight, we must closely consider the stylistics of the film, specifically the sequence in which the Skrulls use one of their machines to tap into Captain Marvel's autobiographical memories. The film uses *morphs* to transition from one intrapsychic scene to another, the same technique it uses to depict the Skrulls' transformation into other alien species. The film suggests, then, that the Skrulls manipulate and rearrange, if not distort, Captain Marvel's memories in such a way as to serve their own tactical interests. The coyness of the film on this matter does not render the Skrulls as villains; rather, it nonjudgmentally suggests that these refugees must exercise an "art of the weak" in order to survive against the much stronger Starforce and search the universe for worlds more agreeable to them than ours. Unlike Trump, these Marvel films, in short, never once suggest that the Earth is full, especially not after the depopulation of the universe in *Avengers: Infinity War*. Curiously, campaign staff on Twitter thought to compare the president to the supervillain in the series responsible for this mass murder. See Tufayel Ahmed, "Trump Campaign Posts Video

of Trump as Thanos—'Avengers' Fans Reminds Him Thanos Was Defeated 'Genocidal Warlord,'" *Newsweek*, December 11, 2019, https://www.newsweek.com/trump-thanos-snap-campaign-ad-inevitable-defeated-genocidal-warlord-twitter-1476653.

52 Jasmine Lee and Jonathan Alexander, "We Are All Abnegation Now: Suffering Agency in the *Divergent* Series," *Journal of the Fantastic in the Arts* 28, no. 3 (2017): 398.

53 "Portals," Amanda D. Lotz's name for internet streaming services, distinguishes their content curation, nonlinear access, and audience nichification features from the conventional formats of network, cable, and satellite television. The remote surveillance devices in *Allegiant* that allow its characters to obtain telepresent data thus speak to the media developments of its release context, in that Caleb and Peter can step through a "portal" at the click of a controller and watch any event occur in real time in Chicago or elsewhere at their discretion. Moreover, through the use of similar devices, other characters can choose to watch "older" content, as Tris does when she enters another "portal" and relives some of the memories of Natalie Prior. See Amanda D. Lotz, *Portals: A Treatise on Internet-Distributed Television* (Ann Arbor: Michigan Publishing, 2017), 8–9.

54 The mirror motif in *Allegiant* corresponds to Gloria Anzaldua's complex formulation of the *Coatlicue* state. Significantly, she starts out with reference to seeing one's own image in the mirror, describing as though it were a door or a wall: "The eye pins down the object of its gaze, scrutinizes it, judges it. A glance can freeze us in place; it can 'possess' us. It can erect a barrier against the world. But in a glance also lies awareness, knowledge." The *Coatlicue* state synthesizes these contradictions; as an archetype for "seeing through" or self-knowledge, it rephrases every "increment of consciousness, every step forward" as a "*travesía*, a crossing" into new territories. Although *Coatlicue* specifically describes the Chicano experience, it also applies to some degree to Tris in this film, as she steps through the "mirror" of the data box to enter into a con-mnemonic relation with a mother figure. After all, Anzaldua couches *Coatlicue* in terms of an earth mother or "cavernous womb," reminiscent of the "consuming" data box. As though at a mirror, Tris stands still and at the same time crosses through a reenactment of Natalie Prior's memories; in so doing, she attains the self-knowledge, emotional wherewithal, and social consciousness to finally collapse the walls enclosing Chicago and acting for its residents as a "barrier against the world." See Gloria Anzaldua, *Borderlands/La Frontera: The New Mestiza* (San Francisco, CA: Aunt Lute Books, 2012), 64, 68, 70–1.

55 Patti Bellantoni, *If It's Purple, Someone's Gonna Die: The Power of Color in Visual Storytelling* (New York: Focal Press, 2013), 67, 141, 173.

56 The monsters, according to Hye Jean Chung, function as metaphors for Hollywood mega-productions, such as *Kong: Skull Island*, in that they *smash through international boundaries* to rip off a chunk of the ticket sales in foreign markets. She argues that in these films, since they rely extensively on digital effects shops from multiple countries, "the body of the monster is an

incarnation of the crisis of national identity, as an image that fluidly crosses national borders through its intertextual connections to Hollywood films and the multinational sources of labor. Its alien body is at once an embodiment of the fantasy of nation and a global imaginary." See Hye Jean Chung, *Media Heterotopias: Digital Effects and Material Labor in Global Film Production* (Durham, NC: Duke University Press, 2017), 119.

57 Bill Randa's dialogue, as well as the entire flight into Skull Island, alludes to Kevin Conner's *The Land That Time Forgot* (1975) and its sequel *The People That Time Forgot* (1977). The first film depicts merchant navy sailors and the U-boat crew who sunk their ship discovering through the Antarctica mists the subcontinent of Caprona, a fantastic realm that dinosaurs and cavemen coinhabit. The sequel, more than the original, informs the action set pieces of *Kong: Skull Island*, as the rescue team in it flies their aircraft over the mountain walls of Caprona, only to face an attack from some sort of *Pterodactylus* (rather than a massive ape).

58 Jeffrey Jerome Cohen, "Monster Culture (Seven Theses)," in *Monster Theory: Reading Culture*, ed. Jeffrey Jerome Cohen (Minneapolis: University of Minnesota Press, 1996), 6, 12.

59 Ibid., 12.

60 Bruno Latour frames the sort of war that Colonel Packard mentions as a climacteric one that Trump was to effectively declare after withdrawing from the Paris Climate Agreement in 2017. Latour argues that this decision fails to address the inability of neoliberalism to modernize all the world's nations, a task that might require the resources of several Earths, not only one: "Now if there is no planet, no earth, no soil, no territory to house the Globe of globalization toward which all these countries claim to be headed, then there is no longer an assured 'homeland,' as it were, for anyone." This crisis means that the colonizers and the subaltern alike, those inside and outside the ambit of the nation-state, now face "a universal lack of sharable space," the deprivation of territories to call their own, and the tribulations of mass migration. The Trumpian response seems the retreat to the "Out-of-this-World," to a state of denial over climate change, meaning that the United States must then act as though *it exists on a different planet* than other nations. Latour thus recommends that we come down to Earth, a course of action that such films as *Monsters* and *Kong: Skull Island* take seriously, as their characters inhabit new spaces, coexist with new species, and develop new forms of social relations. Other films, such as *Elysium* and *Captain Marvel*, take an opposite approach, the characters in them abandoning their "homeworlds" in an attempt to explore new forms of terrestrial existence. See Bruno Latour, *Down to Earth: Politics in the New Climatic Regime* (Medford, OR: Polity, 2018), 5–9, 34–5, 95.

61 Guillermo del Toro's earlier monster film *Pacific Rim* (2013) also features an enormous security wall, this one meant to dispel the "Kaiju" monsters that emerge from the Breach, an interdimensional rift (similar to the one in *Warcraft*) deep in the ocean floor. These sorts of structures, even though they unite the world's nation-states in common cause, fail to deter the Kaiju, as

one of them, for example, easily tears through a wall surrounding Sydney, Australia. The solution in the film seems the construction of "Jaegers," massive robots that resemble the Kaiju in size, strength, and firepower, and that require two copilots to operate them. The task force in charge of the Jaegers must "drift" in order to control them—they must share the mental stress and effort that their use demands. The Jaegers stage for the task force a *virtual interface area*, as the international, multiracial, crosslingual team members struggle to synchronize their thoughts, reactions, emotions, objectives, and movements with one another. One of the team's scientists, Newton "Newt" Geiszler (Charlie Day), even enters into telepathic communication with the nervous system of an infant Kaiju, drifting with it to discover that the DNA of these monsters triggers openings in the Breach that they exploit to devastate the continents and their defense systems. This sort of interface, then, even if it does not reconcile enemies, enables the main characters to obtain information necessary for them to reseal the Breach and expel the Kaiju from the Earth. Newt's mental experiment interestingly stretches the definition of an interface area, as it occurs in a clandestine manner under the noses of the task force's commanders and also with the involvement of the shadowy Hong Kong illegal Kaiju organs market.

62   Chantal Mouffe argues for radicalizing the democratic order in the form of a "chain of equivalence" that respects and energizes the differences among the members of a community, insofar as they oppose the forces that seek to negate them. This common cause—most urgently, in the era of the Anthropocene, the ecological struggle over the "future of the planet"—might then collapse the "political frontier" that separates a "we" from a "they" and thus set the stage for a multitude to form. For example, the Iwi, the expedition members, and the former Second World War combatants in the film unite against the destruction of the environment that Colonel Packard wages. See Chantal Mouffe, *For a Left Populism* (New York: Verso, 2018), 61–3.

63   Graig Uhlin, "The Anthropocene's Nonindifferent Nature," *JCMS* 58, no. 2 (2019): 161.

64   Andrew Britton, *Britton on Film: The Complete Film Criticism of Andrew Britton*, ed. Barry Keith Grant (Detroit: Wayne State University Press, 2009), 87.

65   Timothy Corrigan, *A Cinema without Walls: Movies and Culture after Vietnam* (New Brunswick: Rutgers University Press, 1991), 40.

66   Inga Scharf theorizes the feeling of "homelessness in hope for a home" that Germans were to experience after the completion of the Berlin Wall in 1961, a feeling that the apes also seem to experience after the collapse of their fort. The topoi of the "Heimat" and "border," through their contradictoriness, create "the desire for an as yet unrepresentable home." Even as it thematizes contemporaneous concerns over mass migration, state security, and national identity in the new century, *War for the Planet of the Apes*, as its characters covet and search for an "as yet unrepresentable home," also curiously returns us to the affective thrust of some of the older films under discussion in the introduction of this study, as they each in their own ways took to task the

closing and division of the German nation-state during and after the rise of the Berlin Wall. See Inga Scharf, "Staging the Border: National Identity and the Critical Geopolitics of West German Film," *Geopolitics* 10, no. 2 (2005): 395.

67   Carol Reed's *The Man Between* (1953) follows the attempts of former Nazi soldier Ivo Kern (James Mason) to flee the Soviet zone of East Berlin alongside British citizen Susanne Mallison (Claire Bloom). As in *War for the Planet of the Apes*, they must take tactical advantage of the city's trappings—its traffic, its congestion, and the clamor of its construction sites—in order to mount their escape. The most remarkable fact about the film, though, concerns its extensive use of oblique camera angles to make the diegetic terrain of the Eastern Bloc seem entirely treacherous, as if the closing of the inner German border saw to it to transform the nation's former capital city into a vast interface area, the *very ground* of an unending series of abductions, subterfuges, entrapments, and other meretricious dealings.

68   The film, through these flourishes, repurposes the fact that refugee slaves in the United States were also quick to associate the Underground Railroad with the "Promised Land"—namely, Canada and, for a time, the northern states. See, for example, Renford Reese, "Canada: The Promised Land for U.S. Slaves," *Western Journal of Black Studies* 35, no. 3 (2011): 208–10; and Cheryl Janifer LaRoche, *Free Black Communities and the Underground Railroad: Geographies of Resistance* (Urbana: University of Illinois Press, 2014), 88.

69   Caesar's efforts to free the apes from the concentration camp resemble those of insurance expert and CIA operative James Donovan (Tom Hanks) to coordinate the exchange of a Soviet secret agent for two US citizens in Steven Spielberg's *Bridge of Spies* (2015). Much of the film occurs in 1960s East Germany, the time of the construction of the Berlin Wall, and centers on a dilemma: the CIA wants Donovan to concentrate on the extradition of U2 commander Gary Powers (Austin Stowell), even as the US attorney general also demands that the Soviets release student Frederic Pryor (Will Rogers). Donovan must treat the streets, apartments, and recesses of East Germany as an interface area, secretly meeting with GDR attorney Wolfgang Vogel (Sebastian Koch) and negotiating for a simultaneous exchange at Checkpoint Charlie and the Glienicke Bridge. The CIA insists that Donovan deprioritize the student after the deal almost falls through, and so the insurance man must resort to the tactics of the weak, to use de Certeau's terms, to obtain the release of the two citizens. Much as the apes trick the sentinels in the camp into making irrational snap decisions, so too does Donovan trick the Soviets into following through with the original terms of the exchange. The captive Soviet agent Rudolf Abel (Mark Rylance) assists in the matter, refusing to enter East Berlin until the Soviets agree to meet Donovan's demands, a testament to these characters' mutual respect for each other in the face of the imposing security wall that otherwise separates them. Spielberg's film, then, does not seem as relentlessly cynical and downbeat as *The Spy Who Came in from the Cold*, as it suggests that compromise, reciprocation, and reconciliation might come about from the micropolitical interactions of such state actors, as they share a commitment to such democratic instruments as fair trials, equitable

dealings with others, and the ability to move freely without fear, coercion, or restraint. As Donovan says, slyly indicating the crypto-social tenor of the film, "We have to have the conversations our governments can't."

70 As Dana Polan argues, many twenty-first-century US films in the aftermath of 9/11 "whatever their nominal subject, whatever their historical setting, end up with references to the tensions between security and insecurity and with discussion of governmentality and the proper path to justice, virtue, and personal and political morality" (222). *War for the Planet of the Apes* shows that cultural anxieties over terrorism might dovetail with those over migrant exoduses, resulting in the use of special mission units, indefinite detention, and other such responses to combat them. The concentration camp in the film, for example, evokes at once the internment of terror suspects in Guantanamo Bay during the War on Terror and the caging of families in detention centers under the Trump administration. These security measures, all in all, destabilize the rule of Caesar and the colonel, as well as instill an incessant contempt for those of different faiths, nationalities, ethnoracial complexions, or, in the case of the film, monophyletic species. See Dana Polan, "2009: Movies, a Nation, and New Identities," in *American Cinema of the 2000s: Themes and Variations*, ed. Timothy Corrigan (New Brunswick: Rutgers University Press, 2012), 222.

71 Benedict Anderson argues that such creole communities create the conditions for a "new consciousness" to emerge that chafes against the "depredations" of the older nation-state regimes. The US soldiers in the film thus react to Nova and the apes with ultrapatriotic fervor, "an anticipatory strategy adopted by dominant groups which are threatened with marginalization or exclusion" from this "imagined community." See Benedict Anderson, *Imagined Communities: Reflections on the Origin and Spread of Nationalism* (New York: Verso, 2006), 63, 101.

72 Michael Sragow, "*War for the Planet of the Apes*," *Film Comment* 53, no. 4 (2017): 72.

73 Britton, *Britton on Film*, 107.

Conclusion: The Walls Came Tumbling Down

"*Build the wall, we'll tear it down!*" The ACLU, several activist units, and such 2020 Democratic presidential candidates as Beto O'Rourke and Kirsten Gillibrand spoke some version of this mantra,[1] a sort of counter-promise to Donald J. Trump's campaign oath to finance, construct, and staff a wall along the Southwestern United States. Then, in October 2019, Julie Hirschfield Davis and Michael D. Shear, the authors of *Border Wars: Inside Trump's Assault on Immigration*, were to disclose that the president's vision of the design of the wall was straight out of a Hollywood action-adventure film: a moat full of snakes and alligators surrounding it was to deter asylum seekers from entering the country, and the concertina wire, electrifiable mesh, and rows of spikes atop it were to stop them from climbing over it.[2] Trump also thought to order Border Patrol agents to shoot refugees and immigrants in their extremities in order to slow their movements and make them easier to capture.[3] According to the *Washington Post*, Trump spoke to reporters on September 19 about the wall, calling it "virtually impenetrable" and claiming that someone "could fry an egg on it" due to its absorption of "heat from the broiling sun."[4] These macabre features do not seem out of place in such films as *Monsters*, *The Great Wall*, or *The Maze Runner*; and they fulfill a similar theatrical function, in that they constitute in themselves a terroristic component of these walls. As Alain Badiou argues in relation to the "democratic fascism" that Trump stands for, alongside other far-right statespersons,

> For these new political figures, the aim of language is no longer to explain anything or defend a point of view in an articulate manner. Its aim is to produce affects, which are used to create a fleetingly powerful unity, largely artificial but capable of being exploited in the moment.[5]

As artifacts of our dominant culture industries, the films under discussion in *Walls Without Cinema* tempt us to dismiss them as conservative or tendentially fascist, as examples of a mass media epiphenomenon attempting to inure us to the idea of security walling and to affectively condition us to accept it over time. However, we must resist such temptations, since these films enable us to confront, envision, and test out the effects of these walls on their diegetic universes so that we might improve our ethical imaginations for the times we must debate, repudiate, or vote on administrative decisions relating to immigration, refugee detention, and national security. The walls that we see on-screen might then transform the ways that we see those walls outside the movie theater—without the cinema, these walls might receive more uncritical support than they might otherwise. Of course, careful attention to the details and nuances of these films remains decisive, as close reading, theoretical risk-taking, and sometimes counterintuitive interpretation save us from turning them over to the alt-right.

Moreover, many of these films attain an international reach and reputation due to cofinancing deals or robust ticket sales in foreign markets. These films—in conjunction with our efforts to tease some value from them—might thus contribute to the transnational struggle against racism, cultural isolationism, neocolonialism, and the election in otherwise democratic countries of those far-right ultranationalistic figures in favor of security walling and staunch anti-immigration measures. Such figures include Donald Trump in the United States, Viktor Orbán in Hungary, Benjamin Netanyahu in Israel, Recep Tayyip Erdoğan in Turkey, Narendra Modi in India, Jair Bolsonaro in Brazil, Scott Morrison in Australia, Boyko Borisov in Bulgaria, and Boris Johnson in the UK, among others. These "hyperaggressive" state officials, as William E. Connelly observes, celebrate in their rhetoric "the triumphant nation" only so as to erect "sharp boundaries" against "other perspectives or places."[6] He further argues that the "fascist temptation" this rhetoric represents might excite further demands "to build walls and resist refugee flows," at the same time as it intensifies "race, gender, and class conflict."[7] Some of the most visible films of the twenty-first century, as we can see throughout *Walls Without Cinema*, might then serve to critique the monoculturalism, strongman statecraft, or constant effort to militarize or close off the nation's transit areas so characteristic of their release contexts.[8]

Still, we might turn to an international coproduction, Wim Wenders's documentary *Pope Francis: A Man of His Word* (2018), for some final words (and images) on nation-state security walling and the social injustice and environmental devastation that come of it. At one moment in the film, Pope Francis declares candidly that "building walls is not a solution." He thus echoes earlier comments made ever since 2016 in speeches to the United States and other dominant nations, enjoining all of them "not to build walls but to build bridges."[9] The epilogue of the film sees Pope Francis speaking directly to the camera about our duties to "help others to live better," a cinematographic choice that restyles the audience as the *confessors* to the most important man in the Catholic Church.[10] He thus seeks to *break down barriers* with this final message, including the "fourth wall" that separates the viewer from the images on-screen and usually casts them in a position of privilege and judgment over them. Complementing the fiction films that the chapters of *Walls Without Cinema* cover, this documentary quietly takes to task the spatio-legible diegetic construction of much twenty-first-century Hollywood cinema—as much as these films over the course of their narrative development collapse the security walls, fences, and domes that separate one set of characters in them from another, so too does this documentary, in its final moment, move to collapse *the wall that the cinema screen fundamentally is*.[11] On this note, after a direct encounter with a stranger, with a South American "other," the film sends us once more into the world's expanses to chip away at the cultural-geographic divisions that at once define the nation-state and make it a site of endless fear-mongering, self-policing, and international strife. Of course, more work remains for us to do, as we must investigate the films of the future and the films from other national cinemas[12] to fathom their standpoints on state security walling. Still, the films in these chapters, whether art documentaries or action-adventure franchise entries, with their cross-border appeal, altogether teach us that it does not matter who creates a wall or why or where—in the end, there it stands, separating us from someone else.

Notes

1. See Maki Beker and Matt Gryta, "Dozens Protest Trump's Immigration Order at Buffalo Airport," *Buffalo News*, January 28, 2017, https://buffalonews.com/2017/01/28/dozens-protest-trumps-immigration-order-buffalo-airport/; Jane Morice, "Hundreds Protest Trump's Travel Ban at Cleveland Hopkins International Airport," *Cleveland.com*, January 29, 2017, https://www.cleveland.com/metro/2017/01/hundreds_protest_trumps_travel.html; Robert A. Cronkleton and Matt Campbell, "Protestors at KCI Join Nationwide Rallies against Trump's Immigration Order," *Kansas City Star*, January 29, 2017, https://www.kansascity.com/news/local/article129477569.html; ACLU (@ACLU), "Build a wall? We'll tear it down!" #JFKTerminal4 #NoBanNoWall, *Twitter*, January 28, 2017, 5:34 p.m., https://twitter.com/aclu/status/825472046511579136?lang=en; Nicholas Kulish, "Three Pens, a Notebook and Questions: Inside a Late-Night Assignment," *New York Times*, February 3, 2017, https://www.nytimes.com/2017/02/03/insider/three-pens-a-notebook-and-questions-inside-a-late-night-assignment.html; and David Siders, "Beto's Call to Remove Part of the Wall Provokes Trump's Ire," *Politico*, February 19, 2019, https://www.politico.com/story/2019/02/19/beto-orourke-trump-2020-border-wall-1175846.
2. Julie Hirschfield Davis and Michael D. Shear, *Border Wars: Inside Trump's Assault on Immigration* (New York: Simon & Schuster, 2019), 2–4.

3   See Michael D. Shear and Julie Hirschfield Davis, "Shoot Migrants' Legs, Build Alligator Moat," *New York Times*, October 2, 2019, https://www.nytimes.com/2019/10/01/us/politics/trump-border-wars.html, as well as their *Border Wars*, 336–7.

4   See Philip Rucker, "It's Tall, It's Tough, It's Too Hot to Touch: President Trump Has Just the Wall for You," *Washington Post*, September 19, 2019, https://www.washingtonpost.com/politics/its-tall-its-tough-its-too-hot-to-touch-president-trump-has-just-the-wall-for-you/2019/09/19/3708545e-dae3-11e9-a688-303693fb4b0b_story.html.

5   Alain Badiou, *Trump* (Medford, OR: Polity, 2019), 13–14.

6   William E. Connelly, *Aspirational Fascism: The Struggle for Multifaceted Democracy under Trumpism* (Minneapolis: University of Minnesota Press, 2017), 15.

7   Ibid., 97.

8   In the face of the anti-immigrant sentiment in such countries as Hungary, Germany, Sweden, Italy, the Czech Republic, Slovenia, and Finland, Haley Sweetland Edwards makes a compelling argument for updating the 1967 UN refugee articles, written at a time of extreme US–Soviet tension. She argues that "many of the international migrants arriving at the U.S. border no longer fall neatly into any legal category. The Cold War refugee protocols are silent about migrants fleeing rape or corrupt police harassment, or climate-related destruction, or hunger so severe that kids wake up every night crying." Edwards, in another context, might similarly describe the reasons for migration in such films as *Elysium*, *Warcraft*, or *Warm Bodies*. See Haley Sweetland Edwards, "Dividing Lines: The Human Face of Global Migration," *Time* 193, no. 4–5 (2019): 28, 34.

9   See Philip Pullella, "Don't Build Walls, Pope Francis Says," *Reuters*, February 8, 2017, https://www.reuters.com/article/us-pope-wall-idUSKBN15N1ZW; Rosa Flores, "In Apparent Shot at Trump, Pope Says 'Builders of Walls' Sow Fear and Divide," *CNN*, January 26, 2019, https://www.cnn.com/2019/01/25/americas/pope-walls-panama/index.html; and Eli Watkins, "Pope Francis: 'Those Who Build Walls Will Become Prisoners of the Walls They Put Up,'" *CNN*, April 1, 2019, https://www.cnn.com/2019/04/01/politics/pope-francis-wall/index.html.

10 This shot appears in dialogue with the series of *actualités* made in 1898 of Pope Leo XIII under the camera eye of W. K. L. Dickson. One of the films captures Pope Leo facing the camera and waving the sign of the cross at the viewer. Much as does Pope Francis, Pope Leo also ruptures the shot's fourth wall. However, *in bestowing a blessing*, Pope Leo maintains an air of ecclesiastic distinction, so as to again separate the church authorities in the shot from the film's secular or nonclerical viewers. His successor in Wenders's documentary, in contrast, de-hierarchizes these relations, asking the viewer to assume the role of the confessor and the Pope that of the repentant, imperfect congregation member. For more on the Pope Leo series, see Charles Musser, *The Emergence of Cinema: The American Screen to 1907* (Berkeley: University of California Press, 1994), 218–21; Patrick Loughney, "1898–1899: Movies

and Entrepreneurs," in *American Cinema 1890–1909: Themes and Variations*, ed. Andre Gaudreault (New Brunswick: Rutgers University Press, 2009), 78–81; and Paul Spehr, *The Man Who Made Movies: W.K.L. Dickson* (New Barnet: John Libbey, 2008), 491–518.

11 Monica Hanna and Rebecca A. Sheehan, drawing on the work of Mary Ann Doane, argue that the cinema always already involves the transgression of "borders": it requires us through flicker fusion to overlook the interstices of the otherwise separate frames as we watch the illusion of continuous movement on-screen. See Monica Hanna and Rebecca A. Sheehan, eds., *Border Cinema: Reimagining Identity through Aesthetics* (New Brunswick: Rutgers University Press, 2019), 8.

12 For an introduction to scholarship on the representation of nation-state borders in international cinema, see Rajinder Dudrah, *Bollywood Travels: Culture, Diaspora and Border Crossings in Popular Hindi Cinema* (New York: Routledge, 2012); Jakub Kazecki, Karen A. Ritzenhoff, and Cynthia J. Miller, eds., *Border Visions: Identity and Diaspora in Film* (Lanham, MD: Scarecrow Press, 2013); Nilgun Bayraktar, *Mobility and Migration in Film and Moving Image Art: Cinema beyond Europe* (New York: Routledge, 2015); Ana Cristina Mendes and John Studholm, eds., *Transnational Cinema at the Borders: Borderscapes and the Cinematic Imaginary* (New York: Routledge, 2018); Aine O'Healy, *Migrant Anxieties: Italian Cinema in a Transnational Frame* (Bloomington: Indiana University Press, 2019); and once again Hanna and Sheehan, eds., *Border Cinema*.

BIBLIOGRAPHY

ACLU (@ACLU). "Build a wall? We'll tear it down!" #JFKTerminal4 #NoBanNoWall. Twitter, January 28, 2017. https://twitter.com/aclu/status/825472046511579136?lang=en.

Agamben, Giorgio. *Homo Sacer: Sovereign Power and Bare Life*. Translated by Daniel Heller-Roezen. Stanford, CA: Stanford University Press, 1995.

Agier, Micheal, Yasmine Bouagga, Maël Galisson, Cyrille Hanappe, Mathilde Pette, and Phillipe Wannesson. *The Jungle: Calais' Camps and Migrants*. Translated by David Fernbach. Medford, OR: Polity, 2019.

Agren, David. "Who Is Organizing This Latest Migrant Caravan and Other Questions You Might Have." *USA Today*. October 24, 2018. https://www.usatoday.com/story/news/world/2018/10/24/migrantcaravan/1747721002/.

Agren, David, and Amanda Hulpuch. "Where Is the Migrant Caravan from—and What Will Happen to It at the Border?" *The Guardian*. October 24, 2018. https://www.theguardian.com/us-news/2018/oct/24/caravan-migrants-what-is-it-where-from-guatemala-honduras-immigrants-mexico.

Ahmed, Sarah. *Strange Encounters: Embodied Others in Post-Coloniality*. New York: Routledge, 2000.

Ahmed, Tufayel. "Trump Campaign Posts Video of Trump as Thanos—'Avengers' Fans Reminds Him Thanos Was Defeated 'Genocidal Warlord.'" *Newsweek*, December 11, 2019. https://www.newsweek.com/trump-thanos-snap-campaign-ad-inevitable-defeated-genocidal-warlord-twitter-1476653.

Allen, Richard. "Hitchcock's Color Designs." In *Color: The Film Reader*, edited by Angela Dalle Vacche and Brian Price, 131–44. New York: Routledge, 2006.

Allyn, Bobby. "Federal Judge Rules against Border Wall Construction with Military Funds." *NPR*. June 26, 2019. https://www.npr.org/2019/06/28/737236244/federal-judge-rules-against-border-wall-construction-with-military-funds.

Altman, Rick. *Film/Genre*. London: British Film Institute, 1999.

Anderson, Benedict. *Imagined Communities: Reflections on the Origin and Spread of Nationalism*. New York: Verso, 2006.

Andersen, Gregers, and Esben Bjerggaard Nielsen. "Biopolitics in the Anthropocene: On the Invention of Future Biopolitics in *Snowpiercer*, *Elysium*, and *Interstellar*." *Journal of Popular Culture* 51, no. 3 (2018): 615–34.

Anderson, Stuart. "Trump Plans Far-Reaching Set of New Immigration Regulations." *Forbes*. November 21, 2019. https://www.forbes.com/sites/stuartanderson/2019/11/21/trump-plans-far-reaching-set-of-new-immigration-regulations/#7d7b591262a7.

Anzaldua, Gloria. *Borderlands/La Frontera: The New Mestiza*. San Francisco, CA: Aunt Lute Books, 2012.

Archibold, Randal C., and Marc Lacey. "Obama Requests Money for Border Security." *New York Times*. June 22, 2010. https://www.nytimes.com/2010/06/23/us/23border.html.

Arendt, Hannah. *The Origins of Totalitarianism*. New York: Harcourt, 1976.

Arendt, Hannah. *Eichmann in Jerusalem: A Report on the Banality of Evil*. New York: Penguin, 1994.

Asser, Martin. "Profile: Baghdad's Green Zone." *BBC News*. October 14, 2004. http://news.bbc.co.uk/2/hi/middle_east/3744468.stm.

Badiou, Alain. *Trump*. Medford, OR: Polity, 2019.

Balibar, Étienne. *We, the People of Europe? Reflections on Transnational Citizenship*. Translated by James Swenson. Princeton, NJ: Princeton University Press, 2004.

Barclay, Eliza, and Sarah Frostenson, "The Ecological Disaster That Is Trump's Border Wall: A Visual Guide." *Vox*. February 5, 2009. https://www.vox.com/energy-and- environment/2017/4/10/14471304/trump-border-wall-animals.

Barker, Martin. *A "Toxic Genre": The Iraq War Films*. New York: Pluto Press, 2011.

Bayraktar, Nilgun. *Mobility and Migration in Film and Moving Image Art: Cinema beyond Europe*. New York: Routledge, 2015.

Bazin, André. *André Bazin's New Media*. Edited and translated by Dudley Andrew. Oakland: University of California Press, 2014.

Bégin, Richard. "Digital Traumascape: From the *Trümmerfilme* to *Wall e**." *Space and Culture* 17, no. 4 (2014): 379–87.

Beker, Maki, and Matt Gryta. "Dozens Protest Trump's Immigration Order at Buffalo Airport." *Buffalo News*. January 28, 2017. https://buffalonews.com/2017/01/28/dozens-protest- trumps-immigration-order-buffalo-airport/.

Bellantoni, Patti. *If It's Purple, Someone's Gonna Die: The Power of Color in Visual Storytelling*. New York: Focal Press, 2013.

Benson-Allott, Caetlin. "Dreadful Architecture: Zones of Horror in *Alien* and Lee Bontecou's Wall Sculptures." *Journal of Visual Culture* 14, no. 3 (2015): 267–78.

Bertelsen, Lone, and Andrew Murphie. "An Ethics of Everyday Infinities and Powers: Félix Guattari on Affect and the Refrain." In *The Affect Theory Reader*, edited by Melissa Grieg and Gregory J. Seigworth, 138–60. Durham, NC: Duke University Press, 2010.

Biesecker, Michael, Jake Pearson, and Garance Burke. "Governor Orders Probe of Abuse Claims by Immigrant Children." *AP News*. June 21, 2018. https://apnews.com/afc80e51b562462c89907b49ae624e79.

Biskind, Peter. *The Sky Is Falling: How Vampires, Zombies, Androids, and Superheroes Made America Great for Extremism*. New York: New Press, 2018.

Blitzer, Jonathan. "ICE Agents Are Losing Patience with Trump's Chaotic Immigration Policy." *New Yorker*. June 24, 2019. https://www.newyorker.com/news/news-desk/ice- agents-are-losing-patience-with-trumps-chaotic-immigration-policy.

Blow, Charles M. "Trump's 'Concentration Camps.'" *New York Times*. June 23, 2019. https://www.nytimes.com/2019/06/23/opinion/trump-migrants-camps.html.

Bolstad, Erika. "Trump's Wall Could Cause Serious Environmental Damage." *Scientific American*. January 26, 2017. https://www.scientificamerican.com/article/trumps-wall- could-cause-serious-environmental-damage/.
Boltanksi, Luc. *Distant Suffering: Morality, Media and Politics*. Translated by Graham Burchell. New York: Cambridge University Press, 1999.
"Border Fence Upkeep Costs Millions, Audit Finds." *NBC News*. August 17, 2009. http://www.nbcnews.com/ id/32898302/ns/us_news-security/t/border-fence-upkeep-costs-billions-audit-finds/#.XgmsiM57nDA.
Bradshaw, Peter. "*Rambo: Last Blood* Review—Stallone Storms Mexico in a Laughable Trumpian Fantasy." *The Guardian*. September 19, 2019. https://www.theguardian.com/film/2019/sep/19/rambo-last-blood-review.
Braester, Yomi. "The Spectral Return of Cinema: Globalization and Cinephilia in Contemporary Chinese Film." *Cinema Journal* 55, no. 1 (2015): 29–51.
Brégent-Heald, Dominique. *Borderland Films: American Cinema, Mexico, and Canada during the Progressive Era*. Lincoln: University of Nebraska Press, 2015.
Brice, Makini. "Trump Threatens More Tariffs on Mexico as Part of Immigration Deal." *Reuters*. June 10, 2019. https://www.reuters.com/article/us-usa-trade-mexico/trump-threatens-more-tariffs-on-mexico-over-part-of-immigration-deal-idUSKCN1TB182.
Britton, Andrew. *Britton on Film: The Complete Film Criticism of Andrew Britton*. Edited by Barry Keith Grant. Detroit: Wayne State University Press, 2009.
Brown, Wendy. *Walled States, Waning Sovereignty*. New York: Zone Books, 2010.
Burnett, John. "'I'm Crushed': Migrant Parents, Advocates Press for Family Reunification." *NPR*. June 26, 2018. https://www.npr.org/2018/06/26/623451388/trumps-zero-tolerance- policy-overwhelms-border-agents.
Bush, George W. "Bush's Speech on Immigration." *New York Times*. May 15, 2006. https://www.nytimes.com/2006/05/15/washington/15text-bush.html.
Bush, George W. "Immigration Reform Address." *C-SPAN*. May 15, 2006. https://www.c-span.org/video/?192506-1/president-bush-address-immigration.
Bush, George W. "President Bush Addresses the Nation on Immigration Reform." *The White House: President George W. Bush*. May 15, 2006. https://georgewbush-whitehouse.archives.gov/news/releases/2006/05/text/20060515-8.html.
Caldwell, Alicia A. "Administration to Open Detention Centers for Families Caught Crossing the Border." *PBS*. June 20, 2014. https://www.pbs.org/newshour/politics/administration-open-detention-centers-families-caught-crossing-border.
Campoy, Ana. "Trump's Multibillion-Dollar Border Wall Wouldn't Stop This $5,000 Drone." *Quartz*. August 22, 2017. https://qz.com/1058702/trumps-multibillion-dollar-border-wall- wouldnt-stop-this-5000-drone/.
Carranza, Rafael. "Migrants' Makeshift Shelter in Tijuana Is Nearing Capacity." *USA Today*. November 20, 2018. https://www.usatoday.com/story/news/world/2018/11/19/tijuana-shelter-conditions-worsen-migrants/2064085002/.
Carter, Sean, and Klaus Dodds. *International Politics and Film: Space, Vision, Power*. New York: Wallflower, 2014.
Cavell, Stanley. *Pursuits of Happiness: The Hollywood Comedy of Remarriage*. Cambridge: Harvard University Press, 2003.

Cavell, Stanley. "The Fact of Television." In *Cavell on Cavell*, edited by William Rothman, 87–106. Albany: State University of New York Press, 2005.
Certeau, Michel de. *The Practice of Everyday Life*. Translated by Steven Rendall. Berkeley: University of California Press, 1988.
Chaudhuri, Shohini. *Cinema of the Dark Side: Atrocity and the Ethics of Film Spectatorship*. Edinburgh: Edinburgh University Press, 2014.
Chung, Hye Jean. *Media Heterotopias: Digital Effects and Material Labor in Global Film Production*. Durham, NC: Duke University Press, 2017.
Cohen, Jeffrey Jerome. "Monster Culture (Seven Theses)." In *Monster Theory: Reading Culture*, edited by Jeffrey Jerome Cohen, 3–25. Minneapolis: University of Minnesota Press, 1996.
Cohen, Jeffrey Jerome. "Grey: A Zombie Ecology." In *Zombie Theory: A Reader*, edited by Sarah Juliet Lauro, 381–94. Minneapolis: University of Minnesota Press, 2017.
Combe, Kirk. "Homeland Insecurity: Macho Globalization and Alien Blowback in *Monsters*." *Journal of Popular Culture* 48, no. 5 (2015): 1010–29.
Comentale, Edward P. "Zombie Race." In *Zombie Theory: A Reader*, edited by Sarah Juliet Lauro, 189–211. Minneapolis: University of Minnesota Press, 2017.
Comer, Todd A. "The Disabled Hero: Being and Ethics in Peter Jackson's *The Lord of the Rings*." *Mythlore* 35, no. 1 (2016): 113–31.
Connelly, William E. *Aspirational Fascism: The Struggle for Multifaceted Democracy under Trumpism*. Minneapolis: University of Minnesota Press, 2017.
Cooper, Marc. "Lockdown in Greeley." *The Nation*. February 15, 2007. https://www.thenation.com/article/lockdown-greeley/.
Cordona, Natalia. "The United States Bears Responsibility for the Immigration Crisis." *350*. June 29, 2018. https://350.org/us-responsibility-for-the-immigration-crisis/.
Cornell, Matt. "Where the Z Stands for Zionism." *Al Jazeera*. July 17, 2013. https://www.aljazeera.com/indepth/opinion/2013/07/201371183655144583.html.
Correal, Annie, and Megan Specia. "The Migrant Caravan: What to Know about the Thousands Traveling North." *New York Times*. October 26, 2018. https://www.nytimes.com/2018/10/26/world/americas/what-is-migrant-caravan-facts-history.html.
Corrigan, Timothy. *A Cinema without Walls: Movies and Culture after Vietnam*. New Brunswick: Rutgers University Press, 1991.
Corrigan, Timothy. "Introduction: Movies and the 2000s." In *American Cinema of the 2000s: Themes and Variations*, edited by Timothy Corrigan, 1–18. New Brunswick: Rutgers University Press, 2012.
Crofts, Penny, and Anthea Vogl. "Dehumanized and Demonized Refugees, Zombies, and World War Z." *Law & Humanities* 13, no. 1 (2013): 29–51.
Cronkleton, Robert A., and Matt Campbell. "Protestors at KCI Join Nationwide Rallies against Trump's Immigration Order." *Kansas City Star*. January 29, 2017. https://www.kansascity.com/news/local/article129477569.html.
Da Silva, Chantal. "ICE Agents Frustrated by Trump Using Agency as Political 'Pawn' to Push Anti-Immigration Agenda, Former Official Says." *Newsweek*. May 6, 2018. https://www.newsweek.com/ice-agents-frustrated-trumps-immigration-crackdown- which-putting-communities-831999.

Daisley, Stephen. "Neocon Zombie War: The Surprises of *World War Z.*" *Commentary* 136, no. 2 (2013): 56–7.
Davis, Julie Hirschfield. "Trump Orders Mexican Border Wall to Be Built and Plans to Block Syrian Refugees." *New York Times*. January 25, 2017. https://www.nytimes.com/2017/01/25/us/politics/refugees-immigrants-wall-trump.html.
Davis, Julie Hirschfield, and Michael Tackett. "Trump and Democrats Dig In after Talks to Reopen Government Go Nowhere." *New York Times*. January 3, 2019. https://www.nytimes.com/2019/01/02/us/politics/trump-congress-shutdown.html.
Davis, Julie Hirschfield, and Michael D. Shear. *Border Wars: Inside Trump's Assault on Immigration*. New York: Simon & Schuster, 2019.
Davis, Mike. "Fortress Los Angeles: The Militarization of Urban Space." In *Variations on a Theme Park: The New American City and the End of Public Space*, edited by Michael Sorkin. New York: Hill and Wang, 1992.
Davis, Mike. *Planet of Slums*. New York: Verso, 2017.
Deleuze, Gilles. *Cinema 2: The Time-Image*. Translated by Hugh Tomlinson and Roberta Galeta. Minneapolis: University of Minnesota Press, 2007.
dell'Agnese, Elena. "The US-Mexico Border in American Movies: A Political Geography Perspective." *Geopolitics* 10, no. 2 (2005): 204–21.
Derrida, Jacques. *On Cosmopolitanism and Forgiveness*. Translated by Mark Dooley and Michael Hughes. New York: Routledge, 2001.
Dickerson, Caitlin. "'There Is a Stench': Soiled Clothes and No Baths for Migrant Children at a Texas Center." *New York Times*. June 21, 2019. https://www.nytimes.com/2019/06/21/us/migrant-children-border-soap.html.
Dickinson, Tim. "Trump Administration Argues that Migrant Children Don't Need Soap." *Rolling Stone*. June 20, 2019. https://www.rollingstone.com/politics/politics-news/safe- sanitary-no-soap-beds-court-migrants-trump-850744/.
Dixon, Wheeler Winston, and Gwendolyn Audrey Foster. *21st-Century Hollywood: Movies in the Era of Transformation*. New Brunswick: Rutgers University Press, 2011.
Doane, Mary Ann. *Femmes Fatales: Feminism, Film Theory, Psychoanalysis*. New York: Routledge, 1991.
Driver, Alice. "Trump's Mexico Wall Would Be a Gift to the Drug Cartels." *CNN*. January 9, 2018. https://www.cnn.com/2018/01/08/opinions/border-wall-cartels-trump-opinion- driver/index.html.
Dudenhoeffer, Larrie. *Embodiment and Horror Cinema*. New York: Palgrave Macmillan, 2014.
Dudenhoeffer, Larrie. *Anatomy of the Superhero Film*. New York: Palgrave Macmillan, 2017.
Dudrah, Rajinder. *Bollywood Travels: Culture, Diaspora and Border Crossings in Popular Hindi Cinema*. New York: Routledge, 2012.
Dwyer, Colin. "ICE Carries Out Its Largest Immigration Raid in Recent History." *NPR*. June 20, 2018. https://www.npr.org/2018/06/20/621810030/ice-carries-out-its-largest- immigration-raid-in-recent-history-arresting-146.
Eberwein, Robert. *Armed Forces: Masculinity and Sexuality in the American War Film*. New Brunswick: Rutgers University Press, 2007.
Eco, Umberto. "*Casablanca*: Cult Movies and Intertextual Collage." In *Travels in Hyperreality*, translated by William Weaver. San Diego, CA: Harcourt, 1983.

Edwards, Haley Sweetland. "Dividing Lines: The Human Face of Global Migration." *Time* 193, no. 4–5 (2019): 22–47.
El Nasser, Haya. "Gated Communities More Popular, and Not Just for the Rich." *USA Today*. December 15, 2002. https://usatoday30.usatoday.com/news/nation/2002-12-15-gated-usat_x.htm.
Ellis, John. *Visible Fictions: Cinema, Television, Video*. New York: Routledge, 2000.
"El Paso Sector Border Patrol Encounters New Tactics as Smugglers Keep Sending in Families and Felons." *U.S. Customs and Border Protection*. April 17, 2019. https://www.cbp.gov/newsroom/local-media-release/el-paso-sector-border-patrol- encounters-new-tactics-smugglers-keep.
"Executive Order: Border Security and Immigration Enforcement Improvements." *The White House*. January 25, 2017. https://www.whitehouse.gov/presidential-actions/executive- order-border-security-immigration-enforcement-improvements/.
Fabian, Jordan, and Brett Samuels, "Trump Agrees to End Shutdown without Getting Wall Funding." *The Hill*. January 25, 2019. https://thehill.com/homenews/administration/427004-trump-agrees-to-end-shutdown.
Feltmate, David. "Two Days before the Day before an Irritating Truth: *The Simpsons* and *South Park*'s Environmentalism as a Challenge for Mediating Dark Green Ecological Ethics." *Journal of the Study of Religion, Nature & Culture* 11, no. 3 (2017): 315–39.
Fenwick, Ben. "'Stop Repeating History': Plan to Keep Migrant Children at Former Internment Camp Draws Outrage." *New York Times*. June 22, 2019. https://www.nytimes.com/2019/06/22/us/fort-sill-protests-japanese-internment.html.
Fernandez, Manny. "Lawyer Draws Outrage for Defending Lack of Toothbrushes in Border Detention." *New York Times*. June 25, 2019. https://www.nytimes.com/2019/06/25/us/sarah-fabian-migrant-lawyer-doj.html.
Filkins, Dexter. "2 Bombers Kill 5 in Guarded Area of Baghdad." *New York Times*. October 15, 2004. https://www.nytimes.com/2004/10/15/world/middleeast/2-bombers-kill-5-in- guarded-area-in-baghdad.html.
Fiske, John. *Television Culture*. New York: Routledge, 2011.
Flaherty, Anne. "CBP Investigating Allegation by Young Girl that She Was 'Beaten and Abused' at Clint Border Facility." *ABC News*. July 25, 2019. https://abcnews.go.com/Politics/cbp-investigating-allegation-young-girl-beaten-abused- clint/story?id=64565883.
Flores, Rosa. "In Apparent Shot at Trump, Pope Says 'Builders of Walls' Sow Fear and Divide." *CNN*. January 26, 2019. https://www.cnn.com/2019/01/25/americas/pope-walls- panama/index.html.
Fojas, Camilla. *Border Bandits: Hollywood on the Southern Frontier*. Austin: University of Texas Press, 2008.
Foucault, Michel. *"Society Must Be Defended": Lectures at the Collège de France 1975–1976*. Translated by David Macey. New York: Picador, 2003.
Foucault, Michel. *Security, Territory, Population: Lectures at the Collège de France 1977–1978*. Translated by Graham Burchell. New York: Picador, 2007.
Freda, Isabelle. "Screening War: *American Sniper, Hurt Locker*, and Drone Vision." *International Journal of Contemporary Iraqi Studies* 10, no. 3 (2017): 229–39.
Fredrick, James. "'Metering' at the Border." *NPR*. June 29, 2019. https://www.npr.org/2019/06/29/737268856/metering-at-the-border.

Fredrick, James. "Shouting 'Mexico First,' Hundreds in Tijuana March against Migrant Caravan." *NPR*. November 19, 2019. https://www.npr.org/2018/11/19/669193788/shouting-mexico-first-hundreds-in-tijuana-march-against-migrant-caravan.
Fromm, Erich. *Escape from Freedom*. New York: Holt, 1969.
Fry, Wendy. "Concertina Wire Stolen from Border Fence and Used for Home Security in Tijuana, Authorities Say." *San Diego Union-Tribune*. March 18, 2019. https://www.sandiegouniontribune.com/news/border-baja-california/sd-me-concertina- wire-tj-20190318-story.html.
Frye, Northrop. *Anatomy of Criticism: Four Essays*. Princeton, NJ: Princeton University Press, 2000.
Fuller, Stephanie. *The US-Mexico Border in American Cold War Film: Romance, Revolution, and Regulation*. New York: Palgrave Macmillan, 2015.
Garcia-Navarro, Lulu. "Law Professor Describes Poor Conditions Where Migrant Children Are Held." *NPR*. June 23, 2019. https://www.npr.org/2019/06/23/735191289/law-professor-describes-poor-conditions-where-migrant-children-are-held.
Gellman, Barton, and Walter Pincus. "Depiction of Threat Outgrew Supporting Evidence." *Washington Post*. August 10, 2003. https://www.washingtonpost.com/wp- dyn/content/article/2006/06/12/ AR2006061200932_pf.html.
Genette, Gérard. *Narrative Discourse: An Essay in Method*. Translated by Jane E. Lewin. Ithaca, NY: Cornell University Press, 1983.
Gibson, Suzie. "Stop the Ships: *Elysium*, Asylum Seekers and the Battle over Sovereign Borders." *Screen Education* 78 (2015): 78–85.
Giroux, Henry A. *America at War with Itself*. San Francisco, CA: City Lights Books, 2017.
Goodfellow, Maya. *Hostile Environment: How Immigrants Become Scapegoats*. New York: Verso, 2019.
Gomez, Alan. "Central American Migrants Keep Heading toward USA, Even as Trump Focuses on Stopping Caravans." *USA Today*. January 9, 2019. https://www.usatoday.com/story/news/politics/ 2019/01/09/migrant-caravan-trump-crackdown-has-not-slowed flow-families-us/2523034002/.
Gomez, Alex. "Government Watchdog: Separated Migrant Children Suffered PTSD, Other Mental Trauma." *USA Today*. September 4, 2019. https://www.usatoday.com/story/news/nation/2019/09/04/separated-migrant-children- suffered-ptsd-trauma-report-says/2209669001/.
Graff, Garrett M. "The Border Patrol Hits a Breaking Point." *Politico*. July 15, 2019. https://www.politico.com/magazine/story/2019/07/15/border-patrol-trump- administration-227357.
Graham, Dave. "Mexico Says It Has Deployed 15,000 in the North to Halt U.S.-Bound Immigration." *Reuters*. June 24, 2019. https://www.reuters.com/article/us-usa-trade- mexico-immigration/mexico-says-it-has-deployed-15000-forces-in-the-north-to-halt-u-s-bound-migration-idUSKCN1TP2YN.
Gray, Jonathan. *Watching with* The Simpsons: *Television, Parody, and Intertextuality*. New York: Routledge, 2006.
Gray, Mitchell, and Elvin Wyly. "The Terror City Hypothesis." In *Violent Geographies: Fear, Terror, and Political Violence*, edited by Derek Gregory and Allen Pred, 329–48. New York: Routledge, 2007.

Grewal, Inderpal. *Saving the Security State: Exceptional Citizens in Twenty-First-Century America*. Durham, NC: Duke University Press, 2017.

Grindon, Leger. *The Hollywood Romantic Comedy*. Malden, MA: Wiley-Blackwell, 2011.

Gross, Daniel J. "5 Arrested during 'Build the Wall' Rally and Counter-Protest in Downtown Greenville." *Greenville News*. October 13, 2018. https://www.greenvilleonline.com/story/news/2018/10/13/4-arrested-build-wall-rally-counter-protest-greenville/1629833002/.

Gusain, Renuka. "The War Body as Screen of Terror." In *The War Body on Screen*, edited by Karen Randall and Sean Redmund, 36–49. New York: Continuum, 2012.

Hageman, Andrew. "Ecocinema and Ideology: Do Ecocritics Dream of a Clockwork Green?" In *Ecocinema Theory and Practice*, edited by Stephen Rust, Salma Monani, and Sean Cubitt, 63–86. New York: Routledge, 2013.

Hanna, Monica, and Rebecca A. Sheehan, eds. *Border Cinema: Reimagining Identity through Aesthetics*. New Brunswick: Rutgers University Press, 2019.

Hansen, Claire. "Proposed Trump Rule Limits Eligibility for Asylum." *U.S. News & World Report*. December 18, 2019. https://www.usnews.com/news/national-news/articles/2019-12-18/proposed-trump-rule-limits-eligibility-for-asylum.

Harding, Jeremy. *Border Vigils: Keeping Migrants out of the Rich World*. New York: Verso, 2012.

Harkins, Gina. "Illicit Drone Flights Surge along U.S.-Mexico Border as Smugglers Hunt for Soft Spots." *Washington Post*. June 24, 2018. https://www.washingtonpost.com/world/national-security/illicit-drone-flights-surge-along-us-mexico-border-as-smugglers-hunt-for-soft-spots/2018/06/24/ea353d2a-70aa-11e8-bd50-b80389a4e569_story.html.

Harrington, Rebecca. "Trump Holds Boisterous Saturday Night Rally in '110-Degree' Hot High School in Ohio." *Business Insider*. August 4, 2018. https://www.businessinsider.com/trump-rally-ohio-highlights-quotes-2018-8.

Harris, Adam. "When ICE Raids Homes." *The Atlantic*. July 17, 2019. https://www.theatlantic.com/family/archive/2019/07/when-ice-raids-homes-immigration/594112/.

Henry, Matthew A. The Simpsons, *Satire, and American Culture*. New York: Palgrave Macmillan, 2012.

Henry, Michel. *Barbarism*. Translated by Scott Davidson. New York: Continuum, 2012.

Herrera, Jack. "A Look Inside a Migrant Shelter in Tijuana." *Pacific Standard*. December 20, 2018. https://psmag.com/social-justice/a-look-inside-a-migrant-shelter-in-tijuana.

Higgins, Tucker. "Trump Declares without Evidence That 'Criminals and Unknown Middle Easterners Are Mixed in' with Migrant Caravan Making Its Way from Honduras." *CNBC*. October 22, 2018. https://www.cnbc.com/2018/10/22/trump-says-unknown-middle-easterners-are-mixed-in-migrant-caravan.html.

Higson, Andrew. "Re-Presenting the National Past: Nostalgia and Pastiche in the Heritage Film." In *Fires Were Started: British Cinema and Thatcherism*, edited by Lester Friedman, 91–109. New York: Wallflower, 2006.

Hoberman, J. *The Dream Life: Movies, Media, and the Mythology of the Sixties*. New York: New Press, 2003.

Hoberman, J. *The Magic Hour: Film at Fin de Siècle*. Philadelphia, PA: Temple University Press, 2003.

Hoberman, J. *Army of Phantoms: American Movies and the Making of the Cold War*. New York: New Press, 2011.

Hoberman, J. *Film after Film or, What Became of 21st Century Cinema?* New York: Verso, 2012.

Hoffman, Meredith. "Inside the Trauma-Filled Camp of Migrants Waiting at the US Border." *Vice*. December 28, 2018. https://www.vice.com/en_us/article/439ebg/inside-the-trauma- filled-camp-of-migrants-waiting-at-the-us-border.

Holmes, Jack. "An Expert on Concentration Says That's Exactly What the U.S. Is Running at the Border." *Esquire*. June 13, 2019. https://www.esquire.com/newspolitics/a27813648/concentration-camps-southern-border- migrant-detention-facilities-trump/.

Holland, Steve, and Roberta Rampton. "Trump to Propose Plan to Make U.S. Immigration More Merit-Based." *Reuters*. May 15, 2019. https://www.reuters.com/article/us-usa- immigration-trump/trump-to-propose-plan-to-make-u-s-immigration-more-merit-based- idUSKCN1SL2CX.

Holpuch, Amanda. "Thousands More Migrant Children Separated under Trump than Previously Known." *The Guardian*. January 17, 2019. https://www.theguardian.com/us- news/2019/jan/17/trump-family-separations-report-latest-news-zero-tolerance-policy- immigrant-children.

Horne, Philip. "Martin Scorsese: Catholic Tastes." *Sight & Sound* 27, no. 2 (2017): 16–27.

Horton, Alex. "Why Tear Gas, Lobbed at Migrants on the Southern Border, Is Banned in Warfare." *Washington Post*. November 27, 2018. https://www.washingtonpost.com/national-security/2018/11/26/why-tear-gas-lobbed-migrants-southern-border-is-banned-warfare/.

Horwitz, Sari. "Sessions Vows to Prosecute All Illegal Border Crossers and Separate Children from Their Parents." *Washington Post*. May 7, 2018. https://www.washingtonpost.com/ world/national-security/sessions-says-justice-dept- will-prosecute-every-person-who-crosses-border-unlawfully/2018/05/07/e1312b7e-5216-11e8-9c91-7dab596e8252_story.html.

Huth, Lindsay. "Immigration under Trump: By the Numbers." *U.S. News & World Report*. March 13, 2018. https://www.usnews.com/news/data-mine/articles/2018-03-13/fewer- crossing-border-fewer-deported-immigration-under-trump.

Jameson, Fredric. *Postmodernism or, the Cultural Logic of Late Capitalism*. Durham, NC: Duke University Press, 2001.

Jancovich, Mark. "We're the Martians Now: British SF Invasion Fantasies of the 1950s and 1960s." In *Liquid Metal: The Science Fiction Reader*, edited by Sean Redmond, 337–45. New York: Wallflower, 2007.

Jarvis, Sarah. "'Build the Wall' and 'Fake News': Crowd Fired Up Ahead of Trump Rally in Tampa." *News-Press*. July 31, 2018. https://www.news- press.com/story/news/politics/2018/07/31/donald-trump-crowd-braves-rain-long-wait-ahead-trump-rally-tampa/870189002/.

Johnson, Jenna. "'Build That Wall' Has Taken on a Life of Its Own at Donald Trump's Rallies—but He's Still Serious." *Washington Post*. February 12, 2016. https://www.washingtonpost.com/news/post-politics/wp/2016/02/12/build-that-wall-has-taken-on-a-life-of-its-own-at-donald-trumps-rallies-but-hes-still-serious/.

Johnson, Kevin R. *Opening the Floodgates: Why America Needs to Rethink Its Borders and Immigration Laws*. New York: New York University Press, 2007.

Jones, Reece. *Violent Borders: Refugees and the Right to Move*. New York: Verso, 2017.

Jordan, Miriam. "Trump Threatens Tariffs on Mexico. Have Any of Hid Immigration Measures Worked?" *New York Times*. May 31, 2019. https://www.nytimes.com/2019/05/31/us/border-tariffs-trump-immigration.html.

Jordan, Miriam. "ICE Raids Hundreds in Mississippi Raids Targeting Immigrant Workers." *New York Times*. August 7, 2019. https://www.nytimes.com/2019/08/07/us/ice-raids-mississippi.html.

Kao, Jason, and Denise Lu. "How Trump's Policies Are Leaving Thousands of Asylum Seekers Waiting in Mexico." *New York Times*. August 18, 2019. https://www.nytimes.com/interactive/2019/08/18/us/mexico-immigration-asylum.html.

Kazecki, Jakub, Karen A. Ritzenhoff, and Cynthia J. Miller, eds. *Border Visions: Identity and Diaspora in Film*. Lanham, MD: Scarecrow Press, 2013.

Kendrick, James. *Film Violence: History, Ideology, Genre*. New York: Wallflower, 2009.

Kim, Seung Min, and Missy Ryan. "Trump Says He Wants to 2,000 to 4,000 National Guard Troops to Mexican Border." *Washington Post*. April 5, 2018. https://www.washingtonpost.com/politics/trump-says-he-wants-to-send-2000-to-4000-national-guard-troops-to-mexican-border/2018/04/05/bab01f6a-391a-11e8-8fd2-49fe3c675a89_story.html.

Klein, Naomi. *The Rise of Disaster Capitalism*. New York: Picador, 2007.

Koenigsberger, Kurt M. "Commodity Culture and Its Discontents: Mr. Bennett, Bart Simpson, and the Rhetoric of Modernism." In *Leaving Springfield:* The Simpsons *and the Possibility of Oppositional Culture*, edited by John Alberti, 29–62. Detroit: Wayne State University Press, 2004.

Koulish, Robert. *Immigration and American Democracy: Subverting the Rule of Law*. New York: Routledge, 2009.

Krauze, León. "God Willing, We Can Cross and My Dream Will Come True." *Slate*. November 30, 2018. https://slate.com/news-and-politics/2018/11/migrant-caravan- tijuana-mexico-children.html.

Kristeva, Julia. *Powers of Horror: An Essay on Abjection*. Translated by Leon S. Roudiez. New York: Columbia University Press, 1982.

Kristeva, Julia. *Nations without Nationalism*. Translated by Leon S. Roudiez. New York: Columbia University Press, 1993.

Krstić, Igor. *Slums on Screen: World Cinema and the Planet of Slums*. Edinburgh: Edinburgh University Press, 2017.

Kulish, Nicholas. "Three Pens, a Notebook and Questions: Inside a Late-Night Assignment." *New York Times*. February 3, 2017. https://www.nytimes.com/2017/02/03/insider/three- pens-a-notebook-and-questions-inside-a-late-night-assignment.html.

Langewiesche, William. "Welcome to the Green Zone: The American Bubble in Baghdad." *The Atlantic*. November, 2004. https://www.theatlantic.com/magazine/archive/2004/11/welcome-to-the-green-zone/303547/.

LaRoche, Cheryl Janifer. *Free Black Communities and the Underground Railroad: Geographies of Resistance*. Urbana: University of Illinois Press, 2014.

Latour, Bruno. *Down to Earth: Politics in the New Climatic Regime*. Medford, OR: Polity, 2018.

Lauro, Sarah Juliet, and Karen Embry. "A Zombie Manifesto: The Nonhuman Condition in the Era of Advanced Capitalism." In *Zombie Theory: A Reader*, edited by Sarah Juliet Lauro, 395–412. Minneapolis: University of Minnesota Press, 2017.

Lee, Jasmine, and Jonathan Alexander. "We Are All Abnegation Now: Suffering Agency in the *Divergent* Series." *Journal of the Fantastic in the Arts* 28, no. 3 (2017): 388–401.

Lind, Dara. "The Disastrous, Forgotten 1996 Law That Created Today's Immigration Problem." *Vox*. April 28, 2016. https://www.vox.com/2016/4/28/11515132/iirira-clinton-immigration.

Lombardo, Clare. "U.S. Agents Spray Tear Gas at Migrants, Briefly Close Tijuana Border Entry." *NPR*. November 25, 2018. https://www.npr.org/2018/11/25/670687806/u-s-agents-spray-tear-gas-at-migrants-briefly-close-tijuana-border-entry.

Long, Coleen. "At Least 4,500 Abuse Complaints at Migrant Children Shelters." *AP News*. February 26, 2019. https://apnews.com/6bc34d8c6aaa41d0998d8bce46687e90.

Long, Colleen, Frank Bajak, and Will Weissert. "Ankle Monitors for Immigrants Almost Universally Disliked." *Denver Post*. August 25, 2018. https://www.denverpost.com/2018/08/25/ice-issuing-immigrant-ankle-monitors/.

Lotz, Amanda D. *Portals: A Treatise on Internet-Distributed Television*. Ann Arbor: Michigan Publishing, 2017.

Loughney, Patrick. "1898–1899: Movies and Entrepreneurs." In *American Cinema 1890–1909: Themes and Variations*, edited by Andre Gaudreault, 78–81. New Brunswick: Rutgers University Press, 2009.

Manzanas, Ana M., and Jesús Benito Sanchez. *Cities, Borders, and Spaces in Intercultural American Literature and Film*. New York: Routledge, 2011.

Marcuse, Herbert. *Counterrevolution and Revolt*. Boston, MA: Beacon Press, 1972.

Mason, Jeff, and Makini Brice. "Trump Says He Is Seriously Looking at Ending Birthright Citizenship." *Reuters*. August, 21, 2019. https://www.reuters.com/article/us-usa- immigration-trump/trump-says-he-is-seriously-looking-at-ending-birthright-citizenship- idUSKCN1VB21B.

Masters, Kim. "'The Hobbit': Inside Peter Jackson's and Warner Bros.' $1 Billion Gamble." *Hollywood Reporter*. October 17, 2012. https://www.hollywoodreporter.com/news/hobbit-peter-jackson-warner-bros-379301.

Mauss, Marcel. "Techniques of the Body." Translated by Ben Brewster. In *The Body: A Reader*, edited by Mariam Fraser and Monica Greco, 73–7. New York: Routledge, 2005.

McCarthy, Rory. "Four Gurkhas Die in Baghdad Green Zone Mortar Attack." *The Guardian*. November 26, 2004. https://www.theguardian.com/world/2004/nov/27/iraq.rorymccarthy.

McDonald, Tamar Jeffers. "Homme-com: Engendering Change in Contemporary Romantic Comedy." In *Falling in Love Again: Romantic Comedy in Contemporary Cinema*, edited by Stacey Abbott and Deborah Jermyn, 146–59. New York: I.B. Tauris, 2009.

McGahan, Jason. "Mexicans Storm Migrant Shelter in Tijuana, Shouting for 'Pigs' to Leave." *Daily Beast*. November 19, 2018. https://www.thedailybeast.com/mexicans-storm-migrant-shelter-in-tijuana-shouting-for-pigs-to-leave.

McGowan, Amelia. "After Terrifying ICE Raid, Mississippi Is Still Fighting Back." *USA Today*. October 4, 2019. https://www.usatoday.com/story/opinion/policing/spotlight/2019/10/03/terrifying-ice-raid-mississippi-still-fighting-back/3790692002/.

McNally, David. "Ugly Beauty: Monstrous Dreams of Utopia." In *Zombie Theory: A Reader*, edited by Sarah Juliet Lauro, 124–36. Minneapolis: University of Minnesota Press, 2017.

McSweeney, Terence. *The "War on Terror" and American Film: 9/11 Frames Per Second*. Edinburgh: Edinburgh University Press, 2014.

McWhorter, John. "AOC's Critics Are Pretending Not to Know How Language Works." *The Atlantic*. June 20, 2019. https://www.theatlantic.com/ideas/archive/2019/06/defense-ocasio-cortez-concentration-camp-comment/592180/.

Melesio, Lucina, and John Holman. "Mexican Cartels Recruit Children to Smuggle People to US." *Al Jazeera*. October 30, 2017. https://www.aljazeera.com/news/2017/10/mexico-cartels-recruit-children-smuggle-people-171030103553245.html.

Mendes, Ana Cristina, and John Studholm, eds. *Transnational Cinema at the Borders: Borderscapes and the Cinematic Imaginary*. New York: Routledge, 2018.

Menon, Rajan. "Forget the Wall—the Opioid Crisis Is Trump's Real National Emergency." *The Nation*. January 31, 2019. https://www.thenation.com/article/forget-the-wall-the-opioid-crisis-is-trumps-real-national-emergency/.

Merchant, Nomaan. "Tents, Stench, Smoke: Health Risks Are Gripping Migrant Camp." *AP News*. November 14, 2019. https://apnews.com/337b139ed4fa4d208b93d491364e04da.

Metz, Walter. "'So Shines a Good Deed in a Weary World': Intertextuality in Steven Spielberg's Ready Player One." *Film Criticism* 42, no. 4 (2018). https://quod.lib.umich.edu/f/fc/13761232.0042.402/--so-shines-a-good-deed-in-a-weary-world-intertextuality?rgn=main;view=fulltext.

Mikelionis, Lukas. "Ocasio-Cortez Raises Eyebrows after Comparing Trump's Border Wall to Berlin Wall." *Fox News*. February 19, 2019. https://www.foxnews.com/politics/ocasio-cortez-raises-eyebrows-after-comparing-trumps-border-wall-to-berlin-wall.

Mikelionis, Lukas, and Griff Jenkins. "One-Third of Migrants in Caravan Are Being Treated for Health Issues, Tijuana Health Official Says." *Fox News*. November 29, 2018. https://www.foxnews.com/world/

caravan-migrants-suffer-from-respiratory-infections-tuberculosis-chickenpox-other-health-issues-tijuana-government-says.
"Military Investigates Hostile Fire in 'Green Zone.'" *CNN*. December 25, 2003. http://www.cnn.com/2003/WORLD/meast/12/25/sprj.irq.main/index.html.
Miller, Todd. *Empire of Borders: How the US Is Exporting Its Border around the World*. New York: Verso, 2019.
Minh-ha, Trinh T. *Elsewhere, Within Here: Immigration, Refugeeism and the Boundary Event*. New York: Routledge, 2011.
Mirrlees, Tanner, and Isabel Pedersen. "*Elysium* as a Critical Dystopia." *International Journal of Media & Cultural Politics* 12, no. 3 (2016): 3015–22.
Mohn, Tanya. "America's Most Exclusive Gated Communities." *Forbes*. July 3, 2012. https://www.forbes.com/sites/tanyamohn/2012/07/03/americas-most-exclusive-gated- communities/#874fc4b6fe0e.
Montes, Juan, Santiago Pérez, and Robbie Whelan. "U.S. Border Patrol Uses Tear Gas to Disperse Migrant Caravan." *Wall Street Journal*. November 26, 2018. https://www.wsj.com/articles/u-s-border-patrol-uses-tear-gas-to-disperse-migrant- caravan-1543244902.
Moore, Mark. "Ocasio-Cortez Compares Trump's Border Wall to Berlin Wall." *New York Post*. February 19, 2019. https://nypost.com/2019/02/19/ocasio-cortez-compares-trumps- border-wall-to-berlin-wall/.
"More than 5,400 Children Split at Border, According to New Count." *NBC News*. October 25, 2019. https://www.nbcnews.com/news/us-news/more-5-400-children-split-border- according-new-count-n1071791.
Morice, Jane. "Hundreds Protest Trump's Travel Ban at Cleveland Hopkins International Airport." *Cleveland.com*. January 29, 2017. https://www.cleveland.com/metro/2017/01/hundreds_protest_trumps_travel.html.
Morris, Nigel. "2006: Movies and Crisis." In *American Cinema of the 2000s: Themes and Variations*, edited by Timothy Corrigan, 147–71. New Brunswick: Rutgers University Press, 2012.
"Mortars Strike Baghdad Green Zone." *CBS News*. July 10, 2007. https://www.cbsnews.com/news/mortars-strike-baghdad-green-zone/.
Mortimer, Claire. *Romantic Comedy*. New York: Routledge, 2010.
Morton, Seth. "Zombie Politics." In *The Year's Work at the Zombie Research Center*, edited by Edward P. Comentale and Aaron Jaffe, 315–40. Bloomington: Indiana University Press, 2014.
Mouffe, Chantal. *For a Left Populism*. New York: Verso, 2018.
Murray, Robin L., and Joseph K. Heumann. *That's All Folks? Ecocritical Readings of American Animated Features*. Lincoln: University of Nebraska Press, 2011.
Musser, Charles. *The Emergence of Cinema: The American Screen to 1907*. Berkeley: University of California Press: 1994.
Naficy, Hamid. *An Accented Cinema: Exilic and Diasporic Filmmaking*. Princeton, NJ: Princeton University Press, 2001.
Nagypal, Tamas. "From the Classical Polis to the Neoliberal Camp: Mapping the Biopolitical Regimes of the Undead in *Dawn of the Dead, Zombi 2* and *28 Days Later*." *Journal for Cultural & Religious Theory* 13, no. 2 (2014): 13–24.
Nakamura, David. "Three Presidents, Three Speeches—and an Immigration Debate That Has Grown Courser." *Washington Post*. January 8, 2019. https://www.

washingtonpost.com/politics/three-presidents-one-border--and-an-immigration-debate-that-has-grown-coarser/2019/01/08/d9f3c4a4-1357-11e9-90a8-136fa44b80ba_story.html.

Narea, Nicole. "The Abandoned Asylum Seekers on the US-Mexico Border." *Vox*. December 20, 2019. https://www.vox.com/policy-and-politics/2019/12/20/20997299/asylum-border-mexico-us-iom-unhcr-usaid-migration-international-humanitarian-aid-matamoros-juarez.

Natali, Maurizia. "The Course of the Empire: Sublime Landscapes in the American Cinema." In *Landscape and Film*, edited by Martin Lefebvre, 91–123. New York: Routledge, 2006.

Ndaita, Peter. "Can the Migrant Speak: Ethnic Accents in *Black Panther* and the Quadruple Consciousness of African Immigrants in the United States." *Africology: The Journal of Pan African Studies* 11, no. 9 (2018): 44–7.

Nelson, Elissa H. "The New Old Face of a Genre: The Franchise Teen Film as Industry Strategy." *Cinema Journal* 57, no. 1 (2017): 125–33.

"New Data Show Growing Complexity of Drug Overdose Deaths in America." *CDC*. December 21, 2018. https://www.cdc.gov/media/releases/2018/p1221-complexity-drug-overdose.html.

Nixon, Ron, and Linda Qiu. "Trump's Evolving Words on the Wall." *New York Times*. January 18, 2018. https://www.nytimes.com/2018/01/18/us/politics/trump-border-wall-immigration.html.

Nowicki, Dan, Rafael Carranza, and Ian James. "Trump Says He Now Prefers 'See-Through' Wall." March 13, 2018. https://www.azcentral.com/story/news/politics/border-issues/2018/03/13/donald-trump-visits-san-diego-see-border-wall-prototypes-miramar-otay-mesa-los-angeles/418640002/.

NPR Staff and Wires. "Obama Deploying 1,200 Troops to Mexico Border." *NPR*. May 30, 2010. https://www.npr.org/templates/story/story.php?storyId=127116888.

Obama, Barack. "Remarks by the President in Address to the Nation on Immigration." *The White House: President Barack Obama*. November 20, 2014. https://obamawhitehouse.archives.gov/the-press-office/2014/11/20/remarks-president-address-nation-immigration.

O'Healy, Aine. *Migrant Anxieties: Italian Cinema in a Transnational Frame*. Bloomington: Indiana University Press, 2019.

O'Kane, Caitlin. "Alexandra Ocasio-Cortez: 'The U.S. Is Running Concentration Camps on Our Southern Border.'" *CBS News*. June 18, 2019. https://www.cbsnews.com/news/alexandria-ocasio-cortez-claims-us-running-concentration-camps-on-southern-border/.

Orlando, Valérie K. *New African Cinema*. New Brunswick: Rutgers University Press, 2017.

Ortega, Bob. "Doctor Says Border Patrol Often Misses Early Signs of Illness in Migrant Children." *CNN*. July 1, 2019. https://www.cnn.com/2019/07/01/us/migrant-children-hospitalized-doctor-border-invs/index.html.

Ortega y Gasset, José. *The Revolt of the Masses*. New York: W.W. Norton, 1993.

Oziewicz, Marek. "Peter Jackson's *The Hobbit*: A Beautiful Disaster." *Journal of the Fantastic in the Arts* 27, no. 2 (2016): 248–69.

Peacock, Steven. "The Collaborative Film Work of Greengrass and Damon: A Stylistic State of Exception." *New Cinemas: Journal of Contemporary Film* 9, no. 2/3 (2012): 147–60.

Perrigo, Billy. "Trump Threatens to Cut Off Foreign Aid over Migrant Caravan." *Time*. October 22, 2018. https://time.com/5430841/trump-foreign-aid-migrant-caravan/.

Peters, Robert, William J. Ripple, Christopher Wolf, Matthew Moskwik, Gerardo Carreón-Arroyo, Gerardo Ceballos, Ana Córdova, Rodolfo Dirzo, Paul R. Ehrlich, Aaron D. Flesch, Rurik List, Thomas E. Lovejoy, Reed F. Noss, Jesús Pacheco, José K. Sarukhán, Michael E. Soulé, Edward O. Wilson, Jennifer R. B. Miller, and 2556 Scientist Signatories from 43 Countries. "Nature Divided, Scientists United: US-Mexico Border Wall Threatens Biodiversity and Binational Conservation." *BioScience* 68, no. 10 (2018): 740–3.

Phillips, Kendall R. "'The Safest Hands Are Our Own': Cinematic Affect, State Cruelty, and the Election of Donald J. Trump." *Communication & Critical/Cultural Studies* 15, no. 1 (2018): 85–9.

Pike, Deidre M. *Enviro-Toons: Green Themes in Animated Cinema and Television*. Jefferson, NC: McFarland, 2012.

Pisters, Patricia. "Logistics of Perception 2.0: Multiple Screen Aesthetics in Iraq War Films." *Film-Philosophy* 14, no. 1 (2010): 232–52.

Pokornowshki, Steven. "Vulnerable Life: Zombies, Global Biopolitics, and the Reproduction of Structural Violence." *Humanities* 5, no. 3 (2016): 71–93.

Polan, Dana. "2009: Movies, a Nation, and New Identities." In *American Cinema of the 2000s: Themes and Variations*, edited by Timothy Corrigan, 216–37. New Brunswick: Rutgers University Press, 2012.

Powers, Laura. "Trump's Acting Immigration Director Claims Ending Birthright Citizenship Would Not Require Constitutional Amendment." *Newsweek*. October 16, 2019. https://www.newsweek.com/trumps-acting-immigration-director-claims-ending-birthright-citizenship-would-not-require-1465728.

"President Bush's Plan for Comprehensive Immigration Reform." *The White House: President George W. Bush*. 2007. https://georgewbush-whitehouse.archives.gov/statcoftheunion/2007/initiatives/immigration.html.

Press, Ayal. "Trump and the Truth: Immigration and Crime." *New Yorker*. September 2, 2016. https://www.newyorker.com/news/news-desk/trump-and-the-truth-immigration-and-crime.

Preston, Julia. "U.S. Raids 6 Meat Plants in ID Case." *New York Times*. December 13, 2006. https://www.nytimes.com/2006/12/13/us/13raid.html.

Pullella, Philip. "Don't Build Walls, Pope Francis Says." *Reuters*. February 8, 2017. https://www.reuters.com/article/us-pope-wall-idUSKBN15N1ZW.

Purse, Lisa. "Affective Trajectories: Locating Diegetic Velocity in the Cinema Experience." *Cinema Journal* 55, no. 2 (2016): 151–7.

Rangarajan, Sinduja. "The Trump Administration Is Denying H-1B Visas at a Dizzying Rate, but It's Hit a Snag." *Mother Jones*. October 17, 2019. https://www.motherjones.com/politics/2019/10/h1b-tech-visa-denial-appeal-trump/.

Ravikumar, Vandana. "'Operation Border Resolve' ICE Raids, Touted by President Donald Trump, Net 35 Arrests, Officials Say." *USA Today*. July 24, 2019. https://www.usatoday.com/story/news/nation/2019/07/23/ice-raids-president-donald-trump-35-arrests-officials/1810185001/.

Reese, April. "U.S.-Mexico Fence Building Continues despite Obama's Promise to Review Effects." *New York Times*, April 16, 2009. https://archive.nytimes.com/www.nytimes.com/gwire/2009/04/16/16greenwire- usmexico-fence-building-continues-despite-obam- 10570.html?pagewanted=all&scp=15&sq=mexico%2520security&st=cse.

Reese, Renford. "Canada: The Promised Land for U.S. Slaves." *Western Journal of Black Studies* 35, no. 3 (2011): 208–17.

Reid, Julie. "Decolonizing Education and Research by Countering the Myths We Live By." *Cinema Journal* 57, no. 4 (2018): 132–8.

Reilly, Katie. "Here Are All the Times Donald Trump Insulted Mexico." *Time*. August 31, 2016. https://time.com/4473972/donald-trump-mexico-meeting-insult/.

"Remarks by President Trump in Meeting with Senate Minority Leader Chuck Schumer and House Speaker-Designate Nancy Pelosi." *WhiteHouse.gov*. December 11, 2018. https://www.whitehouse.gov/briefings-statements/remarks-president-trump-meeting- senate-minority-leader-chuck-schumer-house-speaker-designate-nancy-pelosi/.

Rodríguez, Jesús A. "How the Migrant Caravan Built Its Own Democracy." *Politico*. December 12, 2018. https://www.politico.com/magazine/story/2018/12/12/migrant-caravan-tijuana- border-government-222856.

Romo, Vanessa. "Administration Cuts Education and Legal Services for Unaccompanied Minors." *NPR*. June 5, 2019. https://www.npr.org/2019/06/05/730082911/administration-cuts-education-and-legal-services-for-unaccompanied-minors.

Rose, Joel, Carrie Kahn, and Kelsey Snell. "Trumps Tweets on 'Caravans' Crossing the Border, Annotated." *NPR*. April 2, 2018. https://www.npr.org/2018/04/02/598781060/trumps- tweets-on-caravans-crossing-the-border-annotated.

Rosza, Matthew. "The MAGA Fever Dream of 'Rambo: Last Blood.'" *Salon*. September 20, 2019. https://www.salon.com/2019/09/20/the-maga-fever-dream-of-rambo-last-blood/.

Rucker, Philip. "It's Tall, It's Tough, It's Too Hot to Touch: President Trump Has Just the Wall for You." *Washington Post*. September 19, 2019. https://www.washingtonpost.com/politics/its-tall-its-tough-its-too-hot-to-touch-president-trump-has-just-the-wall-for-you/2019/09/19/3708545e-dae3-11e9-a688-303693fb4b0b_story.html.

Rucker, Philip, and Felicia Sonmez. "Trump Calls Wall Only Solution to 'Growing Humanitarian Crisis' at Border." *Washington Post*. January 8, 2019. https://www.washingtonpost.com/politics/trump-declares-a-growing-humanitarian-crisis-at-the-border-in-demand-for-wall-funding-to-end-shutdown/2019/01/08/bdd2767e-1368-11e9-803c-4ef28312c8b9_story.html.

Sacchetti, Maria. "Trump Administration Cancels English Classes, Soccer, Legal Aid for Unaccompanied Child Migrants in US Shelters." *Washington Post*. June 5, 2019. https://www.washingtonpost.com/immigration/trump-administration-cancels-english- classes-soccer-legal-aid-for-unaccompanied-child-migrants-in-us- shelters/2019/06/05/df2a0008-8712-11e9-a491-25df61c78dc4_story.html?arc404=true.

Sakuma, Amanda. "The Failed Experiment of Immigrant Family Detention." *NBC News*. August 2, 2015. https://www.nbcnews.com/news/latino/failed-experiment-immigrant-family-detention-n403126.

Salama, Vivian. "Trump Threatens to 'Call Up the U.S. Military' if Mexico Doesn't Stop Migrants." *Wall Street Journal*. October 18, 2018. https://www.wsj.com/articles/trump-threatens-to-call-up-the-u-s-military-if-mexico-doesnt-stop-migrants-1539866223.

Santiago, Leyla. "Caravan of Migrants Climbs Freight Train for the Next Leg of the Journey." *CNN*. April 15, 2018. https://www.cnn.com/2018/04/14/americas/central-america-migrant-caravan-train/index.html.

Santiago, Leyla, and Catherine E. Shoichet, "Trump Says Caravan Migrants Are Turning Back. Mexico Says Most Are Still at the Border." *CNN*. December 11, 2018. https://www.cnn.com/2018/12/11/americas/mexico-caravan-trump/index.html.

Sarris, Andrew. *"You Ain't Heard Nothin' Yet": The American Talking Film History & Memory, 1927–1949*. New York: Oxford University Press, 2000.

Scharf, Inga. "Staging the Border: National Identity and the Critical Geopolitics of West German Film." *Geopolitics* 10, no. 2 (2005): 378–97.

Segers, Grace. "Kevin McCarthy Says He Will Introduce Bill to Fully Fund Border Wall." *CBS News*. October 9, 2018. https://www.cbsnews.com/news/kevin-mccarthy-introducing- bill-to-fully-fund-border-wall/.

Serres, Michel. *Malfeasance: Appropriation through Pollution?* Translated by Anne-Marie Feenberg-Dibon. Stanford, CA: Stanford University Press, 2011.

Shah, Naureen. "DHS Is Locking Immigrants in Solitary Confinement." *ACLU*. May 24, 2019. https://www.aclu.org/blog/immigrants-rights/immigrants-rights-and-detention/dhs- locking-immigrants-solitary-confinement.

Shapiro, Michael J. *The Political Sublime*. Durham, NC: Duke University Press, 2018.

Shaviro, Steven. *Post Cinematic Affect*. Alresford: Zero Books, 2010.

Shear, Michael D., Abby Goodnough, and Maggie Haberman. "Trump Retreats on Separating Families, but Thousands May Remain Apart." *New York Times*. June 20, 2018. https://www.nytimes.com/2018/06/20/us/politics/trump-immigration-children-executive-order.html.

Shear, Michael D., and Julie Hirschfield Davis. "Shoot Migrants' Legs, Build Alligator Moat." *New York Times*. October 2, 2019. https://www.nytimes.com/2019/10/01/us/politics/trump-border-wars.html.

Shoichet, Catherine E., and Leyla Santiago. "The Migrant Caravan Is Still Coming. Trump Says Don't Let Them In." *CNN*. April 25, 1018. https://www.cnn.com/2018/04/20/us/migrant-caravan-border-arrival-next-steps/index.html.

Siders, David. "Beto's Call to Remove Part of the Wall Provokes Trump's Ire." *Politico*. February 19, 2019. https://www.politico.com/story/2019/02/19/beto-orourke-trump-2020-border-wall-1175846.

Silva, Daniella. "'Like I Am Trash': Migrant Children Reveal Stories of Detention, Separation." *NBC News*. July 26, 2018. https://www.nbcnews.com/news/latino/i-am-trash-migrant-children-reveal-stories-detention-separation-n895006.

Silva, Daniella, Julia Ainsley, Pete Williams, and Geoff Bennett. "Trump Administration Moves to End Asylum Protections for Most Central American Migrants." *NBC News*. July 15, 2019. https://www.nbcnews.com/news/us-news/trump-administration-moves-end-asylum-protections-most-central-american-migrants-n1029866.

Simpson, Audra. *Mohawk Interruptus: Political Life across the Borders of Settler States*. Durham, NC: Duke University Press, 2014.

Skal, David J. "Virtual Gravity." *Fantasy & Science Fiction* 126, no. 1/2 (2014): 179–84.

Slotkin, Richard. *Gunfighter Nation: The Myth of the Frontier in Twentieth-Century America*. Norman: University of Oklahoma Press, 1998.

Sobchack, Vivian. *Screening Space: The American Science Fiction Film*. New Brunswick: Rutgers University Press, 1998.

Sonne, Paul. "Trump Looks to Raid Pentagon Budget for Wall Money Using Emergency Powers." *Washington Post*. February 15, 2019. https://www.washingtonpost.com/world/national-security/trump-looks-to-raid-pentagon-budget-for-wall-money-using-emergency-powers/2019/02/15/cd0fcdb8-3149-11e9-ac6c-14eea99d5e24_story.html.

Spehr, Paul. *The Man Who Made Movies: W.K.L. Dickson*. New Barnet: John Libbey, 2008.

Sragow, Michael. "*War for the Planet of the Apes*." *Film Comment* 53, no. 4 (2017): 72.

Stiegler, Bernard. *Symbolic Misery Volume 1: The Hyperindustrial Epoch*. Translated by Barnaby Norman. Malden, MA: Polity, 2014.

Stiegler, Bernard. *Symbolic Misery Volume 2: The Catastrophe of the Sensible*. Translated by Barnaby Norman. Malden, MA: Polity, 2015.

Stone, Andrea. "Mortars, Rockets Raise Baghdad Tensions." *USA Today*. May 2, 2008. https://usatoday30.usatoday.com/news/world/iraq/2008-05-01-iraqrockets_N.htm.

Stout, Graeme. "Control and Flow: Winterbottom's Migratory Cinema." In *Alien Imaginations: Science Fiction and Tales of Transnationalism*, edited by Ulrike Küchler, Silja Maehl, and Graeme Stout, 209–25. New York: Bloomsbury Academic, 2015.

Stratton, Jon. "Trouble with Zombies: Muselmänner, Bare Life, and Displaced People." In *Zombie Theory: A Reader*, edited by Sarah Juliet Lauro, 246–69. Minneapolis: University of Minnesota Press, 2017.

Suskind, Ron. "Faith, Certainty and the Presidency of George W. Bush." *New York Times*. October 17, 2004. https://www.nytimes.com/2004/10/17/magazine/faith-certainty-and-the-presidency-of-george-w-bush.html.

Tait, Paul. "Baghdad's Green Zone Hit by a Barrage of Blasts." *Reuters*. March 22, 2008. https://www.reuters.com/article/us-iraq-barrage/baghdads-green-zone-hit-by-barrage-of-blasts-idUSL2368975320080323.

Taylor, Diana. *The Archive and the Repertoire: Performing Cultural Memory in the Americas*. Durham, NC: Duke University Press, 2005.

Telotte, J. P. *Replications: A Robotic History of the Science Fiction Film*. Urbana: University of Illinois Press, 1995.

Telotte, J. P. *Robot Ecology and the Science Fiction Film*. New York: Routledge, 2016.

Telotte, J. P. *Animating the Science Fiction Imagination*. New York: Oxford University Press, 2018.

The Project for the New American Century. "Rebuilding America's Defenses: Strategy, Forces, and Resources for a New Century." September 2000. https://archive.org/stream/RebuildingAmericasDefenses/RebuildingAmericasDefenses_djvu.txt.

"Tijuana, Mexico, Declares Migrant 'Humanitarian Crisis.'" *NBC News*. November 23, 2018. https://www.nbcnews.com/news/world/tijuana-mexico-declares-migrant-humanitarian-crisis-n939591.

Toscano, Alberto, and Jeff Kinkle. *Cartographies of the Absolute*. Washington, DC: Zero Books, 2015.

Trump, Donald J. "Here's Donald Trump's Presidential Announcement Speech." *Time*. June 16, 2015. https://time.com/3923128/donald-trump-announcement-speech/.

Trump, Donald J. "Full Text: Donald Trump Immigration Speech in Arizona." *Politico*. August 31, 2016. https://www.politico.com/story/2016/08/donald-trump-immigration-address-transcript-227614.

Trump, Donald J. "Statement from President Donald J. Trump." *WhiteHouse.gov*, September 5, 2017. https://www.whitehouse.gov/briefings-statements/statement-president-donald-j-trump-7/.

Trump, Donald J. (@realDonaldTrump). "… In addition to stopping all payments to these countries, which seem to have almost no control over their population, I must, in the strongest of terms, ask Mexico to stop this onslaught - and if unable to do so I will call up the U.S. Military and CLOSE OUR SOUTHERN BORDER!" Twitter. October 18, 2018. https://twitter.com/realdonaldtrump/status/1052885781675687936?lang=en.

Trump, Donald J. (@realDonaldTrump). "Many Gang Members and some very bad people are mixed into the Caravan heading to our Southern Border. Please go back, you will not be admitted into the United States unless you go through the legal process. This is an invasion of our Country and our Military is waiting for you!" Twitter. October 29, 2018. https://twitter.com/realdonaldtrump/status/1056919064906469376?lang=en.

Trump, Donald J. (@realDonaldTrump). "A big new Caravan is heading up to our Southern Border from Honduras. Tell Nancy and Chuck that a drone flying around will not stop them. Only a Wall will work. Only a Wall, or Steel Barrier, will keep our Country safe! Stop playing political games and end the Shutdown!" Twitter. January 15, 2019. https://twitter.com/realdonaldtrump/status/1085154110108848128?lang=en.

Trump, Donald J. (@realDonaldTrump). "… Mexico must apprehend all illegals and not let them make the long march up to the United States, or we will have no other choice than to Close the Border and/or institute Tariffs. Our Country is FULL!" Twitter. April 7, 2019. https://twitter.com/realdonaldtrump/status/1115057524770844672?lang=en.

Tuan, Yi-Fu. *Landscapes of Fear*. Minneapolis: University of Minnesota Press, 2013.

Turnock, Julie. *Plastic Reality: Special Effects, Technology, and the Emergence of 1970s Blockbuster Aesthetics*. New York: Columbia University Press, 2015.

Uhlin, Graig. "The Anthropocene's Nonindifferent Nature." *JCMS* 58, no. 2 (2019): 157–62.

"US Attorney General Jeff Sessions on Children Separated from Parents at Border, F-1 Visas for PRC Students, and Masterpiece Cakeshop Decision." *Hugh Hewitt*. June 5, 2018. https://www.hughhewitt.com/attorney-general-jeff-sessions-on-the-immigration-policies-concerning-children-apprehended-at-he-border-and-f-1-visas/.

Varela, Julio Ricardo. "Trump's Border Wall Was Never Just about Security. It's Meant to Remind All Latinos That We're Unwelcome." *NBC News*. December 28, 2018. https://www.nbcnews.com/think/opinion/trump-s-border-wall-was-never-just-about-security-it-ncna952011.

Vasquez, Tina. "The New ICE Age: An Agency Unleashed." *New York Review of Books*. May 2, 2018. https://www.nybooks.com/daily/2018/05/02/the-new-ice-age-an-agency-unleashed/.

Vazquez, Maegan. "Trump Defends ICE Raid Strategy." *CNN*. August 9, 2019. https://www.cnn.com/2019/08/09/politics/trump-defends-ice-raid-strategy/index.html.

Virilio, Paul. *The Information Bomb*. New York: Verso, 2006.

Virilio, Paul. *War and Cinema: The Logistics of Perception*. Translated by Patrick Camiller. New York: Verso, 2009.

Virno, Paolo. *A Grammar of the Multitude: For an Analysis of Contemporary Forms of Life*. Translated by Isabella Bertoletti, James Cascaito, and Andrea Casson. Los Angeles: Semiotext(e), 2004.

Vogue, Ariane de. "Supreme Court Clears Way for Trump Admin to Use Defense Funds for Border Wall Construction." *CNN*. July 26, 2019. https://www.cnn.com/2019/07/26/politics/supreme-court-pentagon-border-wall-construction/index.html.

Wagner, John. "Across Five Tweets, Trump Makes a Meandering Case for Border Wall Funding." *Washington Post*. December 11, 2018. https://www.washingtonpost.com/politics/across-five-tweets-trump-makes-a-meandering-case-for-border-wall-funding/2018/12/11/8ea6ad64-fd35-11e8-862a-b6a6f3ce8199_story.html.

Wald, Priscilla. "Viral Cultures: Microbes and Politics in the Cold War." In *Zombie Theory: A Reader*, edited by Sarah Juliet Lauro, 33–62. Minneapolis: University of Minnesota Press, 2017.

Wallace, David Foster. *Both Flesh and Not: Essays*. New York: Little, Brown, 2011.

Walters, James. *Fantasy Film: A Critical Introduction*. New York: Bloomsbury Academic, 2011.

Warner, Marina. *Once Upon a Time: A Short History of the Fairy Tale*. New York: Oxford University Press, 2014.

Wasser, Frederick. *Steven Spielberg's America*. Malden, MA: Polity, 2010.

Watkins, Eli. "Pope Francis: 'Those Who Build Walls Will Become Prisoners of the Walls They Put Up.'" *CNN*. April 1, 2019. https://www.cnn.com/2019/04/01/politics/pope-francis-wall/index.html.

Weber, Cynthia. *Imagining America at War: Morality, Politics and Film*. New York: Routledge, 2005.

Weber, Jared. "Trump Administration Cuts English Classes, Soccer and Legal Aid for Migrant Children at Shelters." *USA Today*. June 5, 2019. https://www.usatoday.com/story/news/nation/2019/06/05/trump-administration-cancels-services-migrant-children/1358114001/.

Weinstock, Jeffrey Andrew. "Zombie TV: Late-Night B Movie Horror Fest." In *Zombie Theory: A Reader*, edited by Sarah Juliet Lauro, 20–32. Minneapolis: University of Minnesota Press, 2017.

Whissel, Kristen. *Spectacular Digital Effects: CGI and Contemporary Cinema*. Durham, NC: Duke University Press, 2014.

Zakaria, Rafia. "How Trump Is Stripping Immigrants of Their Citizenship." *The Nation*. December 21, 2018. https://www.thenation.com/article/denaturalization-trump-citizenship-emma-goldman/.

Žižek, Slavoj. *Violence: Six Sideways Reflections*. New York: Picador, 2008.

Žižek, Slavoj. *Refugees, Terror and Other Trouble with the Neighbors: Against the Double Blackmail*. Brooklyn: Melville House, 2016.

Zohn, Rachel. "Recent ICE Raids Overload Mississippi Legal System." *USA Today*. October 18, 2019. https://www.usnews.com/news/best-states/articles/2019-10-18/recent-ice-raids-by-us-immigration-and-customs-enforcement-overload-mississippi-legal-system.

INDEX

A-Team, The (1983–7) 142
African Queen, The (1951) 138
Agamben, Giorgio 88, 111 n.40
Ahmed, Sarah 195 n.38
Akira (1988) 142
Alexander, Jonathan 177
Alien (1979) 142
Allen, Richard 31–2 n. 30
Altman, Rick 91
America Sniper (2014) 60
Andersen, Gregers 157 n.56
Anderson, Benedict 202 n.71
Anzaldua, Gloria 198 n.54
Apocalypse Now (1979) 125, 179, 184, 186
Aquaman (2018) 158 n.63
Arendt, Hannah 22, 37–8, 46, 48–9
Assignment—Paris! (1952) 29–30 n.24
Atomic Blonde (2017) 10–12, 30 n.25, 30 n.26
Atomic City (1952) 31 n.28
Avatar (2009) 99
Avengers: Infinity War (2018) 140–1, 159 n.66, 197 n.51

Back to the Future (1985–90) 142
Badiou, Alain 203
Balibar, Étienne 133–5
Bandolero! (1968) 197 n.48
Barbarian and the Geisha, The (1958) 5–7, 12–13
Barker, Martin 46
Batman (comics series) 142
Battlestar Galactica (1978–9) 142
Bazin, André 132
Becky Sharp (1935) 32 n.32
Bégin, Richard 71–2 n.56

Belko Experiment, The (2017) 100–5, 116 n.63
Bellantoni, Patti 179
Benjamin, Walter 167–8
Benson-Allott, Caetlin 172
Beowulf (2007) 92
Berlin Wall 3, 4, 7–12, 28 n.19, 30 n.26, 31 n.30, 32 n.31, 59, 108 n.20, 128, 200–1 n.66, 201 n.69
  inner German border 29 n.20, 201 n.67
Bertelsen, Lone 168
BioShock (video game) 142
Biskind, Peter 58–9
Black Panther (2018) 137–42, 158 n.63, 158–9 n.65
Blow, Charles M. 162
Bolsonaro, Jair 204
Boltanksi, Luc 116 n.63
Border, The (1982) 32 n.32
Borisov, Boyko 204
Bradshaw, Peter 116–17 n.66
Braester, Yomi 99
Brégent-Heald, Dominique 70 n.43
Bridge of Spies (2015) 201–2 n.69
Bringing Up Baby (1938) 170
Britton, Andrew 184, 189
Brotherhood of the Wolf (2001) 104
Brown, Wendy 14, 80, 85, 105, 121, 129
Bubble, The (1966) 108 n.20
Burnout (video game) 142
Bush, George W. 1, 3–4, 13, 18, 21–3, 35, 46–7, 58, 70 n.42, 77, 80, 83, 129, 161
  National Security Agency (NSA) wiretapping scandal 196 n.44

PATRIOT Act 39, 41
Secure Fence Act of 2006 1, 13, 15, 21, 80, 124, 129
War on Terror 35–36, 40, 202 n.70

Calais Jungle camp 162
Canada 29 n.20, 86, 110 n.33, 201 n.68
  US-Canada border 70 n.43
Captain Marvel (2019) 197 n.51, 199 n.60
Carter, Sean 68 n.29
Casablanca (1942) 142
Casino Royale (1967) 8
Cavell, Stanley 113–14 n.53, 152 n.33
Chaudhuri, Shohini 153–4 n.37
Chernobyl (2019) 108 n.22
Christmas Carol, A (2009) 154 n.44
Chung, Hye Jean 90–1, 198–9 n.56
Clinton, Bill 108 n.18, 161
  Illegal Immigration Reform and Information Responsibility Act of 1996 108 n.18
Coco (2017) 156 n.54
Code 46 (2003) 15–18
Cohen, Jeffrey Jerome 87, 181
Cold War 4, 7, 10–12, 28 n.19, 29 n.20, 31–2 n.30, 33 n.49, 67 n.23, 108 n.20, 109 n.26, 128, 180, 206 n.8
  Iron Curtain 29–30 n.24, 31 n.30
Cole, Thomas 69 n.37
Combe, Kirk 127
Comentale, Edward P. 111 n.39
Comer, Todd A. 52
Connelly, William E. 204
Cordona, Natalia 120
Cornell, Matt 87
Corrigan, Timothy 2–4, 22, 26, 30 n.26, 155 n.46, 184

Da Vinci Code, The (2006) 57
Das Testament des Dr. Mabuse/The Testament of Dr. Mabuse (1933) 109 n.26
Davis, Julie Hirschfield 203
Davis, Mike 40, 156–7 n.55
Dawn of the Dead (1978) 89
Dawn of the Dead (2004) 89
Day of the Dead (1985) 89

de Certeau, Michel 25, 162–3, 178, 201 n.69
Deadly Mantis, The (1957) 29 n.20
Deepwater Horizon (2016) 108 n.22
Defiance (2008) 49
Deleuze, Gilles 112–13 n.44
Derrida, Jacques 93, 95
Devil's Rejects, The (2005) 196 n.48
Die 1000 Augen des Dr. Mabuse/The Thousand Eyes of Dr. Mabuse (1960) 109 n.26
Divergent (2014) 174–5
Divergent Series: Allegiant, The (2016) 174–9, 197 n.51, 198 nn.53, 54
Divergent Series: Insurgent, The (2015) 174–5
Dixon, Wheeler Winston 68 n.32
Doane, Mary Ann 30 n.25, 207 n.11
Doctor Faustus (Marlowe) 176
Doctor Who (1963-present) 142
Dodds, Klaus 68 n.29
Dog Soldiers (2002) 104
Donkey Kong (video game) 185
Dr. Mabuse, der Spieler/Dr. Mabuse the Gambler (1922) 109 n.26
Dressed to Kill (1980) 30 n.25
Drums Along the Mohawk (1939) 69 n.41
Duke Nukem (video game) 142
Dungeons & Dragons (role-playing game) 145

Eberwein, Robert 74 n.70
Eco, Umberto 142
Edwards, Haley Sweetland 206 n.8
Ellis, John 69 n.36, 109 n.23
Elysium (2013) 133–7, 155 n.50, 155–6 n.51, 156 nn.54, 55, 157 nn.56, 60, 199 n.60, 206 n.8
Embry, Karen 33 n.45
Erdoğan, Recep Tayyip 204
Everest (2015) 108 n.22
Excalibur (1981) 145

Fabian, Sarah 161
Fantastic Beasts and Where to Find Them (2016) 55–9
Feltmate, David 86

Finest Hours, The (2016) 108 n.22
Fiske, John 109 n.23
Flags of Our Fathers (2006) 49
Forbidden Planet (1956) 67 n.23
Fort Apache (1948) 69 n.41
40-Year-Old Virgin, The (2005) 130
Foster, Gwendolyn Audrey 68 n.32
Foucault, Michel 23, 78, 85, 90, 92, 94, 97–8, 103
Frankenstein (1931) 96
Freaks and Geeks (1999–2000) 130
Freda, Isabelle 60
Freud, Sigmund 184
Friday the 13th (1980–2009) 142
Frogs (1972) 180
Fromm, Erich 58
Frye, Northrop 195–6 n.42
Fuller, Stephanie 33–4 n.49
Funeral in Berlin (1966) 8

G.I. Joe: Retaliation (2013) 70–1 n.46
G.I. Joe: The Rise of Cobra (2009) 70 n.46
Garden of Earthly Delights, The (Bosch) 45
Genette, Gérard 42–3
Gibson, Suzie 157 n.56
Gillibrand, Kristen 203
Girl in the Kremlin, The (1957) 29 n.20
Giroux, Henry A. 101, 123, 129
Gods Must Be Crazy, The (1980) 139
Godzilla (1954-present) 142
Goodfellow, Maya 33 n.35
Gorillas in the Mist (1988) 138
Grand Old Party (GOP) 13, 41, 44
Gray, Jonathan 84
Gray, Mitchell 114–15 n.57
Great Escape, The (1963) 128
Great Raid, The (2005) 49
Great Wall, The (2017) 80, 97–100, 114–15 nn.57, 61, 203
Green Berets, The (1968) 46, 69 n.41
Green Hornet, The (2011) 130
Green Zone (2010) 39, 45–50, 69 n.37, 70 nn.42, 43
Grewal, Inderpal 14
Grindon, Leger 169
Gusain, Renuka 63

Hageman, Andrew 81
Halo (video game) 142
Hanna, Monica 207 n.11
Harding, Jeremy 66 n.5
Harry Potter (2001–11) 55–6
Hart's War (2002) 49
Hell in the Pacific (1968) 180
Henry, Matthew A. 108 n.18
Henry, Michel 22, 36–8, 44, 48, 58, 62, 73 n.63
Hercules (2014) 72 n.59
Heumann, Joseph K. 108 n.19
High Sierra (1941) 73 n.69
Higson, Andrew 111–12 n.43
Hobbit, The (2012–14) 54, 56, 71 n.55
Hobbit: The Battle of the Five Armies, The (2014) 50–5
Hobbit: Desolation of Smaug, The (2013) 50, 55
Hobbit: An Unexpected Journey, The (2012) 50
Hoberman, J. 7, 30–1 n.28, 68 n.31, 109–10 n.26
House of 1000 Corpses (2003) 196 n.48
Huntsman, The (2012–16) 56
Huntsman: Winter's War, The (2016) 55–6
Hurt Locker, The (2008) 60

Iliad, The (Homer) 18
Impossible, The (2012) 108 n.22
In the Valley of Elah (2007) 60
Inherit the Wind (1960) 57
Invasion of the Body Snatchers (1956) 31 n.28
Invisible Invaders (1959) 89
Iraq War 22, 35, 39, 42, 46, 60, 63, 73 n.69
 Green Zone (International Zone of Baghdad) 23, 35–6, 38–42, 44, 46–7, 49, 51–3, 55–6, 59, 61, 63–5, 67 n.23, 69 n.36, 70 nn.41, 42, 43, 72 nn.59, 60, 81
It Happened One Night (1934) 124, 152 n.33

Jameson, Fredric 44
Jancovich, Mark 67 n.23
Johnson, Boris 204
Johnson, Kevin R. 28–9 n.19
Jones, Reece 68 n.28
Judge Dredd (1995) 159–60 n.71
Judgment at Nuremberg (1961) 94
Jurassic Park (1993) 142, 144

Kendrick, James 104
Kennedy, John F. 1
   New Frontier 4–5, 7
Kennedy, Robert F. 180
King, Jr., Martin Luther 180
King Kong (1933) 142, 181, 183
Kingdom of the Spiders (1977) 180
Kinkle, Jeff 136
Klein, Naomi 2, 19
Knocked Up (2007) 130
Koenigsberger, Kurt M. 110 n.30
Kong: Skull Island (2017) 179–84, 189, 198 n.56, 199 nn. 57, 60
Kristeva, Julia 24, 121–3
Krstić, Igor 70 n.42

Labyrinth (1986) 171
Land That Time Forgot, The (1975) 199 n.57
Last Judgment, The (Bosch) 45
Latour, Bruno 199 n.60
Lauro, Juliet 33 n.45
Lawnmower Man, The (1992) 144
Le Mépris/Contempt (1963) 42
Lee, Jasmine 177
Lego Movie, The (2014) 159 n.69
Line of Control 163
Lord of the Rings, The (2001–3) 52, 54, 95
Losin' It (1983) 124
Lotz, Amanda D. 198 n.53
Lower Depths, The (1936) 132

Man Between, The (1953) 201 n.67
Man on a String (1960) 31 n.29
Manzanas, Ana M. 74 n.72
Marcuse, Herbert 34 n.53
Mass Effect (video game) 142
Mauss, Marcel 29 n.23

Maze Runner, The (2014) 170–4, 175, 196 nn.44, 46, 203
Maze Runner: The Death Cure (2018) 174
Maze Runner: The Scorch Trials (2015) 172
McCarthy, Kevin 2
McDonald, Tamar Jeffers 130
McGuffin 31 n.32, 142
McKenzie Break, The (1970) 128
McNally, David 167
McSweeney, Terrence 150–1 n.16
McWhorter, John 163
Metz, Walter 160 n.72
Miller, Todd 74 n.71
Minh-ha, Trinh T. 151 n.29
Miracle at St. Anna (2008) 49
Mirrlees, Tanner 155 n.50
Mobile Suit Gundam (1979–80) 142
Modi, Narendra 204
Monroe Doctrine 33 n.49
Monsters (2010) 124–8, 129, 153 nn.34, 37, 156 n.54, 199 n.60, 203
Morris, Nigel 196 n.44
Morrison, Scott 204
Mortimer, Claire 195 n.39
Mouffe, Chantal 200 n.62
Murphie, Andrew 168
Murray, Robin L. 108 n.19

Naficy, Hamid 34 n.50
Natali, Maurizia 69 n.37
Natural Born Killers (1994) 186
Ndaita, Peter 139
Nelson, Elissa H. 174
Netanyahu, Benjamin 204
Nielsen, Esben Bjergaard 157 n.56
Night of the Living Dead (1968) 89
Nightmare on Elm Street (1984–2010) 142
Nightwing (1979) 180
9/11 3–4, 13, 15, 17–19, 21, 49, 69 n.37, 108 n.18, 114 n.57, 124, 150 n.16, 161, 202 n.70

O'Rourke, Beto 203
Obama, Barack 3–4, 13, 129

Affordable Care Act (Obamacare) 157 n.56
internment of minors in detention camps 156 n.54, 161, 172, 176
Ocasio-Cortez, Alexandria 32 n.31, 162
127 Hours (2010) 130
One Missed Call (2003) 113 n.49
Orbán, Viktor 204
Orlando, Valérie K. 158–9 n.65
Ortega y Gasset, José 195 n.40
Oziewicz, Marek 54

Pacific Rim (2013) 199–200 n.61
Peace Lines of Northern Ireland 163
Peacock, Steven 48
Pedersen, Isabel 155 n.50
Pelosi, Nancy 77
People That Time Forgot, The (1977) 199 n.57
Percy Jackson and the Sea of Monsters (2013) 72–3 n.60
Phillips, Kendall R. 174
Pike, Deidre M. 86
Pineapple Express (2008) 130
Pisters, Patricia 60
Pixels (2015) 159 n.69
Point of No Return (1993) 30 n.25
Polan, Dana 202 n.70
Pope Francis 204, 206 n.10
Pope Francis: A Man of His Word (2018) 204
Pope Leo XIII 206 n.10
Pride and Prejudice and Zombies (2016) 89, 111–12 n.43
Project of the New American Century, The 35
Pulse (2001) 113 n.49
Purse, Lisa 11

Rad Racer (video game) 142
Rambo: Last Blood (2019) 116–17 n.66
Ready Player One (2018) 142–7, 159 n.69, 159–60 n.71, 160 n.72
Reagan, Ronald 11
Red Sparrow (2018) 30 n.25
Red State (2011) 57
Redacted (2007) 60

Reid, Julie 21–2
Renoir, Jean 132
Resident Evil: Afterlife (2010) 89
Resident Evil: Apocalypse (2004) 17–20
Rice, Condoleezza 39
Rio Grande (1950) 69 n.41
Robocop (1987–2014) 142
Rogue One: A Star Wars Story (2016) 157–8 n.60
Roma walls 163
Romeo and Juliet (Shakespeare) 165, 170
Roots (1977) 113–14 n.53, 186
Rosemary's Baby (1968) 130
Rosza, Matthew 116–17 n.66

Sanchez, Jesús Benito 74 n.72
Santiago, Leyla 119
Sarris, Andrew 69 n.38
Saturday Night Fever (1977) 144
Scharf, Inga 200–1 n.66
Second World War 49
 Fortress America 15
 Japanese internment camps 162
September 11, 2001 *see* 9/11
Serres, Michel 24, 120–1, 123, 132, 136, 147
Sessions, Jeff 161
Seventh Son (2015) 114 n.54
Shapiro, Michael J. 4
Shaviro, Steven 41
Shear, Michael D. 203
Sheehan, Rebecca A. 207 n.11
Shining, The (1980) 142, 171
Silence (2016) 6–7
Simpson, Audre 110 n.33
Simpsons, The (1989-present) 108 n.18, 110 n.30
Simpsons Movie, The (2007) 80–6, 100, 108 nn.18, 19, 20, 110 n.26, 179
Skal, David J. 155 n.50
Slotkin, Richard 4, 69–70 n.41
Sobchack, Vivian 155 n.46, 155–6 n.51
Some Like It Hot (1959) 170
Sonic the Hedgehog (video game) 144
Southland Tales (2006) 39–45, 68 nn.29, 31, 69 n.36
Spartacus (1960) 186

Spawn (comics series) 142
Speed Racer (1967–8) 142
Spy Who Came in from the Cold, The (1965) 8–11, 13, 32 n.31, 201 n.69
Sragow, Michael 188
Stalag 17 (1953) 128
Starcraft (video game) 142
Star Trek (1966-present) 142
Star Trek Beyond (2016) 153 n.36
Star Wars (1977-present) 142
Stiegler, Bernard 23–4, 78–9, 83–5, 91, 94, 96, 104–5, 109 n.23
Stop-Loss (2008) 60
Stout, Graeme 33 n.44
Street Fighter (video game) 142
Super Mario World (video game) 146
Superbad (2007) 130
Suskind, Ron 35

Taken (2009) 116 n.66
Tarzan the Ape Man (1932) 138
Taylor, Diana 66 n.5
Teenage Mutant Ninja Turtles (comics series) 142
Telotte, J. P. 82, 86, 152–3 n.34, 157 n.59
Terminator 2: Judgement Day (1991) 71 n.55, 130
Thirty Years' War 68 n.28
This Is the End (2013) 128–32, 155 n.46
3 from Hell (2019) 196–7 n.48
300 (2007) 92
Tomb Raider (video game) 142
Torn Curtain (1966) 13, 31 n.30
Toscano, Alberto 136
Toy Story (1995-present) 159 n.69
Trouble in Paradise (1932) 170
Troy (2004) 18–19
Trump, Donald J. 1–4, 13, 15, 21, 26, 32 n.31, 36, 66 n.5, 77–8, 101–2, 115 n.61, 116 n.66, 129, 142, 156 n.54, 161–4, 172, 174, 176, 186, 189, 197 nn.48, 51, 203–4
  Border Security and Immigration Enforcement Improvements Order (Executive Order 13767) 2, 13
  Build the Wall, Enforce the Law Act of 2018 2
  campaign rallies 1
  curtailment of Fourteenth Amendment statue stipulations 119–20
  migrant camps (detention centers) 2, 19, 120–1, 156 n.54, 161, 164, 202 n.70
  National Emergency Concerning the Southern Border of the United States 67 n.27
  response to Northern Triangle migrant caravans 119–22, 141
  response to opioids crisis 196 n.46
  US-Mexico wall 1–3, 7, 13, 23, 28 n.19, 32 n.32, 35, 68 n.29, 70 n.43, 77–8, 80–1, 116 n.66, 119–20, 125, 127, 129, 153 n.37, 156 n.54, 158 n.63, 162, 181, 196–7 n.48, 203
  withdrawal from Paris Climate Agreement 199 n.60
  zero tolerance family separation policy 161–3, 176
Tuan, Yi-Fu 115 n.60
Turnock, Julie 53
28 Weeks Later (2007) 89

Uhlin, Graig 184
Underground Railroad 187, 201 n.68
Underworld (2003–16) 194 n.35
Underworld (2003) 104
Underworld: Rise of the Lycans (2009) 194 n.35
Unfriended (2015) 113 n.49
US Census Bureau 129
US Customs and Border Protection 119
US Department of Defense 45, 49
US Department of Homeland Security 2, 13, 20
US Immigration and Customs Enforcement (ICE) 77–8, 161–2
Us (2019) 115–16 n.61

Vanity Fair (Thackery) 32 n.32
Vera Cruz (1954) 196–7 n.48
Victory (1981) 128

Vietnam War 2–4, 69–70 n.41, 116 n.66, 179
  Ho Chi Minh Trail 116
  Paris Peace Accords of 1973 182
  Strategic Hamlet Program 69–70 n.41
Village, The (2004) 19–21
Virilio, Paul 60, 64, 73 n.63, 74 n.69
Virno, Paolo 25, 163, 171, 179, 184
Voltron (1983–2016) 142, 145

Wald, Priscilla 88–9
Wall, The (2017) 60–4, 74 nn.70, 71
Wallace, David Foster 71 n.55
Walters, James 54
War for the Planet of the Apes (2017) 184–8, 200 n.66, 201 n.67, 202 n.70
Warcraft (2016) 80, 92–6, 114 nn.53, 54, 199 n.61, 206 n.8
Warcraft: Bonds of Brotherhood (2016) 93

Warm Bodies (2013) 165–70, 195 nn.38, 39, 40, 42, 206 n.8
Warner, Marina 113 n.50
Wasser, Frederick 144
Weber, Cynthia 49
Weinstock, Jeffrey Andrew 113 n.46
Whissel, Kristen 92
Who Framed Roger Rabbit (1988) 159 n.69
Wild Bunch, The (1969) 197 n.48
Willy Wonka & the Chocolate Factory (1971) 146, 160 n.72
Windtalkers (2002) 49
World War II *see* Second World War
World War Z (2013) 80, 86–91, 112 n.44, 113 n.46, 115 n.61
Wreck-It Ralph (2012) 159 n.69
Wyly, Elvin 114–15 n.57

Your Highness (2011) 130

Žižek, Slavoj 21, 127–8

www.ingramcontent.com/pod-product-compliance
Lightning Source LLC
Chambersburg PA
CBHW072145290426
44111CB00012B/1983